LEWIS HERBERT THOMAS is a member of the Department of History at the University of Alberta.

When Canada acquired the Hudson's Bay Company territory in 1870 the federal government was faced with the challenge of governing an area comprising more than half the nation. Following the creation of the province of Manitoba, Parliament provided a territorial government for the vast region of northwest Canada and northern Quebec and Ontario. This classic study of the political development of the area now comprising the provinces of Alberta and Saskatchewan describes the complex process of territorial struggle and constitutional change which marked the transition from the administration of imperial authority to the establishment of responsible government in western Canada.

The historical pattern is still in process in Canada's northern territories, and in this new edition Professor Thomas discusses the implications of the western experience for present political and constitutional questions.

The Struggle for Responsible Government in the North-West Territories 1870-97

LEWIS HERBERT THOMAS

SECOND EDITION

UNIVERSITY OF TORONTO PRESS
TORONTO BUFFALO LONDON

Preface to the Second Edition

IN THE TWENTY-YEAR PERIOD following the first publication of this work, little has been published which can be used to modify or correct the original narrative in the preparation of a new edition. Nor has any significant body of archival material come to light which can be used as supplementary material to add to the all too scanty information on men and events. The only exceptions are James Clinkskill's lengthy "Reminiscences of a Pioneer in Saskatchewan," a copy of which is in the Archives of Saskatchewan (Saskatoon office), and the Hillyard Mitchell correspondence in the same location. This was used by D. H. Bocking in his article "Political Manoeuvering in the Territorial Executive 1895," *Saskatchewan History*, vol. XXIV, no. 1 (1971). Clinkskill was an important member of the territorial legislature, 1888–99 and 1902–5. D. H. Bocking has edited selections from the political reminiscences (see *Saskatchewan History*, vol. XXII, no. 1 (1969)). Clinkskill throws much light on election campaigns in Battleford during these years, and comments on Charles Nolin's campaign methods which led to his being unseated in 1892. Clinkskill also describes the work in the Assembly year by year, and on his membership in the executive committees in 1891–2.

Mrs. Jean Larmour's excellent unpublished Master's thesis "Edgar Dewdney, Commissioner of Indian Affairs and Lieutenant Governor of the North-West Territories, 1879–1885" (1971) focuses on Dewdney's relations with the Indians and Métis.

The history of the government of Keewatin from the creation of the district in 1876 until its reabsorption in the Northwest Territories in 1905 was not given adequate attention in my first edition. Since Keewatin was governed by the Lieutenant-Governor of Manitoba, and the focus of this study was the evolution of government in the Territories, the omission perhaps may be excused. Actually the Governor was not very active in either an executive or a legislative capacity. A treatment of the changing boundaries of Keewatin from 1876 to the present will be found in N. L. Nicholson, *The Boundaries of Canada, the Provinces and Territories* (Ottawa, 1964), pp. 71–6, 90.

The supplementary chapter in this edition entitled "Reflections on Territorial Government, 1897–1970" deals in a summary form with the developments in the Yukon and the Northwest Territories (including the Arctic Islands) from 1897 to 1970. It demonstrates the grip which earlier policies and the imperial-colonial relationship had on the thinking of federal ministries, irrespective of party. The result of this persistent conservatism was the postponement of urgently needed action and the reluctant implementation of reforms. The effect on the area involved was to generate regional discontent and the alienation of the people from federal authority—a situation which continues to our own day.

LEWIS H. THOMAS
Edmonton, Alta., November, 1977

Preface to the First Edition

THE ESTABLISHMENT of a territorial government in the Canadian North-West was the first stage in the political development of the area now comprised in the provinces of Saskatchewan and Alberta. The progress of these two provinces owes much to the foundation of democratic experience which was slowly built during the territorial period: in legislation, in administrative practice, in the techniques of the political process, in political leadership, in popular aspirations— in all these spheres there was notable development in the years before provincehood was attained. But in addition to its local significance, the political history of the Territories is a phase of national history, for it involved the administration of a dependency or "colony" by the federal government. The Territories were a creation of the Parliament of Canada, and the latter was responsible for the constitutional structure which determined the objectives of local political leadership. There was therefore a continuous interaction of national policy with local political forces during the period of territorial status.

This study traces the evolution of the system of government in the North-West Territories from 1870 to 1897, or from the date of their acquisition until the achievement of responsible government. The main emphasis throughout is on the movement for local control of the territorial government. The first phase of this movement culminated in the establishment of an elected legislature in 1888; the second phase had as its object the creation of an executive or cabinet composed of members of the Assembly and supported by a majority of that body. This important episode in the political history of Canada has never been treated in detail, although an outline of the subject will be found in a few of the older general histories. A number of other aspects of the development of the Canadian West during this period have been fairly thoroughly investigated, including land policy, settlement, the two Riel Rebellions, and the Canadian Pacific Railway, but the only study of constitutional progress is C. C. Lingard's *Territorial Government in Canada: The Autonomy Question in the*

Old North-West Territories, which deals with the movement for provincial autonomy, and is primarily concerned with the period after 1897.

I am particularly indebted to Professors A. L. Burt and E. S. Osgood of the Department of History, University of Minnesota, for encouragement and counsel in connection with the preparation of this study, which was originally submitted as a doctoral dissertation at that University. I have received very valuable assistance from Dr. Wm. Kaye Lamb and Miss N. Story of the Public Archives of Canada and from the late Dr. J. L. Johnston, Provincial Librarian and Archivist of Manitoba. The officials of the Lands Branch of the Department of Resources and Development, Ottawa, were most helpful in making available to me the records of the Department of the Interior which have been in their custody. I wish also to acknowledge the courtesies of the officials of the Department of the Secretary of State for Canada, the Provincial Archivist of Ontario, and the librarians of the University of Saskatchewan, University of Toronto, University of Western Ontario, and the Legislative Library of Saskatchewan. The assistance of Mr. F. H. B. Dewdney of Trail, B.C., who permitted me to examine the Edgar Dewdney papers in his custody, is much appreciated. Permission to examine relevant portions of the Sir Clifford Sifton Papers was kindly extended by Mr. Victor Sifton, C.B.E., D.S.O., LL.D. of Winnipeg.

The activities sponsored by the Saskatchewan Archives Board since its organization in 1945 have facilitated my research by bringing a variety of important records into archival custody. I am also indebted to the Board for a leave of absence which assisted the completion of the study. The Canadian Social Science Research Council has generously extended financial assistance in the form of a travel grant and a grant in aid of publication. The editorial staff of the University of Toronto Press has given expert assistance in preparing the manuscript for the press.

LEWIS H. THOMAS

Regina, Sask., April, 1955

Contents

Maps

Tables

ABBREVIATIONS

A.S.: Archives of Saskatchewan, in the Archives Office, University of Saskatchewan, Saskatoon, and in the Archives Division, Legislative Library, Regina.

Assembly Journals: *Journals of the Legislative Assembly of the North-West Territories.*

Commons Debates: Official debates of the House of Commons of Canada.

Council Journals: *Journals of the Council of the North-West Territories, 1877–87.*

C.S.P.: *Canada Sessional Papers.*

Interior file: Files of the Department of the Interior, in the Public Archives of Canada and the Department of Resources and Development, Ottawa.

Oliver: *The Canadian North-West, Its Early Development and Legislative Records*, ed. E. H. Oliver, Publications of the Canadian Archives, no. 9, 2 vols. (Ottawa, 1914–15).

Parliamentary Debates: Unofficial report of debates in the House of Commons and Senate of Canada for the years 1870, 1871 and 1872, published by the *Ottawa Times*.

P.A.C.: Public Archives of Canada, Ottawa.

P.A.M.: Public Archives of Manitoba, Winnipeg.

PART 1

The Establishment of the Territorial System

CHAPTER ONE

A Temporary Government for the Territories

WHEN CANADA ACQUIRED Rupert's Land and the North-Western Territory[1] in 1870 it became the largest state on the continent. Without the North-West, Canada would have consisted only of the three maritime provinces and that portion of Ontario and Quebec which lies within the St. Lawrence drainage basin; with it, Canada secured shorelines on Hudson Bay and the Arctic Ocean, and could negotiate for the admission of British Columbia—the last step in expansion from sea to sea. This enlargement of territory had a profound effect on political life, both national and local. To promote national prosperity, the authorities at Ottawa assumed responsibility for peopling and developing the North-West, and this involved a steady increase in the range of federal administrative activity. The long arm of central authority developed sinew and strength in the North-West; in response, there emerged a vigorous self-assertion combined with respect for the substantial benefits of federal activity—two cardinal elements in the political tradition of the North-West. The first of these, self-assertion (from which the desire for self-government issued), found early and dramatic expression in the disturbances at the Red River Settlement in 1869–70 and the founding of the province of Manitoba. In the remainder of the North-West an autonomy movement appeared with the first substantial influx of settlers, continuing until responsible government was secured in 1897 and provincial status in 1905.

Providing a local government was the only new administrative problem created by the acquisition of the North-West. In the years before Confederation, politicians had grappled with land policy, government aid to railways, Indian administration, and the promotion of immigration; but they had never been called upon to establish a government for a dependent territory. Yet in one sense they were not

1For a description of these areas see below, p. 6.

without experience, for they had all lived, and to a certain extent were still living, in a dependent territory, and many of the bonds of colonialism had only recently been discarded. The imperial-colonial relationship and the process of gradual, unsystematic evolution in that relationship were so familiar, and in many of their aspects so acceptable, as to be one of the unconscious assumptions of Canadian political thought. It is not surprising therefore to find the federal government embracing, without any hesitation, the prerogatives of "imperial" authority in the North-West.

This predisposition was strengthened by the well-founded Canadian fear of further territorial expansion by the United States. The American frontier of settlement was now close to the boundary, and an influx of immigrants could make the North-West another Texas. The year before Confederation was consummated, the Macdonald-Brown coalition government recorded its conviction that "the future interests of· Canada and all British North America" were "vitally concerned in the immediate establishment of a strong Government [in the North-West]."[2]

These circumstances explain much of the difference between the Canadian and American systems of territorial government. The American system had been framed in the early years of the republic, in an atmosphere of hostility towards the old colonial system. After 1781, when a number of states surrendered their claims to the country between the Ohio and Mississippi rivers, this area ("the Old Northwest") became the property of the United States. To leave such a vast area under the permanent control of the central government would have produced a fundamental change in the character of the union, and it was decided that new states should be established in the Old Northwest, equal in status to the original thirteen. This constitutional principle, later applied to the Louisiana Purchase and the Mexican cession, was in conformity with the dynamic character of American society, and facilitated the expansion of the republic to the Pacific during the nineteenth century. But in the 1780's it was impossible to establish the apparatus of state government in such an area, for settlers had just begun to enter the Ohio valley. To provide a measure of self-government a "territory" was created, subordinate to the national government, but possessing a constitution which envisaged a steady advance toward statehood. The principles of American territorial government were embodied in an ordinance of 1787 of the Congress of the Confederation which served successive

[2]Order in Council, June 26, 1866, in Macdonald Papers, vol. 101, P.A.C.

generations of frontiersmen as they built new communities in the wilderness. By 1870 this ordinance, or modifications of it, had formed the basis of the constitutions of twenty-eight territories, not only in the Old Northwest but beyond the Mississippi to the Pacific, and eighteen of these had by that year become states of the United States.

In Canada, the influence of the American system did not extend beyond accepting the principle of ultimate provincial status for the North-West.[3] Canadian policy fell into the familiar grooves of the imperial-colonial relationship with its conservative, empirical approach to constitutional matters. This was evident during the period from 1867 to 1869 when the negotiations for annexation of the North-West were proceeding. The records abound with details regarding the terms under which the Hudson's Bay Company might surrender its rights, but we look in vain for any grand scheme or charter for the government of the North-West comparable to Jefferson's 1784 "Report of Government for the Western Territory" or the more famous North-west Ordinance of 1787. The intentions of the Macdonald administration can only be discerned in a few brief pronouncements in various state papers and parliamentary debates and in the abbreviated and hastily improvised legislation of 1869 entitled "An Act for the temporary Government of Rupert's Land and the North-Western Territory when united with Canada."[4]

II

The legislative foundation for Canada's great venture in territorial expansion was laid by section 146 of the British North America Act, and a careful examination of its terms is essential if we are to understand the events which preceded the union of 1870. The section reads as follows:

146. It shall be lawful for the Queen, by and with the advice of Her Majesty's Most Honourable Privy Council, on Addresses from the Houses of the Parliament of Canada, and from the Houses of the respective Legislatures of the Colonies or Provinces of Newfoundland, Prince Edward Island, and British Columbia, to admit those Colonies or Provinces, or any of them, into the Union, and on Address from the Houses of the Parliament of Canada to admit Rupert's Land and the North-western

[3]It is interesting to speculate on the situation which would have arisen with respect to the acquisition of the North-West if the Canadian constitution had been unitary instead of federal, as Sir John A. Macdonald had originally hoped. The problem of governing such a vast territory from Ottawa would have been so formidable that annexation would have been impossible, or if undertaken would have forced the adoption of some type of federal system.

[4]32-33 Vict., c. 3.

Territory, or either of them, into the Union, on such terms and conditions in each case as are in the Addresses expressed and as the Queen thinks fit to approve, subject to the provisions of this Act, and the provisions of any Order in Council in that behalf shall have effect as if they had been enacted by the Parliament of the United Kingdom of Great Britain and Ireland.

There are several important features of this section of the Act. In the first place the existence of two different territorial units in the North-West was recognized—Rupert's Land (the domain of the Hudson's Bay Company), and the North-Western Territory. This distinction had not been observed in the Quebec Resolutions of 1864 or the London Resolutions of 1866, and did not appear in the earlier drafts of the British North America bill prepared by the London Conference;[5] in all of these the North-West was referred to as the North-West or North-Western Territory and no mention was made of Rupert's Land. This last-minute change was a stratagem of William McDougall[6] (the leading advocate of expansion at the Conference) to give recognition to the Canadian contention that there was an area separate from the Hudson's Bay Company's domain which, if not already Canada's by virtue of French exploration and occupation, was at least not legally possessed by the Company. The latter claimed that Rupert's Land consisted of all of the Hudson Bay drainage basin north of the United States—an area overlapping most of the North-Western Territory as defined by Canada.[7] The boundaries of these two areas had never been authoritatively settled. Negotiations conducted by the British government, to incorporate in the former province of Canada land lying west of Lake Superior had culminated in 1865 when the colonial government had been induced to agree to a monetary compensation for extinguishing the Company's claims. But the Canadians had not abandoned their definition of the boundaries of the North-Western Territory, claiming it was contiguous with Upper Canada and included most of the prairie region from the Red River to the Rockies. Since the Act authorized a summary pro-

[5]See Joseph Pope, ed., *Confederation: Being a Series of Hitherto Unpublished Documents Bearing on the British North America Act* (Toronto, 1895). The first mention of Rupert's Land appears in the fourth draft of the Conference, pp. 210–11.

[6]See *Journals of the House of Commons*, 1880, Appendix 1, p. xii.

[7]If the Hudson's Bay Company's claim is accepted, the North-Western Territory consisted of the unorganized crown land lying north and west of Rupert's Land, and bordering on British Columbia, Alaska, and the Arctic coast, i.e., most of the Arctic drainage basin. This area, of course, was not contiguous with the western boundary of the province of Canada.

cedure for the transfer of both areas, the Canadians were proposing to curtail the claims of the Company or to postpone a settlement until after they were in possession of part or all of the North-West.[8]

The second noteworthy feature of this section of the Confederation Act was that Newfoundland, Prince Edward Island, and British Columbia were specifically designated as "Colonies or Provinces," whereas Rupert's Land and the North-Western Territory were not so described. Furthermore, and as a result of this difference in status, there was a distinction in the procedure by which union was to be accomplished in the two cases. The admission of Newfoundland, Prince Edward Island, and British Columbia was to be initiated by joint action of the Canadian Parliament and the legislature of each colony; the admission of Rupert's Land and the North-Western Territory was to be initiated by unilateral action of the Canadian Parliament and effected by summary action of the Imperial government. The framers of the Confederation Act further emphasized the difference in status in the two cases by the terms of the succeeding section (147) which described the representation which the three colonies were to receive in the Senate, but made no provision for the North-West to be represented in that body.

The first official reference to the future government of the North-West was contained in the eight resolutions which William Mc-Dougall (then Minister of Public Works) introduced on behalf of the government during the first session of the first Parliament of Canada in December 1867.[9] These formed the substance of the address which, in accordance with section 146 of the British North America Act, was to convey to the British government the Canadian request for the annexation of Rupert's Land and the North-Western Territory. The third resolution was as follows: "That the welfare of a sparse and widely scattered population of British subjects, of European origin, already inhabiting these remote and unorganized territories, would be materially enhanced, by the formation therein of political institutions bearing analogy, as far as circumstances will

[8]An account of the negotiations up to July 1865 will be found in the documents tabled in the Canadian legislature in 1865. *Journals of the Legislative Assembly*, 1865, pp. 8–16; 44–55. See also the subsequent negotiations as contained in the documents in *C.S.P.* 1869, no. 25. It is significant that a minute of the Canadian cabinet of October 1, 1868, authorizing further negotiations with the British government contemplated the possibility of admitting "the North-West Territory into union with Canada, either with or without Rupert's Land as may be found practicable and expedient": *ibid.*, p. 5; c.f. Macdonald to J. Y. Bown, private, Oct. 26, 1868, Macdonald Papers.

[9]*Journals of the House of Commons*, 1867–8, pp. 66–7.

admit, to those which exist in the several Provinces of this Dominion." It is significant that while the right of self-government was stated in these very general and conveniently elastic terms, the fifth resolution, relating to the role of the federal government in the Territories, was most specific. The British government was requested "to grant to the Parliament of Canada authority to legislate for their future welfare and good government," Canada being willing "to assume the duties and obligations of Government, and Legislation." One additional popular right, though not related to the functioning of government, was admitted in the seventh resolution. The claims of the first Canadians—the Indians—"to compensation for lands required for purposes of settlement will be considered and settled in conformity with the equitable principles which have uniformly governed the British Crown in its dealings with the aborigines."

During the debate on the resolutions the subject of a constitution for the Territories received scant attention, but before it ended two highly significant statements were made, the first by David Mills, a Liberal opponent of the Macdonald administration, the second by the Prime Minister himself. Mills, who represented the Ontario constituency of Bothwell, was a descendant of New England Puritans, whose family had left the United States during the time of the Revolution. A teacher who had turned to the law, he had the rather unusual distinction, for a member of the Canadian Parliament of that period, of being a graduate of an American university (the University of Michigan). He was well acquainted with the principles of territorial government in the United States, and throughout his long career in the House of Commons was the chief Liberal spokesman on matters relating to the government of the Territories. It was during the 1867 debate that he first expounded the principles which in succeeding years he invariably applied whenever territorial government matters were discussed in Parliament. In objecting to the wording of this resolution in 1867, Mills is reported as follows:

This would not give the people there any rights of local self government. He thought the resolutions should express on what principles we intended to govern it; whether or not we were to organize territorial governments like those in the United States, so that the territory to be organized, after acquiring sufficient population, should have the right to have a certain number of Senators in the Senate Chamber, and certain representatives on the floor of this House. He would like, therefore, to add to the 5th resolution words which would secure to the people of the new territory the same rights of local self-government, free from federal control, that are enjoyed by the provinces already within the Dominion.[10]

[10]*Gazette* (Montreal), Dec. 7, 1867, report of debates on Dec. 6.

A few days later the Prime Minister spoke on the resolutions, and in the course of his address referred to the constitutional question in terms which, if they did not define a policy, at least indicated the government's approach to the problem:

As to what the constitution of the territory would be [he remarked] that was a matter for future consideration. . . . Her Majesty would, on receiving this address, make over the sovereignty and right of governing to the legislature of Canada, leaving it to the wisdom of the Parliament of Canada to settle the mode of Government in that territory which, he presumed, speaking on his first impression, and giving his own opinion, would be a provisional one according to the wants of the country.

He concluded as follows:

Of course it would be idle to give the country the same Government as in Canada, but representative institutions should be at once introduced in order that the people might have a voice in their Government; they should all have representation in the Parliament of Canada.[11]

Taken together, these two expressions of opinion neatly epitomize two contrasting philosophies of government—the forthright, rather doctrinaire attitude of Mills, the philosophic liberal; and the cautious, empirical approach of Macdonald, the practical politician and unphilosophic conservative. As Macdonald put it during a similar discussion with Mills many years later, "The hon. gentleman is intensely logical, and I am intensely practical. That is the difference, but somehow my legislation generally gets through."[12] But if the Prime Minister's legislation for the Territories had incorporated a little more of Mills's logic, the constitutional evolution of the North-West would have followed a much steadier and less troubled course.

The address of the Canadian Parliament was based on a strict adherence to the terms of section 146 of the British North America Act; the acquisition of the North-West was to be accomplished by an agreement in which the Canadian and British governments would be the only principals, or "high contracting parties." The interest which the Canadian government had in adhering to this procedure is indicated in a minute of the Privy Council communicated to the Colonial Secretary.[13] "The transfer which the Imperial Parliament has authorized [by section 146] and the Canadian Parliament approved," the minute read, "should not be delayed by negotiations or correspondence with private or third parties [the Hudson's Bay

---

[11]*Ibid.*, Dec. 11, 1867, report of debates on Dec. 9.
[12]*Commons Debates*, 1886, p. 1215.
[13]Minute of the Privy Council of Canada, Dec. 28, 1867, based on a memorandum of Hon. Wm. McDougall, *C.S.P.* 1867–8, no. 59, pp. 2–3.

Company], whose position, opinions and claims have heretofore embarrassed both Governments in dealing with this question."[14] The terms of the address, the minute also stated, could not be altered "without causing injurious delay, and greatly embarrassing the people and Government of Canada in their efforts to open communications with the Territory, to encourage immigration and settlement, to establish law and order, and to provide for the speedy organization of Municipal and Local Governments therein." It is significant that the organization of a government for the North-West appeared last in this list of projects, a position which it certainly occupied in all public discussions of western expansion. The minute concluded with the request that the decision of the British government should be communicated by cable "in order that the Canadian Government may be prepared to submit appropriate measures on the subject on the re-assembling of Parliament in March next."

The hope which the Canadian government entertained that it could acquire the North-West without negotiating with the Hudson's Bay Company, and its high pressure methods for speeding the union, were both frustrated by the law officers of the British government. The latter discovered that the terms of section 146 of the Confederation Act were insufficient to effect the transfer of Rupert's Land, and they recommended that special legislative authority be secured to extinguish the two-hundred-year-old Company charter.[15] The result was the Rupert's Land Act,[16] passed by the Imperial Parliament in July 1868. This Act, which was in effect an amendment of the British North America Act, was passed without prior consultation with the Canadian government. The disappointment felt in Ottawa at this turn of events was later communicated to the Colonial Office, which was informed that "the Canadian government . . . could not understand why it [the Rupert's Land Act] was necessary, and greatly doubted the expediency of passing it."[17]

[14]It is true that one of the terms of the address of the Canadian Parliament was that "the Government and Parliament of Canada will be ready to provide that the legal rights of any corporation, company and individual within [the North-West] shall be respected, and placed under the protection of Courts of competent jurisdiction."

[15]See Cartier and McDougall to Sir F. Rogers, Feb. 8, 1869, in *C.S.P.* 1869, no. 25, pp. 17–18; also *Parliamentary Debates* (Gt. B.), 3rd series, vol. 193 (1868), col. 1101.

[16]31–32 Vict. (Gt. B.), c. 105.

[17]Cartier and McDougall to Sir F. Rogers, Feb. 8, 1869, *C.S.P.* 1869, no. 25, p. 18; also Cartier and McDougall to Sir Stafford Northcote, M.P., March 13, 1869, *ibid.*, p. 34.

This Act established a rather complicated formula for the transfer,[18] involving an agreement with the Hudson's Bay Company and an agreement with Canada, along with provisions to prevent the British government from being saddled with any expenditure in connection with the transaction.[19] But it did more than recognize the position of the Company; the British North America Act had not established federal control of the North-West in specific terms, and the drafters of the later Act decided to dispel any doubt on this point by the following provision: ". . . it shall be lawful for the Parliament of Canada . . . to make, ordain and establish within the Land and Territory so admitted as aforesaid all such Laws, Institutions, and Ordinances, and to constitute such Courts and Officers, as may be necessary for the Peace, Order, and good government of Her Majesty's Subjects and others therein. . . ."[20] The supremacy of the Canadian Parliament in dealing with the North-West as established by this Act was complete, subject only to such conditions as might be imposed by the terms of transfer to be approved by the British government. These conditions, which were accepted by the Canadian negotiators, Cartier and McDougall, in March 1869 and by the Canadian Parliament two months later, were chiefly concerned with protecting the interests of the shareholders of the Hudson's Bay Company; but popular rights were recognized to the extent that land titles granted to the inhabitants of the country by the Company were to be confirmed by the Canadian government, and the latter was to communicate with the Imperial government whenever decisions on Indian claims were to be made.[21]

III

It is clear therefore that, when Parliament was invited in the spring of 1869 to consider the government's measure for "the temporary

[18]The successive steps in the transaction were (1) an agreement between the British government and the Company on terms of surrender, (2) an agreement between the British government and Canada on terms of admission, involving an address from the Canadian Parliament and in practical effect being the same as the terms of surrender, (3) surrender of Rupert's Land to the Crown, (4) acceptance of the surrender by the British government, and (5) admission of Rupert's Land to Canada by Imperial Order in Council within a month after the acceptance of surrender.

[19]Section 3 stated that "no charge shall be imposed by such terms upon the Consolidated Fund of the United Kingdom"; the stipulation that the country was not to remain in the possession of the Crown for more than a month was probably designed with a like purpose in mind.

[20]31–32 Vict. (Gt. B.), c. 105, s. 5.

[21]*Journals of the House of Commons*, 1869, pp. 146–8.

government of Rupert's Land and the North-Western Territory when united with Canada," it possessed unrestricted authority under the Rupert's Land Act to determine the form of local government which should be established in the Territories.[22] It could, had it wished, have passed legislation comparable to the American Northwest Ordinance with its comprehensive provisions for several stages of evolution in the structure of government. A government patterned on one of the British colonies might have been created. Or it could have established a provincial government at once, as indeed was done a year later as a sequel to the Red River disturbances. But none of these possible measures was chosen. Instead, Macdonald avoided making a final decision and submitted a bill to provide for a provisional, or as it was officially called, a "temporary" government. "The Government," Sir John said, when introducing the legislation, "did not intend at present to submit anything like a permanent measure on this subject; but had prepared a short Bill . . . which would sufficiently provide for the organization and government of the country during the few months which might elapse between the issuing of the proclamation [uniting the North-West with Canada] and the convening of Parliament."[23] "The Act," he is also reported as saying, "would only remain in force until the end of the next session, when a measure would be introduced establishing a more permanent government."[24]

This Act, after formally christening the North-West Territories, provided for the appointment of a Lieutenant-Governor who was to administer the local government under periodic instructions from Ottawa. The Lieutenant-Governor could, if necessary, be empowered by the Governor General in Council "to make provision for the administration of Justice . . . and generally to make, ordain, and

[22]The argument which we are advancing here—that a choice of alternative forms of local government for the North-West could have been considered by the Macdonald administration—is not affected by the fact that doubts later arose concerning the competency of Parliament to enact the 1869 Act for Temporary Government and the Manitoba Act of 1870. These doubts resulted in the passage of the first amendment to the British North America Act in 1871, 34–35 Vict. (Gt. B.), c. 28. The Macdonald administration did not consider that it was hampered in any way in 1869 and this view was shared by the law officers of the Crown in London a year later when the Manitoba Act was passed. See Paul Gérin-Lajoie, *Constitutional Amendment in Canada* (Toronto, 1950), pp. 50–8. It is significant, too, that the Liberal opposition raised no objection to the constitutionality of the legislation of 1869.

[23]*Globe* (Toronto), June 5, 1869, report of debate on June 4.

[24]*Ottawa Times*, June 4, 1869, report of debate of same day. The same paper, on May 29, reported Cartier as saying that "he hoped that during the recess a plan would be prepared for submission [to] the next session regarding the opening up of communication and for the government of the territory."

establish all such laws, Institutions and Ordinances as may be necessary for the Peace, Order and good Government of Her Majesty's subjects and others therein."[25] Any power conferred by the federal government in this way and any laws which the Lieutenant-Governor might enact were to be reported to Parliament. A Council "to aid the Lieutenant-Governor in the administration of affairs" could be established, whose members were to be appointed by the federal government. The size of the Council was to be not more than fifteen and not less than seven persons, and its powers were to be defined by the Governor General in Council. Existing laws in the Territories were to remain in force until altered by Parliament or by the Lieutenant-Governor, and unless the latter made new arrangements all existing "Public Officers and Functionaries" were to remain in office.[26] In addition to the verbal assurances given by members of the government, the temporary character of the legislation was specifically referred to in both the preamble and the final section; the former stated that the purpose was "to make some temporary provision for the Civil Government of the Territories until more permanent arrangements can be made by the Government and Legislature of Canada"; the latter stated that the Act was to continue in force only until the end of the succeeding session of Parliament.

It will be seen from this description of its terms that the Act was, on the face of it, chiefly concerned with preventing any hiatus or temporary suspension of government authority as the old régime in the North-West gave place to the new. Fear of a power vacuum, which would stimulate expansionist sentiment in the United States, was a dominant factor in determining government policy during this period. To constitute this provisional government promptly, it was necessary to appoint the Council as well as the Lieutenant-Governor, and so avoid the delay which would have been involved in introducing an elective system. Apart from these considerations, the provisions were designed to give the federal government a free hand for the time being in coping with circumstances and conditions which would remain unknown until after the union had taken place. Here again was the cautious, empirical approach which had been characteristic of the government's policy from the start. On this occasion, however, it was not challenged by Mills or any other member of the opposition,

---

25 32-33 Vict., c. 3, s. 2.
26 *Ibid.*, ss. 5 and 6. The only exception in regard to public officers was "the Public Officer or Functionary at the head of the administration of affairs" (i.e. the Governor-in-Chief of Rupert's Land).

and the bill was passed with scarcely any discussion.[27] Evidently the members of Parliament did not feel they could effectively attack the government's view that no permanent legislation could be passed until after union, when a fund of reliable information could be collected by Canadian officials.

While Parliament gave scant consideration to the bill for the inauguration of territorial government in the North-West, it was not unimpressed with the significance of the impending union. During the debate on the ratification of the terms of transfer, Senator McCully of Nova Scotia, who had been a strong supporter of Confederation, aptly described the general reaction of the members of both Houses.

There was no precedent could be found in history [he declared] for the transfer of so large a tract of territory by a Legislative Act, or by any cession made by one country to another. . . . It will be no easy matter for the Government to be prepared to set up a municipal government there by which the rights not only of the natives, but of immigrants who go there will be protected. . . . Though in the North American Act we contemplated the acquisition of this great country, yet it seems to have come upon us almost before we are prepared for it. We have scarcely organized the institutions necessary for the confederation of these small provinces. . . . Therefore we should not under-estimate the responsibility devolving upon this Legislature in placing that country in a position to invite immigration.[28]

It has been argued that the Temporary Government Act was deliberately intended to fasten despotic rule on the North-West for an indefinite period.[29] Its terms were obviously less liberal than might have been expected from Macdonald's statement of 1867 that "representative institutions should be at once introduced" and parliamentary representation granted. Writing to Tupper about this time he remarked, "He [McDougall] will be for the time paternal despot, as in other small Crown Colonies, his Council being one of advice, he and they however being governed by instructions from Head Quarters."[30] Yet it is clear that he intended to proceed carefully in

[27]The only debate on North-West matters during this session arose from the resolutions relating to the terms of union with Rupert's Land which had been negotiated by Cartier and McDougall. These formed the second of the two addresses to the Queen which were required for the conclusion of the negotiations. In this debate the question of the future government of the Territories was not discussed.

[28]*Ottawa Times,* May 31, 1869.

[29]See A. S. Morton, *A History of the Canadian West to 1870–71* (London [1938]), p. 874 *et passim.* Morton's account of the events leading to the acquisition of the North-West and to the Red River disturbances is coloured throughout by a strong prejudice against the Canadian authorities.

[30]Macdonald to Tupper, private, Aug. 17, 1869, Macdonald Papers; see also Macdonald to Tupper, confidential, July 17, 1869, *ibid.*

forming the Council. In a letter to Hon. Sidney Smith of Peterboro dated July 12, 1869, he wrote:

It will be some months before the Hudson's Bay Co. can surrender to Her Majesty the Western Country, and Her Majesty transfer it to the Dominion. In order to be ready to accept the transfer we have passed a short Bill for the establishment of a provisional Government, and our intention is simply to send up some person as Lieutenant Governor to take command of the Ship. The Act provides that all the officers of the Hudson's Bay Co., of every kind, shall continue to hold their offices under the new *régime* for the present.

We are in utter darkness as to the state of affairs there; what the wants and wishes of the people are—or, in fact, how the affairs are carried on at all.

We shall expect the Lt. Governor to make a report early enough to have legislation of some kind next Session, and to grant them a Constitution suitable to the present scattered state of the few Whites that there are there.

No appointments, therefore, will be made, except under the temporary Act of last Session, until after next Session, and I am as ignorant as possible of the future mode of administering the affairs of that country.[31]

Three months later he wrote to Hon. J. H. Gray: "Until McDougall has time to look about him and report we desire to make no appointments, lest they might jar with the prejudices and feelings of the people at Red River."[32] Moreover, the government was giving heed to Liberal criticisms of the proposed constitution. As early as October 1869 Macdonald was planning to score a point against the *Globe* (the chief Liberal organ) by appointing a certain number of Red River residents as members of the North-West Council.[33] And even the *Globe* (from whom the least charitable interpretation of government policy could be expected) was prepared to recognize the Act of 1869 as a temporary measure:

The inhabitants of the North-West must console themselves that the oligarchy to be established over them cannot last long. Even the members of the Dominion Government do not believe they will be able to maintain the present policy for any considerable period. The right of local self-government must be conceded to them without much delay. The rest of the Dominion enjoys that right, and there is no danger that

---

[31]Macdonald Papers.

[32]Macdonald to Gray, private, Oct. 27, 1869, *ibid.*

[33]See Macdonald to Tupper, private, Oct. 13, 1869, and Macdonald to Archibald, private, Oct. 27, 1869, in Macdonald Papers. See also Instructions issued to Hon. Wm. McDougall as Lieutenant-Governor of the North-West Territories, Sept. 28, 1869, printed in E. H. Oliver, ed., *The Canadian North-West: Its Early Development and Legislative Records* (Ottawa, 1914–15), vol. II, pp. 878–80. This work is cited hereinafter as Oliver.

it will be withheld from the people of the Red River territory even for a few years.[34]

Nevertheless it is unlikely that Macdonald intended to give free play to the elective principle in the constitution of the territorial government for the first few years. On the whole we may regard the Act, not as a crystallization of federal policy, but as a characteristic expression of the Prime Minister's philosophy—cautious, empirical, and, withal, conservative.

IV

The union of the North-West Territories with Canada would have taken place on October 1, 1869,[35] had it not been for the delay which occurred in floating a loan in London to enable Canada to pay the Hudson's Bay Company £300,000, in accordance with the terms under which the company had agreed to relinquish its title to Rupert's Land.[36] As a result, the date of union was postponed to December 1.[37] Meanwhile, the federal government prepared to inaugurate its administration of the North-West. Its first action was the establishment of a land survey administration, and J. S. Dennis was despatched to the Red River Settlement for this purpose, under instructions from McDougall as Minister of Public Works. During the previous autumn, employees of his department had been sent out to construct a road between Fort Garry and the Lake of the Woods without consulting the London headquarters of the Hudson's Bay Company; this time, however, the proprieties were observed, and the consent of the Company was secured before Dennis was appointed.[38] The objective of the survey was threefold: to prepare land for new settlers; to define and determine the holdings of the residents of the Settlement so that these might be formally confirmed; and to enable the Hudson's Bay Company to ascertain what property would remain in its possession under

[34]Editorial of July 26, 1869, "Government of the North-West."

[35]Lord Grenville to Sir John Young, Nov. 30, 1869, C.S.P. 1870, no. 12, p. 140.

[36]The fact that the Canadian government could not raise $1,500,000 to pay the Hudson's Bay Company, without arranging for a loan guaranteed by the British government, throws a significant light on the financial position of the country at the beginning of its national life, and helps to explain Macdonald's desire to avoid large expenditures for North-West administration.

[37]Macdonald to Tupper, private, Aug. 17, 1869, Macdonald Papers.

[38]See House of Commons (Gt. B.), Parliamentary Papers, 1869, "Return of Copy or Extracts of Correspondence between the Colonial Office, the Government of the Canadian Dominion, and the Hudson's Bay Company relating to the Surrender of Rupert's Land. . . ." The Company's protest regarding the Snow road building expedition and the Canadian reply is printed in C.S.P. 1869, no. 25, pp. 10–13.

the terms of the agreement.[39] There was nothing objectionable in this, and the importance of having surveyed lands ready for homesteaders was obvious.

The cabinet next considered the appointments which would be necessary for the government of the Territories. Joseph Howe, then President of the Council, was selected as the cabinet member who should be responsible for the general administration of North-West affairs, it being planned that for this purpose he should assume the portfolio of Secretary of State for the Provinces.[40] It was a curious appointment. Howe had entered the cabinet only a few months before, not to head a particular department, but to strengthen the government's position in Nova Scotia. His fame as an elder statesman was great, but age and ill health had impaired his capacities as an administrator. In the House of Commons in 1867 he had opposed the acquisition of the North-West as involving too great a financial strain, and had favoured the creation of a Crown colony there; after joining the cabinet he accepted the move as a *fait accompli*, but appears to have regarded it with little enthusiasm.

The choice of William McDougall for the position of Lieutenant-Governor was, from one point of view, appropriate. Along with his fellow Liberal, George Brown, he had worked tirelessly for the acquisition of the North-West since the 1840's and had been one of the architects of the terms of union. His assets were vigour, a commanding presence, administrative experience, and oratorical ability, but he was not noted for tact, and this was the one quality which the circumstances demanded above all else, as he himself told the Prime Minister.[41] However, the important powers which he would exercise as Lieutenant-Governor, the larger salary,[42] and the difficulties of his position as a Liberal member of Macdonald's cabinet, led him to relinquish his ministerial post; above all, he must have regarded the appointment as a fitting climax to his long advocacy of western expansion. From Macdonald's point of view the choice had different implications. After the withdrawal of Brown, the Liberal leader, from the coalition and the reappearance of the two-party system, McDougall was of little political value to the administration; "he not

[39]McDougall to Dennis, July 10, 1869, *C.S.P.* 1870, no. 12, p. 1; also Dennis to McDougall, Aug. 21, 1869, *ibid.*, pp. 5–6.

[40]As early as July 17, Macdonald was consulting Howe on North-West matters; see Macdonald to Tupper, confidential, July 17, 1869, Macdonald Papers; see also same to same, Aug. 17, 1869.

[41]See Dougal E. McFee, "The Honourable William McDougall, C.B." (M.A. thesis, Queen's University, 1948), p. 189.

[42]*Ibid.*, p. 113. His salary as Lieutenant-Governor was to be $7,000 per year; as Minister of Public Works he received $5,000 plus a sessional indemnity of $600.

only was troublesome in matters of policy within the Cabinet, but his presence caused jealousy and ill will among the Conservative followers of the Premier."[43] It is apparent that the exigencies of party politics determined the appointment of both of the men who were to be responsible for North-West administration; had fitness for the office been the only consideration it would have been better had their positions been reversed—Howe as the diplomatic Lieutenant-Governor and McDougall as the energetic cabinet minister would certainly have been a happier combination.

The North-West Council was not to be appointed until after the date of union, in order to give McDougall time to submit to the cabinet the names of a number of residents of the Settlement. Unfortunately for the reputation of the Macdonald administration no public statement was made on the policy which had been adopted for selecting members of the Council, with the result that it was rumoured that either all or a majority of the Councillors were to be Easterners; this rumour, assiduously circulated by the *Globe*, had a disastrous effect on public opinion in the Settlement, and has been accepted as true by some historians.[44] The facts are somewhat different. Not only were residents of the Settlement to be members; they were to form a majority of the Council. There were, it is true, three Easterners designated as prospective members, and these men accompanied McDougall. Captain D. R. Cameron of the Royal Artillery, a son-in-law of Tupper, was selected by Macdonald and Howe for a seat on the Council, with special responsibility for organizing a police force. A. N. Richards, a lawyer of Brockville and former Solicitor General of Upper Canada, was chosen by McDougall, with the Prime Minister's approval, for the post of Attorney General. J. A. N. Provencher, a Montreal journalist and nephew of the first Roman Catholic Bishop of St. Boniface, was, unknown to McDougall, selected for the post of secretary. Two residents of the Settlement who were

---

[43]*Globe*, Dec. 31, 1869, editorial "The North-West"; see also Jan. 4, 1870, "The North-West Embroglio," and McFee, *op. cit.*, pp. 186–93.

[44]The government's policy with respect to the appointment of Councillors is set forth in the following documents: Macdonald to Tupper, confidential, July 17, 1869, and Aug. 17, 1869, Macdonald Papers; Richards to Howe, March 11, 1870, and McDougall to John Langton, June 4, 1870, in *C.S.P.* 1871, no. 44, pp. 11–12, 20–1; E. A. Meredith to McDougall, Sept. 28, 1869, *C.S.P.* 1870, no. 12, pp. 2–3; also letter of J. S. Dennis in McDougall to Howe, Nov. 20, 1869, *ibid.*, pp. 55–6. There is no evidence for the statement which appears in Morton (*op. cit.*) and G. F. G. Stanley's *Birth of Western Canada: A History of the Riel Rebellions* (London, 1936) that Alexander Begg of Ottawa was to be a member of the Council; he was an employee of the Inland Revenue Department who was sent to Fort Garry to be Collector of Customs and Inspector of Inland Revenue: see Begg to Howe, Jan. 13, 1870, *C.S.P.* 1871, no. 44, pp. 9–10.

known to the federal government were to be invited to become Councillors—William McTavish the Governor of Assiniboia and John
Black the Recorder of Rupert's Land. If they declined, "one or two
other officers of the Company" were to be nominated by McDougall
along with "several of the residents of character and standing in the
Territory, unconnected with the Company."[45] Whether the government intended to appoint the maximum number of Councillors (15)
provided for in the Act is not apparent, but since the minimum number was seven, the majority of those appointed at the start would have
been residents of the Territories. "The Toronto Globe," Macdonald
wrote, "with its usual anxiety to do mischief, has been representing
that we are going to send a panel of Canadians from the Dominion
to hold all the Offices, to the exclusion of the residents. Such a belief
among the people already at Red River, might cause considerable
dissatisfaction and trouble, so McDougall will proceed with great caution as to appointments."[46]

At the end of September, a few days before his departure for the
West, McDougall received his appointment and commission as Lieutenant-Governor, which were to take effect on the date of union.
Arrangements were made for him to be sworn into office by Governor
McTavish, Judge Black, and Captain Cameron.[47] It was planned
that the Lieutenant-Governor designate would arrive at Fort Garry
at least three weeks before the date of union in order "that no time
should be lost in making the necessary preliminary arrangements for
the organization of the Government of the Territories." McDougall's
instructions ordered him in addition to submitting a list of nominees
for the Council, to report, in consultation with Judge Black, on the
existing system of law, administration of justice, and police arrangements. He was to describe local provisions for taxation, liquor regul-
lation, highways administration, municipal organization, currency
and education, as well as "the relations at present existing between the
Hudson's Bay Company and the different religious bodies in the

[45]E. A. Meredith, Under Secretary of State, to McDougall, Sept. 28, 1869,
C.S.P. 1870, no. 12, pp. 1–5.

[46]Macdonald to Archibald, private, Oct. 27, 1869, Macdonald Papers.

[47]Commission, Dedimus Potestatem, Sept. 29, 1869, appointing McTavish,
Black, and Cameron; copy in Secretary of State for the Provinces file no. 929
in records of the Office of the Secretary of State, Ottawa. There would no doubt
have been a public swearing-in ceremony, and there is no evidence for Morton's
view, op. cit., p. 874, that "the new Government was drafted without making
any arrangements for the ceremony with which one Government usually gives up
the reins of power to another." Such arrangements would have to be made by
McDougall after he reached Fort Garry. The swearing in of the Lieutenant-
Governor was the "ceremony" by which the provinces of Saskatchewan and
Alberta were inaugurated in 1905.

Territories." He was to report the existing situation and make recommendations concerning Indian affairs, land policy, and the personnel required for the administration of the government. Finally, he was to take immediate steps to establish a telegraph line between Winnipeg and St. Cloud, Minnesota (the nearest point on the railway)—a measure which indicates the government's interest in communicating swiftly with its agents in the Territories.[48]

In assessing federal policy for the government of the North-West as it had developed to this point, it is necessary to remember that this subject was never uppermost in the minds of Macdonald and his associates. Their interests lay not in the realm of political invention but in administrative problems which could be comprehended within a framework of previous experience and policy. Communications, surveys, the dispute with the Hudson's Bay Company, even Indian policy, were of more concern than constitutional questions. The temporary government legislation of 1869, obviously hastily drafted, could have been prepared at any time during the previous year and a half. In short, there is no evidence of any deep interest in territorial government as such. The charge that the Macdonald administration was deliberately fastening an undemocratic constitution on the North-West is based on the assumption that the government had devised a fixed policy; the evidence, however, indicates that the policy was not fixed but relatively flexible, but it was a flexibility arising from the lack of firm convictions or deep concern. This was one of the more important reasons why a radical revision in the form of government for a part of the Territories was made within less than a year.

While the policy of the Macdonald administration as revealed in the Temporary Government Act certainly does not exhibit any great devotion to the principle of representative government, and while Mills's approach to the constitutional problem was a much sounder one, it is quite possible that, with effective advocacy, the policy might have been accepted in the North-West with little or no protest. The circumstances of the government's failure in this connection must now engage our attention.

[48]It is one of the ironies of history that of all his instructions this was the only one McDougall was able to act on (see *C.S.P.* 1870, no. 12, pp. 33–7); but had he, as Minister of Public Works, established telegraphic communication with the Red River Settlement in 1868 instead of trying to construct a road between the settlement and the head of the lakes, his career as Lieutenant-Governor would probably not have ended in disaster and the history of the union of the North-West with Canada would have been very different. As it was, he had to wait for five weeks to receive a reply to his letter reporting on the half-breed opposition to his entering the North-West.

CHAPTER TWO

The Evolution of Federal Government Policy

1869-70

THE NORTH-WEST'S RECEPTION of the administration's plans for territorial government revealed the existence of political forces undreamt of in the ministerial offices at Ottawa. Contrary to Eastern opinion, society in the North-West was not completely primitive, even in the isolated trading posts, and social experience and convictions rooted in over fifty years of history existed in the little settlement at the junction of the Red and Assiniboine rivers. Nor was a political tradition lacking, for the North-West had been governed by a system which drew its strength from indigenous forces and the consent of the majority.

The Red River Settlement was the "capital" of the ancient fur trade empire, whose isolated outposts were scattered along the lonely waterways of the North-West, from the international boundary to the Arctic Ocean and from Lake Winnipeg to the Rockies. Founded by Lord Selkirk in 1812 as a haven for evicted Scottish peasants, the Settlement was "reconveyed" to the Hudson's Bay Company in 1836.[1] At the time of union its population consisted of about 5,600 French- and 4,000 English-speaking half-breeds with some 1,600 whites. These last included descendants of the Selkirk settlers, retired employees of the Company, and a few immigrants of the 1860's from Canada and the United States. Differences in language and religion were reflected in the distribution of the population—a series of Roman Catholic and Protestant parishes, lining the rivers' banks like beads on

[1]For a history of the early years of the Settlement see J. P. Pritchett, *The Red River Valley 1811–1849* (New Haven, 1942); the best contemporary description is J. J. Hargrave, *Red River* (Montreal, 1871). Hargrave was private secretary to his uncle, Governor McTavish; he was a careful observer and an effective writer.

a string. Most of the white settlers and the majority of the English-speaking half-breeds were engaged in small-scale agriculture. Most of the French half-breeds led a semi-nomadic existence, finding a livelihood in buffalo hunting on the Plains or as boatmen and labourers for the fur trade; "their parishes were winter homes, their fields sufficient only for self-support at most."[2]

Apart from having the only settlement in the North-West, this area where the Red and the Assiniboine joined their waters was of the greatest strategic importance. Geography made it the door-way to the plains region. It could not be bypassed by Canadians coming from the East. From it radiated the "fluid highways" of the North-West and the overland trail to the Rocky Mountains. It would have to be the first seat of government for the North-West Territories, just as it had been for the Company's administration. This gave to the existing population of the Red River Settlement a significance far beyond mere numbers, and enabled it to exert an unusually strong influence on federal policy, not only at the time of union, but for the first five years of territorial administration.

The Canadians were the most articulate and politically aggressive group in the Red River Settlement. They and the Americans stood· to profit handsomely in the boom which would follow an influx of settlers from the East, and they were imbued with that blatant, sometimes ruthless, "booster" attitude which usually prevails among businessmen in a frontier community. Their views found expression in the only newspaper published in the Settlement, the Nor'Wester. The hostile attitude which this paper assumed towards the government of the Hudson's Bay Company was of great political significance both within the Settlement and in Eastern Canada. There were, for example, a sufficient number of Canadian, American, and native English-speaking residents who disliked the Company that an inflammatory editorial on the administration of justice could produce mob action to release a prisoner from jail. On the other hand, the desire of these expatriated Canadians for annexation of the country by Canada as publicized by the Nor'Wester appears to have been interpreted by Eastern papers as the prevailing opinion in the Settlement. It is probable that the ideas of members of the Macdonald administration regarding North-West affairs were influenced in this way. But though they controlled the press, the Canadian group did

2W. L. Morton, "The Red River Parish: Its Place in the Development of Manitoba" in R. C. Lodge, ed., Manitoba Essays (Toronto, 1937), p. 98.

not control public opinion, nor did the editorials of the *Nor'Wester* even represent the opinion of the majority of the English-speaking element, which was but half the total population.

Occupation, language, and religion combined to make the French-speaking half-breeds a distinct, self-conscious group in the Settlement. During the "happy, bucolic era" which reached its apogee in the 1850's they had no sense of insecurity and lived in amity with their English-speaking neighbours under a primitive, paternal government. In the decade before union, however, the situation had changed. Like the French habitant whose traditional way of life was threatened by the impact of English, Protestant commerce and industry, the French métis, hunters for the most part, had begun to dread the advance of an English, Protestant agricultural frontier. When we consider also the influence of the church, the similarity in circumstances and outlook of the French habitant and the French métis becomes even more significant.

Though the church was the focus of community life in both the Roman Catholic and Protestant parishes, it had a special significance for the métis people. Fifty years of devoted labour had established the French Canadian clergy as their most influential leaders.[3] There was nothing abnormal or unusual in this relationship. A similar situation existed on the banks of the St. Lawrence, and the history of Europe and America exhibits many examples of the process whereby a people, surrounded or threatened by an alien culture, find in their church the chief sustainer of their traditions, aspirations, and sense of importance. Nor is the influence exercised by Bishop Taché surprising; in him the métis possessed a leader who was one of the ablest Canadians of his generation.

From the church the French métis received his concept of minority rights as these were understood by French Canadian Catholics. To his prairie environment he owed the other dominant element in his attitude to life—a sense of independence derived from the democratic group action practiced in the organization of the annual buffalo hunt.[4] The significance of the buffalo hunt for our study lies in the fact that the capacity of the métis for concerted action under leaders

[3]Marcel Giraud, *Le Métis Canadien: son rôle dans l'histoire des provinces de l'Ouest* (Paris, 1945), p. 857; see also Chester Martin, "The First New Province of the Dominion," *Canadian Historical Review*, Vol. I (1920), p. 366, and G. F. G. Stanley, *The Birth of Western Canada: A History of the Riel Rebellions* (London, 1936), pp. 60–1.

[4]See Hargrave, *op. cit.*, p. 169.

of their own choice could be transferred to the realm of politics. This had been demonstrated to a limited extent as early as 1849, when Louis Riel's father led a movement which wrung the concession of free trade in furs from the Hudson's Bay Company.

II

The political institutions of this fur trade society were derived from the very general provisions of the Hudson's Bay Company charter, which permitted the Company to legislate for Rupert's Land and administer justice therein. The Company's institutions of government had evolved gradually, reaching their last stage of elaboration by the middle of the nineteenth century. The supreme governing body consisted of the Governor, Deputy-Governor, and Committee in London, to whom the officers overseas were responsible. The highest functionary in Rupert's Land was the Governor-in-Chief, who possessed "authority over the whole of the Company's Territories for judicial and other purposes, and the exercise of the power vested in him by the Charter."[5] Of the "government" provided for the area beyond the Red River Settlement little need be said here: it was primarily concerned with business matters—the Company had no intention of transforming Indian society, and ancient customs and tribal organization were not disturbed.

The Red River Settlement was the only place in the North-West where the Hudson's Bay Company faced the problem of providing a government for a sizable community. Here, the very general terms of the charter permitted the development of a semi-autonomous political unit called the District of Assiniboia. The office of Governor of Assiniboia had, during the last years of Company rule, been held by the Governor-in-Chief of Rupert's Land. The Councillors were appointed by the Governor and Committee in London on the recommendation of the Governor of Assiniboia, and held office during pleasure. There was no fixed number of Councillors: in 1869 there were twenty, including three ex-officio members—the Recorder of Rupert's Land (the presiding judge of the General Quarterly Court of Assiniboia), the Roman Catholic Bishop of St. Boniface, and the Anglican Bishop of Rupert's Land. The rest had been selected from

[5]Resolution of the General Court of the Hudson's Bay Company, March 13, 1839: extract included in Minutes of the Council of Assiniboia, Oliver, I, pp. 283-7.

among the native-born and long-time residents of the Red River Settlement, both half-breed and white.[6]

The Council was presided over by the Governor, and during the 1860's met at least once every three months and as many as nine times a year. The meetings, which were held at Fort Garry, were not open to the public, but the newspaper of the settlement, the *Nor'Wester*, was supplied with an account of the proceedings by the secretary.[7] The Council engaged in both executive and legislative action at the same sitting. The legislation consisted of short, simply worded resolutions, which were revised and consolidated from time to time and given the dignified title of "laws." These resolutions remained in force unless disallowed by the Governor and Committee in London.[8]

Assiniboia was quite generally viewed as a municipality, and the title "Municipal District of Assiniboia" was used by the Council itself.[9] The term, however, does not convey an accurate conception of the activities of the Council. A number of its "laws," it is true, were of a purely municipal character—those dealing with fire protection, stray animals, the upkeep of roads, police, and the regulation of hay cutting on unoccupied land. But the Council legislated on some subjects quite beyond the sphere of modern municipal government. Among these were the postal service, the administration of justice in the petty courts, the regulation of the manufacture and sale of intoxicants, debtors, marriage licences, and customs duties (the only form of taxation in Assiniboia). The absence of any legislation dealing with land sales and land titles is mute testimony to the dominance of the fur trade economy. Land questions were beyond the competence of the Council as involving the rights of the proprietor, but had an expanding agricultural frontier existed the Council would have been forced to deal with the subject in default of action by the Company in London. Leasehold or freehold titles could be secured,

[6]On the Council, see Report of Select Committee on the Hudson's Bay Company, *Parliamentary Papers* (Gt. B.), 1857, Session 2, pp. 66, 74, and Hargrave, *op. cit.*, p. 86. At a meeting of the Council on Aug. 3, 1865, Governor McTavish requested the members to suggest the names of persons whom he might recommend as Councillors, Oliver, I, p. 557.

[7]Hargrave, *op. cit.*, p. 254. The senior magistrate of each section of the District was supplied with a copy of the Minutes to make public at the sittings of the petty court—Minutes of the Council of Assiniboia, July 4, 1839, Oliver, I, p. 292.

[8]Notification of approval of certain minutes is contained in the letter of R. G. Smith, Secretary to the Governor and Committee, to Major Caldwell, April 5, 1854, printed in Report of Select Committee, 1857, p. 437.

[9]Minutes of the Council of Assiniboia, Oliver, I, pp. 465, 571 *et passim*.

but many of the settlers had not bothered to obtain them, and were simply squatters.[10] They evinced little interest in land policy or systematic land tenure until near the end of the period of Company rule.

The Council's main source of revenue consisted of the customs duties. Of the £1,816 derived from this source during the financial year 1867–8, £708 was paid by the Hudson's Bay Company, as the largest importer.[11] This income was sufficient for the modest public services required by the Settlement. The largest annual expenditure was on roads and bridges, followed by the salaries of the petty magistrates, customs collectors, constables, and a few other officials. The existence of private and church schools in the Settlement permitted the Council to escape the financial burden incident to a system of public education, which it would have been unable to bear without much greater financial resources.[12]

The significance of this description of the government of Assiniboia is apparent when we compare the distinctive features of that government with those of the temporary government established by the Canadian Parliament in 1869. The structure was the same in all essential respects. The head of the administration was an appointed official, responsible in the one instance to London, in the other to Ottawa. In the one case he was an agent of the Hudson's Bay Company, in the other of the federal government. The Council was an appointive one in both cases. In both systems the organ of control and of ultimate authority was geographically remote from the people and country being governed, while at the same time it controlled the fate of all local legislation. The irony of this situation will be evident when we recall that at this time it was generally believed in Canada (thanks largely to the *Nor'Wester*) that the Red River Settlement was groaning under a yoke of tyranny placed upon it by the Company.[13] As a matter of fact, a considerable degree of practical autonomy existed in the District of Assiniboia. The councillors were all local residents, and Bishop Taché, writing in 1869, stated that the Company "has been guided in its selection of councillors rather by the public voice than by its own interests, at least its mercantile in-

[10]See Archer Martin, *The Hudson's Bay Company's Land Tenures* (London, 1898), and Stanley, *op. cit.*, pp. 14–15.

[11]Hargrave, *op. cit.*, p. 96.

[12]See M. P. Toombs, "Educational Policy of the Hudson's Bay Company," *Saskatchewan History*, vol. IV, pp. 7–8.

[13]See for example Cartier's remarks as reported in *Parliamentary Debates* 1870, col. 147.

terests. It has selected several councillors from among those who have been most warmly opposed to its trading."[14]

The Council was permitted to develop a strong sense of its responsibility as a governing body, and the later Governors acted in close concert with it. The institutions of Assiniboia had taken form before the middle of the century under the impress of decisions of the London Committee and Governor-in-Chief Simpson, but once established they were permitted to function rather freely. The London Committee does not seem to have intervened actively in the affairs of the District during the later years, and there were few instances of disallowance of the Council's ordinances. The composition of the Council violated the principles of the separation of powers and of the separation of church and state; but the ill effects, if any, do not seem to have disturbed the people, and a sufficient degree of autonomy existed to satisfy the majority of the population. The Governor and Council expressed no complaint concerning the scope of their powers, though they did protest against the lack of a sufficient constabulary to support their authority.[15] Except for the agitation of the Canadian minority there was no movement for the substitution of an elective for an appointive Council.

The federal government's plan for acquiring the North-West and governing it as a territory was the last of several proposals which had been advanced during the preceding decade with the objective of replacing the rule of the Hudson's Bay Company. Ever since 1857, when a British Parliamentary Committee considered the affairs of Rupert's Land, proposals to establish a Crown colony or to annex a portion of the country to the then Province of Canada had been in the air. There were negotiations between the Company and the Colonial Office, and the question had been raised in the British House of Commons on a number of occasions. The Company had expressed its willingness to relinquish its powers of government, at least in the plains region. But, owing to a combination of circumstances, neither of these proposed changes was effected. The British government was reluctant to increase Imperial commitments by establishing a Crown colony; the Company insisted on substantial compensation for relinquishing title to the land; the Canadian government was hostile to

[14]Mgr Taché, *Sketch of the North-West of America*, translated by Captain D. R. Cameron, R.A. (Montreal, 1870), p. 67.

[15]British troops were stationed on the Red River from 1846 to 1855 and from 1857 to 1861: see Hargrave, *op. cit.*, and Report of the Select Committee on the Boundaries of Ontario, *Journals of the House of Commons*, 1880, Appendix 1, pp. 94 ff.

the Company's claims; and the French Canadians were fearful of being dominated by an enlarged "Canada West." In all these negotiations there was no participation either by the people then living in the North-West or those responsible for its local administration; nor was any attempt made to discover the state of public opinion where such could be said to exist. The emergence of the Confederation movement in eastern British North America offered a third alternative for the government of the North-West, and one which avoided some of the difficulties which the earlier proposals had encountered. But here again the tripartite negotiations proceeded as if the transaction concerned only real estate, or as if the North-West lacked a population living under a system of law and government. The Imperial government and the Hudson's Bay Company were able to escape the consequences of ignoring public opinion in the North-West in this way, but the Canadian government was forced to reckon with it as soon as it attempted to implement its plans for territorial administration.

III

The striking similarity between the temporary territorial government devised by the Macdonald administration and the existing Hudson's Bay Company régime did not lessen the jubilance of the Red River Canadians at the prospect of union with Canada. That in comparison with Company rule, the Canadian government could do no wrong, seems to have been the view of the *Nor'Wester*. That paper, which in May was predicting "an elective Legislature with a representative or two in the House of Commons . . . preparatory to our admission to the full privileges of the Dominion as a province,"[16] was in September defending the temporary government legislation against the *Globe*'s attacks, questioning whether the country was ready for the elective franchise, and welcoming for a few months a pupilage under the experienced statesmen of the East.[17] But it was discreetly silent on the difference between the new system and the "state of semi-vassalage under a powerful monopoly"—the designation which it simultaneously applied to the government of Assiniboia.

The Canadians, however, were the only residents of the Settlement who were exulting over the impending union. The vast majority of

16*Nor'Wester*, May 15, 1869.
17*Ibid.*, Sept. 7, 1869. An editorial of June 26 had described the legislation as "by far the wisest course which could have been adopted for the time being."

the English-speaking population were apathetic; they were "dissatisfied because of the unceremonious nature of the transaction" although not disposed to oppose the change which it effected.[18] A report[19] on their opinions on the eve of the arrival of the Governor designate indicated "a disposition to extend a sincere welcome to Mr. McDougall," but at the same time there was a feeling of chagrin that "The character of the new Government has been settled in Canada, without our being consulted." Though they were prepared "to accept [the new government] respectfully, to obey the laws, and to become good subjects," the report found them unwilling to become involved in any conflict with their French fellow citizens, believing "that the Dominion should assume the responsibility of establishing amongst us what it, and it alone, has decided upon."

The attitude of the French-speaking element in the Settlement to the proposed territorial government was affected not so much by the form of that government as by the prospect of union itself, which they knew would bring in its wake a flood of immigrants—farmers, businessmen, speculators—predominantly Protestant and English speaking. Riel well expressed the views of his people when, having been called before the Council of Assiniboia, he declared "that his party were perfectly satisfied with the present Government and wanted no other; . . . that they were uneducated and only half civilized, and felt that if a large immigration were to take place they would probably be crowded out of a country which they claimed as their own; that they knew they were in a sense poor and insignificant, but that it was just because they were aware of this that they had felt so much at being treated as if they were even more insignificant than they in reality were; that their existence or at least their wishes had been entirely ignored."[20]

Bishop Taché viewed the situation with the keen insight of an analytical mind. "The greatest social crime of our French Half-

[18]See testimony of J. J. Hargrave, Report of the Select Committee on the Causes of the Difficulties in the North-West Territory in 1869–70, *Journals of the House of Commons*, 1874, Appendix 6, pp. 185–6.

[19]This report was made to McDougall by J. S. Dennis on Oct. 27, 1869, see McDougall to Secretary of State for the Provinces, Oct. 31, 1869, *C.S.P.* 1870, no. 12, p. 11; its accuracy is vouched for by McTavish in a letter to McDougall, Oct. 30, 1869, *ibid.*, pp. 23–4, as well as by Hargrave's testimony cited above, and by Riel's remarks before the Council of Assiniboia: "If Mr. MacDougall were once here most probably the English speaking population would allow him to be installed in office as Governor": Minutes of the Council of Assiniboia, Oct. 25, 1869, Oliver, II, p. 617.

[20]*Ibid.*

breeds," he wrote, "is that they are hunters."[21] The advance of agricultural settlement in the North-West, with the resulting extinction of the buffalo hunt, would present a "fearful crisis." "As we love the people more than the land in which they live," he continued, "as we prefer the wellbeing of the former to the splendor of the latter, we now repeat that, for our population, we very much dread some of the promised changes."[22] The Red River Settlement, that "offspring of Rupert's Land," was entitled to considerate treatment:

Yet, although not quite free, the child has acquired certain rights; it possesses or occupies land for which it has not always paid: it has cultivated them with its labor. True,—the labor has not always been great; but we speak of a child of the desert. It commands indulgence; it presumes to hope that here the foreigner shall not be preferred, that in the great and wise plans matured by the Mother Country and Canada— its eldest brother, its past history may not be entirely disregarded.[23]

Thus when some months later Bishop Taché contemplated the territorial government policy of the Macdonald administration so far as it was made public, he found little to allay his disquiet, not only as a friend of the métis, but as a Catholic and a French Canadian.

Puisque le Haut-Canada fournit McDougall et un conseiller [he wrote to Cartier] pourquoi le Bas-Canada n'aurait-il pas aussi ses deux hommes? . . . Pourquoi faire en sorte que toutes les influences puissent devenir prejudiciables à nos compatriotes et co-réligionnaires? . . . J'ai toujours redoute l'entree du Nord-Ouest dans la Confederation parce que j'ai toujours cru que l'élément français catholique serait sacrifié; mais je vous avoue franchement qu'il ne m'était jamais venu à la pensée que, nos droits seraient si vite et si completement méconnus. Le nouveau système me semble de nature à amener la ruine de ce qui nous a coûté si cher.[24]

It is not surprising, therefore, to find Mgr Taché writing to Bishop Grandin at St. Albert: ". . . prenez possession d'autant de terre que vous pourrez dans les différentes localités. Poussez votre peuple à cette measure: que les pauvres métis se saisissent du pays, autrement il leur faudra le laisser, et où iraient-ils?"[25]

The Council of Assiniboia's address of welcome to McDougall[26] (drafted by the Anglican Bishop) reflected these currents of opinion,

[21]Taché, op. cit., p. 106.
[22]Ibid., p. 69.
[23]Ibid.
[24]Taché to Cartier, Oct. 7, 1869, in Dom. Benoit, Vie de Mgr Taché Archevêque de St. Boniface (Montreal, 1904), vol. II, pp. 16–17.
[25]Taché to Grandin, Oct. 26, 1869, in Benoit, op. cit., pp. 25–6.
[26]Minutes of the Council of Assiniboia, Oct. 19, 1869, Oliver, II, pp. 612–14.

and is perhaps one of the most effective proofs that in this part of the North-West a government existed which possessed a sense of responsibility to the community. The language was courteous; the etiquette irreproachable; but the tenor was plain: the head of the new territorial government was to be reminded that he would be living in a community having traditions and rights which were entitled to respect. "We quite feel," the Council declared, "that from the altered circumstances of this country, which has been rapidly changing within the last few years, it is well that its Government has been transferred from the great commercial body on which it hitherto devolved; but the administration of the Honorable Company was we believe, on the whole well suited to the past state of things," and it was a tribute to "the wisdom, discretion and honorable conduct of those who administered the affairs of this country, that a small defenseless settlement even existed for many years among wild tribes of Indians, without annoyance or trouble from them, and that a profitable trade was carried on without difficulty through the length and breadth of the land." In view of this McDougall could "well understand," the address continued, "that there are mingled feelings in our community with respect to the great change that has taken place, and even misgivings as regards the future in the minds of some," but "we have the fullest confidence, not only that all just rights of the old settlers will be respected, but that the transition will be made as easy for them as possible."

IV

The resentment at being ignored during the high-level deliberations which had settled the political destiny of the North-West was the one common factor in the attitude of everyone except the Canadians in the Settlement. The Canadian government, however, cannot properly be criticized for ignoring the Settlement during the tripartite negotiations; if anyone was remiss in this respect it was the Company and the Imperial government. But the negotiations for transfer having been completed, Canada owed its prospective new citizens an explanation of its policy for the North-West. Was such explanation forthcoming? It is true that Canadian newspapers circulated in the Settlement carrying reports of parliamentary proceedings, but, as we have seen, the statements of policy during the session of 1869 were not very revealing. But if the government was oracular, its critics were quite ready with an interpretation of its policy. Thus it was that the *Globe*'s charge that an oligarchy was to be fastened on the North-

West gained wide currency in the Settlement.[27] That no effort was made to counteract the propaganda of the Liberal press must be attributed to the firmly rooted idea in official circles in Ottawa that Hudson's Bay Company rule was unpopular and that union with Canada was unreservedly welcomed. This *idée fixe* explains the government's failure to elicit information from Governor McTavish when he was in Ottawa in June,[28] and also for the indifference with which Cartier received the information proffered by Bishop Taché when he visited the capital in July.[29] Taché's representations, however, may have had something to do with the decision to have Howe visit the Red River Settlement,[30] though in this instance too the government's concern may be measured by the fact that he received no official instructions.

Howe's early October sojourn in the Settlement is certainly the strangest episode in the story of the beginnings of federal policy for the North-West. Though he had been designated as the cabinet minister responsible for that policy, he deliberately left the impression in the Settlement that he was there as a private individual![31] There is every reason to believe that Howe was most uncomfortable in the situation in which he found himself. As soon as he discovered the disturbed state of public opinion (first reported to him at Fort Abercrombie, Minnesota) all his old misgivings about western expansion reasserted themselves, and with the idea of giving no offence to the sensitivities of the Red River people, he represented himself as not having come in any official capacity. When confronted with the com-

[27]See testimony of Archbishop Taché and A. G. B. Bannatyne before the Select Committee of 1874, *Journals of the House of Commons,* 1874, Appendix 6, pp. 14, 22, 123.

[28]The evidence concerning the interview which McTavish had with the government is conflicting. On the one hand there is his statement (quoted by Archbishop Taché in his testimony before the Select Committee of 1874) that "I have not been able to cause any of my recommendations to be accepted by the Government" (p. 14); on the other there is McDougall's statement in the House of Commons that "the Government had an interview with Governor McTavish not long before his [McDougall's] appointment, and he gave no hint of any prospect of trouble" (*Parliamentary Debates,* 1870, col. 1316), also Macdonald's statement in a report of the Privy Council of Dec. 16, 1869, that "When Governor McTavish visited Canada in June last, he was in communication with the Canadian Government, and he never intimated that he had even a suspicion of discontent existing, nor did he make any suggestions as to the best mode of effecting the proposed change, with the assent of the inhabitants": *C.S.P.* 1870, no. 12, p. 142.

[29]See testimony of Archbishop Taché before the Select Committee of 1874, pp. 9 ff.

[30]See Taché's evidence, *ibid.,* pp. 13–14 and Howe's statement in the House of Commons, *Parliamentary Debates,* 1870, col. 112.

[31]Alexander Begg, Red River Journal from Nov. 16, 1869, P.A.C., p. 8.

plaints and fears rife in the Settlement he was in a dilemma: as an old champion of popular rights he sympathized with aspirations for self-government, but as a member of an administration which had developed no plan for territorial government he could offer only the general assurance (as he later reported it) "that the same constitution as the other Provinces possessed would ultimately be conferred upon the country; that in the provisional arrangements to be made, the feeling and interests of the resident population would be considered— that leading men enjoying their confidence, would be at once taken into the Government, and that the young men, without distinction of blood, would be drawn into the public service as they were fitted by education to fill places of trust and emolument."[32] He refused to make speeches, "in consideration," so he later claimed, "of the position of Governor McTavish on the one hand, or of the incoming Governor McDougall";[33] but these were not his only reasons for refusal.

The charge later levelled by McDougall that Howe had preached resistance to the Canadian government's territorial policy has not been firmly established. Yet it is not difficult to see how such a report could originate: the place was a hot bed of rumours, and with the local press in the hands of a partisan minority, public opinion was formed largely by word of mouth communication. To the little settlement a visit from the President of the Privy Council of Canada was a great event. The consequences, therefore, of his deliberately refraining from fraternizing with the leaders of the Canadian party can easily be imagined; not only that, but he "disclaimed any connection" with Schultz and Mair,[34] the *bêtes noires* of the French. What Howe regarded as a proper attitude of neutrality to local feuds would be interpreted as a blow at the Canadians. No doubt too the slightest hint of sympathy with prevailing complaints, coming from the champion of better terms for Nova Scotia, would be eagerly seized on and magnified by those who were dissatisfied with the conditions of union.

Howe's position was a delicate one, but he could have done more than he did to influence public opinion, even by his deliberately chosen method of informal conversations. He reported to Macdonald that "by frank and courteous explanations to leading men, who largely represent the resident population, I have cleared the air a good deal,

[32]Howe to McDougall, Dec. 11, 1869, *C.S.P.* 1870, no. 12, pp. 58–9.
[33]*Parliamentary Debates*, 1870, col. 113.
[34]Howe to McDougall, Oct. 31, 1869, in Beckles Willson, *The Life of Lord Strathcona and Mount Royal* (London, 1915), pp. 175–6.

and I have done my best to give McDougall a fair start."[35] Yet the "leading men" did not include Riel, Bruce, or Father Ritchot, and he only saw the Anglican Bishop (the most influential English-speaking member of the Council) for a few moments, despite the fact that he spent about ten days in the Settlement.[36] His two days spent in studying the records of the Council of Assiniboia could have been better employed; and the procuring of a copy of the existing laws and the names of the Councillors were details which could have been left to McDougall's care.

Howe's real feelings, which explain his evasiveness while in the Settlement, are revealed in a letter to a friend:

My visit to Red River [he wrote] has utterly cured me of any lingering hope I may have had of a peaceable transfer. The only thing we can do now is to minimize the extent of the mischief. Trouble is bound to come either before or after, and if it were not for Mr. McDougall and the extent to which we have pledged ourselves, I would say let us keep our hands out of this Manitoba business into which we have been hurried and which promises to jeopardise our Government and the interests of Confederation. It will be hard to pull out now, but if we see a chance of it we must do it. This country is not necessary to us, and at this stage it will only be a drag upon our energies and resources.[37]

These sentiments, however, could scarcely be communicated to McDougall, who would have scorned them as treasonable. Moreover, Howe had no way of knowing that McDougall would not be allowed to enter the Settlement and form his own conclusions before assuming office. Consequently, when they met on the prairie trail between Georgetown and Fort Abercrombie, he did no more than warn that the Canadians in the Settlement had aroused the hostility and fears of the métis.[38]

V

Macdonald's scheme for the government of the Territories was one of the central issues during the disturbances of 1869–70 in the Red River Settlement. These disturbances forced the federal authorities to

[35]Howe to Macdonald, Oct. 16, in Joseph Pope, *Memoirs of the Rt. Hon. Sir John Alexander Macdonald* (revised ed., Toronto, 1930), p. 407.

[36]See Howe to McDougall, Dec. 11, 1869, *C.S.P.* 1870, no. 12, p. 58, and the Bishop of Rupert's Land to the Governor General of Canada, March 18, 1870 in J. A. Roy, *Joseph Howe* (Toronto, 1935), p. 293.

[37]Howe to Edward O'Brien, Oct. 23, 1869, in Willson, *op. cit.*, p. 173.

[38]See Howe's and McDougall's statements in *Parliamentary Debates*, 1870, at cols. 117 and 119. Howe's letter to McDougall written at St. Paul on Oct. 31, 1869, contained only general observations and a similar warning.

undertake a formal defence of their policy, while at the same time the people of the Red River Settlement, and particularly the métis group, fashioned a set of constitutional principles more to their liking than those embodied in the Temporary Government Act.

When McDougall was stopped at the border of the North-West on October 30 by half-breeds who asserted that their rights had been ignored, he was in the same position as Joseph Howe had been a couple of weeks earlier—he could offer only the general assurance of "the determination of the Government to deal justly with all classes, and to respect existing rights, without reference to race or religion."[39] Provencher, having been sent forward to interview the leaders of the movement, told them that "many members of the New Council would be taken from amongst the population of this country, so as to represent as faithfully as possible all the various interests of the people, and that the policy of the Canadian Government could be ascertained by their general dealings with other Provinces, and by the speeches of ministers on this very question." "The people of Canada," he told them, "would be only too glad to be relieved of a portion of their responsibility, by granting to those people free political institutions and self-government as soon as practicable."[40] But the métis, even at this early stage of the movement, were determined not to be put off with promises and general declarations, and informed Provencher that these explanations had come too late, and that they were even then in consultation with the English-speaking residents "to arrange all matters relating to languages, nationality or religion," following which they would be prepared to negotiate with some acceptable representative of the Canadian government.[41] In this statement are to be found the principles upon which the leaders of the movement, Riel and Abbé Ritchot, based their strategy, and with brilliant results. While they never secured the whole-hearted co-operation of the English-speaking population, their propaganda effectively neutralized overt opposition. In the battle for the mind of the Settlement, Mc-Dougall and his supporters were decisively defeated.

At the instigation of the métis leaders a joint council or convention consisting of twelve English-speaking and twelve French-speaking representatives from the several parishes was organized, which met periodically from November 16 to December 1, 1869.[42] It was not a

39Instructions to J. A. N. Provencher, reported in McDougall to Howe, Oct. 31, 1869, C.S.P. 1870, no. 12, p. 6.
40Provencher to McDougall, Nov. 3, 1869, ibid., p. 28.
41Ibid.
42The minutes of this "convention" in French, prepared by the secretary, Louis Riel, are in the Riel Papers, P.A.M.

harmonious assembly, but on the last day it accepted a "List of Rights." In contrast to the generalities of McDougall and Provencher, the List was detailed and specific:

1. That the people have the right to elect their own Legislature.
2. That the Legislature have the power to pass all laws local to the Territory over the veto of the Executive by a two-thirds vote.
3. That no Act of the Dominion Parliament (local to the Territory) be binding on the people until sanctioned by the Legislature of the Territory.
4. That all Sheriffs, Magistrates, Constables, School Commissioners, &c., be elected by the people.
5. A free homestead and pre-emption land law.
6. That a portion of the public lands be appropriated to the benefit of schools, the building of bridges, roads, and public buildings.
7. That it be guaranteed to connect Winnipeg by rail with the nearest line of railroad, within a term of five years; the land grant to be subject to the Local Legislature.
8. That, for the term of four years, all military, civil, and municipal expenses be paid out of the Dominion funds.
9. That the military be composed of the inhabitants now existing in the Territory.
10. That the English and French languages be common in the Legislature and Courts, and that all public documents and Acts of the Legislature be published in both languages.
11. That the Judge of the Supreme Court speak the English and French languages.
12. That treaties be concluded and ratified between the Dominion Government and the several tribes of Indians in the Territory, to ensure peace on the frontier.
13. That we have a fair and full representation in the Canadian Parliament.
14. That all privileges, customs, and usages existing at the time of the transfer, be respected.[43]

The French representatives proposed that steps be taken to confront McDougall with the choice of guaranteeing these rights (if his commission permitted it) and being welcomed to Fort Garry, or of being told "to remain where he is, or return, [to Canada] till the rights be guaranteed by Act of the Canadian Parliament."[44] When the English refused to agree to the despatch of a delegation of the Convention with this object in view, the French countered by printing and distributing the List throughout the Settlement where, since it clarified the objectives of the métis, it prevented the Canadians from rallying

43C.S.P. 1870, no. 12, p. 100.
44Ibid., p. 101.

the English-speaking population in a counter movement.[45] The List had this effect because it appealed to the majority of the English as being, on the whole, a statement which embodied their own aspirations.

From the standpoint of popular political ideas the List of Rights exhibits several interesting and significant features. American influence is evident in the relationship of the executive to the legislature (2), the election of sheriffs, magistrates, and constables (4), the land law (5), and the land grant for railway construction (7); of these, the first two were foreign to prevailing constitutional practice in Canada, but the remaining two were to become prominent features of federal land policy. The French interest in minority rights is to be found in the 10th, 11th, and 14th items. The 3rd and 9th were extreme measures to protect local vested interests. The use of public lands as a means of securing revenue for schools (6) had precedents in both American and Canadian administration. The demand for railway communication has an interesting parallel in the conditions under which British Columbia later entered Confederation, though in this case the fact that the nearest connecting line was American may not be without significance. The 8th item, relating to the financial position of the territory, was in conformity with the nature of territorial status, particularly if (as was implied) the land was to remain under federal control. Finally, the 1st, 12th, and 13th items were in the main stream of British political and administrative tradition.

This List of Rights, hurriedly composed, obviously the work of a "committee" with each member contributing his quota of inspiration, in part naïve, in part unreasonable, is also a striking example of the mingling of American,[46] British, and French Canadian political ideas in this little settlement at the crossroads of the Canadian and American frontiers. In this document the three traditions had not been merged in a consistent and mature synthesis—their first contact was still too recent for that—but its authors had no reason to be ashamed of a product so thoroughly democratic in spirit.

At about the same time that this List of Rights was circulating in

[45]See "Record of Proceedings under Commission from Lieutenant-Governor McDougall, dated 1st December, 1869" by J. S. Dennis, C.S.P. 1870, no. 12, pp. 111–13.

[46]An indication of Riel's attitude to the Americans was given in one of his conversations with Donald A. Smith: "Do not attempt to prejudice us against the Americans," Smith reported him as saying, "for although we have not been with them—they are with us, and have been better friends to us than the Canadians." Report of Donald A. Smith to Hon. Joseph Howe, April 12, 1870, C.S.P. 1870, no. 12, hereinafter cited as D. A. Smith, "Report."

the Red River Settlement, and before copies of it had reached Ottawa, Joseph Howe and his colleagues were preparing a belated explanation of their policy in response to the reception which had been accorded to their unfortunate colleague McDougall. The "explanations" involved printing copies of McDougall's Instructions for distribution in the Settlement and formulating general assurances of representation of all interests in the composition of the Council and of respect for civil and religious liberties and property rights. These assurances, which McDougall was instructed to convey, had already, as we have seen, been communicated by him to the métis. The only new particulars which he was permitted to mention were that a "most liberal policy" would be followed in granting titles to land already occupied, that the Council would have the power to establish municipal self-government immediately and that, contrary to an earlier decision, the existing customs duties, except on liquor, would be continued unchanged for two years. Finally, the temporary character of the existing arrangements was re-emphasized, with the promise of "a liberal constitution" as soon as the Lieutenant-Governor and Council could report fully "on the wants and requirements of the Territory."[47]

The Macdonald administration had not, of course, abandoned the idea of establishing a territorial form of government applicable to the Red River Settlement along with the rest of the North-West. This is clearly indicated in the only general exposition of the theory of territorial status which can be found in the pronouncements of federal ministers, in this case penned by Joseph Howe as Secretary of State for the Provinces:

All of the Provinces of the British Empire which now enjoy Representative Institutions and Responsible Government have passed through a probationary period, till the growth of population, and some political training, prepared them for self-government.

In the United States, the Territories are ruled from Washington till the time arrives when they can prove their fitness to be included in the family of States, and, in the Halls of Congress, challenge the full measure of power and free development which American Citizenship includes.

It is fair to assume that some such training as human society requires in all free countries may be useful, if not indispensable, at Red River; but of this you may be assured, that the Governor-General and his

---

[47]Howe to McDougall, Dec. 7, 1869, *C.S.P.* 1870, no. 12, pp. 42–3. To give weight to these assurances, a proclamation of the Governor General in the Queen's name, dated Dec. 6, promised that "on the union with Canada all your civil and religious rights and privileges will be respected, your properties secured to you, and . . . your country will be governed, as in the past, under British laws, and in the spirit of British justice," *ibid.*, p. 44. The original policy respecting the tariff and the subsequent change are contained in Orders in Council dated Sept. 28, 1869, and Dec. 7, 1869, respectively.

Council will gladly welcome the period when the Queen can confer, with their entire approbation, the largest measure of self-government on her subjects in that region, compatible with the preservation of British interests on this Continent, and the integrity of the Empire.[48]

The federal government's reaction to the List of Rights is indicated in a letter of January 2, 1870, from the Prime Minister to Donald A. Smith, General Manager of the Eastern (Montreal) Department of the Hudson's Bay Company.[49] About the middle of December, the government, now anxious to utilize all sources of influence to remove the obstructions to union, had formally commissioned Smith to report on the difficulties, to explain to the people the principles of the scheme of territorial government, and to arrange with McDougall and McTavish "one system of concerted action in the pacification of the country."[50] The letter indicated that Macdonald was still hopeful that explanations, rather than radical concessions, could produce this "pacification." In this connection he claimed that by the terms of the Temporary Government Act the Council of Assiniboia was continued in existence, [51] and would be McDougall's Council until such time as it was reconstituted. While such an interpretation of the Act was quite possible, this was the first time that anyone had advanced it, and there is no reason to believe that it represented the original intention of the government. When reconstituting the Council, Macdonald stated, the government would be guided by the advice of the old members and would be willing to select two-thirds of the Councillors from residents of the North-West. Introduction of the "elective principle" would have to await a report from "the existing Council" (except in the case of municipal bodies, where it could be established at once) and would also depend on the Territory being in a position to "bear the burdens and assume the responsibilities" of an elective legislature. Under these circumstances the expenses of the territorial government would be "for the present" paid from the federal treasury. The question of representation in Parliament Macdonald regarded in a different light—it would, he stated, be "a matter for discussion

[48]Howe to The Very Rev. Grand Vicar, Mr. Thibault, Dec. 4, 1869, *C.S.P.* 1870, no. 12, p. 46.

[49]Sir Joseph Pope, *Correspondence of Sir John Macdonald* (New York and Toronto, 1921), pp. 116–19.

[50]Howe to Smith, Dec. 10, 1869, *C.S.P.* 1870, no. 12, p. 48.

[51]Section 6 stated that "All Public Officers and Functionaries holding office in Rupert's Land and the North-Western Territory, at the time of their admission into the Union, excepting the Public Officer or Functionary at the head of the administration of affairs, shall continue to be Public Officers and Functionaries . . . until otherwise ordered by the Lieutenant-Governor, under the authority of this Act."

and arrangement" with a delegation which Smith was authorized to invite to Ottawa. The implication was that such representation would not be delayed.

At the mass meetings at Fort Garry on January 19 and 20, 1870, it was decided to elect what was, in effect, a constitutional convention, which met from January 25 to February 10 at Fort Garry.[52] Composed of twenty English-speaking and twenty French-speaking delegates elected by the several parishes, it was the first fully representative body to meet in the North-West to consider political matters.[53] The majority of the English-speaking representatives insisted on preparing a new List of Rights—a course favoured by Smith. It appears that Smith, as a confidant of some of the members, was able to influence the drafting of this document. He reported to Macdonald: "We have succeeded in getting expunged some of the most objectionable points in their demands."[54] The most important question which arose during the deliberations of the Convention was Riel's proposal, now advanced for the first time, that provincial status should be demanded. The majority, however, favoured territorial status, with the result that the second List of Rights was based on this premise. This document was longer (19 articles) and exhibited much greater discernment and realism than its predecessor. American influence was less in evidence, with the result that most of the terms were consistent with British political usage. Nevertheless about half of the provisions of the first List were incorporated in the second.[55]

The new clauses dealt with practical issues: no direct taxation except for municipal purposes during the territorial period; continuance of existing customs duties for at least three years; local control of the public domain within a circle whose radius was to be the distance between Fort Garry and the international boundary; no liability for the £300,000 payable by Canada to the Hudson's Bay Company or for the public debt of Canada. On the other hand

[52]The English delegates to the convention were elected at public meetings in the various parishes, the apportionment of delegates among the parishes being fixed by a committee appointed at the meeting on January 20: *New Nation*, Jan. 21, 1870. The apportionment and election of the French delegates appears to have been arranged by the métis council.

[53]The proceedings and debates of the Convention are fully reported in the *New Nation*. These reports form the basis of Thomas Spence's manuscript "Manitoba Missing Links or The True Story of the Red River Troubles of 1869–70, Containing Interesting Speeches of Riel and Others," P.A.C.

[54]Smith to Macdonald, Feb. 1, 1870, quoted in A. S. Morton, *op. cit.*, p. 902.

[55]The second List is printed as an Appendix to D. A. Smith's "Report." The 2nd, 5th, 10th, 11th, and 12th items in the first List appeared also in the second; the 3rd, 7th, 8th, 13th, and 14th appeared with some modifications.

measures for protecting the interests of the old residents were spelled out in greater detail: the franchise for elections to the territorial legislature and to the House of Commons was to be restricted to those who had resided in the North-West for at least three years, and was to be subject to amendment only by the local legislature; existing local customs and usages were not only to be respected but to be placed under local legislative control; representation in Parliament was to consist of one Senator and three members of the House of Commons. This List also described the form and powers of the territorial government: it was to consist of a Lieutenant-Governor, a legislature (elected in the manner already described), and a three-man executive (heads of departments) chosen by the Governor General in Council from among the members of the assembly. The powers of the territorial legislature were indirectly defined by the stipulation "that there shall be no interference by the Dominion Parliament in the Local Affairs of this Territory other than is allowed in any of the Provinces in the Confederation." The List did not specify how long territorial status was to continue, but defined it as an "exceptional period" upon whose expiration provincial institutions with responsible government should be instituted.

On the whole, this second List was a well-considered and reasonable presentation of popular rights and legitimate local interests. Smith, somewhat unwillingly forced into the role of spokesman for the federal government, reported to the Convention that most of its terms would be accepted.[56] In this he was later supported by Howe, who when the List was communicated to him stated that it was "in the main satisfactory."[57] The government, of course, had no thought of conferring anything but territorial status on the North-West. Writing privately to Bishop Taché on February 16, as the latter prepared to depart on his mission of pacification, Macdonald stated, "It is obvious that the most inexpensive mode for the administration of affairs should at first be adopted. As the preliminary expense of organizing the Government after union with Canada, must, in the first, be defrayed from the Canadian treasury, there will be a natural objection in the Canadian Parliament to a large expenditure."[58]

[56]D. A. Smith, "Report," Appendix. Smith gave the convention his views on each of the nineteen articles ("such answers as I believed would be in accordance with the views of the Canadian Government").

[57]Howe to Taché, telegram, Feb. 25, 1870, *Journals of the House of Commons*, 1874, Appendix 6, p. 20.

[58]Macdonald to Taché, private, Feb. 16, 1870, *ibid.*, p. 19. The official communication from the government to Taché on the subject of the bishop's mission is a letter from Howe dated Feb. 16, 1870, printed in *C.S.P.* 1870, no. 12, pp. 128–9.

Had the three delegates chosen by the Convention left immediately for Ottawa it is probable that the demand for provincial status would not have been advanced during the negotiations, and the whole of the North-West would have entered the union under a territorial form of government. The delay in the delegates' departure is reported to have been due to the receipt of news of Taché's mission: "It was decided to await his arrival," in the expectation that he might have "sufficient authority to arrange matters."[59]

VI

Over six weeks elapsed before the delegates left the Red River Settlement, it having been discovered that the Bishop had no authority to negotiate on political matters. Meanwhile the Settlement was in a ferment of political activity: a provisional government was formed, a legislative assembly elected, and a constitution adopted for "Assiniboia," as the whole North-West was designated. To describe the events of this period and how Riel, as President of the provisional government, accomplished what the constitutional convention had thwarted —the preparation of a bill of rights demanding provincial status— would lead us beyond the proper limits of this study.[60] The main point to be noted is that Riel and his associates became convinced that their rights were safer under a provincial constitution than under a territorial form of government, and that the Macdonald administration was placed in a position where it found it expedient to concede this demand. Indeed the concession was an inescapable necessity, for without it the whole ambitious scheme of western expansion was in imminent danger of collapse: the Red River Settlement, the key to the North-West, was in Riel's firm grasp; the Imperial government demanded a political settlement before the despatch of an expeditionary force; and in French Canada there was a rising tide of sympathy with the métis cause. The decision to create a province was a disagreeable one, for as we have seen the government had all along been considering a form of territorial administration. "Sir George Cartier told me," Bishop Taché wrote later, "how the Government of Ottawa was embarrassed and annoyed when the delegates refused to negotiate on the

---

[59]Rev. J. B. Thibault to Hon. Joseph Howe, March 17, 1870, *ibid.*

[60]The best account of these developments is in Stanley, *op. cit.* See also Chester Martin, "The First 'New Province' of the Dominion," *Canadian Historical Review*, Vol. I, pp. 364–71, and Rev. Geo. Bryce, *Two Provisional Governments in Manitoba* (Transactions of the Historical and Scientific Society of Manitoba, no. 38, 1890).

Bill of Rights prepared by the Convention."[61] Having been forced to establish a province, the government determined that it should not be a large one and that it should be unable to obstruct immigration or "interfere with the general policy of the Government in opening up communication to the Pacific."[62]

Expediency rather than political conviction produced the Manitoba Act. As Macdonald himself remarked in the House of Commons, "This Bill contains very few provisions, but not too few for the object to be gained, which is the quiet and peaceable acceptance of the new state of things by the mass of the people there. . . ." In private, he declared that provincial status was "a little premature,"[63] but politician-like he made a virtue of necessity and in public described the measure as "a boon and convincing proof of the liberality of the people and the Legislature of the Dominion";[64] but he could not and did not claim that it was part of a plan for the government of the North-West. That no such plan existed was made evident by the provisions which the Manitoba Act contained for the government of the territory outside of the new province. The Lieutenant-Governor of Manitoba was to be the Lieutenant-Governor of the North-West Territories and was to administer it under the provisions of the Temporary Government Act, which was re-enacted and continued in force until the end of the parliamentary session of 1871.[65] As to the future of the North-West, nothing was said except that it "should be divided into Provinces with as restricted a boundary as possible," though the enlargement of Manitoba was also mentioned as a possible development.[66]

The Liberal leader, Alexander Mackenzie, likened the diminutive new province to "some of the incidents in Gulliver's Travels." "The Government," he declared, "were proceeding now as much in the wrong direction as last session, when passing a Bill practically ignoring the right of the people of that Territory." For the time being, he favoured "a state of tutelage . . . such as was in existence in the Territories of the United States" but with a "Legislative Assembly chosen by the popular voice" and representation in Parliament, so that when a provincial constitution was later established the views of regularly

[61]Open letter of Archbishop Taché to James Taylor, in *Manitoba Daily Free Press*, Jan. 15, 1890.
[62]Sir John A. Macdonald, *Parliamentary Debates*, 1870, col. 1318.
[63]Macdonald to Robert Bown, private, Jan. 4, 1871, Macdonald Papers.
[64]*Parliamentary Debates*, 1870, col. 1294.
[65]33 Vict. c. 3, ss. 35 and 36.
[66]Sir John A. Macdonald, *Parliamentary Debates*, 1870, cols. 1309–10.

elected representatives could be taken into consideration.[67] The theoretical grounds of Mackenzie's opposition were reinforced by his dislike of Riel and his belief that the three delegates were spokesmen for the Riel faction and did not accurately represent North-West opinion. However, his amendment to substitute a temporary territorial government for provincial institutions was defeated by a vote of 95 to 35.[68] McDougall, now back in his seat as a private member, admitted the defect of the earlier scheme and his share of responsibility "for not more strongly recognizing the rights of the people there to some share in the Government of their country."[69] Like Mackenzie, he criticized the government's bill and proposed instead a territorial government built on the foundation of the Temporary Government Act, but with the addition of an elective assembly to serve the district of Assiniboia.[70] His scheme, which was worked out in detail, was designed to erase the impression that he favoured an autocratic government for the North-West. His professions on this point were undoubtedly genuine, but the point of greatest concern to the métis was obviously not popular rule but rather minority rights, and McDougall showed no interest in these.

Having failed in their attempt to postpone provincial status for Manitoba, neither the opposition nor McDougall paid any attention to the form of government under which the rest of the North-West would be administered.

Thus was concluded the Canadian government's first essay in territorial administration. The initial venture in applying measures conceived in Ottawa without reference to the experience and convictions of the North-West population had ended in dramatic defeat. The lesson, however, was never completely taken to heart, and so while the next twenty-seven years saw no such sudden change in the political evolution of the North-West, a peaceful struggle developed which after many vicissitudes forced the concession of self-government within a framework of territorial status.

[67]*Parliamentary Debates*, 1870, cols. 1296, 1501 ff. See also Mackenzie to Morris, April 16, 1874, Mackenzie Papers, P.A.C.

[68]*Journals of the House of Commons*, 1870, p. 325. Four years later Mackenzie still deprecated the decision to establish Manitoba as a province; writing to Lieutenant-Governor Alexander Morris on April 16, 1874, he declared that he still felt that some "simple and inexpensive machinery of government is still what is needed for Manitoba if the Province would consent to surrender the system now in operation": Mackenzie Papers.

[69]*Parliamentary Debates*, 1870, col. 1494.

[70]See *Journals of the House of Commons*, 1870, pp. 322–4. Mackenzie supported McDougall's proposal, but the majority of the Liberals did not follow him, the vote being 120 to 11.

CHAPTER THREE

The Territorial Government at Winnipeg

1870-76

THE MACDONALD ADMINISTRATION had been compelled to concede provincial status to the Red River Settlement, but amid the excitement of the political crisis it had escaped the necessity of adopting any definite plan for the government of the rest of the North-West. The Temporary Government Act, despite the odium which it had incurred in 1869, became the basis for the administration of an area incomparably more important, potentially if not actually, than the diminutive province of Manitoba.

At this time there was no need for an elaborate structure of territorial government now that provincial autonomy had been granted to the chief settlement in the North-West. The population was small and widely scattered: there were a few venturesome white settlers at Prince Albert and Edmonton; the population of the Hudson's Bay Company's trading posts usually consisted of from three to forty men with their families; at or near such places as Fort Qu'Appelle, Fort Pelly, Fort Edmonton, Stanley, Fort à la Corne, and Norway House, Protestant or Roman Catholic missions existed, and Indians had been induced to settle near some of them, although most remained nomadic. In 1870 the Indians of the Territories numbered perhaps 25,000,[1] few in relation to area but posing an administrative problem as many lived in the path of advancing settlement. The maintenance of order and the suppression of crime were also important, in view of

[1]The statistics for Indian population at this time are estimates rather than exact enumerations; the first Canadian statistics are in the 1871 Report of the Indian Branch of the Department of the Secretary of State for the Provinces (*C.S.P.* 1872, no. 22) in which the Indians of Manitoba and the western part of the Territories number 18,357 and those in the area north of Ontario and Quebec 4,370, or a total of 22,727. To these should be added the estimated 2,000 plains Indians killed by the smallpox epidemic of 1870.

the penetration of the south-western corner of the Territories by American whiskey traders from Montana, and the proximity of American Indians who were resisting the white man's westward progress. In this situation the direct exercise of federal authority was both possible and desirable, but it did not eliminate the need for some measure of local government. In a frontier area, speedy action and prompt adaptation of policy to local circumstances were not likely to be achieved by federal agencies. There was thus a real need for a territorial government with clearly defined powers (even if only modest in their scope), competent to deal with emergencies, and in a position to provide information and advice in connection with the formulation of federal policies.

This need for a territorial government was met in part by the existence of a local executive authority in the person of the Lieutenant-Governor. The policy of having the Lieutenant-Governor of Manitoba act as Lieutenant-Governor of the North-West Territories had much to commend it. The two areas were bound together by social and economic ties; Winnipeg was the only possible administrative centre at this time, for the Territories extended east and north of Manitoba, as well as west; for a time at least a close relationship between the governments of the Territories and of Manitoba would be mutually beneficial; lastly, the arrangement was economical—an administrator for the Territories was secured at a salary of $1,000, the amount which the Governor of Manitoba was granted in his capacity of Lieutenant-Governor of the Territories.

Thus far the policy of the federal government was on sound ground, but in several other important respects it lacked precision and substance. The executive needed official local advisers, for an eastern Governor, no matter how able, could not be expected to have a sufficient knowledge of conditions in the Territories to administer the area effectively; yet over two years were to elapse before such advisers were appointed. In the second place, local legislative power was only vaguely and imperfectly defined in the Temporary Government Act; it appeared to be vested solely in the Lieutenant-Governor, but could not be exercised until its extent was defined by a federal Order in Council. There was no good reason for excluding the Governor's advisers (council) from sharing the exercise of this legislative power, yet two years elapsed before the matter was clarified.

The new Lieutenant-Governor of Manitoba and the North-West, Adams G. Archibald,[2] had scarcely assumed office before an event

[2]Archibald was appointed to the two offices of Lieutenant-Governor of Manitoba and the North-West Territories on May 20, 1870: see copies of his Com-

occurred which demonstrated the need of having a local government for the Territories whose constitution would command general respect. A devastating smallpox epidemic began to rage through the Indian settlements between the North Saskatchewan and the American border, and its possible spread eastward caused universal dread in Manitoba. Legislation to restrict the movement of infected persons and goods was urgently required. The constitution described in the Temporary Government Act was a poor instrument to meet this crisis, but in any event no copy of it could be found at Fort Garry and Archibald's papers had not yet arrived. The Governor took a leap in the dark, and, assuming that the constitution conformed with the normal colonial pattern in its simplest form, swore in three men as Executive and Legislative Councillors on October 21, 1870.[3] He and his Council then proceeded to legislate on the smallpox menace, and also improved the occasion by passing an ordinance establishing prohibition in the Territories.[4] Six days later when the Governor's papers arrived, he discovered to his horror that whatever the Temporary Government Act meant (and he was not very sure what sort of legislative power it did establish) it did not empower him to appoint a Council.[5] Meanwhile, however, the smallpox "law" was being enforced with good effect in the Territories. The Governor's ignorance of the law and his willingness to grapple with a crisis had saved the day!

This episode demonstrated the need for a local legislature in some form, since there was no telling when a similar crisis might recur. But though Archibald was invited to nominate persons for appointment as a regularly constituted Council, Howe, as spokesman for the gov-

missions in volume labelled "Records" in the Public Archives of Manitoba. He arrived at Fort Garry by canoe on September 2, a few days after the expeditionary force under Colonel Wolseley.

[3]See North Western Territory, Register of Commissions, P.A.M. The council consisted of Judge F. G. Johnson, Q.C., a Superior Court Judge in Quebec and a former Recorder and Governor of Assiniboia, who had returned to the province on a mission for the federal government, Pascal Breland, a prominent French half-breed (though not a supporter of Riel) and former Councillor of Assiniboia, and Donald A. Smith of the Hudson's Bay Company. Archibald gave them separate commissions as Executive and Legislative Councillors. He reported to Howe that he had given "a fair representation of the three great interests of the West, the English, the French and the Hudson's Bay interest": Archibald to the Secretary of State for the Provinces, Oct. 22, 1870, printed in Oliver, II, pp. 975–6. Fearing that his appointments might not be valid, Archibald did not have them gazetted: see personal letter to Macdonald, Dec. 6, 1870, Macdonald Papers.

[4]The smallpox ordinance is printed in Oliver, II, pp. 977–9; the liquor law is printed in the *Manitoba Gazette*, vol. I. This legislation, along with a proclamation warning against the violation of the liquor law, was published in the *Manitoban*.

[5]See Archibald to Secretary of State for the Provinces, Nov. 22, 1870, Oliver, II, pp. 982–5.

ernment, would say no more about it than that it was to be "a mere consultative Body, with such additional powers, as may be from time to time conferred upon it by order of the Privy Council of Canada."[6]

The indifference to local government in the North-West which prevailed at Ottawa was demonstrated during the parliamentary session of 1871, when the Temporary Government Act was due to expire. Instead of replacing it by a more carefully drafted bill, its terms were simply re-enacted to provide a permanent constitution for the Territories.[7] For convenience we will refer to this Act hereafter as the North-West Government Act.

II

Since there was no disposition in Ottawa to speed the appointment of the Council, the full weight of responsibility for North-West affairs devolved, for two full years, on Lieutenant-Governor Archibald. Archibald had been selected for the post during the time of Macdonald's severe illness in the spring of 1870, when Sir George Cartier was acting Premier. The appointment was a matter of great concern, for it was necessary to secure a person who would consummate the policy of conciliation represented by the Manitoba Act; at the same time proven ability and detachment were important qualifications. The government probably felt that it would be difficult for a man from Ontario or Quebec to maintain a position of neutrality, or to convince others of his neutrality, amid the animosities produced in the Red River Settlement by the troubles of the preceding six months. Archibald was a member of Parliament from Nova Scotia, of long experience in public life, a Father of Confederation, and had had no previous connection with North-West affairs. When first approached, he was reluctant to accept, and is said to have given way only at Cartier's earnest request, and on the understanding that he would be relieved of the position at the end of a year.[8] He is described as a "man of broad views, of strong will but cool judgment, courteous and dignified in bearing."[9] His policy as Lieutenant-Governor was forecast in an eloquent speech on the Manitoba bill. In discussing the causes of the insurrection he declared, "I can not say I am astonished that

[6]Howe to Archibald, Nov. 17, 1870, in Oliver, II, p. 980.
[7]34 Vict., c. 16. See remarks thereon in *Parliamentary Debates*, 1871, cols. 274, 298–9.
[8]See John Boyd, *Sir George Etienne Cartier, Bart.: His Life and Times* (Toronto, 1914), p. 305; also *Parliamentary Debates*, 1872, col. 38, and telegram from Archibald to Macdonald, March 30, 1872, Macdonald Papers.
[9]Biographical sketch in *Dictionary of National Biography*, Supplement, vol. I.

under the circumstances in which these men were placed, and with the fears they entertained, just such things should occur as have occurred."[10] There was now "a stern duty" to "vindicate the supremacy of the national flag." "But the readiest mode of doing so," he continued, "is, at the same time, to show these people that their fears are unfounded, that their rights shall be guaranteed, their property held sacred, and that they shall be secured in all the privileges and advantages which belong to them, as Britons and as freemen." From this it may be gathered that, in appointing Archibald, the government was determined that conciliation should be the order of the day.

As Lieutenant-Governor of the North-West Territories, Archibald's first instructions were substantially the same as those given to his ill-fated predecessor McDougall.[11] His chief duty was to collect information on the North-West for the use of the cabinet. In Archibald's case the Indian question occupied a more prominent position: he was instructed to establish friendly relations with them and report "the course you may think most advisable to pursue, whether by treaty or otherwise, for the removal of any obstructions that may be presented to the flow of population into the fertile lands that lie between Manitoba and the Rocky Mountains."

Much of Archibald's activity at Fort Garry was in connection with the establishment of the elaborate apparatus of a provincial government amid a small population divided into warring factions; the circumstances of the time also forced him to advise on the activities of various federal agencies, and he was expected to keep an eye on the matter of parliamentary representation, for in all this the political aspect of affairs (the welfare of the Macdonald administration) was not to be neglected.

With the pressure of all these responsibilities, the Lieutenant-Governor would have had some excuse for neglecting North-West affairs. The careful attention which Archibald gave them is a measure of his ability and high sense of public duty. A considerable portion of his correspondence with Ottawa was concerned with Indian affairs, including the question of local administration, the Indians' reaction to the influx of surveyors and settlers, and the effects of the whiskey trade in the area between Fort Benton and Edmonton. His recommendations led to the negotiation of the first two treaties with western Indians, the first involving the surrender of all land in Manitoba, and

[10]*Parliamentary Debates*, 1870, cols. 1425–6.
[11]See Under Secretary of State for the Provinces to Archibald, Aug. 4, 1870, in Oliver, II, pp. 974–5.

the second that part of the Territories situated immediately north and west of the province. In these negotiations, which took place on the 3rd and 21st of August 1871, he personally assisted the Indian Commissioner, Wemyss M. Simpson. Archibald's philosophy of Indian administration was based on two points—fulfilment of the government's obligations "with scrupulous fidelity," and the provision of a source of authority accessible to the Indians.[12]

Mr. Simpson [he complained to the government] is under the impression that by being out of the way of being called upon, he saves a great deal of importunity and some expense to the Government. This may be true, but if the saving is made at the cost of friendly relations with the savages, we shall not be much the better for the Treaty. The Government of Canada succeed[ed] to the position of the Hudson's Bay Company with the Indians. And the usage of easy access to the representative of the governing power, which has continued for over a century, cannot be broken up at once without danger.[13]

On this issue of on-the-spot authority *versus* government by remote control the Governor developed strong views, since in the absence of the Indian Commissioner he had to spend a great deal of time receiving Indian delegations.[14] A perusal of his correspondence evokes admiration for his grasp of the essentials of successful Indian administration and for his sensitivity to human need. A strong humanitarianism is evident in all his references to the Indians, and in the interests of friendly relations he was willing to make personal sacrifices.[15]

In his position as local administrator for the North-West Territories Archibald was granted only meagre powers. In September 1870 an Order in Council empowered him to appoint justices of the peace and also to appoint Judge F. G. Johnson as Recorder for the Territories[16]—the latter being a temporary measure based on the Hudson's

[12]Archibald to Secretary of State for the Provinces, Feb. 12, 1872, Lieutenant-Governor's Papers, P.A.M.
[13]*Ibid.*
[14]See his letters to Secretary of State for the Provinces of Feb. 17, Feb. 23, and March 18, 1872, protesting vigorously against Simpson's absence: Lieutenant-Governor's Papers, P.A.M.
[15]See his letter to Secretary of State for the Provinces of July 6, 1872, relating to his reception of an Indian delegation and offering to pay the cost of the presents given on this occasion: *ibid.*
[16]Order in Council, Sept. 13, 1870. In 1839 the Hudson's Bay Company appointed a lawyer with the title of Recorder of Rupert's Land, to be the presiding judge of the General Quarterly Court of Assiniboia, which became the court for all of the Company's territory. In England a Recorder was the presiding judge of the court of quarter sessions of a borough. Johnson had been Recorder under the Company régime from 1854 to 1858.

Bay Company's system of judicature. Following the episode of the irregular Council in the autumn of that year Archibald suggested that legislative power be conferred on him under the terms of the Temporary Government Act, but though Howe promised early consideration of the request,[17] no action was taken until August 1871, and the power then conferred was confined to legislation respecting infectious diseases.[18]

With these limited powers, there was no opportunity for Archibald to intervene in North-West affairs in any extensive way. Several justices of the peace and a board of health for the North-West were appointed;[19] a proclamation warning disturbers of the peace was issued;[20] and an ordinance prohibiting the import and use of poisons for killing fur-bearing animals was published.[21] His most important measure was the appointment of Lieut. W. F. Butler to undertake a fact-finding expedition through the Saskatchewan valley.[22] Archibald hoped by this means to obtain much of the information required by his instructions as Lieutenant-Governor of the Territories. To obtain it promptly, with winter coming on, was no easy task, and it was fortunate that a person of Butler's qualities was available to undertake a journey full of hazard and hardship. He covered the 2,700 miles from Fort Garry to Rocky Mountain House and back between late October and early February, and had his report ready for Archibald on March 10. It is a remarkable document, a careful yet vivid account of social and economic conditions in the plains region of the Territories at a fateful era in its history. Butler's analysis of the needs of the North-West in terms of police protection, more effective administration of

[17]Howe to Archibald, Dec. 13, 1870, Oliver, II, p. 987.

[18]Order in Council, Aug. 3, 1871. See Howe to Archibald, Aug. 5, 1871, Lieutenant-Governor's Papers, P.A.M.

[19]See North Western Territory, Registry of Commissions, and Lieutenant-Governor's Papers, P.A.M. The Board of Health consisted of Bishop Grandin, Rev. George McDougall, and W. J. Christie.

[20]Proclamation of Dec. 21, 1870, published in English, French, and Cree; another proclamation of Feb. 26, 1872, warned against breaking the law regarding wood cutting within and outside Indian Reserves.

[21]In this instance Archibald went to the length of publishing an ordinance allegedly enacted by the Lieutenant-Governor and Council in March 1871 (the day was omitted) though no council existed at the time: see the *Manitoban*. In a letter to Howe on March 6, 1872, he referred to this "law" and the one prohibiting the liquor trade as having "had good effect" and urged the federal government to "give them the force of law": Despatch Book of Lieutenant-Governor Archibald to Secretary of State for the Provinces, P.A.M.

[22]Butler's instructions and his official report are printed as an Appendix to his book *The Great Lone Land: A Tale of Travel and Adventure in the North-West of America*, first published in 1872.

justice, and negotiations with the Indians, was no more than plain common sense—ultimately embodied in federal policy but, characteristically, only after some unfortunate delays.[23]

As an energetic and conscientious administrator, Archibald could not but be irritated by his lack of authority to deal adequately with the needs of the North-West, which in some instances required legislation. "At this moment," he wrote to Howe in November 1871, "I am governing that Territory with very undefined authority. It is doubtful what is at this moment Law in the North-West."[24] His only legislative power, he pointed out, was confined to the subject of health and quarantine. "Meanwhile applications have been made to me," he continued, "with a view to Legislation on several matters connected with the Territory and which ought to be dealt with, but which cannot be touched till Legislative power is conferred." He did not request further powers for the Lieutenant-Governor alone, but pressed instead for the establishment of the Council, which would act with him in a legislative capacity. To the membership of that body he devoted considerable attention.

III

The selection of Councillors was not, of course, a simple matter under the circumstances which prevailed at this time. The majority could hardly be residents of the Territories in view of the difficulty which they would have in attending meetings, and with mail delivery (by the Hudson's Bay Company) once in six months. Those whose character and competence were known were Hudson's Bay employees, and Archibald thought that while the Company was entitled to representation it was unwise to give it a preponderant influence.[25] Consequently, most of the Councillors would have to be Manitobans. Here further complications presented themselves: the province was a hotbed of warring factions, and the animosities generated during the insurrection and after the arrival of the military expedition were bitter and pervasive. The tendency was to judge every government measure, whether federal or provincial, not for its effect on the general welfare, but for its effect on the prestige and influence of the several rival groups. Thus it happened that knowledge of the North-West

[23]For example the Cypress Hills massacre of May 1873 would probably not have occurred if the N.W.M.P. had been organized, and if it had occurred the criminals would hardly have escaped apprehension with police in the vicinity.

[24]Archibald to Secretary of State for the Provinces, Nov. 23, 1871, Interior file no. 4 (N.W.T.), 1871.

[25]Archibald to Howe, March 24, 1871, Macdonald Papers.

was not always the chief qualification which led to the appointment of a Councillor, and in some instances it was conspicuously absent.

Archibald submitted his first list of nominees in December 1870.[26] This was followed by a revised list in March 1871,[27] and finally by another revision (this time accompanied by a plea for early action) in November of the same year.[28] His correspondence with Macdonald and Howe throws some light on the considerations which influenced his nominations. At first he was anxious to include Bishop Taché and Bishop Machray ("the best men the Country affords") because of their knowledge of the North-West derived from the supervision of widely scattered mission stations.[29] In this it will be observed that he was following the Hudson's Bay Company's precedent, since both men had been Councillors of Assiniboia. While admitting that "theoretically they are objectionable" he contended that there would be no local opposition to their selection and that it would be better "to make them directly responsible—instead of taking their tools—and giving them the power—without the responsibility."[30] The cabinet refused to consider their appointment, though Macdonald was prepared to appoint persons who would enjoy the Bishops' confidence.[31] In the end this issue of ecclesiastical influence seems to have been confined to the selection of one man as "the mouthpiece" of Bishop Taché.[32]

Archibald's final recommendations included three Hudson's Bay employees, because, he argued, of the "enormous influence" of the Company "on which we require to count for the Good Government of the Country." The Company's officers, he reported, "have got on well, not only with the Native Indians, but with the French Half Breeds who constitute a large portion of the partially civilized population of the Saskatchewan, and to some extent may be considered as representatives of them."[33] Another consideration which the Governor pointed out was that future immigration would be largely from Ontario, and he declared "under these circumstances it would hardly

26Archibald to Secretary of State for the Provinces, Dec. 9, 1870, Interior file no. 3 (N.W.T.), 1870. Archibald suggested that only the minimum number of seven be appointed at the start.
27See Archibald to Howe, March 24, 1871, in Macdonald Papers.
28Archibald to Secretary of State for the Provinces, Nov. 23, 1871, Interior file no. 4 (N.W.T.), 1871. See also Archibald to Macdonald, Dec. 17, 1871, and May 14, 1872, Macdonald Papers.
29See Archibald to Macdonald, private & confidential, Feb. 15, 1871, Macdonald Papers.
30Ibid.
31Macdonald to Archibald, private, Jan. 25, 1871, ibid.
32This was Joseph Dubuc; see Archibald to Macdonald, Nov. 23, 1871, ibid.
33Ibid.

be judicious, particularly considering the feverish state of feeling in Ontario, to give to the Council of the North-West a complexion which would subject the Government at Ottawa to misconstruction." Since the Government had a free hand in the Territories as distinguished from Manitoba, Archibald contended that it was possible "to adopt such measures as are best adapted to develop the Country, whether they be or be not pleasing to a population not particularly qualified to judge what is the best in the interests of the Country." This was dangerous doctrine, and the Governor sensed it, for he hastened to add: "Of course you must not forget the character or situation of the population of the interior in estimating their power for mischief. They live in remote and inaccessible districts. They might be induced by agitators to create disturbances and if once created they would be difficult to suppress." It was a warning that Archibald's successors were to repeat, but with little effect, as the events of 1885 were to demonstrate.

The Council was finally constituted on December 28, 1872, by the appointment of eleven members: Marc A. Girard, Donald A. Smith, Henry J. Clarke, Pascal Breland, Alfred Boyd, Dr. John C. Schultz, Joseph Dubuc, Andrew G. B. Bannatyne, William Fraser, Robert Hamilton, and William J. Christie.[34] Seven of these were among those recommended by Archibald, who by this time had left the province. His successor (Alexander Morris), Dr. Schultz, and D. A. Smith are also known to have made suggestions; apparently the final choice was not dictated by any one person.[35]

Things had been quiet at Fort Garry at the turn of the new year, Morris reported to Macdonald, "till the news of the Council for the North-West reached [us] & then there was a storm."[36] But Macdonald vigorously defended the cabinet's decision: replying to the criticism that Ontario was not represented he wrote:

Dr. Schultz is an Ontario man. There is a large preponderance of English and Protestant over French and Catholic in the Council, and that is all that can be fairly required by the English speaking inhabitants up there. We must discountenance these sectional cries as soon as possible or you will never have any peace in Manitoba.

It must be remembered that no individual in Manitoba has any right, as such, to be a Member of the North-West Council. That Council is to

[34]Order in Council of Dec. 28, 1872.

[35]See Morris to Macdonald, telegram, Dec. 1, 1872, and Schultz to Macdonald, Dec. 4, 1871, Macdonald Papers; also memorandum by Macdonald in Interior file no. 4 (N.W.T.), 1871.

[36]Morris to Macdonald, confidential, Jan. 9, 1873, Macdonald Papers.

govern territories beyond the bounds of Manitoba, and a Manitoban, as such, has no more claim of right to a seat in the Council than a Nova Scotian.[37]

He warned another complainer: "Take care not to mix yourself up too much with this so-called Ontario party. They seem to think that the whole of the North West was made for that Province alone."[38] From another quarter a different complaint reached the Premier: Dr. Schultz, the pre-1870 leader of the Canadians, was a bitter foe of the métis, and Archbishop Taché vigorously protested his appointment—"a very unfair proportion of French members," he wrote, "is the compensation for the insult."[39]

Had Macdonald adhered strictly to the principle which he had enunciated—that knowledge of the North-West was the only proper qualification for membership in the Council—he would have created a more efficient body and had a stronger defence against partisan critics. However, even as it was, the first members were not an inferior group. Only two (Hamilton and Christie) were residents of the Territories, but this was inevitable; nor was it a serious defect since suitable men with a knowledge of the North-West were mostly residents of Manitoba. While the French and Catholic element was not represented in proportion to their numbers in the North-West, they possessed four competent and influential spokesmen in Girard, who had been designated by the government as the senior member of the Council, Clarke, Breland, and Dubuc.[40]

When the government was pressed to make additional appointments it was discovered that under the terms of the North-West Government Act it had exhausted its power, even though the maximum number had not been appointed.[41] This "blunder," as Macdonald called it, was corrected by an amendment during the spring session of 1873, and at the same time the maximum number of councillors was increased from fifteen to twenty-one.[42]

Macdonald had not been unmoved by the criticisms which had been levelled at his first appointments, and in the autumn of 1873

[37]Macdonald to Morris, Jan. 22, 1873, *ibid.* Four of the eleven Councillors were Roman Catholics.
[38]Macdonald to G. McMicken, private, Jan. 13, 1873, *ibid.*
[39]Taché to Macdonald, Jan. 25, 1873, printed in *Journals of the House of Commons*, 1874, Appendix 6, pp. 49–50. Taché claimed that at a meeting in the Prime Minister's office on Dec. 7, 1871, Macdonald had assured him that Schultz would not be appointed.
[40]Howe to Girard, Jan. 2, 1873, Interior file no. 66292.
[41]Macdonald to Morris, Jan. 22, 1873, Macdonald Papers.
[42]36 Vict., c. 5.

five new members were added to the Council:[43] Pierre Delorme, James McKay, Joseph Royal, Dr. W. R. Bown, and Wm. N. Kennedy. As in the previous instance the government received representations from various sources and the Lieutenant-Governor was consulted.[44] The first three were Roman Catholics and in sympathy with the French-speaking element of the population. The latter two were immigrants from Ontario. None of the five were residents of the Territories, but Delorme had hunted buffalo on the plains and McKay was born on the Saskatchewan and was intimately acquainted with the North-West, as well as having great influence among the Indians.

The Mackenzie administration appointed three members to the Council in April 1874: William Tait, Robert Cunningham, and John H. McTavish, the last being a replacement for Christie, who had retired to Ontario.[45] These were the last appointments made during the life of the Council;[46] the reason for them is not apparent, but was probably the same political and factional pressures which had played such an important role in Macdonald's appointments; only one, McTavish, was acquainted with the North-West. Morris had felt that no further increase in the membership was necessary for the time being, and was opposed to the three nominees on the ground that they increased the number (already a majority) who were influenced by the interests of the Hudson's Bay Company; he would have preferred to see the recent Ontario immigrants given greater representation.[47] He regretted the necessity of having to recognize such distinctions but believed it was the only way "to ensure harmony and encourage the people in united efforts for the advancement of the North-West."[48]

[43]Orders in Council of Oct. 22 and Oct. 30, 1873.

[44]Rev. George Young recommended Kennedy; Girard recommended Delorme and Royal (among others); Morris urged the selection of McKay and Kennedy; Bishop Grandin is also known to have made representations: see Campbell to Morris, Aug. 20, 1873 (2 letters), Lieutenant-Governor's Papers and Morris Papers, P.A.M., and Morris to Campbell, private, Sept. 4 and Oct. 24, 1873, in Morris Papers. Unless otherwise indicated, all references to Morris Papers are to those in the Public Archives of Manitoba.

[45]Order in Council, April 3, 1874.

[46]These last appointments increased the Council to eighteen members.

[47]Morris to Mackenzie, confidential, March 16, 1874, Morris Papers, and Morris to A. A. Dorion, Dec. 15, 1873, entitled "Strictly confidential memorandum for the Privy Council." This document presents a detailed analysis of the composition of the Council with regard to the background and interests of each member. The memorandum has been separated from its three schedules—the former is in the Morris Papers in the Public Archives of Manitoba and the latter in the Morris Papers in the Public Archives of Ontario.

[48]Ibid.

IV

When the Council was constituted in 1873 there was no definition of the nature and scope of its activities, for on this the North-West Government Act was silent. Was it to be "a mere consultative body"? This matter was settled by an Order in Council of February 12, 1873, prepared under Macdonald's direction.[49] The Lieutenant-Governor and the Council were empowered,

to make provision for the administration of justice . . . and generally to make and establish such ordinances as may be necessary for the peace, order and good government of the said North-West Territories, and of Her Majesty's subjects and others therein. Provided first that no such ordinance shall deal with, or affect any subjects which are beyond the jurisdiction of a Provincial Legislature, under the "British North America Act, 1867", and provided second, that all such ordinances shall be made to come into force only after they have been approved by the Governor-General in Council, unless in cases of urgency, and in that case the urgency shall be stated on the face of the ordinance.

The order also specified that ordinances (presumably those passed under the emergency clause) could be disallowed at any time within two years of their passage. The Lieutenant-Governor was to preside at all meetings (later modified to permit the senior member to preside in his absence)[50] and all proceedings were subject to his approval.[51]

The grant of power was an equivocal measure, indeed almost grotesque; for on the one hand the territorial legislature was placed on the same footing as a provincial legislature in terms of the subject matters with which it could deal (with the exception of public lands and the power to tax)[52] while on the other hand any legislation it might enact was to remain in a state of suspended animation (except in emergencies) until the federal cabinet got around to approving it! It would be hard to find a more striking example of distrust of local self-government—all the more striking because the local body was the creature of the federal government, and also because that government appointed one of the members (the Attorney General of Manitoba)

[49]Macdonald to Campbell, Dec. 30, 1872, and Jan. 29, 1873, Macdonald Papers.
[50]Order in Council of Aug. 6, 1873.
[51]The order also established a quorum consisting of the majority of the members of the Council; it also required the Council to meet at least once every six months in Winnipeg with a provision for emergency meetings called by the Governor. The Order in Council of Aug. 6, 1873, modified this to the extent of requiring only an annual meeting to be held on the first Monday in June.
[52]This restriction was imposed by 36 Vict., c. 34, s. 3.

as legal adviser with a salary, whose chief duty would be to prepare the legislation in proper form.[53]

The terms of this order illustrate again the relative indifference to the problem of the structure of the territorial government first exhibited in the Temporary Government Act. The order failed to provide for oaths of allegiance and of office, with the result that the first meeting of the Council took place in March without the members being sworn in. This deficiency was corrected by an amending order on August 6, 1873, but the oath of office provided therein enjoined secrecy regarding both legislative and executive proceedings, with the result that another order had to be passed (on October 1, 1873) limiting secrecy to executive business.[54]

Still another amendment to the North-West Government Act was passed during this session.[55] The February Order in Council was confirmed, and the application of federal legislation to the North-West was defined. Inasmuch as the prevailing law of the Company period was still in force, the North-West Council during its March session had recommended "that the Criminal Laws now in force in the other portions of the Dominion of Canada should be extended to the North-West Territories."[56] The amendment met this request by providing that an important part of the criminal law of Canada should be applicable in the Territories.[57] As regards federal legislation generally, this Act delegated to the Governor General in Council the power (with certain exceptions) "either to make new laws (on subjects beyond the competence of the North-West Council) or to extend and apply and declare applicable to the North-West Territories, with such amendments and modifications as may be deemed necessary, any Act or Acts of the Parliament of Canada, or any parts thereof."[58] Though this extraordinary power of legislation by Order in Council was not

[53]These legal advisers were H. J. Clarke (1873–4), and Joseph Dubuc (1874–5), who were successively Attorneys General of Manitoba; see Orders in Council of July 10, 1873, and Sept. 22, 1874.

[54]This change was advocated by Morris in order to permit of legislative sessions open to the public: Morris to Minister of the Interior, Sept. 6, 1873, *C.S.P.* 1877, no. 121. Such sessions were, however, not held during the existence of this Council.

[55]36 Vict., c. 34.

[56]Minutes of the North-West Council, March 10, 1873. The minutes of the Council during the period when the seat of government was at Winnipeg are printed in Oliver, II, pp. 990–1075; these are cited hereafter by date of the minute.

[57]See Schedule A of the Act.

[58]36 Vict., c. 34, s. 2.

exercised to any extent,[59] it is significant as a further evidence of the dominance of centralized authority in Macdonald's philosophy of territorial administration.

While the parliamentary session of 1873 cannot be said to have given any notable impetus to the development of self-government in the North-West, it was distinguished by three other acts of a constructive character. One established prohibition in the Territories, with the object of protecting the welfare of the Indians.[60] It superseded a similar measure passed by the North-West Council at its first session,[61] and it was not until 1891 that the territorial government regained the power to legislate in this field. This act also inaugurated the liquor permit system under the control of the Lieutenant-Governor —a duty which was to plague successive incumbents of the office.

The second measure was entitled an "Act respecting the Administration of Justice and for the establishment of a Police Force in the North-West Territories."[62] In addition to giving limited judicial powers to certain officers of the police force, the government was empowered to appoint stipendiary magistrates, each with the powers of two justices of the peace; the most serious crimes were to be tried by the Court of Queen's Bench of Manitoba. Since the Territories lacked prisons, sentences of imprisonment imposed by the magistrates were to be carried out in an institution in Manitoba. Some years elapsed before the stipendiary magistrates were appointed, so that the first effective law enforcement was by the police exercising their judicial powers. This force later became a Dominion-wide organization, the Royal Canadian Mounted Police, but its greatest contribution was made during the period when the frontier of settlement was moving across the Western plains and penetrating the forest and mining regions of the far North. Against the indifference and narrow con-

59The only case was the proclamation of May 28, 1874, extending provisions of certain acts relating to Indians.

6036 Vict., c. 39, s. 3; the other sections dealt with customs duties in Manitoba and the Territories. The curious feature of this legislation is that while it was directed at the consumption of liquor by the Indians it also applied to all residents of the North-West, with the exception of what might be secured (presumably for medicinal or sacramental purposes) under permit from the Lieutenant-Governor. When prohibition was inaugurated in 1873 it was possible to ignore the non-Indian population, but with the spread of settlement in later years the familiar problem of enforcement arose.

61Minutes of the North-West Council, March 10, 1873. See also minutes of Sept. 8, 1873, and March 14, 1874, for the Council's views on the defects of the federal law.

6236 Vict., c. 35.

servatism which was too often evident in the North-West policy of the Macdonald administration must be set this wise and constructive measure; the North-West Mounted Police was to suffer at times from growing pains—it was not a perfect organization—but it did not fail the people of the Territories. In 1873, Parliament builded better than it knew.

The third important measure relating to the North-West was the act establishing the Department of the Interior.[63] In May, Joseph Howe had retired from the post of Secretary of State for the Provinces, after an undistinguished period of service, though one which was undoubtedly useful from the point of view of Macdonald's broad political strategy. This event provided an opportunity to unite under one department all the agencies dealing with North-West affairs. Howe's department was abolished; apart from routine correspondence with the provinces, its activities had concerned Indian affairs, the Geological Survey, and the administration of the Territories. These were now transferred to the Department of the Interior, which at the same time took over from the Department of the Secretary of State the management of Dominion Lands (crown lands in Manitoba and the North-West Territories), and ordnance and admiralty lands. The influences which prompted this change are not as yet satisfactorily documented; during the previous autumn Macdonald's objective was limited to replacing Howe by a more vigorous incumbent.[64] The impending change in the American system was probably influential, for in 1872 President Grant had recommended that the supervision of territorial affairs, hitherto exercised by the Department of State, be transferred to the Department of the Interior, which since its creation in 1849 had controlled Indian affairs and public lands.[65] This was accomplished in 1873, just before the Canadian measure was introduced in Parliament. Certainly in naming the new department the Macdonald administration was following the American precedent. However, in so far as the supervision of a territorial govern-

---

[63]36 Vict., c. 4. See also the first report of the Department of the Interior for 1873–74, C.S.P. 1875, no. 8.

[64]On Oct. 9, 1872, Macdonald wrote to Tupper, "I wish . . . that you would quietly have a talk with Howe. If you could manage to get him to write a note, asking if it would be convenient to be relieved of the onerous duties of his Department and get a less onerous one, I might make arrangements for his successor." Macdonald Papers. The new incumbent, Macdonald stated, was to "settle the policy for Manitoba & the Great West" with Archibald, who was returning from Manitoba after relinquishing the governorship.

[65]See Earl S. Pomeroy, The Territories and the United States, 1861–1890, Studies in Colonial Administration (Philadelphia and London, 1947), pp. 14–15.

ment was concerned, the policies of the two departments were quite different: in the United States, control was confined within narrow limits, inspired by the philosophy that "in construing provisions for the self government of an inchoate state, under our principle of administration, every intentment is to be made in favor of the powers of the local legislature. . . ."[66] In Canada, however, the system of close centralized control which has been delineated in the preceding pages was to continue—territorial autonomy having to be wrested from the federal government in piecemeal fashion. Senator Campbell, the first Minister of the Interior, expressed the prevailing Canadian philosophy when he referred to his position as "Secretary for the Colonies"[67]—a term which was meant to imply the full measure of imperial control of dependent territory.

V

Interest in territorial self-government during Archibald's two-year sojourn in the West was confined to the Governor himself: it was he who raised the issue, and who first encountered that Ottawa inertia which was to be the continuing obstacle for advocates of autonomy. Alexander Morris, his successor, was to encounter this inertia in a much more serious form, and consequently the issue was sharply defined during his term of office.

It had not been easy to secure a suitable successor to Archibald. Unlike the Lieutenant-Governors of other provinces, who were immune from political attacks and whose duties were purely formal, the governorship of Manitoba during these formative years was a post involving close contact with both politics and administration.[68] Macdonald had expected Archibald to be "a paternal despot," even to the extent of "taking a personal interest in the result of the elections, so as to secure the return of a body of respectable men representing the various races and interests."[69] Archibald's efforts to protect the rights of the métis (and thus fulfil the spirit of the Manitoba Act) and his recognition of Riel's services during the threatened Fenian invasion of October 1871 had resulted in bitter attacks both in Manitoba and Eastern Canada. There was thus little inducement for him to remain beyond the limited period of service which he had promised to the

66Quoted in *ibid.*, p. 12.
67Campbell to Macdonald, July 27, 1873, Macdonald Papers.
68See Frank Archibald Milligan, "The Lieutenant-Governorship in Manitoba, 1870–1882," M.A. thesis, University of Manitoba, 1948.
69Macdonald to Archibald, Nov. 1, 1870, Macdonald Papers.

government. In addition to the political and administrative problems of Manitoba there was the responsibility for the Territories, as well as a share in the management of Indian affairs. "It is very humiliating," one Winnipeg editor wrote, "to think that whilst the Lieutenant-Governorships of the other Provinces are prizes eagerly contended for and struggled for, the Governorship of our Province should be held in such despite as that the ministers cannot get anybody to accept— no, not even after hunting through the Government offices at Ottawa."[70]

Happily for Manitoba and the North-West, the government's good fortune and good judgment led to the appointment of Alexander Morris, then Chief Justice of Manitoba and a former member of the federal cabinet.[71] Ill health had led to his retirement from politics and, in part, to his migration to a region whose climate, even at this early date, was becoming celebrated for its salubrious properties; equally important was his deep interest in the West, dating from his early youth.[72] For over a decade Morris had been the leading advocate of Confederation and western expansion in the Liberal-Conservative party, and had done much by speeches and writing to publicize the resources of the North-West. For him, it was a happy chance which offered an opportunity of launching the judicial system of a land which had been one of the chief enthusiasms of his life. "It is given to comparatively few men," one paper declared, "to see the full realization of early hopes and aspirations, and to fewer still to be privileged in moulding the destiny which they themselves pictured as of the future. Mr. Morris has had both those advantages, and his first charge [to the first Grand Jury of Manitoba] in his official character has the ring about it of a man who can not only dream of national grandeur, but who has the will and character to aid in its development."[73] During the debates on the acquisition of the North-West in 1867, Morris had suggested that Parliament should "organize a local

[70]*Manitoban*, Nov. 30, 1872.

[71]Archibald's resignation was accepted in April and the government selected F. G. Johnson as his successor (see *Canada Gazette*, April 13, 1872), but the policy of appointing a man who would also retain his post as a judge in Quebec became an issue in Parliament and the commission was cancelled before Johnson took the oath of office. (See Judge Johnson's statement of May 28, 1872 reported in the *Manitoban*, June 1, 1872). Consequently Archibald retained the position until Dec. 2, 1872, when Morris assumed office. Morris had acted as administrator following Archibald's departure in October; he had been Chief Justice of Manitoba since July 2, 1872.

[72]See Alexander Morris, *Nova Britannia* (Toronto, 1884).

[73]Quoted in Morris, *Nova Britannia*, p. 152.

government there, and give the people the benefit of a constitutional authority, and so aid them in the great work of colonizing that fertile region."[74] As Governor he adhered to this policy by inaugurating responsible government in Manitoba and championing a measure of self-government for the Territories.

During the four years of Morris's governorship of the Territories there was considerable bustle and stir in what Captain Butler had termed "the Great Lone Land." These were the years which will be forever associated with the heralds of the frontier—the surveyors and explorers, the mounted police, and the makers of Indian treaties. In many parts of the prairies, from the 49th parallel where the International Boundary Commission was operating, to the Saskatchewan valley where a route for the Pacific railway was being marked, men were laying the foundations of one of the world's great topographical surveys. Then in 1874 the Police made their famous march across the plains, their patrols and prompt prosecutions soon restoring confidence and a sense of security. Meanwhile, the whole of the southern portion of the Territories from Lake Superior to the Rocky Mountains and from the international boundary into the forest belt was being opened by a series of Indian treaties—from 1873 to 1877 a new treaty was signed every year. At the same time an effort was made to improve communications (essential for a system of centralized administration); in 1871 Winnipeg and Ottawa were linked by telegraph via American lines, and in 1875 construction began on a line westward to Edmonton following the projected railway. A tri-weekly mail between Winnipeg and the East was established in 1871, though it was necessarily a slow service until rail connections with Minnesota were completed in 1878. In the Territories a government mail service was not inaugurated until 1876 when it was arranged that Edmonton, Winnipeg, and intermediate points would be served once every three weeks.

Manitoba absorbed the bulk of the immigrants during these years, and the Territories experienced no large influx of population. Yet some people were on the move. Métis were trekking from Manitoba and establishing new communities on the South Saskatchewan, where they hoped to continue their old way of life; here they were joined by others who had discovered that a provincial constitution was but a frail support for their particular interests. The old centres such as Edmonton and Prince Albert drew a few venturesome newcomers; embryo communities appeared near some of the police posts; and in

74*Ibid.*, p. 142.

1875 an important Icelandic settlement was established on Lake Winnipeg just north of the Manitoba boundary. But it was the trader and the prospector rather than the settler who was attracted to the Territories during this period. Rumours of gold on the upper Saskatchewan and Peace rivers caused a stir, but no large rush developed. Much more significant was the influx of men who were attracted by the Indian trade, so long monopolized by the Hudson's Bay Company. Soon it was only at the more remote posts in the far north that the Company retained its dominant position, and even there it was challenged in later years. The result of all this was that it was no longer possible to assume, as Archibald had done, that Hudson's Bay Company officers still had the prestige and representative character which they had possessed before 1870.

VI

In the administration of North-West affairs during these years the federal government, because of its powers under the constitution (with control of Dominion lands added thereto), had a much more important and dramatic role than any local government which it would then have been possible to create. It is important to note, however, that the activities of the federal authorities were not completely divorced from the territorial government, particularly in regard to the Indian treaties, for Morris was a Commissioner in all cases, and in three of the four treaties a member of the Council also participated as a Commissioner.[75] Moreover, in these negotiations the government had the benefit of advice offered by the Council.[76] Indeed the Council's interest in Indian affairs was so great that it pressed for a recognized supervisory role in Indian administration,[77] being strongly supported in this request by the Lieutenant-Governor.[78] Both the Macdonald and Mackenzie administrations rejected this proposal, but the Council, undaunted, continued to make recommendations on various matters which it believed were being overlooked by the Indian Branch, or where dangerous delays had occurred. In this the members

[75]These were W. J. Christie (Treaty No. 4), James McKay (Treaty No. 5), and McKay and Christie (Treaty No. 6). The selection of North-West Councillors for this work had been urged by Morris in a letter to the Minister of the Interior on Jan. 24, 1874: Morris Papers.

[76]See Minutes of the North-West Council, Sept. 8, 1873, March 14, 1874, June 1, 1874, and Dec. 7, 1874.

[77]Ibid., Sept. 8, 1873, March 16, 1874.

[78]See Campbell to Morris, Aug. 6, 1873, and Morris to Minister of the Interior, Jan. 24, 1874: Morris Papers.

were undoubtedly encouraged by Morris, who had great confidence in the soundness of their views and advice.

In addition to Indian affairs the Council proffered carefully considered recommendations to the federal government on such matters as administration of justice, surveys and land policy, enforcement of the federal liquor legislation, postal service, fish conservation, and the maintenance of trails. Though not always successful in its representations, the Council certainly made a sustained effort to express North-West opinion on the issues of the day.

Since the legislation of the Lieutenant-Governor and Council had to be approved at Ottawa before it could come into force, unless designated urgent, we have a real measure of the interest of the federal authorities in the development of territorial self-government. At its first session in March 1873 the Council passed three acts: one authorized the appointment of justices of the peace and coroners, the second prohibited the import and sale of liquor, and the third prohibited the import and use of strychnine and other poisons. Months passed, and no word concerning "His Excellency's pleasure" was received. The Council was due to meet in September, so Morris wrote Campbell in August asking for "something more than a mere formal acknowledgement" of the previous proceedings. Ignoring them, he stated, "will discourage the Council very much."[79] Six weeks later Campbell replied: "The proceedings of your meeting in March . . . have only today been found. They have been mislaid in Sir John Macdonald's office."[80] The decision, for which Macdonald as Minister of Justice was directly responsible, was made three weeks later—of the three acts, only the one relating to poisons was approved.[81] It was reasonable enough to insist that the federal liquor legislation should supersede the territorial act, but the decision regarding the appointment of justices and coroners exhibited a callous disregard of the rights of the local legislature, since it was admitted that the act was *intra vires*. Fear that the Council was not going to select enough French-speaking justices may have had something to do with this blunt assertion of federal power,[82] but control of party patronage was

---

[79]Morris to Campbell, confidential, Aug. 18, 1873: Lieutenant-Governor's Papers, Indian Affairs and N.W.T., P.A.M.

[80]Campbell to Morris, private and confidential, Sept. 24, 1873, Morris Papers.

[81]Order in Council of Oct. 13, 1873. The government ignored the fact that the act relating to justices of the peace had been marked urgent and so had come into force—justices having been appointed under its authority.

[82]See Campbell to Morris, telegram, Oct. 28, 1873, Lieutenant-Governor's Papers, 1873, Indian Affairs and N.W.T., P.A.M.

probably the real reason. To the cabinet this decision may have been a small matter, but a vital principle was involved, as Morris clearly perceived. It was, he wrote to Campbell, "a very unfortunate" proceeding. The declared reason for disallowance—the undeveloped state of the country[83]—applied "with much greater force against selections made in Ottawa." "The appointments," he asserted, "should be made here." "The communication is so difficult with the interior, and changes of residence so frequent that important revisions of the list will be necessary."[84] There had been no discrimination on racial grounds, the Governor added; indeed a special effort had been made by the Council to secure as many French justices as possible. In this interchange Morris had championed the right of the territorial government to a reasonable measure of autonomy, even though a contrary view was held by his political friends at Ottawa, and in this matter his attitude did not waver during his term of office. His governorship thus may be said to mark the beginnings of the movement for self-government in the Territories.

In view of the criticism which the Liberals had levelled at Macdonald's policy of centralizing authority at Ottawa, a marked change might have been expected in the attention given to the acts of the North-West Council after November 7, 1873, when the Mackenzie administration was formed. At the time of Macdonald's resignation no action had been taken on the legislation passed at the September session.[85] Yet when the Council met again the following March there was still no word from Ottawa. The members therefore resolved to make a respectful but vigorous protest against the indifference of the federal authorities:

The Council are aware that exceptional circumstances [the change of government and the general election] may during the past few months, have prevented that prompt action which they trust will, in future, characterize the dealings of the Privy Council with North-West affairs.

Sensible as they are of the great importance of the duties which they are called upon to perform, and earnestly desirous, as they are, to dis-

---

[83]The order read, "that until the settlement of the country shall have reached a more advanced stage, it will be inexpedient to allow the Act to go into operation." Campbell in a private letter to Morris of Oct. 28, 1873, stated, "It was thought better to keep the appointments directly under the Crown as a matter of prerogative": Morris Papers.

[84]Morris to Campbell, private, Oct. 29, 1873, Morris Papers. The government at the time of disallowance proposed to soften the blow by appointing as justices those who had been named by the Council; this was done, after further consultations with Morris, by an Order in Council of Dec. 23, 1873.

[85]Three acts were passed at this session, two of them designated as urgent.

charge those duties loyally and efficiently, the Council feel that they will be unable to do so, if matters which they believe to be of urgent importance, and which they have taken occasion to represent as such, be permitted to remain altogether unnoticed for a period of six months.[86]

The Council passed two acts at this session, but these also were ignored at Ottawa, and by June, Morris reported that the Council had become "very much discouraged in consequence of the Government, past and present, not having disposed of the matters submitted for their consideration in September and March last." In supporting their plea for action he remarked, "The Council can be of great service and are desirous of doing their best for the Territories."[87]

The final and most sharply worded protest was made during the session of December 1874.

The Council deeply regret [the resolution read], that the Privy Council has not been pleased to communicate their approval or disapproval of the Legislation and many resolutions adopted by Council . . . and they respectfully represent that such long delay has paralyzed the action of the Council. The Council have given their best attention to the weighty interests entrusted to them and have acted with a sincere desire to contribute to the advancement of the North-West Territories and the establishment of Law and Order, but they represent that to enable them to discharge their important mission they must be sustained by the prompt action and active support of the Government of Canada.[88]

Some indication of the Mackenzie government's interest in the Council as a legislative body may be gleaned from the fact that of the eleven acts passed after the Liberals assumed office only one was approved, and no action was taken on the rest.[89]

With its restricted legislative power, there was little opportunity for the territorial government to establish an administrative programme. Furthermore it had practically no money to spend, since it

[86]Minutes of the North-West Council, March 12, 1874.

[87]Morris to Mackenzie, confidential, June 3, 1874, Morris Papers. The Council had renewed its request for action: see Minutes of the North-West Council, June 1, 1874.

[88]Minutes of the North-West Council, Dec. 4, 1874.

[89]The lone approval (by Order in Council, Nov. 5, 1874) was of an amendment to the Poisons Act, the original having been approved by the Macdonald government. Even this would not have been approved had it not been for Morris's urgent request: see Morris to Laird, telegram, Oct. 19, 1874, Lieutenant-Governor's Papers, P.A.M.; see also Council Journals, 1877, pp. 8–9; and C.S.P. 1876, no. 70. During the life of the Council a total of seventeen acts were passed; of these five became operative either by being approved by the federal government or by having been designated as urgent; two were disallowed; how many of the remaining ten became operative de facto is not certain, but at least one did: see Interior file no. 82510.

lacked local sources of revenue and the amount received from the federal treasury was a mere pittance. Morris had first raised the financial issue in the spring of 1873, when he proposed to the federal government that a sum be placed at the disposal of the Council.[90] Some time later he was asked to name an amount; he consulted the Council, and $10,000 was requested.[91] Amid the distractions of the Pacific Scandal the Macdonald ministry seems to have overlooked this request, and it was not until after further pressure from Morris that the Mackenzie government placed $4,000 to his credit for the balance of the fiscal year 1873–4.[92] The following year, however, less than $700 was made available by the new administration, and this only after repeated requests from Morris.[93] Other expenses connected with the North-West government were paid directly from Ottawa, but these never amounted to much—the largest items were the salaries of the Clerk of the Council and the legal adviser, who constituted the territorial civil service of this period.[94] For the year 1874–5 the total expended on behalf of the territorial government, exclusive of the Governor's salary, amounted to less than $3,000, and even this was too much in the opinion of the parsimonious Mackenzie.[95]

VII

After 1876 the Lieutenant-Governor in his capacity as chief executive officer of the territorial government was given various administrative responsibilities under the authority of local ordinances. But during Morris's term the Council was not encouraged to use its legislative power in this way. At no time, however, was there any lack of activity in the Governor's office. To it came a steady stream of requests, warnings, complaints, and information—from missionaries, traders, métis, the Mounted Police, and settlers at Prince Albert and Edmonton—pertaining to such matters as the regulation of buffalo hunting, squatters' rights, grants to mission schools, postal com-

[90]Morris to Secretary of State, June 24, 1873, C.S.P. 1877, no. 121, p. 8.
[91]See Campbell to Morris, telegram, Sept. 10, 1873, Lieutenant-Governor's Papers, Indian Affairs and N.W.T., P.A.M. Morris to Minister of the Interior, Nov. 22, 1873, C.S.P. 1877, no. 121, p. 25, and Minutes of the North-West Council, Sept. 11, 1873.
[92]See "Account Book for the North-West Territories, 1873–75," P.A.M.
[93]Ibid.
[94]W. T. Urquhart was Clerk of the Council from Nov. 28, 1872, till his death on Sept. 21, 1874; he was succeeded by F. G. Becher, private secretary to the Lieutenant-Governor.
[95]See Dominion Public Accounts, 1874–5, C.S.P. 1876, no. 1, and Mackenzie's remarks in Commons Debates, 1875, p. 656.

munication, seed grain relief, and law enforcement. Being unable to deal with such questions directly, Morris referred them to Ottawa, accompanied by carefully considered recommendations based on the best local advice he could obtain. In addition to this there were his "agency duties" arising from federal policies or federal legislation: he was responsible for regulating the amount of liquor which could be legally imported into the Territories; and he had to give general supervision to the administration of justice, a matter of some difficulty since the delay in appointing the stipendiary magistrates left the Territories without local courts, except that provided by the justices of the peace with their limited jurisdiction.

The Governor's heaviest responsibilities, however, were in the field of Indian administration. During these years the federal government was feeling its way towards a system for the administration of Indian affairs at the local level, since it was not clear how far the system operating in Eastern Canada could be applied in the West. The first Indian Commisioner for the North-West, W. M. Simpson, had confined his activities to the negotiation of treaties. Archibald had occupied a prominent role in these negotiations as a Commissioner, but had no authority to participate in day-to-day administration, nor did he desire any; despite this he felt obliged to fill the gap created by the absence of a resident representative of the Indian Affairs Branch. Morris shared his predecessor's views and advocated the appointment of a resident Commissioner of businesslike qualities, and two Assistant Commisioners of half-breed origin.[96] Macdonald, however, was determined that the Lieutenant-Governor should be given a measure of responsibility, and proposed the appointment of an "Indian Board" or Commission for Manitoba and the Territories, consisting of the Lieutenant-Governor, a resident Commissioner or agent, and the head of the Dominion Lands Branch in Winnipeg. The Prime Minister outlined his plan in a letter to Morris:

The Governor is not expected to work in the Indian Office or Department. He is simply to preside over a Commission which will regulate the general policy with respect to the Indians under instructions from Head Quarters here. The working part of it will be done by the Indian Commissioner who will succeed Simpson. . . .

Unless this arrangement is made the Indian Dept. must be managed directly from here, and the Lt. Governor of Manitoba will cut a sorry figure, having no control or voice in one of the main features connected with the administration of the affairs of the great Nor'West.[97]

[96]Morris to Secretary of State for the Provinces, Dec. 13, 1872, Lieutenant-Governor's Papers, P.A.M.
[97]Macdonald to Morris, March 1873, quoted in Milligan, *op. cit.*, pp. 194–5.

The Board was established in June 1873,[98] but never functioned effectively.[99] Morris preferred to consult the North-West Council, which he declared was "far more competent to advise on such subjects,"[100] and, as we have already noted, he supported the Council in its unsuccessful efforts to replace the Board as the recognized advisory agency. Meanwhile, he became more and more involved in administration, both as a negotiator of treaties and as adviser on the host of special problems appearing wherever whites and Indians mingled in the vast plains region. Describing his position to Mackenzie on one occasion, he wrote: "I have more work and grave responsibilities in a month than the Governors of the other Provinces have in a couple of years. . . . In fact I am by force of circumstances your Chief Indian Agent."[101] In the end he became convinced, as Macdonald had been, that the continuinig participation of the Lieutenant-Governor in Indian administration was of the greatest importance, though he remained critical of the amount of detailed supervision which had devolved upon him. When the Mackenzie administration abolished the Indian Board in February 1876, and established two superintendencies (Manitoba and the Territories) on the Ontario model, with Superintendents directly responsible to Ottawa, Morris criticized it because it failed to provide any form of local control over policy.[102] The Ontario model was not applicable, he contended, because the Indians of the North-West insisted (very shrewdly) on carrying their grievances to the Queen's representative and would not be satisfied with a Superintendent; a supervisory board for each of the superintendencies should be created, consisting of the Governor, the Superintendent, and someone well acquainted with Indian character, with the Governor possessing a veto power. While the government did not accept this proposal, Morris's views, based on a brilliant record of treaty negotiations, could not be ignored, and when the government of the North-West was reorganized later in the year Morris was made honorary Chief Superintendent of Indian Affairs for Manitoba and Keewatin with powers to investigate grievances and make recommendations, while on the other hand the new

---

[98]Order in Council, June 16, 1873.

[99]See statements of the Minister and J. A. N. Provencher in *Annual Report of the Department of the Interior*, 1873–4.

[100]Morris to Minister of the Interior, Jan. 24, 1874, Lieutenant-Governor's Papers, P.A.M.

[101]Morris to Mackenzie, confidential, Aug. 20, 1875, Morris Papers.

[102]Morris to Minister of the Interior, Feb. 18, 1876, Lieutenant-Governor's Papers, P.A.M.

Lieutenant-Governor of the Territories was commissioned as Superintendent of Indian Affairs for that area.[103]

VIII

The North-West government of 1870–6 suffered from several severe handicaps, none of them self imposed. First was delay in establishing the Council; but this was of minor importance compared with the limitations placed upon that body when it finally was created. Endowed with a weak constitution, it led a frustrated, starved existence, and was ultimately dismissed with the suggestion that it had been a failure. While it was not a failure, its usefulness would have been greatly increased by a few simple reforms. Its membership should have been restricted to those who were acquainted with the North-West (there were about six such out of the eighteen); instead, an attempt was made at the start to make it conform to the divisions in the Manitoba population—a quite irrelevant consideration from the administrative point of view. Once having yielded, the government was forced to make further additions to satisfy "neglected interests" in that province, until the Council reached a size quite out of proportion to the needs of the situation. The size of the Council may have had something to do with preventing a second reform—payment of the members; not only did they not receive a sessional indemnity but some had to pay their hotel bills out of their own pockets; apparently their only compensation was the title "Honourable."[104] This, no doubt, was one reason why the sessions were so brief, which in turn explains why the press was barred from the meetings—legislative and executive matters being discussed at the same sitting.[105] As a consequence of this lack of publicity, there was no public opinion to back demands for action by the federal government.

Though the Mackenzie administration did not ignore the Governor and Council as an advisory or consultative agency, it made no attempt to remove the handicaps which prevented it from becoming a more effective governing body. For some reason Mackenzie disliked this creation of his predecessor, and within a year after taking office he began to think of introducing "some form of government more effective than that now in operation."[106] So determined was he to sub-

---

103See report of the Deputy Superintendent General of Indian Affairs in *Annual Report of the Department of the Interior*, 1875–6.
104Morris to Secretary of State, Dec. 24, 1875, *C.S.P.* 1877, no. 121, pp. 43–4.
105See Minutes of the North-West Council, Nov. 25, 1875.
106Mackenzie to Morris, confidential, Dec. 11, 1874, Mackenzie Papers.

stitute his own scheme that Morris was not permitted to complete his five-year term as Governor of the North-West, although he was most anxious to do so. While this scheme was being matured the existing territorial administration dragged out an exasperatingly futile existence as a governing body for nearly three years, without the federal support which was necessary for it to meet the problems within its jurisdiction. Though the preparation of plans for a new territorial government suited to the future development of the North-West was a commendable policy, there was no excuse for sabotaging the existing system. Whether by accident or design the experiment of governing the Territories from Winnipeg was not given a fair trial under the Mackenzie administration.

Despite the brief existence of the first Council of the North-West Territories, the lack of publicity given to its activities, its impotence as a legislative body, and the federal government's indifference to its activities, it nevertheless has a significant place in the evolution of self-government in the North-West, for it demanded a measure of autonomy for the Territories and challenged the principle of centralizing authority in Ottawa. In defining these issues it had the wholehearted support of Alexander Morris, who thus became the first champion of territorial autonomy as well as the father of responsible government in Manitoba.[107] The ablest of all the Lieutenant-Governors of the North-West, he was also the only one who gave unqualified and continuous support to the movement for self-government. A man of strong convictions, he refused to sacrifice his lifelong concern for western development and his belief in constitutional principles on the altar of political expediency and personal popularity at Ottawa, for in supporting legitimate local interests he did not hesitate to challenge ignorance or indifference, whether displayed by his former cabinet associates or their Liberal successors. With the severance of Morris's connection with the North-West, interest in territorial autonomy, lacking vigorous leadership from the chief executive, subsided for a time.

---

[107]Morris's contribution to the constitutional development in Manitoba is described in Milligan, op. cit., chaps. viii and ix. His correspondence contains many references to his efforts to secure greater recognition for the North-West Council—see for example his private letter of Feb. 25, 1874, to the Postmaster General with respect to soliciting the Council's views on postal services: Morris Papers.

CHAPTER FOUR

The Territorial Government at Battleford

1876-82

THOUGH THE MACKENZIE ADMINISTRATION disliked the existing system of territorial government, it did not spend much time in preparing its own scheme. Its chief concern was that "there should be a firm Government established within the territories and that the Governor should reside several hundred miles west of the present point of authority,"[1] but this policy was not carefully worked out in detail. The North-West Territories Act of 1875[2] was, on the admission of the Minister of the Interior "too hastily prepared,"[3] and neither personal acquaintance with the North-West nor knowledge of the American system (such as Mills possessed) influenced its terms to any great extent. No sooner had the Act come into operation (October 7, 1876) than defects became apparent, so that at the succeeding session of Parliament it had to be amended—the first of a series of piecemeal changes by which the territorial constitution evolved during the next two decades.

The Act of 1875 was drafted by the Prime Minister with the assistance of the Deputy Minister of Justice. David Laird, the Minister of the Interior, seems to have had little to do with it, and indeed was anxious to shift the supervision of the territorial government from his department to the Secretary of State, on the ground that he had "quite enough to do with the Indians and the Lands."[4] Nor did Alexander Morris have any influence in drafting the measure, perhaps because he had made bold to suggest that the views of the Deputy Minister

[1] Hon. Alexander Mackenzie, *Commons Debates*, 1875, p. 657.
[2] 38 Vict., c. 49, "An Act to amend and consolidate the laws respecting the North-West Territories."
[3] Laird to Morris, private, March 15, 1875, Morris Papers.
[4] *Ibid*. When the Act came into force in October 1876, Laird directed that the supervision of the territorial government be transferred to the Secretary of State under the mistaken impression that section 2 of the Act required it. This continued

of Justice were "only theoretical at best" since he had "never set foot in the North-West and knows nothing of its peculiar conditions";[5] moreover, Morris was of the opinion that until railway facilities were available the government of the Territories should continue to be administered from Winnipeg, and this ran counter to the Prime Minister's views. The Governor's preference was for a reform of the existing constitution by instituting "a Council of five, having the power to pass statutes coming into operation *at once*, only subject to be vetoed if beyond the power of a local legislature." "Such a Council," he stated, "enacting a simple municipal law adapted to the peculiar [condition?] of the people, and other laws of like character could deal with North-West questions, until population enabled another government to be established on a substantial basis."[6] The fact that preparation of the bill was not completed until after the session was well advanced explains, although it does not justify, the failure of the government to submit a draft for Morris's consideration;[7] though its main principle was at variance with his own views he would have accepted the government's policy and made every effort to improve the measure in its detailed operation, and there was no one whose judgment was of more value in this connection.

Mackenzie advanced several reasons for establishing an independent government in the Territories: existing settlement and an expected influx of population required a "centre of authority . . . nearer than Winnipeg"[8] (initially, at Fort Pelly); the measure would appeal to prospective settlers and so encourage immigration; it was inconvenient and expensive to have the Governor of Manitoba travelling in the Territories; and the existing system was costing "as much as a Government in the territory without being as efficient."[9] Though this last argument was vitiated by a large increase in the estimates for govern-

---

for several months until Laird's successor, David Mills, pointed out that the Lieutenant-Governor's connection with the Secretary of State did not extend beyond the formal instructions given at the time of appointment. Consequently the jurisdiction of the Department of the Interior was restored early in 1877: see Mills to Scott, private, Jan. 5, 1876, Mills Papers, University of Western Ontario Library.

[5]Morris to Mackenzie, Dec. 25, 1874, Lieutenant-Governor's Papers, P.A.M.

[6]Morris to Mackenzie, confidential, Nov. 29, 1874, *ibid*. Morris coupled this reform with recommendations for a resident judge or stipendiary magistrate at Carlton, Edmonton, Qu'Appelle, and Fort Francis, jurisdiction for Manitoba courts north and east of the province, and a reorganized Indian service.

[7]Despite repeated requests, Morris was not given an opportunity to see the bill until after it was introduced in the House: see telegraph book for February 1875, Lieutenant-Governor's Papers, P.A.M.

[8]Mackenzie to Morris, confidential, Dec. 11, 1874. Mackenzie Papers.

[9]*Commons Debates*, 1875, p. 656.

ment in the North-West[10] and by the government's failure to test the efficiency of the existing system, the others rested on the undoubted fact that an independent authority would have to be established sooner or later in the North-West. The real issue, therefore, was the timing of the change, as Macdonald pointed out. He believed it could be postponed for a few years, particularly since the Governor of Manitoba was in the best position to administer that disputed portion of the Territories east of Manitoba through which ran the Dawson road—an area which his government had regarded as extending to the head of the Lakes.[11]

The structure of the new government was set forth in the first thirteen sections of the Act; the rest of it was a consolidation and amplification of previous legislation on the administration of justice and the prohibition of intoxicating liquors, along with new provisions relating to procedure in civil matters, real property law, wills, and the property of married women. In the rest of Canada most of these matters were within provincial jurisdiction, but Parliament was not restricted in its legislative dealing with the North-West, and it was regarded as conducive to the settlement of the country to introduce this body of law without delay instead of leaving it to the territorial legislature.[12]

There was to be no immediate change in the system of government by a Governor and an appointed Council. The Governor was to be the active head of the administration, aided, but not necessarily controlled, by the Council:[13] the Act gave no indication that all

[10]The appropriation for 1875–6 was $33,800 as compared with $10,000 for 1874–5.

[11]*Commons Debates*, 1875, pp. 655 ff.

[12]Another example of this type of legislation was the Act of 1878 "to provide for the creation and registration of Homestead Exemption Estates in the Territories of Canada" (41 Vict., c. 15). In discussing this measure Mills claimed that the reason for intervening in this field was "in consequence of Parliament having superior facilities through the library for ascertaining what was the actual condition of the law in other countries, [and] it was considered desirable to establish a system of real property, and, afterwards, give the North-West Government power to amend or change it, as experience might suggest": *Commons Debates*, 1878, p. 1516. This particular Act was modelled on American law, and was drafted by Mills in an effort to place the North-West on an equal footing with the American West in the competition for settlers.

[13]The Act conferred a number of specific duties on the Lieutenant-Governor in addition to his general administrative power and any responsibilities which might be conferred by territorial legislation. He was responsible for creating electoral districts, issuing writs of election, defining election procedure (until superseded by local law), appointing justices of the peace, securing reports on all civil and criminal proceedings in the territorial courts, and issuing liquor permits. In addition, he could control the local disposition of the Mounted Police for any purpose connected with the administration of justice or the general peace, order, and good government of the Territories.

executive matters required Council approval, though on the other hand there was no continuance of the requirement that all proceedings were subject to the Governor's approval. Like its predecessor, the new Council possessed both legislative and executive powers, and as the amendment of 1877 put it, the Governor "shall sit in Council with the Councillors as an integral part thereof, and not separately from them."[14] The Council was to be composed initially of not more than five members (later changed to six)[15] appointed by the federal government; three of these were to be judges (this being the number of stipendiary magistrates to be provided for the North-West), undoubtedly to save the cost of appointing a law officer and more than two salaried councillors.[16]

The Liberals made great claims for the feature of the Act which provided that as soon as any area of not more than 1,000 square miles (i.e. about 28 townships) contained 1,000 adults (exclusive of aliens or unenfranchised Indians) the Governor could establish it as an electoral district to return one member to the Council for a two-year term.[17] All adult male householders (other than aliens or unenfranchised Indians) resident within the electoral district for at least one year could vote and qualify as candidates.[18] Since no minimum value was placed on the property owned or occupied by the householder this was probably a slightly more liberal franchise than prevailed elsewhere in Canada, and it remained in force until 1888 when the Legislative Assembly was established and the householder qualification eliminated. As soon as there were twenty-one elected members, the Council was to become the Legislative Assembly of the North-West Territories. Whether this would also mean the introduction of responsible government was not stated, and the obscurity of the Act in this respect later resulted in the establishment of the Assembly without any parallel change in the executive powers of the Governor; had the probable intention of the Mackenzie administration been more clearly

[14]40 Vict., c. 7, s. 4.

[15]Ibid., s. 2. The judges (stipendiary magistrates) were *ex officio* members.

[16]Section 5 (modified by s. 89 of 43 Vict. c. 25) permitted payment of a salary of up to $1,000 for councillors; by Order in Council of July 10, 1884 appointed members received $200 per annum and elected members $400 (Interior file no. 66292).

[17]Section 13.

[18]Section 13, ss. 3 and 4. The clause defining the qualifications of voters is, like some other parts of the Act, not carefully worded. That the right to vote belonged to householders (rather than mere residents) is made clear in paragraph 30 of the instructions issued by the Lieutenant-Governor on the occasion of the first election in 1881: see proclamation of Feb. 5, 1881, also *Commons Debates*, 1886, p. 1249.

expressed the later constitutional development of the Territories would have been very different.[19]

The principle of steadily increasing the number of elected representatives with the growth in population was true liberal doctrine, and the authors of the Act no doubt hoped this would make it a charter of territorial liberty, comparing favourably with the American system, and a little more care in preparation would have made it such. As it was the elective principle was confined within rigid limits: not only was the area and population of the future constituencies arbitrarily fixed, but their boundaries, once established, could not be altered. The fact that a second member could be elected when the population reached 2,000 did not meet the real requirements of the situation as it developed in the next ten years.

What with careless drafting and inept changes in committee, the sections of the Act relating to the legislative powers of the Lieutenant-Governor and Council were complicated and contradictory,[20] so much so that all of the legislation (twelve ordinances) of the first (1877) session of the Council was discovered to be inoperative.[21] Since the Act had been in force only a few months when the enumerated powers of the Council were repealed, there is no need to consider them here. However, there were certain restrictions on the legislative power of the Council imposed in 1875 which had a marked effect on later political history. The first was an attempt to control the organization of municipalities and school districts. Instead of conferring power on the territorial legislature to make laws in relation to municipal institutions and education, complicated restrictions were imposed: no municipality could be established except in one of the electoral districts in spite of the fact that municipal institutions might be needed in areas not included within these districts; school districts, moreover, could not be established except in areas where a system of taxation prevailed, and this made school district organization dependent on municipal organization, since the territorial government did not impose any taxes. The other restriction had more lasting significance, for it established the right (at that time enjoyed in Ontario, Quebec, and

19Though Mackenzie was silent on this point, Mills probably expressed the intention of the government when he wrote in 1877, "when a Legislative Assembly supersedes the Council, then the Governor will of course simply be an Executive Officer as in the Provinces": Mills to G. W. Wicksteed, Chief Law Clerk, House of Commons, Feb. 10, 1877, Mills Papers.

20Particularly the relationship of sections 3 and 7.

21Under Secretary of State to Laird, telegram, Aug. 9, 1878, Attorney General's file G 694, A.S.

Manitoba) of a Roman Catholic or Protestant minority to organize separate schools. This provision, like the one relating to prohibition[22] and a later one (1877) placing the English and French languages on an equal basis in the courts and in the records and proceedings of the Council,[23] were evidences of how Parliament could succumb to pressure from special interests and use its unlimited legislative authority to intervene in matters of local concern.[24]

In one respect only did this Act produce an immediate improvement in the status of the territorial government—ordinances did not require prior approval at Ottawa before coming into effect.[25] On the whole the Act was a conservative measure—too indefinite in many of its provisions to be a blueprint of future constitutional evolution. As Mills pointed out during the debate on the bill, there was no provision for future representation in Parliament, no indication of "the terms and conditions under which these people would be formed into a Province," and no clarification of the financial relationship of the Territories and the Dominion. By comparison, he continued, "Those who observed the American territorial system of government would notice that from the time the first government was organized under the ordinance enacted by Congress in 1787, till the establishment of the last territorial government, there was scarcely any difference in the plan of government and they never found it necessary to depart from

[22]In connection with the liquor law Mackenzie remarked that it "would give the Dominion a fair opportunity to commence with a clean slate in this enormous territory, and test practically the operation of a prohibitory liquor law where there has been no law on that or any other subject before": Commons Debates, 1875, p. 655.

[23]40 Vict., c. 7, s. 11: "Either the English or the French language may be used by any person in the debates of the said Council, and in the proceedings before the Courts, and both those languages shall be used in the records and Journals of the said Council, and the ordinances of the said Council shall be printed in both those languages." This section was not part of the government's bill and was introduced by Senator Girard of Manitoba. The government would have preferred to leave the matter under local control, but it was too late in the session to send the bill back to the Senate, and it was allowed to pass: Commons Debates, 1877, p. 1872.

[24]The only opposition to the separate school clause was in the Senate, where an unsuccessful effort was made to eliminate it, with George Brown contending that the matter should be left to the people of the Territories to settle. Senator Miller, speaking in support of the clause, argued with admirable candour that "They could do now safely and easily what they might not hereafter be able to accomplish when powerful conflicting interests had grown up in the territory." Senate Debates, 1875.

[25]The Act also dropped the provision whereby the Governor General in Council could legislate on any subject not under the control of the territorial government—this power however had never been exercised; the power to proclaim acts of Parliament to be in force in the Territories was retained.

the general principle laid down in the ordinance of 1787." "It seemed to him," he concluded, "we ought not to refuse to profit by the experience of others under similar circumstances to our own."[26] Apart from D. A. Smith, who also advocated representation of the Territories in Parliament, Mills received no support from other members, while Macdonald, representing the opposition, contented himself with questioning the principle of a separate government and warning the administration that they "should not clog themselves" with "the clause introducing the popular element." "At the right time," he declared, "they could pass an Act introducing the popular element into the Government of the North-West"[27]—an observation which is the complete epitome of his philosophy of government.

The North-West Territories Act of 1875 was undoubtedly an honest attempt to improve the territorial constitution and guide its future development. It is fair to state, however, that Mackenzie would have been better advised to have retained the services of an experienced administrator such as Morris till the end of his term of office in 1877,[28] meanwhile maturing the legislation under which a new system could be established. By more attention to detail, by soliciting the views of men acquainted with the West, and by incorporating some of the American principles in British political forms, a true charter of territorial progress could have been produced which would have been a monument to the Mackenzie administration. Instead, the opportunity was fumbled: as a contribution to the advance of self-government the Act was only partially effective and in some of its features was, directly or indirectly, an obstacle to the movement.

II

The North-West Territories Act was passed in April 1875, but it was not until October 7, 1876—a year and a half later—that the proclamation was issued bringing it into force. The government, it appeared, had developed some reservations concerning the suitability of Fort Pelly as the first territorial capital, and was gathering further information on the location of existing and prospective settlements, in order to establish the seat of government at a more central point.

[26]*Commons Debates*, 1875, p. 661.
[27]*Ibid.*, p. 656.
[28]"My sphere has lost its attraction," Morris wrote Macdonald in 1875, "by the proposed cutting off of the North West. I wish I had been left to complete my work there, during the remainder of my term of two years": quoted in F. A. Milligan, "The Lieutenant-Governorship in Manitoba, 1870–1882," M.A. thesis, University of Manitoba, 1948, p. 202.

"The place," the Prime Minister stated, "must be one favourable for the location of a considerable town; it ought also to be favourable as an agricultural district, with an abundance of fuel and timber, and easy access from the different posts established by the Government in the Territories."[29] In October 1876 Battleford was chosen[30]—it being a point on the transcontinental railway as then surveyed, and also on the telegraph line which followed the projected railway route. Pending the provision of suitable quarters there the new Lieutenant-Governor established himself some ten miles from Fort Pelly—at Swan River Barracks (Livingstone), also on the railway route, where part of the Mounted Police barracks was available for his use. Here the first session of the new Council was held in March 1877, and it was not until August of that year that the Governor moved on to Battleford.

The problem of securing a Lieutenant-Governor may have been a factor in delaying the inauguration of the new régime. Little is known concerning this appointment, except that David Laird did not seek out the position. "I did not want to leave the Government at that time," he later wrote to Mackenzie, "but you urged me to accept, and, like a loyal supporter, I yielded, supposing that you, somehow, thought it would be in the interest of the country."[31] Laird had been catapulted into the office of Minister of the Interior following the sudden resignation of the Macdonald administration in 1873; the editor of a Charlottetown newspaper, he had had only the briefest experience of public office before being elected as one of Prince Edward Island's first members of Parliament. As Minister he had taken very little interest in the territorial government, with Mackenzie assuming the major responsibility for policy in this field;[32] the negotiation of three important Indian treaties and the consolidation of the Indian Act were the only major events of his period of office. His selection as Lieutenant-Governor was probably determined by quali-

[29]*Commons Debates*, 1876, p. 197.

[30]Order in Council of Oct. 7, 1876, designating Battleford as the seat of government from and after that date. An Order in Council of Feb. 28, 1876, had reserved a block of land at this point for government use, in anticipation that Battleford would be chosen as the capital.

[31]Quoted in Wm. Buckingham and G. W. Ross, *The Hon. Alexander Mackenzie: His Life and Times* (5th ed., Toronto, 1892), p. 436. Cartwright wrote to Mackenzie on Sept. 25, 1876: "Probably Laird's objections to the Nor. West might be much lessened if you could promise him Manitoba as soon as Morris leaves which will be somewhere in 1877": Cartwright Papers, Public Archives of Ontario.

[32]Laird did not take part in the debates in 1875 on the North-West Territories bill or in 1876 on the Keewatin Territory bill.

ties of personality and character which appealed to the Prime Minister—stern morality, caution, and devotion to duty. His successor as Minister of the Interior was David Mills, seemingly an appropriate choice in view of that gentleman's interest in the theory of territorial administration.

The new North-West Council as constituted in 1876 consisted of only three members—Lt. Col. Hugh Richardson and Mathew Ryan, Stipendiary Magistrates, and Lt. Col. J. F. Macleod, Stipendiary Magistrate and Commissioner of the Mounted Police.[33] Since all three were federal officials the government was saved the expense of salaries— undoubtedly one reason why Mackenzie was blind to the fact that this Council was remarkably similar to the one which he and his fellow Liberals had castigated Macdonald for appointing in 1869; the other reason was that he had a mistaken notion of the readiness of any part of the Territories to elect Councillors under the restrictions imposed by the Act of 1875.[34] Though the three members possessed some useful qualities for the position of Councillor, none of them had been in Manitoba or the North-West before 1873. Morris was shocked at the failure to appoint any half-breeds—he had repeatedly urged it in letters to Mackenzie and Laird while the latter was still Minister of the Interior, "to obviate," as he said, "any repetition of the McDougall difficulty which in its initiation largely arose from a fear of a *foreign* Council."[35] Yet though many of the half-breeds of the Territories had sympathized with the movement of 1869–70 and had moved out of Manitoba to continue their old free life of buffalo hunting and casual husbandry, their position was now quite different: scattered over a vast area, controlling no strategic centre, above all without the leadership of Louis Riel, they were not in a position to offer the sort of opposition to the new territorial government which had been so effective in 1869.

Nevertheless, representation of the métis in the new Council was but simple justice. Not only were they the largest single group in the non-Indian population but they also were busily demonstrating their capacity for self-government while Conservative and Liberal administrations at Ottawa were witlessly assuming that nobody but an Ontario immigrant would worry about such matters. With the moral

33Macleod became a Stipendiary Magistrate on Jan. 1, 1876, and became Commissioner on July 22, 1876, holding the latter office until Oct. 1, 1880.
34See for example his comments as reported in *Commons Debates*, 1878, p. 1534.
35Morris to Mackenzie, confidential, Aug. 20, 1875, Morris Papers; see also Morris to Minister of the Interior, July 24 and Aug. 3, 1875, Lieutenant-Governor's Papers, P.A.M.

support of the Roman Catholic missionaries, local "councils" had been formed in all the major métis settlements and simple rules for the government of these communities were adopted by popular consent. The first of these local councils was formed at St. Albert (near Edmonton) in 1871;[36] another was established at Qu'Appelle, headed by one John Fisher.[37] Late in 1873 the métis on the South Saskatchewan (St. Laurent) took a similar step and Gabriel Dumont, a renowned hunter, was elected president of the council.[38] Though Morris was worried lest this last council should develop into another provisional government on the Red River model, he was prepared to admit that "in the absence of all law hitherto the people will naturally make a law to themselves and they cannot be severely blamed therefor."[39]

Arriving in the Territories as Lieutenant-Governor, Laird belatedly discovered the unsatisfactory composition of his Council. "It appears to me highly desirable," he wrote to Mackenzie, "that we should have a local member of the Council—one for some time resident in the Territory and either a French or Scotch Halfbreed. . . . I find there is a little feeling here that all the present members of the Council are outsiders."[40] Since the government had not responded by the beginning of 1878, the people of St. Laurent petitioned the Governor-General that two old residents of the North-West be selected for the remaining positions in the appointive section of the Council, and that at least one be "un métis français."[41] A similar petition was received from the St. Albert settlement. Laird said the request should be given consideration, and in April the government appointed Pascal

---

[36]See W. J. Christie to Archibald, Nov. 21, 1871, Lieutenant-Governor's Papers, P.A.M.; both Bishop Grandin and Christie gave support to this venture. Archibald was sympathetic, though he stressed that the "laws" must rest on voluntary consent—Archibald to Christie, Jan. 11, 1872, *ibid.* A copy of the by-laws adopted in St. Albert is enclosed in a letter from Frank Moberly to Archibald, Jan. 8, 1872, *ibid.*

[37]Petition of May 5, 1873, to Morris from the council of the half-breeds at Qu'Appelle, also Morris to Fisher, June 4, 1873, *ibid.*

[38]This council is described in G. F. G. Stanley, *The Birth of Western Canada: A History of the Riel Rebellions* (London, 1936), pp. 180–2 and correspondence relative to it is in the Lieutenant-Governor's Papers, P.A.M.

[39]Morris to Minister of the Interior, Aug. 3, 1875, *ibid.*

[40]Laird to Mackenzie, private, July 10, 1877, Laird Papers, A.S.

[41]Interior file no. 13985, petition of Feb. 1, 1878. During the federal election of 1878 the political interests of the métis in the Territories were an important issue in the Marquette (Man.) constituency; it was proposed that the population requirement for the election of councillors be changed from 1,000 adults to 1,000 souls, and that in appointments to the council there should be Catholic representation in proportion to the population: see Joseph Royal to Macdonald, Sept. 28, 1878, Macdonald Papers.

Breland, a French half-breed who had been a member of the old Council.[42] Breland, though widely known and possessing some experience in public office, was by this time an old man who spent most of his time in Manitoba.[43] Since he had been opposed to the Riel movement, it is unlikely that he had much influence in the important métis settlement on the South Saskatchewan, and no one living in that settlement ever became a member of the North-West Council. The lesson of the Red River troubles, which had influenced the appointments to the first Council, was lost sight of in the composition of the second, and was unfortunately but the first of a series of neglected opportunities which led directly to the Rebellion of 1885. But the only warning voice was Morris's, and it awoke no response. His final verdict was prophetic: "It is a crying shame that the half breeds have been ignored. It will result in trouble and is most unjust."[44]

III

Some months after the passage of the North-West Territories Act of 1875 and while Mackenzie was still in charge of territorial government policy, Morris drew attention to the problem of administering the vast district lying north and east of Manitoba. "Insuperable geographic difficulties," he wrote, "will prevent their efficient government from any part of the Western Territories proper."[45] His solution involved two measures; the enlargement of Manitoba east, west, and north, and the creation of a separate territory north and east of the enlarged province "to be known as the Territory of 'Kee-wa-tin' which means in the Cree and Chippewa dialects the 'North Land'."[46]

[42]Laird to Minister of the Interior, Feb. 13, 1878, ibid.; see also Order in Council of April 5, 1878. Breland's appointment was to date from July 1, 1878, and his salary was set at $800 per annum. See Interior file no. 66292.

[43]A biographical sketch of Breland is given in Oliver, I, p. 122. He is referred to in the Council Journals, 1878, p. 5, as a "Merchant of Cypress Hills" but his residence in the Territories appears to have been, at most, intermittent.

[44]Morris to Hon. H. L. Langevin, private, June 8, 1878, Morris Papers. As a result of a suggestion from Morris (following his retirement as Governor in December 1877), Langevin had raised the issue in the House of Commons (see Commons Debates, 1878, pp. 2542–6). Mills defended the government's policy on the ground that the half-breeds of the Territories were uneducated, had no fixed habitation, and were satisfactorily represented by Breland; Blake claimed that the elective principle in the constitution of the Council would result in two or three elected members "within some few months from this time." During the brief discussion neither side discussed the issue on its merits, each being more concerned with making charges to embarrass the other.

[45]Morris to Secretary of State, Oct. 13, 1875, Lieutenant-Governor's Papers, P.A.M.

[46]Ibid. The name was suggested to Morris by James McKay: see Milligan, op. cit., p. 202.

He proposed as a practical and inexpensive arrangement that the new district be governed by the Lieutenant-Governor of Manitoba and a Council of three members with the seat of government at Winnipeg. "The people inhabiting the country," he explained, "hold no intercourse with the Western portion of the Territories, and their only communications are with Fort Garry or in the case of the Moose Factory and York Factory (on Hudson Bay) with Great Britain."[47] Morris's arguments for a new territory gained greater weight by the delay in settling the Ontario boundary, which prevented the enlargement of Manitoba and thus isolated the Icelandic settlement on Lake Winnipeg as well as the Dawson road country. It was this aspect of the problem which induced Mackenzie to prepare a bill which was passed at the 1876 session creating the Territory of Keewatin.[48] This legislation simply maintained the status quo in the area by reviving the provisions of Macdonald's North-West Government Act, with the exception that the size of the Keewatin Council was limited to between five and ten members. Though the government had seemingly accepted Morris's recommendation, its conception of the need was quite different—Keewatin was to be only a temporary creation,[49] whereas Morris believed that some permanent provision should be made for the far north, which would not likely be included in either Manitoba or Ontario when their boundaries were settled.[50]

Keewatin Territory came into existence on the same day as the new North-West government—October 7, 1876. The wisdom of its creation was immediately demonstrated, for Morris had scarcely assumed his new office before he was faced with a smallpox epidemic among the Icelanders and Indians of the Lake Winnipeg area. As a consequence, the government was induced to appoint a Council of six members to deal with the emergency;[51] their legislative powers,

[47]Morris to Secretary of State, Oct. 13, 1875, Lieutenant-Governor's Papers, P.A.M.

[48]39 Vict., c. 21, "An Act respecting the North-West Territories, and to create a separate Territory out of part thereof." Section 12 of 40 Vict., c. 7, extended the jurisdiction of Manitoba courts into Keewatin, as had been suggested by Morris.

[49]See preamble to the Act and remarks of Mackenzie and Blake, *Commons Debates*, 1876, pp. 194–5.

[50]The salary as Governor of Keewatin ($1,000) was also important to Morris; he reported to Blake that he had spent $4,000 more during 1875 than he had received from public sources, and saw no means of economizing: Morris to Blake, confidential, Feb. 18, 1876, Blake Papers.

[51]Order in Council of Nov. 25, 1876. The members were J. A. N. Provencher, A. G. Jackes, M.D., Lt. Col. W. Osborne Smith, William Hespeler, Gilbert McMicken, and Alfred Codd, M.D.

much to Morris's disgust, were restricted in the same manner as those of the old North-West Council.[52] The Keewatin Council grappled manfully with the epidemic and succeeded in preventing it from invading Manitoba. However in constituting Keewatin the Mackenzie administration had really no intention of inaugurating a second territorial government, and when the smallpox epidemic was over the Council was summarily dismissed.[53] But it was soon discovered that the needs of the people of Keewatin could not be completely ignored, and in 1878 Mills introduced a bill to permit municipal and school district organization in the Icelandic settlement, where in the absence of any existing law the people had, in typical frontier fashion, resorted to voluntary organization to meet their requirements.[54] In the heated atmosphere of the pre-election session the government gave priority to other business; the bill was not brought to third reading, and the Icelanders were left to their own devices until 1881, when their district was included in the enlarged province of Manitoba. Meanwhile the Lieutenant-Governor of Manitoba continued to give a limited measure of oversight to affairs in Keewatin (the Council was never reinstituted)—a system which continued until the time of the general reorganization of territorial administration in 1905.[55]

IV

Some of the defects and omissions of the Act of 1875 became apparent to both Laird and Mills as soon as they assumed their new offices, the one as Governor and the other as Minister.[56] But instead

[52]Order in Council, Nov. 25, 1876. Morris protested against the provision that ordinances (unless marked urgent) were to come into effect only after approval at Ottawa; "that restriction," he wrote, "hampered and fettered the action of the late North-West Council, and led to great delays": Morris to Secretary of State, Dec. 6, 1876, Morris Papers.

[53]The resignations were accepted in April 1877: see *Annual Report of the Department of the Interior*, 1876–7, p. ix. Copies of the minutes of the Council of Keewatin and correspondence relative thereto are in the Morris Papers and Lieutenant-Governor's Papers, P.A.M.

[54]Mills stated that there were some 1,500 settlers in the settlement when he visited it in 1877: *Commons Debates*, 1878, p. 1384; see also at p. 427. Instead of assisting the passage of the bill the members wrangled over the merits of the ballot and the respective advantages of Ontario and Quebec municipal systems.

[55]A small appropriation was made each year for expenses in Keewatin—chiefly for the salary of the Governor's secretary and the care of the insane. Beginning in 1890 an annual report by the Governor was published in the *Report of the Department of the Interior*.

[56]See Laird to Blake, private, Nov. 29, 1876, Blake Papers, University of Toronto Library; Laird to Mackenzie, confidential, Jan. 2, 1877, Attorney General's file G 545, A.S.; Mills to G. W. Wicksteed, Feb. 10 and Feb. 28, 1877, Mills Papers.

of thoroughly overhauling the Act, the amendment which Mills sponsored in 1877 corrected only a few obvious imperfections.[57] Provision was made for the appointment of an Administrator in the absence of the Governor and for oaths for the Councillors, and the position of the Governor as "an integral part" of the Council was clarified. The only important provision concerned the jurisdiction of the Council: the enumerated powers of 1875 were repealed and the previous system of conferring powers by federal Order in Council was restored. In May the new powers (which continued unchanged until 1886) were defined as follows:

1. The establishment and tenure of Territorial Offices, and the appointment and payment of Territorial Officers.

2. The establishment, maintenance and management of prisons in and for the *North-West Territories*.

3. The establishment of Municipal Institutions in the Territories, in accordance with the provisions of "The *North-West Territories* Acts, 1875–1877".

4. The issue of Shop, Auctioneer and other Licenses, in order to the raising of a revenue for territorial or municipal purposes.

5. The solemnization of marriage in the Territories.

6. The Administration of Justice including the constitution, organization and maintenance of Territorial Courts of civil jurisdiction.

7. The imposition of punishment by fine, penalty or imprisonment for enforcing any territorial Ordinance.

8. Property and civil rights in the Territories, subject to any Legislation by the Parliament of *Canada* upon these subjects. . . .

9. Generally on matters of a merely local or private nature in the Territories.[58]

It will be observed that these powers were selected, with certain modifications, from the list of provincial powers in the British North America Act, and this at least established a standard for purposes of comparison and definition. The powers possessed by a province but withheld from the territorial government were the amendment of the constitution, direct taxation, borrowing money, management and sale of public lands, establishment of hospitals, asylums, and charitable institutions, local works and undertakings, and the incorporation of companies. In addition, the powers relating to municipalities, property and civil rights, administration of justice, and imposition of fines were restricted either by provisions of the North-West Territories Act or by other special legislation for the Territories.

[57]40 Vict., c. 7. The largest part of the Act dealt with the administration of justice.
[58]Order in Council, May 11, 1877.

These powers would have been sufficient to meet the needs of the Territories for a few years had the amendment of 1877 removed the restrictions of 1875 on the organization of municipalities and school districts. Mills toyed with the idea of inaugurating a simple form of municipal government, but allowed the opportunity to pass.[59] When later in the year the difficulty of organizing schools was drawn to his attention(the métis of St. Laurent being the first people in the North-West to ask for school grants) he had no satisfactory solution to offer.[60] Altogether the legislation of "the philosopher from Bothwell" does not live up to the expectations aroused by his earlier speeches on the proper theory of territorial government, though his brief term of office is an extenuating circumstance.

V

Though the Mackenzie administration made much of the removal of the capital from Winnipeg to a point in the Territories, this of itself had little constitutional significance. As Mackenzie himself said, "practically the legislation of the territory would be in the hands of the Government here at Ottawa."[61] Had the change been accompanied by a substantial increase in legislative power, by the establishment of a representative council, and by adequate financial assistance, the period of Laird's governorship (1876–81) might have seen significant political progress. Instead it was on the whole a period of frustration, for both the Governor and the people of the North-West. The contrast between the administrations of Morris and Laird is not in the degree of discontent with federal "colonial policy" but rather in its expression. In the former it was the Governor and Council who were dissatisfied with their powers; in the latter it was the people themselves who initiated the complaints and requests which Laird and his Council supported with varying degrees of vigour.

This dawning of popular interest in territorial affairs was promoted by the influx of several thousand new settlers and the appearance of newspapers. By 1881 the most populous of the new settlements were situated just beyond Manitoba in the region between the provincial boundary and the Minnedosa (Little Saskatchewan) River, and a

[59]Mills to Laird, private, Jan. 30, 1877, Mills Papers.
[60]Mills to Laird, Jan. 14, 1878, Council Journals, 1878, Appendix A. Mills suggested the establishment of "School Corporations" with power to levy taxes— a proposal of dubious constitutionality when viewed in relation to section 11 of the Act of 1875, which is probably why it was not acted upon.
[61]Commons Debates, 1875, p. 658.

few settlers had gone even farther west—almost to Fort Ellice.[62] During the same period the older districts—Prince Albert, St. Laurent, and Edmonton—were attracting newcomers, and in the south-west an important ranching community appeared, the second phase of the northward thrust of American enterprise in that region. When the census was taken in 1881 there were, exclusive of Indians, perhaps eight thousand people in the area immediately west of Manitoba and close to six thousand scattered throughout the rest of the prairie region.[63] Newspapers were founded in these pioneer settlements with amazing promptitude—the *Saskatchewan Herald* (Battleford) in 1878, the *Edmonton Bulletin* in 1880, the *Macleod Gazette* and the *Prince Albert Times* in 1882. The early editors were men of intelligence and vigour, and usually highly competent writers. No aspect of national or territoral affairs was foreign to their interests, and their columns immediately became the most effective single force in evoking and communicating a North-West point of view on public affairs.[64]

Laird had not been long in the Territories before he discovered that the provision in the Act of 1875 for electing members of the Council was incapable of providing early popular representation, and, worse still, was a barrier to municipal and school district organization since these depended on the existence of electoral districts; such was the result of legislating without an accurate knowledge of conditions in the West. "I am inclined to the opinion," he wrote, "that a less number than one thousand inhabitants of adult age within an area of one thousand square miles . . . might properly have the privilege of electing a member to the Council. Both in British Columbia and Manitoba there are smaller constituencies than half the above number represents."[65] Since the Macdonald administration made no effort to

---

[62]See A. S. Morton, *History of Prairie Settlement* (Toronto, 1938), chap. III, and map at pp. 46–7.

[63]*Census of Canada*, 1880–1, vol. I. The non-Indian population in the census districts in the plains region was: Cumberland South, 130; Qu'Appelle, 648; Wood Mountain, 409; Prince Albert, 2161; Battleford, 852; Edmonton, 800; Bow River, 400. The population in the area of the Territories annexed to Manitoba in 1881 is given under the heading "Manitoba Extension."

[64]See Earl G. Drake, "The Territorial Press in the Region of Present Day Saskatchewan," M.A. thesis, University of Saskatchewan, 1951.

[65]Laird to Minister of the Interior, Jan. 1, 1879, *Council Journals*, 1879, Appendix A. Laird had taken a census of Prince Albert and St. Laurent in December 1878, but the population fell short of the required number: see *Saskatchewan Herald*, Jan. 13 and March 10, 1879. Councillor Mathew Ryan had also suggested that the population requirement be reduced—from 1,000 to 500: Ryan to J. S. Dennis, private, Jan. 25, 1879, Interior file no. 16873.

liberalize their predecessor's measure, it was not until 1880 that districts having the necessary qualifications were found. Salisbury and Kimberley were established as electoral districts in the country bordering on Manitoba, and a third, Lorne, included the Prince Albert and St. Laurent settlements.[66] Before elections were held, however, the first two districts became part of the enlarged province of Manitoba. In March 1881, the election was held in Lorne, so that for the final Council session during Laird's term an elected member was present.

The restrictions on municipal and school district organization caused, perhaps, more discontent in the Territories than the lack of popular representation in the Council: the need for educational facilities and local public works touched the isolated frontier communities even more closely than control of a government located, for many, at a remote point and possessing but meagre legislative powers. "If Parliament," wrote the editor of the *Saskatchewan Herald* in exasperation, "will only take time to amend the North-West Territories Act so as to permit of the creation of municipalities and the organization of school districts on a more reasonable basis than can at present be done, we will try and bear patiently the wrangling about the N.P. and other nightmares."[67] Inability to establish tax supported schools, however, did not prevent the people from creating some educational facilities: in almost every settlement a school was established on a voluntary basis, and by the same type of co-operative effort a few essential local public works were provided.[68]

Though Laird was a conscientious administrator, he had but a slight interest in constitutional problems, and, unlike Morris, he made no effort to discuss broad issues of territorial policy with the federal government. Nor could leadership in this matter be expected from the Council, though Richardson in his capacity as legal adviser may have had some influence in the changes made in the North-West Territories Act in 1880. The only occasion during Laird's régime when the Council expressed itself on the powers of the territorial government was in 1881, after some technical difficulties had arisen in connection with the effect of the Act of 1880.[69] Its recommendation

66Proclamation of the Lieutenant-Governor, Nov. 13, 1880; see also Interior file no. 186 (N.W.T.), 1880, and no. 184 (N.W.T.), 1880, memorandum of J. S. Dennis, Oct. 1, 1880.

67*Saskatchewan Herald*, Jan. 26, 1880.

68See news from various points in the Territories carried in the *Saskatchewan Herald*.

69See *Council Journals*, 1881, pp. 26–7. It was on this account that Laird had not summoned the Council into session during 1880: see Laird to Minister of the Interior, Feb. 11, 1881, Interior file no. 186 (N.W.T.), 1880.

on this occasion was confined to a slight revision in the enumeration of legislative powers, the incorporation of companies being the only new power requested.[70]

When the Macdonald administration sponsored a consolidation of the North-West Territories Acts in 1880[71] there was some concession to North-West opinion: the sections of the Act of 1875 relating to municipal organization were dropped,[72] and a procedure was adopted for vesting the control of road allowances and old trails in the territorial government. But though the restriction on the Council's powers in the field of municipal legislation was removed, the drafters of the new Act failed, no doubt from carelessness rather than deliberate intent, to eliminate the related restriction on the organization of public schools; it was not until 1885[73] that this last vestige of the enforced and unnecessary relationship between electoral districts, municipalities, and school districts disappeared.

VI

The financial relationship of the Dominion and the Territories during Laird's term assumed a pattern which was to continue without major change until 1891. Since local sources of revenue were limited by constitutional restrictions and the reluctance of the Council to impose direct taxation, the expenses of government were met in large part by the annual parliamentary appropriation. This appropriation was not paid over as a grant to the territorial government, but was a fund administered by the Department of the Interior, with the Lieutenant-Governor acting as its agent. The management of the fund was designed to effect strict departmental control: instead of transferring the whole amount, the Governor made periodic requisitions which were provided by placing a sum to his credit in a Winnipeg

[70]See recommendation of the Council in June 1881, in Lieutenant-Governor's Orders, pp. 89–91. The Council asked for power to enact statute labour legislation, probably to remove any doubt that it already possessed this power.

[71]43 Vict., c. 25. There was no discussion of this act at any stage of its passage through Parliament. On the question of municipal law see J. S. Dennis to Macdonald, Dec. 23, 1879, Macdonald Papers, and Interior file no. 176 (N.W.T.), 1880, memorandum of Hugh Richardson, Jan. 8, 1880.

[72]This did not fully emancipate the Council, for doubts were later expressed concerning the power to authorize municipalities to levy taxes; during the session of 1884 D. L. Scott (the mayor of Regina) and N. F. Davin went to Ottawa and secured a declaratory amendment (s. 10 of 47 Vict., c. 23) which settled this matter: see Interior file no. 71293 and 73000; Regina Leader, May 1 and June 26, 1884.

[73]48–49 Vict., c. 51, s. 2. See memorial of the Executive Council of the North-West Territories, Aug. 2, 1884, Interior file no. 79134.

bank; against this account he could issue cheques, but he was required to transmit all his vouchers to the department for inspection and audit. Any unexpended balance at the end of the year reverted to the federal treasury. The Council had no control over this money; unofficially the Governor might ask for its recommendations, but this did not affect his responsibility to the department for all expenditures. Similarly, he, and not the Council, advised the department on the estimates upon which the annual appropriation was based, though in this case too there was nothing to prevent the Governor from eliciting the views of the Councillors for his own guidance. In the absence of records of executive proceedings it is not possible to discover whether Laird consulted the Council on these matters or not;[74] whatever his inclinations might have been, the difficulty and expense of securing the attendance of members at Council meetings undoubtedly prevented regular and consistent consultation.[75]

The financial resources of the territorial government during Laird's term, though larger than those of its predecessor at Winnipeg, were still small considering the vast area to be administered. Local revenues were confined to what could be collected from licences and fines for the infraction of territorial ordinances: during the four-year period 1877–81 these averaged about $233 per year.[76] Though the *Saskatchewan Herald* frequently complained of the inadequacy of federal assistance, it was Laird's caution rather than niggardliness at Ottawa which helped to keep expenditures low, and a sizable proportion of the appropriation remained unexpended at the end of every year. On the other hand it was during his term that Ottawa agreed to permit the use of federal funds for education and local public works. The first request for government aid for schools had come from the métis of St. Laurent in 1877;[77] they repeated it the following year,

[74]The original record of executive acts of the Territorial Government beginning in 1876 is contained in a series of volumes labelled Proclamations and Orders of the Lieutenant-Governor of the North-West Territories. Reports of a few decisions in which the Council participated are contained in these volumes, but in general no record of executive proceedings of the Council down to 1888 was kept: see Secretary to the Lieutenant-Governor to Sir Joseph Hickson, April 10, 1894, Attorney General's file G 809, A.S.

[75]For example, Breland's travelling expenses for attending one Council session in 1879 were $720: Interior file no. 210 (N.W.T.), 1880. In September 1878 Laird wrote to the Secretary of State: "A majority of the members of the North-West Council reside at places so remote from the seat of Government that it is scarcely possible to hold meetings more frequently than once a year": Attorney General's file no. G 691, A.S.

[76]See appendices to *Council Journals*, 1878, 1879, and 1881.

[77]See *Council Journals*, 1877, pp. 10, 24, and Interior file no. 13985.

supported this time by their fellows at St. Albert. This was an aspiration which aroused Laird's strongest sympathy, and he pressed the matter on Mills and later on Macdonald. The result was that in November 1880 the government authorized him to pay half of the teacher's salary in each school voluntarily organized by the settlers and having a minimum attendance of fifteen pupils.[78] During 1878–9 Laird spent some money on roads and bridges (ferries being provided by private enterprise); nothing was spent the following year, but during 1880–1 a number of bridges were constructed.[79] The reason for such a limited public works programme was probably the difficulty of appraising the needs of distant communities and of supervising the expenditure, for the only officials of the territorial government were the Governor and the Clerk of the Council.

As long as the Territories had no representation in Parliament (the *Saskatchewan Herald* began to advocate it in 1880), federal policies as they affected the West were a natural and entirely proper concern of the North-West Council, and the Council at Winnipeg had established a notable precedent in this respect. The sharp reduction in the number of memorials addressed to the government at Ottawa during Laird's régime as compared with the record of the earlier Council was the result of less vigorous leadership by the Governor and the predominance of federal officials among the membership; of the non-official element, Breland was an amiable nonentity, and Lawrence Clarke (the representative for Lorne) did not become a member until 1881. But the salutary effect of having even one elected member was evident in the session of that year, when Clarke ventilated some of the settlers' grievances pertaining to Dominion lands administration.[80]

The legislative record of Laird's Council is contained in three slight volumes of ordinances—1878, 1879, and 1881.[81] Though in bulk it is not an impressive achievement, it was sufficient for the relatively simple needs of the period and was favourably received. Since only one of the old Council's acts was in operation,[82] the new Council

[78]The negotiations leading to this decision are recorded in the following records: *Council Journals*, 1878, Appendix A; *ibid.*, 1879, Appendix A; Interior files nos. 184 (N.W.T.), 1880, and 85869.

[79]See the *Public Accounts* of the Dominion of Canada for the details of expenditure of the appropriation for the government of the North-West.

[80]See *Council Journals*, 1881, pp. 22 and 25–6. The representations of the Council on this occasion resulted in the opening of the Dominion Lands Office in Prince Albert: Interior file no. 36304(238).

[81]The form of numbering and enacting the ordinances was based on British Colonial Office regulations for colonies having nominated councils: Laird to Minister of the Interior, March 26, 1877, Interior file no. 74 (N.W.T.), 1877.

[82]The Minister of Justice's report on the legislation of the Council at Winnipeg is printed in *Council Journals*, 1877, pp. 8–9.

perforce dealt with such elementary and pressing frontier problems as infectious diseases, care of the insane, prairie and forest fires, marriage regulations, fences, stray animals, brands, registration of deeds, appointment of notaries, the administration of civil justice, prohibition of gambling, chattel mortgages, and sale of drugs. The legislation seems to have been carefully prepared, as indeed it should have been with three judges among the Councillors.

VII

Though the territorial government had undoubted shortcomings, the decision to locate the capital within the Territories proved to be a popular one, and in this respect Mackenzie's policy was vindicated. A demonstration of public feeling on this subject was occasioned by the proposal of the *Toronto Mail* (a leading government organ) late in 1879, that the system of government from Winnipeg be restored at the expiration of Laird's term.[83] The *Saskatchewan Herald* sprang to the attack in a long and vigorous editorial:

Our Lieutenant-Governor resides in the centre of the Territories, and has opportunities of consulting with people from all parts of the country. He is able to observe the working of the laws from day to day, and to hear suggestions as to amendments or to new legislation that may be required. Most of the members of his Council are called by their duties to visit different sections of the country; and are thus in a position to gain knowledge which non-residents could not readily obtain. . . .

The people of this country, the Mail may rest assured, will not be satisfied with a Lieutenant-Governor and Council residing and legislating outside their borders. They look for a greater, not a less direct influence on the management of their local affairs. The system of government which they possess is upon the whole adapted to a sparsely settled country, but instead of being abolished or handed over to Manitoba, it should be placed upon a more liberal basis.[84]

Proof that these views were shared by the people of the central Saskatchewan area was provided by the mass meetings which were held early in the new year at Prince Albert, Duck Lake, and St. Laurent for the purpose of approving petitions to the House of Commons opposing any legislation "which would have the effect of depriving the people of the North-West Territories of a resident local Government."[85] At the St. Laurent meeting Father André, the in-

---

[83]Macdonald intended to take this step at one time: see Macdonald to Dewdney, private, July 10, 1880, Dewdney Papers (Trail).

[84]*Saskatchewan Herald*, Feb. 23, 1880.

[85]The petition is printed in the *Saskatchewan Herald*, Feb. 23, 1880. See also *Journals of the House of Commons*, 1880, p. 231, and 1881, p. 67.

fluential parish priest, praised the territorial government and declared that "their acts so far had been marked by the greatest impartiality towards all, irrespective of religion or nationality."[86]

These expressions of opinion must have given satisfaction to Laird, for his position in many respects was not a happy one. To begin with there had been physical hardships—for example, his first winter in Battleford had been spent in a house without storm windows: "When the high winds and cold come together we are all nearly perished," he wrote Mackenzie.[87] Then there was the high cost of living, and the isolation, for both mail and telegraph service left much to be desired. His position as Indian Superintendent was a severe trial: economy in government administration, he discovered, could be carried too far— to keep his efficient assistant from quitting, he had to give him free board, and since there was no Indian office and store house, visiting Indians had to be entertained at the expense of his private larder. Up to this time he had received no remuneration as Indian Commissioner: "Continuing on in this self-denying sense is something that I do not think any person is called upon to offer for his country," he told Mackenzie.[88] Moreover there was enough work "to engage a man's undivided time" and "an amount of drudgery, too, above the office with its present staff which is incompatible with the position of Lieut. Governor." He submitted his resignation as Superintendent to the Mackenzie administration, but it was not accepted, and he continued to hold this office until early in 1879, when Macdonald acceded to his renewed application for release.[89] Added to all this was the absence of congenial relations with his successors in the Ministry of the Interior. Mills, he claimed, treated him "with scant consideration,"[90] and with the defeat of the Mackenzie government he had no friends at Ottawa. The new Minister of the Interior, Sir John A. Macdonald, regarded his appointment as a "useless expense,"[91] and consequently their correspondence was confined to a few formal communications on minor administrative matters.

In the history of the North-West Laird occupies an honourable if

[86]*Saskatchewan Herald*, April 12, 1880.
[87]Laird to Mackenzie, private, Jan. 24, 1878, Laird Papers, A.S.
[88]Laird to Mackenzie, private, April 20, 1878, *ibid.*
[89]His resignation took effect on March 31, 1879. For comments on his resignation see *Commons Debates*, 1879, p. 1687.
[90]Laird to Mackenzie, private, April 20, 1878, Laird Papers, A.S.; c.f. Order in Council, Oct. 31, 1881. Macdonald claimed that Mills "did all the business from here" (Ottawa): see Macdonald to Dewdney, confidential, Oct. 28, 1881, Dewdney Papers (Trail).
[91]*Ibid.*

not a distinguished position. The negotiation of Treaty No. 7 (with the Blackfeet), the promulgation of regulations for the election of Councillors, and the inauguration of grants in aid of education are the highlights of his administrative activity. His real contribution was in the realm of morale—in the influence which high character in public office can have on the life of a society, and particularly of a frontier society. It was an influence which the pioneers of the Territories valued and respected.

VIII

During the last year of Laird's term of office the federal government had made a change in the boundary of Manitoba which, as we have seen, had an important effect on the political development of the Territories by severing from it the area where the most populous settlements had appeared. This decision also had an important bearing on contemporary thinking regarding future provinces in the North-West.

Having satisfied the demand for provincehood in the largest settlement in the North-West in 1870, the federal government had been under no immediate pressure to formulate a policy for the establishment of additional provinces. There were two other considerations which promoted delay: it had been conceded in 1870 that the area of Manitoba might later be increased, and secondly, the dispute between the federal government and Ontario over the western boundary of that province made it impossible to determine the precise area of the Territories; pending decisions on one or both of these points it was impossible to formulate any plans for new provinces. The Macdonald administration had been considering an enlargement of Manitoba's boundaries as early as 1873, but it had been driven from office before any decision was made.[92] The Mackenzie administration was more concerned with effecting a settlement of the Ontario boundary than with satisfying Manitoba's aspirations for enlargement. Nevertheless a decision on that boundary was not made before the general election of 1878, and the victorious Macdonald administration was not disposed to make any concessions to the aggressive demands of the Liberal premier of Ontario, Oliver Mowat. It proved to be quite amenable, however, when Manitoba renewed its application in 1880.[93] Concurrent legislation extending Manitoba's

92See Morris Papers for 1873, and the Manitoba statute 37–38 Vict., c. 2.
93See Interior file no. 7349 and the *Statutes of Manitoba* for 1880, c. 1.

boundaries east, west, and north was passed by Parliament and the provincial legislature in 1881, and took effect on July 1 of that year.[94] The eastern extension was to be coterminous with the western boundary of Ontario whenever that was settled, and for the present was made to include all of that part of Keewatin adjacent to Ontario; on the other two sides the province was extended some one hundred miles west and one hundred and sixty miles north. It was a wise decision: Manitoba as it was originally established was certainly too small to support the apparatus and services of a provincial government, and its enlargement in 1881 was a logical move.[95] There is no doubt too that it was a boon to the settlers living just beyond the old northern and western boundaries, who were not in a position to derive much benefit from the governments of Keewatin and the North-West Territories as then constituted.[96]

This decision paved the way for a plan for the future subdivision into provinces of that portion of the Territories situated between Manitoba and British Columbia. In this there is an interesting parallel with early American territorial policy: the Ordinance of 1787 had provided for not less than three and not more than five states in the area between the Mississippi and Ohio rivers, and had indicated their approximate boundaries; in the case of the Louisiana Purchase and the Mexican cession, however, no such specifications seem to have been drawn up in advance. In Canada no statement of policy had been made in 1870, although Macdonald had remarked during the Manitoba bill debate that the North-West "should be divided into Provinces with as restricted a boundary as possible."[97] He was quite aware of the importance of the question, however: "Canada," he wrote on one occasion, "is the paramount power and has a distinct interest in the size, population and limits of every Province within her bounds."[98] A few months after the change in the Manitoba boundary, J. S. Dennis, Deputy Minister of the Interior, prepared "a scheme showing the proposed subdivision of the North-West Territories of Canada into Provinces," which formed the basis for the "Provisional Districts" created in the following year.

[94]The Dominion statute was 44 Vict., c. 14, brought into operation by proclamation; the concurrent Manitoba statute was 44 Vict., c. 1.

[95]The original area of Manitoba was 13,900 sq. miles; with the boundaries as given in 1881 it was over 123,000 sq. miles, later reduced by the settlement of the Ontario boundary to 73,732 sq. miles, at which size it remained until 1912.

[96]In the western settlements there was some opposition to inclusion in Manitoba chiefly because of the difference in the liquor laws of Manitoba and the Territories.

[97]See above, p. 43.

[98]Macdonald to Campbell, private, Jan. 14, 1882, Macdonald Papers.

The great objects to be aimed at [Dennis wrote] in devising the most expedient apportionment of the Territories, with a view to self-government in the future, are:

1. Reasonable areas for the different Provinces.
2. The equalization of such areas as far as possible.
3. Securing to each Province as nearly as possible an equal share of the great natural resources of the Territories.[99]

Dennis outlined the boundaries of four provinces—three in the area below the 55th parallel between Manitoba and British Columbia, and one, traversed by the Peace River, extending from the 55th to the 60th parallels. Their areas varied from 95,000 to 122,000 square miles —not out of proportion to the government's current estimate of the areas of Manitoba (150,000 sq. mi.), Ontario (109,480 sq. mi.), and Quebec (193,355 sq. mi.). Though Dennis did not make the comparison, the size of the proposed provinces was also similar to that of the neighbouring American territories—Dakota (147,712 sq. mi.), Montana (147,138 sq. mi.), and Wyoming (97,914 sq. mi.).

On the basis of Dennis's scheme of division the government issued an Order in Council on May 8, 1882, stating that "for the convenience of settlers and for postal purposes, a portion of the North-West Territories should be divided into provisional Districts." The names given to the Districts were Assiniboia, Saskatchewan, Alberta, and Athabasca. The Order in Council was submitted to Parliament for its approval, on the ground that the step which had been taken "might result in those divisions becoming hereafter Provinces,"[100] although the Prime Minister stressed that Parliament was not thereby bound in any way and could, as he put it, subsequently "subdivide them into Provinces or do as they please." The measure was approved after the briefest discussion; Blake, speaking for the opposition, merely remarked that the arrangement should be flexible, since it was very difficult to say where the future centres of population would be.[101]

Unlike Keewatin, which had its own "government" in the person of the Lieutenant-Governor of Manitoba, these four Provisional Districts were not, and never became, independent jurisdictions during

99Interior file no. 37906, memorandum of Oct. 15, 1881. Dennis stated that he had submitted a scheme in 1876 at the request of the Minister, based on the original Pacific railway route; now that the route was changed a different subdivision was required.

100*Commons Debates*, 1882, p. 1567.

101*Ibid.*, pp. 10 and 1567. The Liberal organ, the *Globe*, had in 1881 suggested a provisional outlining of boundaries of future provinces: see editorial reprinted in *Saskatchewan Herald*, Nov. 26, 1881. The government had also received suggestions on the subject in 1880 from Marcus Smith, a surveyor for the Pacific railway: Smith to Macdonald, March 18, 1880, Macdonald Papers.

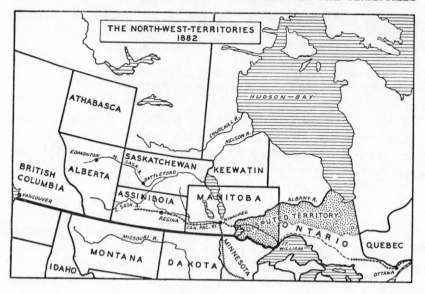

the territorial period; nor did they, in the end, become provinces. Nevertheless they played an important role in later Territorial politics, since they became centres of sectional feeling or what may be termed "district consciousness." This development was due in part to the fact that in terms of resources, communications, and historical development the Districts represented natural divisions of the North-West. Defining and naming these divisions no doubt increased the sense of identity, to which their use for purposes of representation in the House of Commons also contributed.

With respect to the territorial government itself, Macdonald maintained his customary attitude of cautious conservatism. The enlargement of Manitoba, he contended, had so reduced the responsibilities of the territorial government that "the chief duties of the Lieutenant-Governor will be the protection and advancement of the Indians, and the keeping of the peace between them and the whites who are scattered over the country."[102] This ignored the remaining settlements, and was as well in curious contrast to the administration's current policy of promoting the immediate construction of the Pacific railway across the prairies and of encouraging immigration. Nevertheless it was the dominant consideration in the selection of Laird's successor, Edgar Dewdney. Dewdney had been appointed Indian Commissioner

[102]Order in Council, Oct. 31, 1881.

following Laird's resignation in 1879, and it was Macdonald's belief that the previous policy of uniting the two offices in one person should be reinstituted "at all events for the present."[103] Actually this arrangement was continued throughout Dewdney's term of office (1881–8).

The new Governor was an English civil engineer, who during his early twenties had migrated to British Columbia. In three successive general elections he had won the Yale seat in the House of Commons for the Conservative party; his record in the House did not exhibit much interest in public affairs beyond minor matters of local concern, though his surveying experience enabled him to make some contribution to the discussions of the Pacific railway route through the Rockies. However, he became a close friend of Macdonald, and the latter developed a high opinion of his capacities as an administrator. From this point of view his selection as the head of the territorial government was appropriate, since his term of office coincided with the period of greatest executive power and responsibility enjoyed by the Governors of the North-West.

103*Ibid.* Dewdney's formal appointment dated from an Order in Council of Dec. 3, 1881. He was allowed an extra $2,000 in addition to his salary as Indian Commissioner; beginning in 1883 this was increased to $4,000 or a total from both sources of $7,200.

PART 2

The Movement for Territorial Autonomy

CHAPTER FIVE

The Ascendency of the Lieutenant-Governor

1883-88

THE EARLY YEARS of Dewdney's term coincided with important changes in the social and economic conditions of the plains region of the North-West. One of these was the painful revolution in the life of the Indians which had been foreshadowed in the terms of the treaties, whereby the freedom of the plains was exchanged for the restraints of the reserve. As long as buffalo could be obtained there had been little inclination to settle on reserves, but by 1881 the great herds had disappeared. Dewdney's first work as Indian Commissioner was to induce the reluctant bands to move away from the American border, where many of them had lived and hunted for years and where the last of the buffalo had been seen, to reserves north of the Canadian Pacific Railway, where they would be in an area under the firm grip of government authority.[1] By 1883 the dismal business was completed, and the Indians were confronted with the new way of life which the white man had imposed.

Meanwhile a profound change was taking place in the pattern of white settlement as a result of the construction of the railway. The route as originally surveyed had, after crossing the Red River near Lake Winnipeg, proceeded in a north-westerly direction, crossing the South Saskatchewan a few miles upstream from the métis settlements and continuing through Battleford, paralleling the North Saskatchewan to Edmonton, and thence headed for the Yellowhead Pass through the Rockies. It was in this region that the bulk of the non-Indian population lived in 1881. By changing the route to run due west from Manitoba, the flow of immigration was suddenly and dramatically

[1]See G. F. G. Stanley, *The Birth of Western Canada: A History of the Riel Rebellions* (London, 1936), chap. XI.

shifted in favour of the District of Assiniboia and the southern part of the District of Alberta. The District of Saskatchewan, with its large métis population and the aspiring settlements at Battleford and Prince Albert, along with the Edmonton area of northern Alberta, were cut off from the main stream of development which followed the building of the railway. The resulting stagnation and sense of frustration were important influences in the political and economic affairs of this part of the North-West for many years to come.

The influence of the C.P.R. can be traced by comparing the census figures for 1881 and 1885. In the former year the non-Indian population of Assiniboia, Saskatchewan, and Alberta numbered 5,400; in the latter year 28,192. Assiniboia naturally exhibited the greatest increase, and also became the most populous of the districts, growing from 1,057 in 1881 to 17,591 in 1885, exclusive of Indians. In the same period Alberta increased from 1,200 to 6,115, while in Saskatchewan the figures were 3,143 and 4,486 respectively.[2] Immigration did not continue at the same rate for the rest of Dewdney's term, but despite rebellion, drought, and frost, people continued to come, and by 1891 the population of the three districts had risen to 66,799, including some 15,000 Indians.

The political significance of this increase in population was heightened by the fact that most of the new settlers were British subjects (see Table A). Unlike the European immigrants (who made their first appearance during this period), they did not have to acquire citizenship and familiarity with the language and constitution before participating in public life. There were well-educated and well-to-do men among them, and all of them had a lively interest in politics. There was an element of truth in Nicholas Flood Davin's oratorical flourish—"Were they—*an immigration d'élite*—a select immigration —the flower of the old pioneers of Canada—to remain 'disestablished and disendowed' and outside the pall of the Constitution?"[3] There was independence and intellectual vigour aplenty among the Ontario and British immigrants, sufficient to challenge traditional political loyalties and create a lively public opinion. This latter was stimulated by further additions to the ranks of North-West journalism—the *Regina Leader* (1883), the *Calgary Herald* (1883), the *Moose Jaw News* (1883), the (Fort) *Qu'Appelle Vidette* (1884), the *Moosomin Courier* (1884), the *Lethbridge News* (1885), the *Qu'Appelle*

---

[2]These comparisons are secured by correlating the census districts named in the Census of 1881 with the areas of the Provisional Districts.
[3]Speech before the Old Guard Club, Ottawa, *Regina Leader*, Jan. 20, 1885.

TABLE A

Birthplace of the North-West Population Other Than Native Born, 1885 and 1891

	British Isles		Ontario		Quebec		Maritimes		Manitoba		U.S.A.		Europe	
	1885	1891	1885	1891	1885	1891	1885	1891	1885	1891	1885	1891	1885	1891
Assiniboia	5,635	7,714	6,967	8,209	717	725	615	554	1,013	1,201	481	110	365	2,970
Saskatchewan	359	593	722	902	147	184	47	98	1,624	1,517	106	600	27	65
Alberta	1,164	4,041	1,134	4,473	476	906	233	858	507	842	420	1,215	170	785
Total	7,158	12,348	8,823	13,584	1,340	1,815	895	1,510	3,144	3,560	1,007	1,961	562	3,820

SOURCES: *Census of the Three Provisional Districts of the North-West Territories, 1884-85; Census of Canada, 1891.*

Progress (1885), the *Calgary Tribune* (1885), the *Medicine Hat Times* (1885), and the *Regina Journal* (1886). Among editors of the period Davin of the *Regina Leader* was unique.[4] This talented Irishman with his enthusiasm, oratorical power, and political connections at Ottawa, soon attained a pre-eminent position, moving easily from the editor's chair to a seat in the House of Commons as one of the North-West's first representatives. Smaller in literary stature than Davin but his peer in political influence was Frank Oliver, the doctrinaire and vituperative editor of the *Edmonton Bulletin*.[5] An uncompromising reformer of the George Brown school, and thus a sworn foe of Conservatism, he too made journalism the foundation of a political career, but at first in the less exalted sphere of the North-West Council and Assembly, where he made a significant contribution to the legislation and debates of the period.

The rise of partyism was a notable feature of this period of North-West politics, and it had an important influence on the movement for increased territorial autonomy. Among the circumstances which stimulated the spirit of partisanship was the fact that the policies of the federal government had such a pervasive influence on so many aspects of everyday life that differences of opinion inevitably developed either hostile or friendly to the government at Ottawa. Though there were a few even at this early date who dreamed of a party devoted to North-West or farmers' interests, traditional loyalties predominated. Government patronage was also important in this connection. There were numerous appointments to be made, embracing not only the ordinary federal civil service, but also such local officers as sheriffs, clerks of court, land titles office and jail employees, and the clerks and other officials of the territorial government. For some years there was a strong tendency to appoint easterners who had some claim on the party in power at Ottawa, but this was most unpopular in the West, and increasing consideration was given to residents. In the latter case the Macdonald administration was not disposed to ignore claims of party allegiance.[6] The ground was therefore well prepared for a contest along traditional party lines when the first election of members for the House of Commons took place in 1887.

---

[4]See Norman Ward, "Davin and the Founding of the *Leader*," *Saskatchewan History*, vol. VI, pp. 13–16.

[5]See William S. Waddell, "The Honourable Frank Oliver," M.A. thesis, University of Alberta, 1950, pp. v, 356. While still a boy Oliver was employed in the *Globe* office in Toronto; in 1873, at the age of twenty, he migrated to Manitoba and for three years worked for the *Free Press*. He moved to Edmonton in 1876 and established the *Bulletin* there in 1880.

[6]See Thos. White to Macdonald, private, Nov. 9, 1885, Macdonald Papers.

II

Amid the stirring events of the 1880's in the North-West, the Lieutenant-Governor occupied a central position: in administration, in legislation, and in politics he was the most influential figure. Under these circumstances some criticisms of the Governor's policies and actions were bound to be made, but Dewdney was a figure of more than ordinary controversy in an era noted for the virulence of political animosities. Most of the attacks on him were inspired by the first major decision of his career as Governor—the selection of Regina as the Territorial capital, made in 1882 and formally confirmed in 1883.[7] The abandonment of Battleford was made necessary by the change in the route of the railway, and Dewdney was asked to select a new site for the capital in consultation with W. C. Van Horne, the general manager of the C.P.R. As soon as the choice was known, it was vigorously attacked by newspapers in Winnipeg, and the cry was taken up by the Liberal press and politicians in Eastern Canada. It was alleged that Dewdney had been influenced by his investments in lands along the railway (purchased from the Hudson's Bay Company), and not by the merits of the site in question.[8] Although there is no evidence that Dewdney was swayed by personal considerations, he should not have participated in the decision without previously divesting himself of his real estate holdings; as it was, he left himself vulnerable to periodic attacks throughout the rest of his career as Governor. Liberal criticisms were doubtless also stimulated by Dewdney's half-concealed political proclivities; the Governor's highest loyalty was to "Sir John" and the Conservative party, which not only coloured his attitude to territorial government affairs but also resulted in his active participation in dispensing federal patronage,[9] as well as important behind-the-scenes efforts in connection with the first election of members of Parliament from the Territories.[10]

The conditions which during Laird's régime had prevented the Council from assuming an active role in administration continued to operate during Dewdney's term. With the Council steadily increasing in size (twenty members exclusive of the Governor by 1887), the difficulty and expense of securing attendance meant that execu-

[7]The selection was made in June 1882 and became effective by Order in Council of March 27, 1883. Dewdney discussed the matter in several private letters to Macdonald; see Macdonald Papers, vol. 211.

[8]See *Commons Debates*, 1883, pp. 273 ff.

[9]See for example Dewdney to Macdonald, Sept. 8, 1885, Macdonald Papers, and Attorney General's file no. G 363, A.S.

[10]See his letters to Macdonald during the fall of 1886, Macdonald Papers, vol. 213.

tive business was transacted only during or after the annual legislative sessions. In 1885 Dewdney referred to the need for some system whereby advice could be secured between sessions, and suggested the formation of a committee consisting of members living within easy reach of Regina.[11] It is not surprising that this proposal, which would hardly appeal to the remoter districts, was rejected, and the Council endorsed the existing system of having each member assist "with any particular advice required as to purely local matters concerning his District, either personally or by letter."[12]

The circumstances just described meant that the Council was under the necessity of conferring extensive executive duties on the Governor if the objects sought in much of its legislation were to be achieved. This process had begun during Laird's term and was perforce greatly extended after 1881. The list of powers delegated to the Governor as they appear in the various ordinances is a long one, and a few examples must suffice to indicate the variety of activities. They included the appointment of a Queen's Printer, notaries public, game guardians, fire guardians, licence issuers, poundkeepers, and health officers; the establishment of health districts, statute labour districts, stock districts, and pound districts; the licensing of druggists, ferry operators, and auctioneers; the establishment of school districts; the empowering of school trustees to borrow money, and the registration of advocates and physicians. Under the terms of the School Ordinance the Governor was also chairman of the Board of Education, which was the equivalent of a department of education. While theoretically responsible to the Council for the exercise of all these powers, and while his decisions were hedged in by the terms of the law, the Governor could exercise his own judgment in many instances. No doubt some consultation with Councillors either individually or as a body took place from time to time, but there is no evidence that his decisions were ever questioned.

When to these powers are added those which the Governor possessed under the terms of federal legislation, the real measure of his supremacy becomes apparent.[13] He controlled the expenditure of a large part of the parliamentary appropriation for the expenses of government; he decided when and where electoral districts should be established, and appointed the returning officers; he controlled the use of intoxicating liquor; he appointed justices of the peace and coroners; he had a large measure of responsibility in connection with

[11]*Council Journals*, 1885, pp. 8, 51.
[12]*Ibid.*, p. 46.
[13]See above, p. 75, n. 13.

the administration of justice;[14] and he could, within limits, direct the disposition of the North-West Mounted Police.[15] The significance of all these powers was heightened during Dewdney's term by the growth of population. Laird's opportunities for executive action were limited by the small and scattered population, and he issued some fifty orders and proclamations from 1876 to 1881; during the next five years Dewdney issued over 570.[16]

This increase in administrative activity necessitated a gradual growth of the territorial civil service, which was also controlled by the Governor. The lone clerk and the part-time legal adviser of Laird's period were now joined by others whom Dewdney was able to select at will by virtue of his access to federal funds. During the last year of his governorship (1887–8) there were, in addition to the Clerk of the Council, eleven full-time employees in the offices in Regina, as well as a number of persons who provided part-time services, such as the auditor and the legal adviser. The Board of Education, which appointed its own officers, had by this time a permanent secretary and two full-time and a number of part-time inspectors of schools.[17]

The practice of requiring the submission of an official annual report provides a means of scrutinizing and controlling the actions of an executive agency, but the North-West Council was handicapped in this respect because the Governor derived so much of his authority from the federal government. The only report which the Council received apart from the local financial accounts was the one submitted by the Board of Education. Dewdney's speeches at the opening of Council sessions[18] contained information on a variety of subjects, but there was no uniformity of content from year to year, and not infrequently they were more concerned with emphasizing the beneficent effects of federal policies than conveying information on local administration.[19] During the session of 1885, as we shall see,[20] this not too

[14]See Attorney General's files, G series, A.S.

[15]Attorney General's files, nos. G 270, G 347, and G 369, A.S., are among those which indicate the nature of this responsibility.

[16]See Lieutenant-Governor's Orders, A.S.

[17]Public works services were secured by contracts for specific projects.

[18]Laird delivered a speech at the opening of the first session in 1877, but did not do so for the other sessions during his term.

[19]The speech of 1883 lauded the decision to establish the capital at Regina; the 1884 speech decried "exaggerated reports of Indian difficulties" and claimed that the administration of Indian affairs was in a satisfactory state (nine months before the Rebellion); the 1885 speech claimed that those who participated in the Rebellion had no grievances, and lauded "the patient and statesman-like manner in which the Minister of the Interior has inquired into the wants of the settlers"; the 1886 speech, reported Macdonald's *first* visit to the North-West "for whose advancement he has devoted so much of his life."

[20]See below, p. 133.

subtle political propaganda recoiled on Dewdney, and the Council, in framing its address in reply, became involved in a long and acrimonious argument over a number of grievances against the federal government which were current at that time.

It is true that in 1883 the practice was inaugurated of having the Governor submit an annual report which was published as part of the report of the Department of the Interior. Its purpose, however, was not quite ingenuous, as Macdonald made clear to Dewdney: "I think also that as you govern 'a Crown Colony' it would be well to introduce the practice of having a well considered short report from you as Lt. Governor of the progress of the Territory under your sway. This will give you an opportunity of answering indirectly any attacks made on your management."[21] No doubt this was to be prepared in the same spirit as the Indian Commissioner's report, which, Macdonald suggested, should be "full and favorable" and should indicate a "prospect of diminishing expenditures."[22]

Though the Governor overshadowed the Council in the matter of administrative activity, the latter did not completely relinquish its executive powers to him. By the terms of its ordinance establishing the General Revenue Fund it retained control over the collection and disbursement of revenue from local sources, and it also reserved the right to appoint the members of the Board of Education and approve its regulations.[23] Beyond this it could not go to any significant extent without hampering public business by delaying decisions until meetings of the full Council could be held.[24] In the matter of disbursing the moneys in the General Revenue Fund, the Council in 1884 adopted an expedient which though unorthodox continued as a distinctive feature of territorial public life until 1896.[25] Equal sums were appropriated annually for each electoral district, and the expenditure was controlled by the local member subject to a few simple regulations. Most of the money was spent on roads and bridges and grants to agricultural societies, and occasionally for fireguards, dams, and public wells. The members secured suggestions for projects from their con-

[21]Macdonald to Dewdney, private, Sept. 17, 1883, Macdonald Papers.
[22]Ibid.
[23]Changes in the constitution and powers of this body and its Roman Catholic and Protestant sections were made almost every year by amendments to the School Ordinance, and the powers over educational administration reserved for the Lieutenant-Governor in Council varied during the period.
[24]The Municipal Ordinance provided that municipalities might be proclaimed either by the Lieutenant-Governor or the Lieutenant-Governor in Council, but in practice the proclamations were issued by the Governor alone.
[25]Council Journals, 1884, p. 66.

stituents and, insofar as they were able, checked on the performance of the work. In the absence of a regular public works staff the system had much to commend it, for the centres of settlement were scattered over such an immense area that centralized administration from Regina was difficult. However, the honesty and impartiality of the members was the chief factor in the success of the system. There were two obvious defects: the principle of equal appropriations did not take into account differences in need; and before 1888 there were many needy settlements which were outside of electoral districts. However, the hardship arising from these circumstances was mitigated by projects undertaken by the Governor and paid for out of federal funds.

III

Before considering the autonomy movement during Dewdney's régime, some attention must be given to the composition of the Council during this period. The "official" members (the three judges and those who were specially appointed) reached the maximum number of six in 1883. Stipendiary Magistrate Ryan, who had been a prominent Liberal before his appointment, was dismissed in 1881, and in 1883 Charles B. Rouleau, a Quebec lawyer and former District Magistrate in Ottawa, became the third judge and ex-officio member.[26] In 1882 Lt. Col. A. G. Irvine, who had succeeded Macleod as Commissioner of the Mounted Police, was appointed to the Council along with Hayter Reed, an Indian agent at Battleford who became Assistant Indian Commissioner at Regina.[27] Irvine, and probably Reed also, was appointed on Dewdney's recommendation.[28] In 1886 the office of Stipendiary Magistrate was abolished when Parliament effected a general reorganization of the administration of justice in the Territories,[29] but despite vigorous protests from Liberal members

[26]The number of stipendiary magistrates was increased to four by an amendment to the North-West Territories Act in 1885 (48–49 Vict., c. 51, s. 4) in order to meet demands originating in Alberta. Despite protests from the Liberals, the government intended to increase the maximum number of appointed members to seven to permit the new judge to sit in the Council, but in the end it neglected to make the change, so that Stipendiary Magistrate Travis (appointed July 30, 1885) did not become a member. See *Commons Debates*, 1885, pp. 2926 ff. and Interior file no. 92182.

[27]Order in Council, April 8, 1882.

[28]Dewdney to Macdonald, Jan. 26, 1882, Interior file no. 66292.

[29]49 Vict., c. 25. This Act created the Supreme Court of the North-West Territories with original and appellate jurisdiction, consisting of five judges. The Act came into force on Feb. 18, 1887, and the first judges were Richardson, MacLeod, Rouleau, E. L. Wetmore, and T. H. McGuire.

the judges of the new Supreme Court were made eligible for membership in the Council. When it was pointed out that this was a characteristic of the most primitive form of colonial government when judges and bishops were members of the Council, the Minister of Justice, Hon. John Thompson, agreed that this was so, and claimed that it was appropriate to the existing condition of the Territories; even the inclusion of bishops, he said, would be "no great calamity."[30] The result was that Richardson, Macleod, and Rouleau, who were members of the new court, were appointed for the last (1887) session of the Council.[31]

There was no unanimity of opinion in the Territories concerning the presence of ex-officio and appointed members in the Council. The more radical spirits, whose spokesmen were Councillors Frank Oliver of Edmonton and J. H. Ross of Moose Jaw, were openly critical of the "official element" on principle.[32] The Prince Albert Times, before it became a supporter of the status quo, spoke of "that wretched farce the North-West Council whose pitiful powers are controlled by Government officials."[33] Though some other sections of the press echoed this sentiment from time to time, no real movement developed to oust this element in the Council. Criticism was naturally more widespread before 1884, when the elected members were still in a minority.[34] Richardson was, throughout the period, the most influential member, since he not only drafted much of the legislation but also participated actively in the debates. Rouleau and Macleod were heard from frequently, and in addition were regarded to some extent as representing the interests of the Battleford and Macleod districts. "Irvine," Dewdney reported to Macdonald in 1884, "is worse than nobody for he can't understand what is going on and half the time does not know which way to vote."[35] Three years later he declared that Breland and Irvine "are of very little use to the Council and reside out of the Territories."[36] For Breland, membership in the Council had become

30Commons Debates, 1886, p. 1463. Thompson also argued that they were simply keeping things as they were until the Legislative Assembly was created.

31Order in Council, Sept. 17, 1887. See also Dewdney to Macdonald, Sept. 11, 1887, Macdonald Papers.

32See Council Journals, 1884, p. 61.

33Editorial of May 23, 1884.

34In 1883 there were six elected members, balanced by five appointed members and the Governor. In 1884 there were eight elected members and six appointed members.

35Dewdney to Macdonald, private, Aug. 5, 1884, Macdonald Papers; see also letter of Sept. 27, 1883, ibid.

36Dewdney to Macdonald, April 7, 1887, ibid.

little more than a pension, and the initiative in bringing half-breed grievances to the attention of the federal government came not from him but from the three elected members—Oliver, Macdowall (Lorne), and Jackson (Qu'Appelle)—who had important métis settlements in their constituencies.[37] It is little wonder, therefore, that Riel during the earlier phase of his agitation suggested that he be appointed in Breland's stead as one means of satisfying his people.[38]

Though scepticism concerning the value of the North-West Council became vocal at times, there was a general desire to be represented in that body. Settlers in at least seven areas are known to have presented petitions to Dewdney on this subject, and at Battleford and Moose Jaw the petitioners compiled a census for his guidance. As will be seen from Table B, only eleven districts, returning a total of fourteen members, had been established by the end of Dewdney's term. Since there were probably between 18,000 and 19,000 adults,[39] exclusive of aliens and Indians, in Assiniboia, Saskatchewan, and Alberta as early as 1885, the principle of one representative per thousand was not operating with any degree of precision. Not only were there discrepancies in the population of the districts, but there was a considerable number of people not included in any district. Complaints regarding this situation began to appear in the press as early as 1883. From some unrepresented areas like Battleford came suggestions that the population requirement be reduced to some figure below a thousand,[40] but neither this change nor the alternative of increasing the maximum area of the districts was extensively advocated. Dewdney suggested to the government that both the area and population requirements be increased: his proposal involved dividing the Territories into 21 districts, each to be given a member when its population reached 5,000.[41] Though ostensibly designed to give complete representation, its main result would have been to slow up the growth of the elected section of the Council, which indeed was part of his intention. Fortunately for the political progress of the North-West, Mac-

[37]See Dewdney to Macdonald, private, July 22, 1884, *ibid.*
[38]See Dewdney to Macdonald, private, Sept. 19, 1884, *ibid.*
[39]This calculation is based on the proportion of adults to children in the Moose Jaw district as given in the census of 1885.
[40]See *Saskatchewan Herald*, June 24, 1883; editorial in *Macleod Gazette* reprinted in the *Qu'Appelle Vidette*, Nov. 6, 1884; also Oliver-Ross motion, *Council Journals*, 1884, pp. 60–1.
[41]Dewdney to Macdonald, private, Dec. 13, 1883, Macdonald Papers. In 1884 Dewdney proposed that the population requirement be increased to 2,000 adults— see annotated copy of memorial of Executive Council of Aug. 2, 1884, in Macdonald Papers, vol. 113.

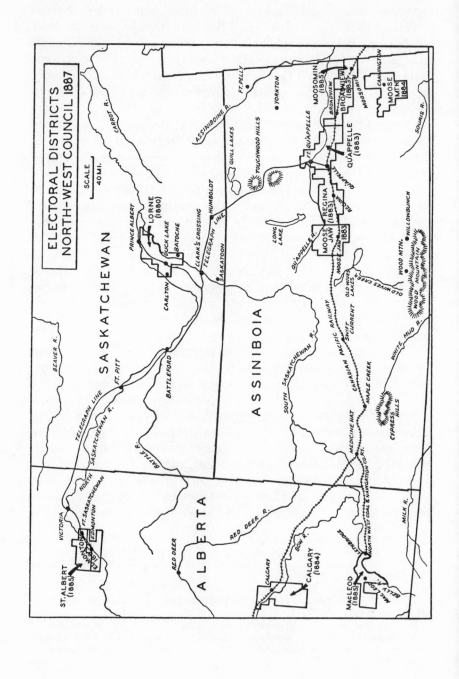

ELECTORAL DISTRICTS
NORTH-WEST COUNCIL 1887

SCALE
40 MI.

TABLE B

NORTH-WEST COUNCIL ELECTIONS

Electoral district	Date of creation[1]	Dates of elections
Lorne	Nov. 13, 1880	March 23, 1881; June 5, 1883; Sept. 15, 1885
Edmonton	Jan. 22, 1883	March 29, 1883; Sept. 15, 1885
Broadview	June 2, 1883	Aug. 13, 1883; Sept. 15, 1885
Qu'Appelle (2 members in 1885)	June 2, 1883	Aug. 13, 1883; Sept. 15, 1885; Oct. 14, 1886;[2] May 24, 1887[2]
Regina (2 members in 1885)	June 2, 1883	Aug. 13, 1883; Sept. 15, 1885
Moose Jaw	July 14, 1883	Aug. 13, 1883; Sept. 15, 1885
Calgary (2 members in 1886)	May 29, 1884	June 28, 1884; July 14, 1886
Moose Mountain	May 29, 1884	June 28, 1884; July 8, 1886
Macleod	April 30, 1885	Sept. 15, 1885; Sept. 5, 1887[2]
St. Albert[3]	Aug. 4, 1885	Sept. 15, 1885
Moosomin[4]	Aug. 7, 1885	Sept. 18, 1885

[1]Date of Lieutenant-Governor's proclamation.
[2]By-elections.
[3]Established by dividing the electoral district of Edmonton.
[4]Established by dividing the electoral district of Broadview.

kenzie's population-area ratio was not replaced by this more restrictive one.

Dewdney's policy was one of cautious concession to popular demands. In 1883 he established five electoral districts (see Table B) and he invariably investigated all representations which were made to him; yet he did not go out of his way to increase the number of representatives, except perhaps in the case of the division of the Edmonton district in 1885 (after the Rebellion), which enabled the métis to elect a representative and may have contributed to the defeat of "the fire brand," Frank Oliver.[42] The case of Lorne, which was apparently entitled to a second member by virtue of having the requisite 2,000 population, reveals a neglected opportunity to give representation to the métis of St. Laurent before the troubles of 1885.[43] After the Rebellion was over, Dewdney reported that he saw "no object to be gained by doing it, the French part being almost abandoned."[44]

The question of representation was first aired in the Council by Frank Oliver and J. H. Ross in 1884. Their motion asserted that "changes should be made in the method of qualifying districts for the election of members . . . so that important localities, such as Medicine Hat, Fort Macleod and Battleford, should not be debarred from securing representation on the North-West Council, while full representation should be given other localities in accordance with the spirit and intent of the North-West Territories Act."[45] Though this motion was not passed, the Council endorsed the principle of more adequate representation in its 1884 memorial to the federal government, and to that end recommended a census of the Territories and a change in the law to permit a general redistribution.[46] One factor

42See report of the Lieutenant-Governor in *Annual Report of the Department of the Interior*, 1885, and editorial in the *Prince Albert Times*, May 27, 1887. The term "fire brand" was Dewdney's—see private letters to Macdonald, Sept. 27, 1883, and July 22, 1884, Macdonald Papers.

43That Dewdney realized there was an opportunity here is revealed in his private letter to Macdonald, March 23, 1885, Macdonald Papers; cf. *Saskatchewan Herald*, March 20, 1885, report from Duck Lake. He may, however, have been waiting for power to subdivide the district: see private letter to Macdonald, May 3, 1884, Macdonald Papers.

44Dewdney to Macdonald, private, Aug. 7, 1885, *ibid*.

45*Council Journals*, 1884, p. 61. The motion also contained several controversial proposals and criticized the Macdonald administration, see below, p. 124.

46Memorial of the Executive Council, Aug. 2, 1884, Interior file no. 79134. The territorial census which was taken in 1885 must have been of little value in establishing new electoral districts since it did not give the population by townships. See *Census of the Three Provisional Districts of the North-West Territories, 1884-5* (Ottawa, 1886).

which hampered the growth of the representative element was that the Governor had no power to divide or rearrange the boundaries of existing electoral districts and the Council also complained about this defect in the law.[47]

All this discussion was not without effect, for in the following year Dewdney established three new districts and made Qu'Appelle and Regina into two-member districts. Moreover, the government proposed, among other changes in the North-West Territories Act, in 1885, that the Lieutenant-Governor be empowered to subdivide a district where the adult population had reached the 2,000 mark. Under pressure from Blake and Mills, the amendment was widened to permit the Lieutenant-Governor in Council to rearrange district boundaries, provided the existing ratio of area to population was maintained.[48] Mills tried to increase the maximum area to 2,000 square miles, but the government refused to accept the proposal.[49]

During the 1885 session, without Frank Oliver to prod it into action, the Council did not exercise its new power of redistribution.[50] The following year redistribution was again considered, but by this time, as we shall see,[51] it became involved with the more important issue of establishing a Legislative Assembly.

IV

The question of representative in the North-West Council was a phase of the broader movement whose object was to secure an increased measure of autonomy for the Territories. The main issues of this movement were not long in emerging—in fact they were all placed on record during the first session of Dewdney's term. In 1883 when the Council first met under Dewdney's presidency, seven years had elapsed since a voice had been raised in the territorial capital in support of the right of self-government for the North-West. The conditions under which these aspirations were now expressed differed from the days of Alexander Morris—there was no sympathetic Governor to add his voice to those of the local members, and federal party

---

[47]Memorial of the Executive Council of the North-West Territories, Aug. 2, 1884, Interior file no. 79134; see also annotated copy enclosed in Dewdney to Secretary of State, Aug. 11, 1884, Macdonald Papers.
[48]48–49 Vict., c. 51, s. 3; *Commons Debates*, 1885, pp. 2964–5.
[49]*Ibid.*, p. 2967.
[50]Oliver had introduced a bill in 1884 to effect a redistribution, but the committee to which it was referred declared it to be *ultra vires*, as indeed it was. Oliver was defeated in the election of 1885.
[51]See below, pp. 138–9.

politics had become a factor in the situation. Consequently there were cross currents within the Council which affected the form and nature of the agitation. Most of the members had identified themselves as either Liberals or Conservatives, and since the Conservatives were greatly in the majority there was a tendency to prevent any representations on North-West matters from being couched in language which would give aid and comfort to the Liberal party. On the other hand many of the Conservative members were, within the limitations of party allegiance, genuinely concerned about territorial rights and grievances, with the result that the years from 1883 to 1887 saw the development of a vigorous movement for increased autonomy, both in the Council and throughout the country.

Dewdney had quietly done his best to see that "suitable" men were elected to the Council in 1883. His candidate in Qu'Appelle was defeated,[52] but on the whole he was pleased with the result, and he wrote to Macdonald, "I think with the exception of Oliver who is a Grit from Edmonton they are all pretty good men."[53] "Ross is in for Moose Jaw," he reported; "he is I believe of a Grit family, but is sent here to support me." In the end his fond hopes for the Moose Jaw member were not realized, for Ross allied himself with Oliver. But the Governor's manœuvres were not confined to the elections. Macdonald had sent him "hints" on how he should "manage" the official members, and he promised "to let the appointed members understand the position I consider that they should occupy."[54] But though Dewdney was an adept political manipulator of the Macdonald school and never lost an opportunity to advance the cause of Conservatism, he did not try to bludgeon the Councillors into line. The latter moreover were not sycophants, and had a genuine desire to serve their constituents, as their 1883 memorial to the federal government fully demonstrates.

The initiative in preparing this memorial came from T. W. Jackson of Qu'Appelle and D. H. Macdowall of Lorne, both friends of the Macdonald administration. Since these two led the moderate Conservative element in opposition to Oliver during the following session,

[52]Dewdney favoured Major Bell as against T. W. Jackson, and had attempted to secure the métis vote for him by soliciting Archbishop Taché's intervention; apparently this was not secured, as Dewdney later reported to Macdonald that Jackson had received the support of the métis through the influence of Father Hugonard: Dewdney to Macdonald, July 11, 1883, and Aug. 14, 1883, Macdonald Papers. For the background of the Dewdney-Jackson feud see Interior file no. 60302.

[53]Dewdney to Macdonald, Aug. 14, 1883, Macdonald Papers.

[54]Dewdney to Macdonald, Aug. 30, 1883, *ibid.*

their tactics may have been designed to take the wind out of the Edmonton member's sails. A committee consisting of all the elected members was formed, with instructions to prepare a memorial dealing with a number of complaints regarding various federal policies and several constitutional matters. The result was a unanimous report which, in regard to constitutional issues, requested the grant of legislative power to incorporate companies with territorial objects and to impose imprisonment for breaking territorial ordinances, as well as full control over roads and trails, a per capita subsidy to be expended by the Council, and representation in Parliament.[55] The members also took up the matter of the control of the federal funds with the Governor. Dewdney telegraphed to Ottawa for instructions, asking, "Is it not under control of Lieutenant-Governor who advises with members in regard to payment made for public improvements in their district to a limited extent? Greater portion of Territories are outside of electoral districts and must be protected."[56] The reply from the Department of the Interior was, "Whatever money is voted by federal Parliament for North-West purposes must of necessity be expended by Lieutenant-Governor, under instructions from this Department."[57] Throughout the period of his governorship Dewdney maintained the stand which he took at this time—that his control of the federal funds was necessary to ensure proper attention to the needs of unrepresented areas. His argument appeared to be strengthened by the fact that the Council in 1884 and succeeding years confined its appropriations of local revenues largely to grants to the elected members for expenditure in their districts, but since it was doubtless assumed that the Governor would look after the intervening areas, Dewdney's case rested on the questionable supposition that such areas would be ignored if the Council had complete control of all funds.

Before the members dispersed they dealt with another question having a constitutional aspect, and which for a number of years caused the sharpest of all divisions of opinion in the North-West on a local issue, viz. liquor policy. A petition had been received which proposed that the Council request the federal government to modify the prohibition law so that beer and ale could be manufactured and sold in the Territories. The committee which considered the petition recommended that the government be asked to empower the Lieutenant-Governor in Council to issue licences for the manufacture and sale of

55*Council Journals*, 1883, pp. 40–2.
56Dewdney to Minister of the Interior, telegram, Sept. 19, 1883, Interior file no. 65702.
57A. M. Burgess to Dewdney, telegram, Sept. 27, 1883, *ibid.*

beer and ale. The committee's report was adopted after a vote which found Oliver (a prohibitionist) allied with Richardson, Macleod, and Irvine, in opposition to Dewdney, Reed, and the other elected members.[58] Dewdney viewed the measure, as others have done before and since, as a means of reducing the amount of smuggling and illicit distilling which he claimed were beyond the control of the Mounted Police.[59]

The Governor felt strongly about the liquor issue and pressed the matter at Ottawa, but his attitude to the constitutional aspirations of the Council was one of indifference. "I hope the 'Memorial' as passed will not give you any annoyance," he wrote to Macdonald at the end of the session. "I found the Elected Members had all something they wished to bring before the Govt. & they all agreed to back each other."[60] To prevent the Prime Minister from becoming annoyed and worried over agitation in the North-West by discounting local criticisms of federal policy, was to become one of Dewdney's main preoccupations.

That none of the constitutional objectives which the Council approved at this 1883 session were in advance of territorial public opinion may be proved by reference to the press of the period. There was complete unanimity on the need for parliamentary representation —a very natural objective since so many of the settlers' grievances could be solved only by adjustments in federal policies. Of the several proposals relating to the position of the territorial government, all had been advocated at one time or another by the press, and as one session succeeded another, interest in these proposals increased. The papers carried fairly adequate reports of Council proceedings, and all the important questions were made the subject of frequent and often lengthy editorial comment.

Nicholas Flood Davin did not limit himself to editorializing, and during the parliamentary session of 1884 he acted as an unofficial lobbyist for the North-West, and succeeded in getting one of the requests of the Council brought to the attention of Parliament.[61] At his prompting, Senator Plumb, a Conservative from Ontario, urged the granting of parliamentary representation in a long and able speech which analysed the early history of Upper Canada and the territorial system of the United States from the point of view of representative government.[62] The government's reply was given by Senator Mac-

[58]Council Journals, 1883, pp. 17, 57, 63–4.
[59]Ibid., 1884, pp. 7–8.
[60]Dewdney to Macdonald, private, Sept. 27, 1883, Macdonald Papers.
[61]Regina Leader, June 26, 1884. See also p. 90 above, footnote 72.
[62]Senate Debates, 1884, pp. 143–52.

pherson, the Minister of the Interior, who congratulated the speaker on his researches, and agreed that representation, when granted, should place the Territories on a basis of full equality with the rest of Canada, as distinguished from the American system which prevented a territory from participating in presidential elections and confined its representation to a voteless delegate in the House of Representatives. However, he rejected the proposal for immediate representation, stating that there should be an inquiry first, and that the government would take the matter into consideration before the next session. At about the same time, the issue was brought before the House of Commons in the form of a private bill giving the Territories one member for each provisional district, with the first election before the end of the year. Its author was M. C. Cameron, a Liberal member from Ontario who had business interests in the Territories, and who during his last visit there had promised to bring the matter before Parliament.[63] For the Prime Minister, the bill was nothing more than an occasion for jocular comment at the expense of the opposition; it was, he asserted, merely an insidious attempt on Cameron's part to make himself the next Liberal Minister of the Interior.[64] Needless to say, the bill did not progress beyond its first reading.

V

The North-West Council met in July and August 1884, amid an atmosphere of rising discontent throughout the North-West.[65] In both Manitoba and the Territories a general business depression had followed the collapse of the land boom of 1882. Early frosts, low prices, and a decline in immigration dashed many high hopes and encouraged a critical attitude towards government policies which seemed to be aggravating the settlers' hardships. Such issues as the monopoly position of the C.P.R., the reservation of large tracts of land for colonization companies, bureaucratic rigidity in the land regulations, the tariff on agricultural implements and lumber, were debated with increasing heat. In some quarters there was talk of secession and rebellion. The discontent found one avenue of expression in local farmers' unions, which at a convention in Winnipeg late in 1883 formed the Manitoba and Northwest Farmers' Union, thus inaugurating the first of the agrarian protest movements of Western Canada.

[63]*Commons Debates*, 1884, pp. 598 ff.
[64]*Ibid.*, p. 692.
[65]See Stanley, *op. cit.*, chap.xii, and Morton, *History of Prairie Settlement* (Toronto, 1938), pp. 93–4.

Due to a combination of circumstances, the agitation in the District of Saskatchewan, and particularly in the electoral district of Lorne, reached an intensity unequalled elsewhere in the Territories. This area, which comprised the white and English half-breed settlement around Prince Albert and the métis colonies on the South Saskatchewan, derived its distinctive character from certain well-defined social and economic characteristics. Prince Albert, founded in 1866, was the centre to which most of the Eastern Canadian (chiefly Ontario) immigrants had come in the period before the construction of the C.P.R. The change in the railway route and the delay in building a branch line had caused a sharp drop in the rate of immigration, had kept transportation costs high, and had restricted the market for surplus grain.[66] Even including the French-speaking area, it was soon surpassed in population by several areas in Assiniboia. Thus the general depression was aggravated in this locality and there was keen disappointment among farmers, merchants, and speculators. Moreover, government favours and the attentions of ministers and officials appeared to be showered on the upstart settlements along the main line, thus heightening the feeling of inferiority and neglect.

The French-speaking portion of the district had its own peculiar grievances. It was even older than the Prince Albert settlement, but it did not grow to any significant extent until after 1870, when it attracted the more nomadic element from Manitoba.[67] These, like their fellows elsewhere in the Territories, had come, not as land seekers, but to continue their old free life based on the buffalo hunt. Here too the Catholic missionaries had done their utmost to induce them to give up their nomadic habits in favour of agricultural enterprise, but had been only partially successful.[68] Consequently the disappearance of the buffalo left many of the métis in a demoralized and maladjusted state, without financial resources or the knowledge necessary to begin successful farming operations. A large number had resorted to freighting, but the decline in immigration and general business activity threw many of them out of employment in 1884.[69] Like the English settlers, they were annoyed by the terms of the land law as it applied to old

66D. H. Macdowall, writing to Dewdney, Jan. 14, 1885 (Dewdney Papers, Trail) stated that, without communication with the Eastern market, the district was utterly at the mercy of the Hudson's Bay Co. for the price of grain and the mode of payment.

67See M. Giraud, Le métis canadien: son rôle dans l'histoire des provinces de l'Ouest (Paris, 1945), pp. 1138 ff.

68Ibid., pp. 1142 ff.

69Ibid., p. 1172. See also Hayter Reed to Dewdney, private, Aug. 25, 1884, enclosed in Dewdney to Macdonald, private, Sept. 5, 1884, Macdonald Papers.

residents, particularly since they believed that they shared with the Indians the aboriginal title to the soil and were therefore entitled to special consideration. Another source of discontent among many of them was the reluctance of the government to extend the river lot survey beyond the area which had been subdivided in that fashion in 1877 and 1878.

The missionaries, almost the only ones who saw the situation of the métis as a social problem comparable to the Indian problem, had given every aid to their people in making representations to the government, but without result, at least in Saskatchewan.[70] Consequently by 1884 many were in a mood to accept a more aggressive type of leadership than their clergy were prepared to supply. The initiative in bringing together the discontented elements in the two parts of the district was provided by some of the settlers from the East, who now saw more reasons for opposing Macdonald than they had dreamed of in Ontario. Thus was born a temporary alliance which by the spring of 1884 resulted in an invitation to Louis Riel, the founder of Manitoba, to come to the Saskatchewan; he, it was hoped, could organize a movement of sufficient power to cause a stir even along the remote and tranquil shores of the Ottawa.

The extremes to which righteous indignation (not unalloyed with political partizanship) carried some of the Western critics of the federal government is revealed in the columns of the *Edmonton Bulletin* and the *Prince Albert Times*. Replying to an Ontario paper which had asserted that the pioneers of that province had overcome difficulties by "persistent perseverance" rather than by appealing to the government or threatening rebellion, Oliver wrote:

If it was not by—not threatening, but actual—rebellion and appeals to the British government for justice that the people of Ontario gained the rights they enjoy today and freed themselves from a condition precisely similar to that into which the North-West is being rapidly forced, how was it? Was it not by armed rebellion coupled with murder, that Manitoba attained the rights she enjoys today from the very men who now hold the reins of power at Ottawa. If history is to be taken as a guide, what could be plainer than that without rebellion the people of the North West need expect nothing, while with rebellion successful or otherwise they may reasonably expect to get their rights.[71]

[70]The St. Albert (Alberta) métis secured some concessions in 1883 by sending a delegation to Ottawa consisting of Father Leduc and M. B. Maloney: see Stanley, *op. cit.*, p. 258.
[71]Editorial in the *Edmonton Bulletin* reprinted in the *Prince Albert Times*, Feb. 22, 1884.

"There is the ring of true metal about it, which indicates pretty plainly the temper of the Nor'Wester," the *Prince Albert Times* remarked in commenting on this editorial (which was reproduced in full). "We doubt," this paper declared a month or two later, "if anything we can say will make the Government understand the strong feeling they have excited against themselves throughout all classes of the people in the Territories. Where they get the information which induces them to believe the people likely to submit tamely much longer we do not know, but we can assure them that they need not look for their friends among the Canadians, Half Breeds or Indians, as they are likely soon to be made aware of in a manner at once startling and unpleasant."[72]

The widespread feeling that just grievances were being ignored by the federal government was reflected in the proceedings of the Council during this 1884 session. The extenuations in Dewdney's opening speech were not very convincing when the record of federal action on the 1883 memorial was examined, and the Governor soon sensed that another and possibly more critical memorial was in the offing. With his usual political resourcefulness he suggested that in future all memorials should be prepared by the Council in its executive capacity, a stratagem which would prevent criticisms of federal policy from being expressed in sittings open to the press and public.[73] This was agreed to, since the majority, as the Governor reported to Macdonald, were "anxious to do nothing to complicate your government."[74] Oliver and Ross, however, refused to be gagged in this manner, and a few days later during a legislative sitting they tried to get the Council to reiterate the requests of the previous year in much more blunt and vigorous language.

The Council [their resolution[75] read] should forthwith assert its rights to the legislative and executive control of all matters relating to the Government of the North-West Territories, such as is exercised by representative Legislative Bodies of all the Provinces within the British Empire as well as of the Empire itself, and at once inform the Minister of the Interior for Canada, or such other Minister or official as may be proper or necessary, of their desire to have the funds granted or to be granted by the Parliament of Canada for the expenses of Government in the North-West, placed under their control as the representatives of the people of the North-West, instead of in the hands of the Lieutenant-Gov-

---

[72]*Prince Albert Times*, May 23, 1884.
[73]See Dewdney to Macdonald, private, July 22, 1884, Macdonald Papers.
[74]Dewdney to Macdonald, private, Sept. 6, 1884, *ibid*.
[75]*Council Journals*, 1884, pp. 47–9. Oliver had discussed this, and other resolutions which he introduced, with his constituents before the session: see *Edmonton Bulletin*, June 28, 1884.

ernor. . . . Although the North-West has not been admitted into Confederation as a Province, the people being governed directly from Ottawa
are held to be, as they hold themselves to be, Canadians; they therefore
are entitled to be placed upon the same footing, and treated as Canadians
elsewhere in Canada, whether the organization provided for their local
self government is called a Council or Legislature.

Then came a demand for a subsidy under local control, of an amount
proportionately greater than the provincial subsidies because of the
higher incidence of federal taxation and the absence of revenues from
Crown lands; also a special grant for school purposes, or, alternately,
control of the school lands. The final demand was for control of the
federal funds during the current session "as the people of the country
desire the responsibility to be assumed at once by the Council." The
two reformers were unable to muster any support for their resolution,
the rest of the Council voting for an amendment sponsored by Jackson and Macdowall which declared that the subject had already been
referred to the Executive Council.[76]

Nothing daunted by this rebuff, Oliver and Ross returned to the
attack a few days later with another long and sharply worded resolution[77] dealing with various federal policies and demanding as well the
immediate establishment of a Legislative Assembly, reform in the
system of representation, and expulsion of the official members.[78]
Jackson again led the embattled majority, supported this time by
J. G. Turriff of Moose Mountain. Their amendment[79] reiterated the
policy of having the Executive Council deal with the several problems
which, it claimed, arose from "the extraordinary growth and development of the country" (in other words not from any failure on the part
of the federal government). The motives of the two reformers, it was
alleged, were political: "We believe," the amendment continued in a
pious tone, "the feeling of the Country to be strongly against the introduction of party politics into the Council as well as against any action
of the Council being taken in such a way that either Political Party
in the Dominion Parliament could use it for political purposes." It
was a cunning argument, but hardly a candid one in view of the associations and political sympathies of the majority of the Councillors.

[76]*Council Journals*, 1884, pp. 49–50.
[77]*Ibid.*, pp. 60–1. See above, p. 116.
[78]The resolution also stated "that while the location and boundaries of the
different Provisional or Postal Districts in the North-West make those Districts
well suited for erection into Provinces some time, it is not advisable at present to
separate them from each other and place each one under the control of a petty
Provincial Government."
[79]*Ibid.*, pp. 61–2.

Even this second rebuff did not subdue Oliver and Ross, for during the same week they presented a third critical resolution relating to federal land policy[80] and concluding with the assertion that, while it was expedient for the present to have public lands administration vested in the federal government, yet "as soon as Responsible Representative Government is obtained by the North-West it should be assumed by that Government."

Despite the defeat of their three motions, the two "agitators" had succeeded in putting their views on record, and also had embarrassed the majority by making them appear in the role of defenders of the federal government. The result was that while the majority of the Council had asserted that the 1883 memorial "fairly set forth the requirements of the Territories,"[81] their deliberations in executive session produced another long memorial reiterating most of the requests made the previous year and adding several new ones.[82] Its tone, while not as peremptory as that of the Oliver-Ross resolutions, was nevertheless much more emphatic than in 1883.[83] And it included the Oliver-Ross proposals for a special grant for school purposes and more complete representation in the Council. All in all, Oliver's "wild talk"[84] (as Dewdney called it) had not been without effect.

Shortly after transmitting an official copy of the memorial to the Secretary of State, Dewdney sent his private comments on it to the Prime Minister. "I hope that after it has been considered," he wrote, "you will see that an answer is sent other than the formal acknowledgement. . . . I had to make the best of the last year's in referring to it in my speech."[85] Concerning constitutional matters in the memorial, he supported the plea for power to incorporate companies but suggested that it not include railway companies; he did not support the proposal for increased representation, claiming that a census

[80]*Ibid.*, pp. 71–2.

[81]*Ibid.*, p. 62.

[82]Memorial of the Executive Council of the North-West Territories, Aug. 2, 1884. There is a difference between the copy in Interior file no. 79134 (presumably the official copy) and the annotated one in the Macdonald Papers, vol. 113. The latter contains a request that "the powers generally given to the legislatures of the several provinces should be given to the North-West Council."

[83]That public opinion was forcing the hands of some of the members may be illustrated by the criticisms of Macdowall's stand in the 1883 session, appearing in the *Prince Albert Times*. After hearing him defend his record, a meeting at Colleston school early in 1884 gave him a vote of confidence, but also passed a series of resolutions critical of various federal policies and requesting representation in Parliament, exclusion of official members from the Council, provincial powers, and a larger grant from federal funds. See *Prince Albert Times*, Feb. 29, 1884.

[84]Dewdney to Macdonald, private, Aug. 5, 1884, Macdonald Papers.

[85]Dewdney to Macdonald, private, Sept. 6, 1884, *ibid.*

would satisfy the people for the present, and advocated instead an increase in the population requirement from 1,000 to 2,000 adults; with respect to the plea for control of the federal grant he claimed that "only those [districts] who have members would derive the benefit" and cited the Council's policy in appropriating local funds for public works as proof of his claim. Regarding parliamentary representation he simply remarked, "Council expect an opinion on this."

The Governor had succeeded in his effort to save the Macdonald administration from embarrassing criticism by having the North-West Council memorial of 1884 prepared in secret session. But his effort in this direction was not confined within the walls of the Council chamber. The *Prince Albert Times* was a thorn in the flesh to him personally, as well as to the government. It was being published in the area of greatest unrest, and its vehement, intemperate editorials supplied ample fuel for the flames of discontent. Somehow the raucous voice had to be silenced, and this was accomplished by extending government patronage to the necessitous publishers.[86] The result was striking, for not only was there a marked change in editorial policy, but news reports on the course of the agitation soon disappeared from the columns of the *Times*. But the dragon's teeth had been sown: the vituperative editorials and threats of rebellion had done their work, and the abrupt change of policy merely strengthened the charge that a conspiracy was afoot to suppress popular rights.[87]

The agitation which had been so marked during the spring of 1884 in no wise abated during the summer and autumn. Parliamentary representation, responsible government, and provincial status were debated at public meetings and in the press in all parts of the North-West. The people at Wolseley and Moosomin were reported as favouring responsible government, control of the federal funds, an elective assembly, and the retention of one government for the three provisional districts.[88] The *Saskatchewan Herald* did not favour the last of these, claiming that it would not suit the districts remote from Regina, and proposing instead that one province be organized and the less populous areas be placed under a reorganized territorial government with greater powers and a council composed chiefly of elected members.[89] In Alberta, the *Edmonton Bulletin* advocated the immediate grant of

[86]See Dewdney to Macpherson, Sept. 13, 1884, Dewdney Papers (Trail); see also Dewdney to Macdonald, July 23, 1884; also Dewdney to Macdonald, Oct. 19, 1886, reporting that Macdowall had control of the paper: Macdonald Papers.
[87]See W. H. Jackson's manifesto of July 28, 1884 in Stanley, *op. cit.*, p. 302.
[88]*Regina Leader*, Nov. 20 and Dec. 11, 1884; *Qu'Appelle Vidette*, Dec. 18, 1884.
[89]*Saskatchewan Herald*, Jan. 16, 1885.

provincial powers, but the retention of one government "until such time as one or more of the different [provisional] districts shall have attained a sufficient population to warrant the expense, or make necessary, a separate local government." "The territories," wrote Oliver, "have attained a sufficient population, of sufficient intelligence to warrant the assumption by them of responsible local government having all the powers of the different provincial governments, without further delay." Oliver did not specify that power to deal with public lands should be granted immediately, but declared that "the control of the land of the North-West belongs to the people of the North-west . . . the federal government is only entitled to act as administrator until with the permanent establishment of provinces the people are in a position to take hold of and control their own lands to advantage."[90]

Viewed in this setting, the movement headed by Louis Riel in the District of Saskatchewan involved no unique constitutional proposals, except for a vague threat of secession and formation of "a separate federation of our own in direct connection with the Crown."[91] The main proposal for constitutional change was the grant of provincial status to each of the provisional districts, including local control of natural resources. Other proposals, contained in the petition or bill of rights forwarded to the federal government in December, consisted of various reforms which had been advocated from time to time in the Territories: scrip and patents for the half-breeds, representation in Parliament and in the cabinet, vote by ballot, lower tariffs, a Hudson Bay railway, modification of the homestead laws, and more generous treatment for the Indians.[92] Riel's contribution to the movement was his power to sway the métis by his oratory and magnetic personality. The only statement of objectives which is definitely associated with his name, apart from the demand for provincial status, is largely taken up with detailed proposals for improving the social and economic position of his people.[93]

The news policy of the *Prince Albert Times* and the *Saskatchewan Herald* as well as the secrecy which surrounded some of Riel's movements make it difficult to trace the trends of opinion among the agitators, and the relative influence of Riel and the spokesmen for the discontented white and English half-breed settlers. W. H. Jackson of

[90]*Edmonton Bulletin*, Nov. 1, 1884.
[91]Jackson's manifesto, Stanley, *op. cit.*, p. 301.
[92]*Ibid.*, pp. 306–7.
[93]Memorandum of Louis Riel to Bishop Grandin, handed Sept. 7, 1884, at Gabriel's Crossing: copy with Dewdney to Macdonald, private, Sept. 19, 1884, Macdonald Papers.

Prince Albert, the secretary of the movement, claimed that the December bill of rights represented a compromise.[94] The process by which this compromise was arrived at was evidently a matter of negotiation between the leaders of the agitation, since no general convention comparable to the Red River constitutional convention of 1870 was held.

During the autumn of 1884 Dewdney and Reed, as the local representatives of the Indian administration, investigated Indian grievances and made some attempt to alleviate various hardships;[95] as a result of these efforts they reported that if the half-breed complaints were also dealt with, the danger of serious trouble in the North-West would disappear. Unfortunately, action in regard to these complaints was beyond the powers of the territorial government. Macdonald had promised the North-West Council in July that the Minister of the Interior (Senator Macpherson) "will take into his serious consideration the claims of the Half Breeds at Prince Albert and elsewhere in the North-West Territories,"[96] but as one month succeeded another no action was forthcoming.

Dewdney saw the essential remedies for the métis discontent clearly enough, and stated them in private letters to the Prime Minister: work for the unemployed and investigation of land claims. "In any negotiations you have with the Manitoba and North Western [Railway]," he wrote Macdonald in September, "an effort might be made to induce them to do some work (grading the Road) from the South Branch south; this would give plenty of work to the Half Breeds."[97] The latter were very anxious to work, he reported: "In the north it would circulate a little money among them & the want of it is the secret of their uneasiness." "If the Half-breed question is arranged this winter," he wrote a few days later, "it will settle the whole business; if not, a good force in the North will be necessary."[98] But his loyalty to the Macdonald administration prevented him from criticizing the government's dilatory tactics. He did not reiterate his advice, and his subsequent letters gave the impression that action could be postponed till the following year.

The federal government bears the greater share of responsibility for the delay in dealing with the grievances. Dewdney's reports during the early fall provided important information on the movement, in-

94W. H. Jackson to Secretary of State, Dec. 16, 1884, in Stanley, *op. cit.*, p. 306.
95See Reed to Dewdney, Sept. 10, 1884, copy in Macdonald Papers.
96*Council Journals*, 1884, p. 67.
97Dewdney to Macdonald, private, Sept. 5, 1884, Macdonald Papers.
98Dewdney to Macdonald, private, Sept. 19, 1884, *ibid.*

cluding the alarming fact that the missionaries had lost their influence to Riel and could no longer control the course of the agitation.[99] But Macdonald took the view that "no amount of concession will prevent . . . people from grumbling and agitating," and thought more about increasing the strength of the Police than about the need for prompt action.[100] This was the final scene before the last tragic act of the Riel agitation. Under the strain of continued frustration, reason deserted the folk hero of the métis, and he made the fatal choice of open resistance by forming a provisional government and arming his followers, hoping apparently to repeat his successful tactics of 1869–70.

The North-West Council was no more successful than the métis and white settlers in securing a response to its proposals from the federal government. The Executive Council memorial of August 1884 was pigeon-holed in Ottawa until May 26, 1885, when Macpherson prepared a report on it. The métis, who had resorted to arms in March, had finally been subdued in the early part of May,[101] and the Minister showed no disposition to make large concessions to Western opinion now that open revolt had been quelled. His comments on the proposed constitutional reforms were much the same as Dewdney's: he refused to take a stand on the grant of power to incorporate companies, saying this was a matter for the Minister of Justice; increased representation in the Council and representation in Parliament should await the results of the census—the latter being one proposal which was accepted. On the all-important question of financial control, the response was emphatic: ". . . it would be inexpedient to entrust the expenditure of money voted by the Parliament of Canada to anybody not responsible to it."[102]

VI

It was inevitable that discussion of North-West affairs during the session of Parliament which dragged out its weary course during the spring and summer of 1885 should be largely concerned with the causes of the rebellion, and the conduct of the campaign to suppress it. The government was kept busy repelling opposition attacks on its past policy respecting Indian and métis grievances, and there was

[99]Dewdney to Macdonald, private, Sept. 14 and Sept. 19, 1884; also Forget's report of Sept. 18 enclosed in latter: *ibid.*
[100]Macdonald to Dewdney, private, Sept. 2, 1884, Dewdney Papers (Trail).
[101]A full and authoritative account of the Rebellion is contained in Stanley, *op. cit.*
[102]Memorandum of May 26, 1885, in Interior file no. 79134.

little disposition to consider any current constitutional problems of the North-West. Early in the session, before the outbreak of hostilities, the government rejected M. C. Cameron's renewed attempt to give parliamentary representation to the Territories, which was declared to be premature pending the taking of a census.[103] Actually the measure was premature for another reason—Parliament could not grant representation under the existing terms of the constitution, and an amendment to the British North America Act had to be secured the following year in order to permit this legislation to be passed. There was some evidence that the government was not completely impervious to North-West opinion; in addition to the census bill[104] and an amendment clarifying the clause of the North-West Territories Act respecting the powers of school districts,[105] the grant for expenses of government was doubled, increasing from $32,000 to $65,450. The main item in the increase was for school purposes, thus meeting one of the requests in the Executive Council memorial of 1884 which had also been supported by Dewdney.[106]

The North-West Council elections of September 1885 (see Table B) provided an occasion for public discussion of the constitutional position of the Territories. Dewdney had established three new districts—Macleod, St. Albert, and Moosomin—and given Regina and Qu'Appelle each a second member; altogether, eleven seats were open out of a total of thirteen. In all but one there was a contest; however, there was a remarkable unanimity in the views of the candidates, and the voters were doubtless influenced more by personal qualifications and thinly disguised political preferences. The *Regina Leader* reported that the platforms of the candidates all agreed on parliamentary representation, full representation in the Council, and provincial organization at an early date.[107] Actually in some cases the *Leader* was probably equating expressions favouring a Legislative Assembly with a desire for provincial status—a distinction which was not always observed in public discussions of the future constitutional development of the Territories. The results of the elections were very satisfactory from Dewdney's point of view: most of the successful candi-

---

[103]*Commons Debates*, 1885, pp. 491 ff. Cameron's bill (no. 45) gave Alberta, Saskatchewan, and Athabasca one member each and Assiniboia two members; the first election was to take place not later than Dec. 1, 1885: copy of bill in Macdonald Papers.

[104]48–49 Vict., c. 3.

[105]48–49 Vict., c. 51.

[106]See Dewdney to Minister of the Interior, Nov. 26, 1884 and Jan. 24, 1885, Interior file no. 81692.

[107]*Regina Leader*, Aug. 27, 1885.

dates were friends of the government or of the Governor.[108] Dewdney's hope that Oliver would be defeated[109] was realized, by a process which Oliver claimed was "a combination of gerrymander, bribery, intimidation, perjury and whiskey . . . to put the case mildly."[110] The significant point about this contest, however, was that the successful candidate, Dr. H. C. Wilson, had not challenged Oliver's constitutional reform programme, and the chief difference between them seems to have been Oliver's temperance principles. Wilson advocated a non-partizan approach to constitutional reform, the implication being that his opponent's antipathy to the Conservative party had affected his attitude in Council deliberations.[111] In the two-member district of Qu'Appelle, the candidate who attacked Dewdney's policies and criticized Jackson for not supporting Oliver and Ross[112] received very limited support, and Jackson and W. D. Perley, both professed Conservatives, headed the poll; here as elsewhere, however, the winners were supporters of responsible government and local control of the federal funds.

Shortly after the elections another opportunity was provided for an expression of opinion on reforms in the territorial constitution. In August, Thomas White, the member for Cardwell (Ontario), succeeded Senator Macpherson as Minister of the Interior. The new minister took his new duties sufficiently seriously to pay a visit to the Territories—the first incumbent of the office to do so—and his forthright manner and evident interest in the problems of the settlers created a favourable impression, even in circles hostile to the administration.[113] At Regina and Fort Qu'Appelle he was presented with memorials which had been previously adopted at meetings specially called for the purpose.[114] These advocated both parliamentary representation and provincial organization. In his reply, White declared himself in favour of the former. In regard to the latter, he stated that there was no doubt the existing system would soon have to be replaced, and though it had not been adopted as government policy, he himself favoured an experiment "of a more simple system of Provincial Government than can be obtained in other and older provinces of the Dominion," but with the same powers as the provinces possessed. The apparatus of

[108]Dewdney to Macdonald, private, Aug. 7, 1885, Macdonald Papers.
[109]Dewdney to Macdonald, private, Aug. 5, 1884, *ibid.*
[110]*Edmonton Bulletin*, Sept. 19, 1885.
[111]*Ibid.*, Sept. 5, 1885.
[112]See speech of Leslie Gordon reported in the *Regina Leader*, Sept. 10, 1885.
[113]See *Edmonton Bulletin*, Nov. 14, 1885.
[114]*Regina Leader*, Oct. 8 and 15, 1885.

provincial government, he argued, was a serious drain on the resources of the people.[115]

The petition presented to him when he arrived in Prince Albert revealed not only a lively interest in the constitutional question but also the extent to which "district consciousness" had developed in that vicinity. Each of the provisional districts, it was represented, should be given provincial status, with control of the public lands; and in the case of Saskatchewan its boundaries should be extended to Hudson Bay, and Prince Albert established as the capital. White's reply was similar to the one he had already given in Assiniboia—that the districts would ultimately become provinces but for the present a simpler and less expensive form of government was desirable, embodying local control of local affairs.[116] The *Edmonton Bulletin* concluded from the minister's speeches in various parts of the Territories that "at once or very shortly" there would be (in addition to various changes in the land law) parliamentary representation, a "more representative, more fully empowered and more liberally endowed local government," and "generally a more just and less arbitrary method of dealing with the territories by the federal authorities."[117]

Though the Council which met during the last two months of 1885 was composed largely of members who were Conservatives in federal politics, it exhibited a marked independence in expressing current North-West aspirations. That it was not a pliant tool was demonstrated by the episode of the address in reply to the Governor's opening speech. Dewdney had incautiously undertaken a general defence of federal policies, partly no doubt to divert attention from the absence of any reply to the memorial of 1884. The Council, however, refused to echo some of the views expressed by the Governor and used its reply to ventilate a number of popular grievances.[118] Dewdney's reference to the increase in the elected membership drew the following comment:

While congratulating ourselves and the Country on the increased representation afforded us we cannot omit to point out to Your Honor the still greater rights of representation which we feel we are entitled to, but have not yet received. Settled as these Territories in a large measure are by men who have been accustomed to the constitutional rights and privilges of the British Empire and its Colonies, it is inevitable that a feeling of distrust and uneasiness should be prevalent owing to our not enjoying the same.

115*Ibid.*, Oct. 29, 1885.
116*Prince Albert Times*, Oct. 23, 1885.
117*Edmonton Bulletin*, Nov. 14, 1885.
118*Council Journals*, 1885, pp. 43–5.

The taking of the Census we are confident will show that our longings and aspirations for local Self-Government are not the outcome of a few individuals but the desire of a country settled as largely as some of the present Provinces of the Dominion.

We confidently look forward to the next Session of the Federal Parliament granting our requests and calling to their Councils representatives of these Territories. As Canadians we shall cherish the day when we shall receive the same rights and privileges as the rest of our beloved Dominion, and be permitted to take part in moulding its destinies.

With respect to "the very handsome subsidy . . . for School purposes" (as the Governor described it), the response was: ". . . we only regret that any restrictions should be placed upon moneys which should certainly be at the disposal of this Council"—a reference to the fact that school grants as fixed by the School Ordinance were subject to federal approval.[119] The sharpest retort, however, was to the references to the Rebellion contained in the speech ("designing men seeking their own ends," "lawlessness and disloyalty in the far West"):

Knowing, as we do, the great influence always had over the Indians by the Half-Breeds, we have to regret that the repeated representations heretofore made to the Government of Canada by the North-West Council, on behalf of the Half-Breeds and their claims, did not receive more immediate attention. We trust Your Honor will join with this Council in bringing the matter of the many existing unsettled claims to the notice of the Dominion Government by memorial or resolution.

All this caused a long, and at times acrimonious, debate, with Rouleau taking up the cudgels on behalf of Dewdney and federal policies.[120] At one point, the discussion of Indian administration provoked a violent altercation between Jackson and Dewdney, the Governor even descending to the level of questioning the genuineness of the Qu'-Appelle member's devotion to the Conservative party.

Early in the session Jackson and Bedford (of Regina) secured the formation of a committee consisting of Richardson, Macleod, and the elected members to prepare a new memorial to the federal government. This time there was no suggestion that the matter be handled in executive session. Twenty-seven resolutions were subsequently approved, covering a range of complaints similar to that of previous years.[121] The familiar requests—power to incorporate companies,

119See Order in Council of March 12, 1886, and Interior file no. 85869.
120Regina Leader, Dec. 10, 1885. Dewdney attempted to rebut some of the criticisms in his reply to the address from the members: Council Journals, 1884, p. 51.
121Council Journals, 1885, pp. 65–72.

parliamentary representation (with due regard for area as well as population), and local control of federal funds—were repeated. There was also a request for a territorial court of appeals, and a recommendation that the government "fill appointments to positions of trust and emolument from amongst the residents of these Territories." In forwarding his comments on the resolutions, Dewdney again opposed local control of federal funds, and stressed the fact that his practice was to consult the members regarding expenditures in their districts;[122] however, he suggested that when the Council was replaced by the Assembly other arrangements would have to be made.

With the experience of the previous two years in mind, the Council decided to give weight to its recommendations by sending a delegation to Ottawa.[123] The councillors selected for this purpose were W. D. Perley, H. C. Wilson, and J. H. Ross, and in February 1886 they laid the various proposals before the members of the government. Fortunately for their mission, the government was more inclined to give a favourable reception to representations from the North-West than at any time in the past: the new Minister of the Interior was an energetic and alert administrator, and the political repercussions of the Rebellion prompted a closer attention to conditions in the Territories. Not only was a detailed official reply given to the Council's submissions, but action was taken on a number of them.[124]

VII

Parliamentary representation, so long and so generally desired, was at last conceded at the 1886 session of Parliament. An act giving Assiniboia two members and Alberta and Saskatchewan one each was passed,[125] and the following year Parliament granted the Territories

122Dewdney to Minister of the Interior, Dec. 31, 1885, Interior file no. 103598.

123See *Council Journals*, 1886, Appendix B, p. 83. The *Prince Albert Times* had stressed the advantage of sending a delegation as early as 1883: see editorial of Nov. 23, 1883.

124*Council Journals*, 1886, Appendix C.

12549 Vict., c. 24. The franchise was the same as that for elections to the North-West Council; amendments introduced by the Liberals in both the Commons and Senate to abolish the property (householder) qualification were defeated, along with amendments to introduce the ballot. Macdonald argued that no change in the franchise should be made until the North-West Council had expressed itself on the subject; the Liberals, however, pointed out that Parliament had recently adopted the policy of setting its own qualifications without reference to provincial franchises. *Commons Debates*, 1886, pp. 1249 ff. See also memoranda of Wm. Wilson, assistant law clerk, April and May 1886, Macdonald Papers, vol. 113.

two members in the Senate.[126] "The population," Macdonald said in discussing the bill of 1886, "would scarcely allow of so many members, but, although the settlers are very few in number, the country is large and has many different interests requiring different legislative measures."[127] Since the 1885 population was 48,362, the measure was not particularly generous if compared with the four members given to Manitoba in 1870 (with its 1871 population of 25,228) and the six members given to British Columbia in 1871 (with its population in that year of 36,247). On the other hand, if the current representation quotient had been applied, the Territories would have been entitled to only two members. Since area as well as population had been recognized, there was little disposition in the North-West to criticize the number which had been granted, although the *Saskatchewan Herald* claimed that each of the three districts should have had one additional member, or a total of seven.[128] But the satisfaction of having four members instead of none at all was probably the dominant feeling in most parts of the country.

The power to incorporate companies with territorial objects, with the exception of transportation and certain other companies, was conferred by Order in Council in July.[129] The Order also conferred the power of direct taxation, which had been included in the Act of 1875 but eliminated by Mills in 1877 apparently in deference to the principle of no taxation without representation.[130] This was one power which had not been requested by the North-West Council; it had

[126]50-51 Vict., c. 3. The Council memorials of 1883 and 1884 had referred simply to representation in Parliament; the resolution of 1885 specified representation in both the Commons and Senate. In introducing the measure, Macdonald stated that the government originally intended to postpone representation in the Senate until provincial status was granted, but was deferring to opinion in the North-West; doubtless he was not uninfluenced by the political advantages of the move. Mills opposed the bill, claiming that the government could change the constitution by appointing an indefinite number of senators from the North-West, that there was no necessity for it, that the American territories did not possess it, and that it involved unnecessary expense. *Commons Debates*, 1887, pp. 197 ff.

[127]*Commons Debates*, 1886, p. 1205.

[128]*Saskatchewan Herald*, March 8 and June 14, 1886.

[129]Order in Council, July 7, 1886. The exceptions were, insurance, railway, tramway, steamboat, canal, transportation, telegraph, and telephone companies, in addition to companies which could not be incorporated by a province. As in the case of the Order of May 11, 1877 which authorized the Council to levy licences (see above, p. 86), this order permitted the Council to levy taxes to secure a revenue for municipal as well as territorial purposes, since there were only a few municipalities in the Territories and the territorial government frequently supported activities normally undertaken by municipal bodies.

[130]*Commons Debates*, 1885, p. 2961.

empowered municipalities to levy direct taxes but, as in the provinces during this period, federal subsidies were expected to provide most of the funds for the financing of all non-municipal activities.[131] No doubt the initiative in conferring this power came from the federal authorities—Macdonald for example had suggested some years previously that "a wise system of taxation" would enable the Council to provide the sessional indemnities for its members instead of having them paid from federal funds.[132] The request for a territorial court of appeals was granted, and the question of civil and criminal law in force in the Territories was also clarified for the first time.[133]

On the financial issue, however, the government hedged. Its official reply to the Council ran as follows:

With the growth of population in the North-West Territories, and the establishment of the provincial system, which in the nature of things must soon take place, control over all public moneys will naturally become vested in the representatives of the people, whether those moneys be voted by way of subsidy by the Parliament of Canada or be derived from local taxation as in the other Provinces.[134]

Evidently there was to be no change in the prevailing system as long as the Council continued in existence. The delegates described the position in somewhat different terms: "We were informed," they reported, "that the Government had under consideration a scheme whereby all monies voted for Governmental purposes in the Territories would be vested in the Council";[135] apparently they gave the impression that the concession had been granted, for reports to that effect appeared in the territorial press.[136] Perhaps to counteract the effect of the refusal of financial autonomy, the government approved

[131]See D. G. Creighton, *British North America at Confederation* (Ottawa, 1939), pp. 85–7, 94 ff.

[132]See Dewdney to Minister of the Interior, Aug. 30, 1883, Interior file no. 66292.

[133]49 Vict., c. 25. This Act declared that English civil and criminal law as it existed in 1870 (subject to federal and territorial legislation) was to be the basic law of the Territories; also that all acts of the Canadian Parliament, unless specifically exempted, were thenceforth to apply to the Territories. The government also seized the opportunity offered by this reorganization of the judicial system to increase its patronage in the North-West, taking over the power to appoint clerks of court (s. 20) hitherto possessed by the judges under the terms of territorial legislation: see Dewdney to Macdonald, Sept. 8, 1885 and G. W. Burbidge to Macdonald, private, Aug. 26, 1885, Macdonald Papers.

[134]*Council Journals*, 1886, Appendix C, p. 111.

[135]*Ibid.*, Appendix B, p. 92.

[136]See *Regina Leader*, April 6, 1886, report of banquet for J. H. Ross in Moose Jaw, also *Saskatchewan Herald*, March 8, 1886.

Dewdney's estimates for 1886–7, which involved a moderate increase in the parliamentary appropriation.[137]

When the North-West Council met again towards the end of 1886, it appeared that the movement for increased self-government had come to an impasse, at least for the time being. The government had hinted that "the establishment of the provincial system . . . must soon take place," but it gave no indication how soon this was to be. The Council, having led the movement so far, felt impelled to continue in its role of chief advocate. It therefore seized on a suggestion which Dewdney made in his opening speech that, in view of the necessity of holding elections in a large number of seats before the next session, the boundaries of the electoral districts should be revised "with a view to a more completely representative character being given."[138] As we have already seen, Dewdney had in mind merely adding a few additional seats (the number of elected members now stood at fourteen), but the Council saw it as an opportunity to prove that they were entitled to the Legislative Assembly:

We unite in believing [it declared in its reply to the Governor] that the time has come when that character should be given to [the] Council which appertains to the Legislative Assemblies of the older Provinces. The census of the Territories, recently taken, seems to show that a redistribution of electoral boundaries will bring the Elective Members of the Council up to that number which would bestow on the Territories the Assembly indicated in the North West Territories Act. It seems to be a matter only of such a distribution of seats, as will leave no qualified voter in the country unenfranchised, to secure the result desired by the framers of the Act.[139]

A few days later a committee consisting of all the elected members was appointed to deal with this matter, and also to report on "a well considered scheme . . . [for] responsible Government" which could be submitted to the next session of Parliament.[140] When the committee got down to business, however, it was found that it lacked adequate information on the population of some of the proposed districts, so it was impossible to do more than draw tentative boundaries until after Dewdney had taken a special census.[141] Since the committee did not bring in a report, the Council decided to take action

---

[137]From $65,450 to $74,400. See Interior file no. 100754.

[138]*Council Journals*, 1886, p. 9.

[139]*Ibid.*, p. 15.

[140]*Ibid.*, p. 21. See also report of the debate in the *Regina Journal*, Oct. 29, 1886.

[141]Dewdney to Macdonald, private, Nov. 22, 1886, and April 7, 1887, Macdonald Papers. See also T. Brown to Minister of the Interior, June 16, 1887, Interior file no. 66292.

on part of the terms of reference in an executive session. Having been balked in its attempt to create an Assembly by redistribution, it made an effort to secure the same result by the familiar device of a memorial to the federal government. Evidence concerning the content of the memorial indicates only that "a purely representative Government" was requested and that a subdivision of the North-West into electoral districts was drawn up.[142] Three of the members were designated as spokesmen to arrange details with the federal government if the latter proceeded with the scheme. The Council also went on record during its legislative sittings in favour of the ballot, abolition of the property (householder) qualification for voting, and reduction of the residence qualification from one year to six months.[143]

Consideration of the autonomy movement as it developed from this point on is reserved for the following chapter, but it should be noted here that the memorial of 1886 occasioned the first significant conflict of opinion between the three provisional districts. In order to give complete representation, the old population-area ratio had to be discarded and the whole of the settled area of the North-West divided into constituencies. But the Council soon found that it was not easy to devise an acceptable scheme since it started from the assumption that each provisional district should be treated as an independent unit and separately subdivided, with no constituency including parts of two provisional districts. It appears that the councillors from Saskatchewan and Alberta refused to accept the distribution favoured by their Assiniboia colleagues, and it was reported that the compromise finally arrived at gave Assiniboia thirteen, Alberta seven, and Saskatchewan four.[144] Compared with the non-Indian population of each district, this distribution was a fair one.

142Dewdney to Macdonald, private, Nov. 22, 1886, and April 7, 1887, Macdonald Papers.

143*Council Journals*, 1886, pp. 36, 72–3. It was also recommended that persons who had resided anywhere in the Territories during the previous year should be eligible as candidates in any constituency. For a comment on the franchise proposal see *Regina Journal*, Dec. 3, 1886. Earlier criticisms of the length of residence qualification are made in the *Saskatchewan Herald*, June 24, 1883, *Regina Leader*, May 31, 1883, and *Prince Albert Times*, March 14, 1883 (report of meeting at Batoche).

144Though the matter had been dealt with in executive session, some news had obviously leaked out since the newspapers carried references to the dispute: see *Saskatchewan Herald*, Nov. 22, 1886, *Prince Albert Times*, Nov. 19, 1886. One of the *Leader*'s main criticisms of J. H. Ross, Davin's opponent in the 1887 election in Western Assiniboia, was his alleged betrayal of Assiniboia in the proposed distribution: *Regina Leader*, March 15, 1887. See also Macdowall's election address promising to press for adequate representation for Saskatchewan, *Prince Albert Times*, Feb. 4, 1887, and Perley's remarks reported in the *Qu'Appelle Vidette*, Feb. 24, 1887.

VIII

The interest of the North-West Council in federal matters, so marked during the Morris period, was also a notable feature of the years of Dewdney's governorship. There was, however, a significant difference in the circumstances surrounding the discussion of these issues in the two periods: in the former, the Governor identified himself with local interests and aspirations and encouraged the preparation of submissions to the federal authorities; in the latter, the Governor did not depart from his role of federal representative, and was usually lukewarm and sometimes hostile to the remonstrances and recommendations which were prepared. Referring to the drafting of the Executive Council memorial of 1884 he wrote to Macdonald: "I expect you will receive a very lengthy document (confidential) embodying all the petty grievances each member thinks he is suffering from."[145] It is sufficient commentary on this remark to point out that the memorial consisted of specific proposals on such matters as constitutional reform, half-breed claims, construction of branch line railways, settlement of squatters claims, fish conservation, grain inspection, encouragement of tree planting, Saskatchewan River navigation, and amendment of the liquor law.

The interest which the Council was to take in federal matters was foreshadowed during its first meeting under Dewdney's presidency. The reply to the Governor's opening speech asserted that the people were "looking anxiously forward to the course legislation may take in this Council, as well as to the action which may be taken by us toward assisting to remove laws and regulations over which we as a Council have no direct power." To this end, the members declared that they proposed to adopt means "to convince the Dominion Government of the necessity that exists of some definite action being taken with regard to those matters on which repeated Memorials have been presented by the people, as well as matters and complaints which have arisen as the result of more recent legislation by the Federal authorities."[146] The distinctive needs and economic interests of the plains region were taking root in popular consciousness during this period, and the overwhelming importance to the average settler of such matters as land regulations, transportation facilities, freight rates, and the tariff explains the persistent and vigorous representations which the Council made to the federal government, friendly though the majority were to Macdonald and the Conservative party.

Some of the Council's views were endorsed by the Governor in his

[145]Dewdney to Macdonald, private, July 22, 1884, Macdonald Papers.
[146]Council Journals, 1883, p. 15.

despatches accompanying the memorials; others, as we have already noted, he condemned; while many were allowed to pass without comment. The only occasions when he encouraged the Council to deal with matters under the control of the federal government were in 1883 and 1884 when he supported representations for relaxing the provisions of the prohibition law, and in 1887 when at Macdonald's suggestion he tried to secure a resolution condemning Premier Norquay of Manitoba for his railway policy.[147] In connection with this latter manœuvre, he boasted to Macdonald that he could get a committee "as will do what I want," but the members did not co-operate in the manner expected, and the resolution avoided any reference to the controversy then raging between the federal government and Manitoba.[148]

The perseverance of the Council in pressing half-breed claims, despite the fact that these people had no elected representatives of their own race, should have indicated to the federal government the serious view which was taken of this problem in the Territories. The memorial of 1883 dealt with the question, but the continued inaction of the government seemed to demand more vigorous representations in 1884. Both Oliver and Macdowall prepared resolutions, but the latter brought his to Dewdney who "tempered it" as much as he could, and by a parliamentary manœuvre was able to prevent Oliver's "much stronger" one from being presented.[149] The claims and remedies, however, were reviewed in the memorial prepared during executive session—"the Council," it was stated, "cannot too strongly impress upon Your Excellency's Government the urgent necessity of an immediate settlement of this question."[150] The Council's interest did not cease with the Rebellion; at its 1885 session it urged prompt completion of the claims investigation which at long last had been begun, and, while it approved Riel's execution, it urged clemency for those Indians and métis who were serving sentences for political crimes and whose families were suffering from neglect.[151]

With the advent of Thomas White as Minister of the Interior the Council was at least accorded the courtesy of an official reply to its

147Dewdney to Macdonald, private, Oct. 20 and Nov. 3, 1887, Macdonald Papers.

148Council Journals, 1887, p. 70; see also Dewdney to Macdonald, private, Nov. 20, 1887, Macdonald Papers.

149Dewdney to Macdonald, private, July 22, 1884, Macdonald Papers; see Council Journals, 1884, p. 39.

150Memorial of the Executive Council of the North-West Territories, Aug. 2, 1884, Interior file no. 79134.

151Council Journals, 1885, pp. 59, 61. In 1886 and 1887 it renewed its representations on behalf of the métis: ibid., 1886, pp. 60–1 and 1887, pp. 56–7.

representations. The resolutions of 1885 covered the whole range of western grievances and the reply dealt with each one.[152] The same treatment was accorded the 1886 representations.[153] Moreover, it was obvious from the replies that federal policy, at least in some of its practical applications, was being modified to suit western opinion. With the grant of parliamentary representation there was no longer the same need for the Council to act as a forum for the discussion of federal matters, but the habit had become established, and was fortified by the peculiarly dominant role of the federal government in Western Canadian affairs. The Council at its last session in 1887 forwarded its views to Ottawa on the use of the ballot in federal elections in the North-West, the settlement of half-breed claims, the proposal to establish the head office of the Land Board in the Territories, and the extension of time for the payments on pre-emptions.[154] Its successor, the Legislative Assembly, continued the custom.

IX

The relationship between Dewdney and the elected members in regard to federal-territorial relations presents a diverting panorama of manœuvres and sorties. In the legislative and administrative fields, however, there was little conflict or agitation. With respect to legislation, the responsibility of the Governor was an important one. Under British constitutional practice the preparation and introduction of legislation is very largely controlled by the executive, and in the circumstances of the North-West during this period it was particularly desirable to have a legislative programme prepared at Regina and ready for each Council session. A number of bills were submitted each year by the Governor (see Table C), which included most of the more important measures. Many of these were prepared with the assistance of one of the judges (usually Richardson), but on occasion a lawyer in the capital would be employed for the purpose.[155] There seems to have been plenty of scope for participation by the elected members (the first school bill, for example, was prepared by Oliver),[156] and of the sixty-four bills introduced by them during the five sessions from 1883 to 1887, forty-three were passed. It is not clear how their bills were drafted: some were probably drawn up during the session

152*Ibid.*, 1886, Appendix C.
153*Ibid.*, 1887, Appendix G.
154*Ibid.*, pp. 42, 56–7, 60, 70.
155Dewdney to Macdonald, Aug. 30, 1883, Macdonald Papers.
156The final bill as passed in 1884 was a compromise between Oliver's bill and one introduced by Judge Rouleau, cf. Dewdney to Macdonald, private, July 22, 1884, *ibid.*

TABLE C

INTRODUCTION OF BILLS: NORTH-WEST COUNCIL SESSIONS, 1883–7

Session	By Governor	By appointed members	By elected members	By committee	Total
1883	13	5	13		31
1884	18	4	19	2	43
1885	9	2	8	4	23
1886	6	2	13	3	24
1887	16	3	11	1	31
Total	62	16	64	10	152

with the assistance of one of the judges, but apparently many were prepared by the member himself. Since only three of the twenty-five elected councillors who served during this period were lawyers, there was a tendency to leave legislation of a more technical character to the judges, or to the Governor acting with the judges' assistance.

One defect of the system was that there was no law clerk available to prepare the legislation and scrutinize all bills before they were presented; and there does not seem to have been any consultation between sessions as to the bills to be introduced by the members. Under these circumstances, and considering the general structure and resources of the territorial government, the results were better than might be expected. Without attempting to evaluate the ordinances of this period, it can nevertheless be said that a considerable amount of important and valuable legislation was produced. Of the 125 ordinances, only one was disallowed by the federal government; the Minister of Justice recommended some changes in a few others, but most of these were of minor importance.

The amicable relations between the Governor and Council and between the Council and the federal government in the matter of local legislation were in part due to the fact that bills of dubious validity were nipped in the bud by the judges, thus eliminating occasions for conflict.[157] Moreover, the Governor does not appear to have interfered to any extent with the bills introduced by the elected members. Nevertheless the existing system, or lack of system, did not meet

157The report of the Minister of Justice on the Revised Ordinances of 1888 stated that "the legislation as a whole is remarkably free from any attempt to usurp authority in respect to subjects that are exclusively within the jurisdiction of the Dominion parliament": Correspondence, Reports of the Minister of Justice and Orders in Council upon the Subject of Dominion and Provincial Legislation, 1867–95 (Ottawa, 1896), p. 1249.

with the approval of the elected members when they reviewed the situation at their last session in 1887, and one of the arguments advanced for an executive council operating under the principles of responsible government was that "the present method of introducing legislation . . . has been proved by a number of years' experience to be unsatisfactory and leads to an ill-considered and inconsistent body of legislation."[158] Though the defects of the existing system were obvious, this was an over-harsh judgment of the legislative record of these years, inspired no doubt in part by a desire to advance the cause of responsible government.

As director of the day-to-day administrative activities of the territorial government, Edgar Dewdney seems to have discharged his duties in a manner which gave general satisfaction. The *Saskatchewan Herald*, the least biased if not the most influential paper of the Territories, stated in 1886 that the Governor's administration of schools and public works had been above criticism.[159] J. H. Ross, who advocated control of federal funds by the Council, admitted that Dewdney had done his best to spend the money in an acceptable manner.[160] His practice of consulting the members in connection with the spending of federal funds for public works in their districts gave general satisfaction, and he took an interest in the development of the educational system.[161] The extent to which he consulted the Council in preparing the estimates submitted to the Department of the Interior is not apparent, but the steady yearly increase during the last half of his term indicates that he was not unmindful of the more pressing requirements of the Territories.

One measure of Dewdney's industry and administrative capacity is provided by his tenure of the two offices of Governor and Indian Commissioner. Though some of his decisions as the chief representative in the Territories of the Indian Affairs Department were criticized, no major charges of maladministration were brought against him; though recent scholarships has dealt severely with some of the policies devised at Ottawa during this period, Dewdney has escaped cen-

[158]*Council Journals*, 1887, p. 72.
[159]Editorial of Oct. 11, 1886.
[160]*Regina Leader*, April 6, 1886. In 1886 and 1887 the papers reported some sentiment in favour of a second term for Dewdney. The Dewdney Papers (Trail) contain numerous petitions to the federal government in 1887, from groups in various parts of the Territories, asking for his reappointment; there is also a letter dated Nov. 9, 1886, to the Prime Minister, to the same effect, signed by eight of the fourteen elected members of the Council.
[161]See Dewdney to Minister of the Interior, June 10, 1886, Interior file no. 118859, supporting a proposal to establish a combined high school and teacher training school at Regina.

sure.[162] It was undoubtedly a mistake, however, to continue the union of the two offices so long. "The [Indian] work is incessant and increasing," he wrote to Macdonald in 1885, "and with the North-West Government business, which is also rapidly on the increase, requires my constant attention to keep the run of things—so much so that it is impossible for me to visit the Indians as much as I ought."[163] Though the Prime Minister agreed that the time had probably arrived to make a change,[164] nothing was done about it until 1888.

Dewdney's contribution to the government of the Territories can best be understood if we remember that he belonged to that school of competent, forceful, shrewd men who played such an important part in the political and business life of Canada during the formative years of the Dominion. Unlike Morris, who brought to the office a generous sympathy for western aspirations and an intense awareness of the dynamic character of prairie development, Dewdney saw only a series of administrative duties, which he discharged with a cold efficiency coupled with an astute regard for the advancement of the Conservative party.[165] Like many others in the public life of the day, his ideas and ideals were cribbed in a loyalty to the person and cause of Sir John A. Macdonald. He was more than half serious when, writing to the chief about the qualifications of voters in the first federal elections in the North-West, he remarked, "A man who lives in a tepee should not be considered a householder unless he is a Conservative";[166] and his advice to Perley on the same occasion was equally self-revealing: "I have told him," he reported to Macdonald, "that he must put himself straight with the Party and have no half measures or he will be left."[167] From the point of view of the federal government, on the other hand, Dewdney's tenure of office represented the realization of the ideal in federal-territorial relations—a man of "prudence and firmness"[168] working in close concert with Ottawa. Macdonald and his colleagues had every reason to be satisfied with Dewdney's discharge of his function as "a paternal despot . . . governed by instructions from Head Quarters."

162See G. F. G. Stanley, op. cit., chaps. XI and XIII.
163Dewdney to Macdonald, private, Aug. 7, 1885, Macdonald Papers. See also his letter to Macdonald of Jan. 10, 1888, ibid.
164Macdonald to Dewdney, private, Aug. 17, 1885.
165See for example his policy for distributing relief to the métis: Dewdney to Macdonald, private, Oct. 26, 1886, Macdonald Papers. The shrewdest contemporary estimate of Dewdney's character is contained in an editorial in the Regina Journal, May 31, 1888, "Dewdney as Minister of the Interior."
166Dewdney to Macdonald, private, Nov. 4, 1886, Macdonald Papers.
167Dewdney to Macdonald, Dec. 21, 1886, ibid.
168Macdonald to Dewdney, confidential, Sept. 1, 1886, ibid.

CHAPTER SIX

The Establishment of the Legislative Assembly

1888

DISCUSSION OF THE FUTURE form of government for the North-West entered a new phase with the beginning of 1887. Hitherto none of the various proposals had had any chance of being adopted, and while there was much talk of responsible government, the particular form or constitutional structure within which this principle would operate had not been given very much attention. As we have seen, there had always been advocates of provincial status; some of these favoured one government for the three provisional districts with a possible division of the province at a later stage—in other words, a "provisional province"; some proposed that the districts be forthwith established as provinces. There were others who favoured some halfway house to full provincehood, such as a continuance of territorial status with an improved constitution. Since all of these proposals were at times referred to as "responsible government," it is not always possible to determine which one was being advocated at any given time, or which one was gaining in popularity.

That no one plan had gained general acceptance was illustrated by the views of the candidates who ran in the 1887 federal general election. Two of the Liberal candidates (J. H. Ross in Western Assiniboia and David Laird[1] in Saskatchewan) favoured "a constitution similar to that of Manitoba and Ontario."[2] Lafferty, the Liberal candidate

[1]According to reports in the *Saskatchewan Herald* and the *Prince Albert Times*, Laird had been induced by the Liberals of Prince Albert to come west and contest the election; the Liberals at Battleford claimed that they had not been consulted in the matter, and it is apparent that Laird's campaign proceeded under severe handicaps—both of the papers were hostile, and his non-resident status counted heavily against him.

[2]See Ross's speech as reported in the *Regina Journal*, Feb. 17, 1887, and Laird's platform published in the same paper on Feb. 3. The *Regina Journal* was founded in 1886 to promote the cause of the Liberal party in the Territories. It never became as large or influential a paper as the *Leader*.

in Alberta, merely proposed "that some more representative and extensive form of government be devised."[3] Davin, the Conservative candidate in Western Assiniboia, favoured "an elective chamber and full responsible government,"[4] presumably without full provincial powers—a proposal which was also endorsed by both the Liberal and Conservative candidates in Eastern Assiniboia.[5] Davis, the Conservative standard bearer in Alberta, promised to support all efforts "in the direction of granting a complete system of self-government to the Territories."[6] Macdowall, Laird's opponent in Saskatchewan, pronounced in favour of "the formation of a Legislative Assembly for the Territories in which Saskatchewan shall have full and proper representation."[7] The Territories elected four Conservative members. The fact that the advocates of provincial status (Ross and Laird) were defeated had little significance, however, since the constitution of the North-West was not the sole or dominant issue in the contests. Nevertheless before the year was out it became fairly clear that most people who took an interest in the problem did not favour immediate provincehood.

The next development in the discussion took place when Davin, now the member for Western Assiniboia, introduced a bill providing for a legislative assembly of twenty-four members, elected for a four-year term, and an executive council. It was, in effect, a proposal for provincial status.[8] Apparently it was introduced without prior consultation with the other territorial members,[9] for Macdowall later proposed a different measure. Meanwhile there was a reaction in the territorial capital where a public meeting had been called to consider various measures then pending in Parliament. Davin's bill was discussed, but it was apparent that its supporters were in the minority. The majority view was reported in the press in the following terms:

That the expense of a Provincial Government would be too great to be borne by the small population at present in the Territories.

That as a Province we would be compelled to bear the expense of the administration of justice, supporting the Mounted Police, etc., that we could not expect a sufficient increase in subsidy to do this, and direct taxation would result.

[3]*Macleod Gazette*, March 8, 1887.
[4]*Regina Leader*, Jan. 4, 1887. See also editorials of Sept. 28 and Oct. 19, 1886.
[5]See *Regina Journal*, Feb. 3, 1887, and *Qu'Appelle Progress*, Feb. 10, 1887.
[6]*Macleod Gazette*, Feb. 15, 1887.
[7]*Prince Albert Times*, Feb. 4, 1887. The *Times* commented in the same issue: "If Assiniboia is allowed to outvote Alberta and Saskatchewan in the first Assembly it will continue to do so."
[8]See *Regina Leader*, May 3, 1887.
[9]See Perley's remarks as reported in the *Qu'Appelle Progress*, Aug. 18, 1887.

That if the whole of the Territories were united into one Province there would be difficulties in subdividing it into smaller Provinces, as would be necessary as the country developed.

That with the present system the people elected the majority of the Lieut. Governor's advisers, and that the Lt. Gov. was responsible to the Dominion Parliament where the Territories were represented.[10]

A resolution was then passed stating "that the time has not arrived for introducing a Provincial form of Government into the Territories." This expression of opinion sealed the fate of Davin's measure, although even without this setback there was little likelihood of it being passed, since the government regarded it as premature.[11]

Davin was not the only North-West member bent on making a name for himself as a constitution maker. Later in the session Macdowall introduced a bill of more modest character which proposed to divide the Territories into nineteen electoral districts for purposes of representation in the Council. The members were to be elected for a three-year term and the number of appointed members reduced from six to four. Apparently he did not intend to change the powers or functions of the Council, but was thinking of a scheme which would be a temporary improvement and give time for further consideration of a more comprehensive change.[12] The government regarded this bill with some favour, but due to the pressure of other business it was decided that it could not be adequately discussed during the 1887 session. The Prime Minister, however, promised to introduce a measure the following year and, pending this development, proposed that those members whose terms were due to expire should be continued in office until 1888.[13]

When the Council assembled for its last session in the autumn of 1887 it was clear that the federal government was not in favour of provincial status for the North-West. "I have been requested to confer with you," Dewdney told the members in his opening speech, "as it was thought from your knowledge of the wishes of the people and the requirements of the Country, that you could suggest some inexpensive form of Government, which would give the people a greater control over the management of their affairs and, by subdividing the whole of the Territories into Electoral Districts, would enable every Settler to have a voice in the Government of his Country."[14] A committee

---

[10]*Regina Journal*, May 19, 1887.

[11]See report of the proceedings of the committee of the North-West Council in the *Regina Leader*, Nov. 22, 1887.

[12]*Commons Debates*, 1887, p. 925.

[13]*Ibid.*, p. 1075. The Act was 50–1 Vict., c. 29.

[14]*Council Journals*, 1887, p. 7.

consisting of all the elected members and Hayter Reed, one of the appointed members, was formed to deal with the question.[15] Its deliberations do not seem to have been very lengthy or controversial, probably because most of the ground had been covered in executive session the previous year, and also because there was no sharp conflict of opinion.[16] Davin, who was present at one of the meetings, was questioned on his bill, and he reported on the attitude of the government and of the other North-West members of Parliament. After the report of the committee had been submitted and during the last stages of the discussion there was a flurry over the number of seats in the new legislature; the number recommended the previous year (24) had again been adopted, but a new member, F. W. G. Haultain (who had just been elected for the Macleod district),[17] proposed that an additional seat be added to give representation to the Lethbridge area. Since this reopened the delicate question of the balance between the provisional districts there was some sharp debate, but in the end Haultain's amendment carried and the total proposed membership was raised to twenty-five.[18]

The recommendations as approved for submission to the federal government proposed that the Council be made a purely elective body consisting in the first instance of twenty-five members chosen for a four-year term and presided over by one of their number. The franchise was to be widened by abolishing the householder qualification and reducing the term of residence to six months. The recommendation concerning the executive was set forth in the following terms:

That the Lieutenant-Governor carry on his executive functions by and with the advice of an Executive Council of three, who shall be from time to time chosen and summoned by the Lieutenant-Governor and sworn in as Privy Councillors, and who shall hold seats in the North-West Council.[19]

Measures were suggested to give the Council full control over all public funds; the existing method, it was asserted, was one which "excludes the people of the country from any control in their disposal." The object sought was control of the federal funds, since there was no difficulty over local revenues.[20] A schedule outlining the boundaries

[15]Ibid., p. 45.
[16]See report of the committee's deliberations in the Regina Leader, Nov. 15 and 22, 1887.
[17]The member for Macleod, Viscount Boyle, had resigned during the summer and an election had been held in September to fill the vacancy.
[18]Regina Journal, Nov. 24, 1887.
[19]Council Journals, 1887, p. 73.
[20]To achieve this object it was recommended that the provisions of the British North America Act relating to appropriation and tax bills and the recommenda-

of nineteen one-member and three two-member electoral divisions was adopted, giving Assiniboia thirteen members, Alberta eight, and Saskatchewan four. Finally, it was recommended that the Council be given authority to amend its constitution, presumably a more limited power than that of amending the constitution of the territorial government as a whole. Not included in this submission, but recommended for incorporation in any federal legislation dealing with the constitution, were proposals for the use of the ballot in territorial elections and the granting of power to legislate on the liquor question.[21]

In considering the significance of these proposals it should be noted in the first place that they did not involve any novelties—the main principles had been endorsed in previous years, and consequently could be regarded as representing the considered judgment of the Council.[22] In the second place, it was apparent that an attempt was being made to arrive at some acceptable form of government short of provincehood, or, as the Governor had suggested, "some inexpensive form of Government." This was clear from the use of the name "Council" instead of "Legislative Assembly," and from the absence of any demand for full provincial powers or for any financial settlement. Thirdly, while proposing something short of provincial status, there was an unequivocal demand for the establishment of a cabinet or executive council operating under the principles of responsible government—this being stated not only in the paragraph quoted above, but also in the declaration that the existing system of introducing legislation was unsatisfactory. Moreover, the discussions in the committee were very clear on this point: there was complete agreement on the necessity of having ministers, the only difference of opinion was over the number. The decision was reported as follows: "Dr. Wilson moved that the first Government consist of three Ministers, which being seconded by Mr. Bedford was carried."[23] All in all, these proposals represented a reasonable and practical elaboration of the territorial constitution, based on the admission that provincehood was premature both in the nature of things and because of recent expressions of opinion on the subject.[24] Yet to have asked anything

tion of money votes (sections 53 and 54) be made applicable to the North-West Council. But since the object was to secure control of the federal funds this proposed remedy was insufficient, as later events were to prove.

[21]*Ibid.*, pp. 42, 68.

[22]The *Regina Journal* (Nov. 24, 1887) reported that the recommendations were the same as those made during the previous session.

[23]*Regina Leader*, Nov. 22, 1887.

[24]*Saskatchewan Herald*, June 18, 1887 and *Prince Albert Times*, April 13 and June 10, 1887.

less would have been a betrayal of five years of agitation for increased autonomy. It was not mere rhetoric when the editor of the *Regina Journal* wrote: "The North-West is being settled by a liberty-loving people, educated in self-government, who will be satisfied with nothing short of an administration responsible to the people in the fullest sense of the word. And if any makeshift is given, it will invite agitation and lead to an early struggle for the rights and privileges enjoyed by the Provinces."[25]

II

A critical juncture had now been reached in the affairs of the Territories. The representatives of the people had spoken, and the next step was up to the federal government. But there was another influence emanating from the North-West: though he had no constructive proposals to offer, Dewdney consistently belittled the autonomy movement. "There is no doubt in my mind," he had written Macdonald following the session of the previous year, "that the majority of the Council do not expect at once representative Government, but they think the time has arrived to make a move for it, especially as eight of them have to go back to their Constituents this year."[26] Every expression of opinion hostile to the movement was diligently reported to the Prime Minister.[27] And the tactics of the elected members at the 1887 session displeased him: "They objected to the nominated members being in the committee," he wrote Macdonald.[28] The latter, he declared, "had better opportunities of knowing the feeling of the people than any others in the Territories." "They [the elected members] appeared to be afraid of too much ventilation of the subject. . . . They don't want to tax themselves in any way but think that you should give them plenty of money to divide up among themselves." Not content with private representations, he went to the length of using his official annual report to the Minister of the Interior to oppose the Council's recommendations:

During the sitting of the Council a memorial was adopted [he wrote] recommending that a purely representative form of government take the place of our present Council. I think it my duty to inform you that my information from the several scattered centres of population in the Ter-

25*Regina Journal*, Nov. 10, 1887.
26Dewdney to Macdonald, private, Nov. 22, 1886, Macdonald Papers.
27Dewdney to Macdonald, private, April 7, 1887; telegram, May 19, 1887, *ibid.*
28Dewdney to Macdonald, private, Nov. 20, 1887, *ibid.*

ritories does not indicate that such is the general feeling of the people. A strong fear is expressed that the establishment of a purely representative form of government will lead to direct taxation, and thus impose on the settlers burdens which they are at present unable to bear.[29]

All this was calculated to reinforce the government's temporizing and conservative approach to the constitutional progress of the North-West. It is hardly surprising, therefore, to find Macdonald announcing, when the legislation was introduced the following spring, that "the object of the Government has been to alter the original Act as little as possible." The measure, he declared, "is not intended to be in any way a perfect constitution. It cannot by any possibility be so." Moreover, he reiterated the proposition that "the true theory . . . of the territorial system both here and in the United States, is that Government proceeds from here."[30]

The bill[31] which was introduced with these rather disparaging comments was a typical example of the makeshift legislation which had plagued the Territories since the Temporary Government Act of 1869. It provided for an Assembly having the same legislative powers as its predecessor. It was to be composed of twenty-two elected members and three "legal experts" appointed by the federal government from among the territorial judges. The elected membership was three less than that recommended by the Council, and the proportions from the three provisional districts differed. There were to be sixteen one-member and three two-member constituencies: eleven members for Assiniboia, six for Alberta, and five for Saskatchewan; as compared with the Council scheme this meant a reduction of two each for Assiniboia and Alberta and an increase of one for Saskatchewan. The boundaries of the electoral divisions, however, were in many cases the same or substantially the same as those suggested by the Council. The Assembly was to be presided over by a Speaker, and its relations with the Lieutenant-Governor in respect to legislative activity were to be the same as those of a provincial house.[32] The term of the Assembly was fixed at three years, and the Lieutenant-Governor could not dissolve

[29]*Annual Report of the Department of the Interior*, 1887; report dated Dec. 31, 1887.
[30]*Commons Debates*, 1888, pp. 1474 and 1477.
[31]51 Vict., c. 19.
[32]For some reason the Governor was not empowered to withhold assent to bills—he could only assent to them or reserve them for the assent of the Governor General; see *ibid.*, s. 4. A situation involving this point arose in 1895: see *Correspondence, Reports of the Ministers of Justice and Orders in Council upon the Subject of Dominion and Provincial Legislation, 1867–1895* (Ottawa, 1896), pp. 1276–9, and *Assembly Journals*, 1896, pp. 94–5.

it before that time. The sessional indemnity, like that of members of the old Council, was to be paid out of the consolidated revenue fund of Canada, and was fixed at $500—an increase of $100 over that received by the councillors. The Council's recommendation for the franchise was accepted in part: the property qualification was eliminated, but the voter was to be a resident of the Territories for twelve months and of the electoral district for three months. Manhood suffrage had by this time been adopted in Prince Edward Island, Ontario, Manitoba, and British Columbia, so its adoption in the Territories was not a novel principle.[33] There was no residence qualification for candidates, but a hundred dollar deposit was required (no deposit had been required in North-West Council elections). Macdonald refused to assume the responsibility for introducing the ballot—the Assembly could do so if it wished,[34] but the government contended that the vast area and scattered population would make it too expensive. Open voting would not involve abuses, Macdonald claimed, since there would be no "government" to intimidate the electorate.[35]

The curious feature of having three judges as members of a Legislative Assembly (they did not have the right to vote) was to save the expense of appointing a law clerk; a suitable person to draft bills could not be secured, Macdonald argued, without offering a very large salary.[36] It was to be a temporary measure, he stated, to make up for the anticipated dearth of lawyer members, a condition which he hoped would be corrected by the time of the second term of the Assembly.[37] It was planned that the three judges who had been members of the Council—Richardson, Rouleau, and Macleod—would be asked to serve in this capacity.

Up to this point the Act of 1888 was, with some modifications in detail, a reasonably accurate reflection of the views of the North-West Council. Its provisions respecting the executive, however, deviated sharply from what had been recommended. There was no provision for an executive council; and when questioned by the opposition on this omission Macdonald declared that the Assembly would "have the

[33]*Regina Journal*, April 26, 1888; *Canadian Gazette* (London), May 24, 1888.
[34]The North-West Council possessed the power to introduce the ballot under s. 2 of section 13 of the North-West Territories Act, 1875.
[35]*Commons Debates*, 1888, p. 1474. The Liberals moved an amendment to introduce the ballot but it was defeated, *ibid.*, p. 1481. Perley was the only North-West member who voted with the Liberals.
[36]The legal experts received a sessional indemnity of $250.
[37]*Commons Debates*, 1888, p. 454. It is probable that this provision of the Act was suggested by N. F. Davin; he had proposed just such a measure in an editorial of Oct. 19, 1886, in the *Regina Leader*.

same administrative as well as legislative powers which they had when under the name of the council."[38] How this extraordinary arrangement was to operate with an Assembly sitting separately from the Lieutenant-Governor was not explained, and it appears that the problem of executive authority had been completely ignored in the drafting of the bill. At this juncture Davin stepped into the breach with a proposal for an executive council of not more than three members, but Macdonald refused to consider it;[39] instead, he produced a new clause creating an "advisory council in matters of finance," whose status was defined as follows:

The Lieutenant-Governor shall select from among the elected members of the Legislative Assembly four persons to act as an advisory council on matters of finance, who shall severally hold office during pleasure; and the Lieutenant-Governor shall preside at all sittings of such advisory council and have a right to vote as a member thereof, and shall also have a casting vote in case of a tie.[40]

The difference between this body and the one proposed by Davin was that its authority did not cover the whole field of local administration; since the idea of having the Assembly exercise executive powers was dropped,[41] this meant investing the Lieutenant-Governor with an even wider jurisdiction than he already had. The function of the Advisory Council was made clear by the Prime Minister during the course of the debate. Its authority was to be confined to the management of the general revenue fund of the Territories (local revenues); to this extent only was there to be responsible government.[42]

[38]*Commons Debates*, 1888, p. 455.

[39]The bill had been given first reading on March 27; on May 8 the *Regina Leader* carried the announcement of Davin's proposal for an executive council; the government's reaction was described by Davin some years later in a speech in the House of Commons: *Commons Debates*, 1897, cols. 4116–18. Dewdney's reaction was typical: "I notice in the papers Davin's proposition for three Executive Advisers to be appointed by the Lieutenant-Governor. I am sure this would not work. . . . Any privileges not shared in by the whole Body would I am sure lead to jealousies": Dewdney to Macdonald, private, May 7, 1888, Macdonald Papers. Dewdney's comment applied with equal force to the Advisory Council which Macdonald created.

[40]51 Vict., c. 19, s. 13. This clause was introduced on May 16 when the bill was being considered in committee: see *Commons Debates*, 1888, pp. 1474 ff.

[41]Royal, Dewdney's successor, raised the question of executive sessions during a visit to Ottawa in September 1888, before the first session of the Assembly, and was told that he was "not to call any executive meetings of the Legislature." The government also considered amending section 2 of the Act to make it clear that the Assembly was to have no executive powers. See Macdonald to Dewdney (Minister of the Interior), Sept. 24, 1888, Macdonald Papers.

[42]*Commons Debates*, 1888, pp. 1474; 1483.

That "matters of finance" did not include the federal fund then being administered by the Lieutenant-Governor was clearly indicated in the following exchange with a member of the opposition:

Sir John A. Macdonald. . . . The revenues that are at the disposal of the Council, and will be at the disposal of the Legislature, are very small. . . . The expenditure for the opening of that country [the parliamentary appropriation for the North-West government] is guided here. It does not come within the purview or control of a Local Government or Legislature any more than in any votes here it would come within the control of a Provincial Legislature. . . .

Sir Richard Cartwright. What I meant to have inquired was, as these people have, as it appears to me, very small funds of their own, does the hon. gentleman intend to allow them to dispose of all or a considerable part of this vote of $140,000 [the sum in the estimates for 1888–9], or is he going to supervise that, as we are the parties who furnish the money?

Sir John A. Macdonald. Of course the vote is here and the responsibility is here, and that money will be appropriated on the responsibility of the general Government.

Sir Richard Cartwright. This Local Legislature, as I understand it, will not receive a lump sum to divide at their pleasure?

Sir John A. Macdonald. No. . . .[43]

The government's failure to grapple with the problem of executive authority was brought to the attention of the House by David Mills and Wilfrid Laurier. "The power of legislation and administration," Mills pointed out, "should go hand in hand. If the community are entitled . . . . . to complete legislative control over those matters which are exclusively assigned to them, they should have equally independent control over the executive and administrative affairs of the Territory, within the same limits." The absence of such control "would be simply Downing street over again."[44] Macdonald's defence was that the principle of a responsible executive had not been embodied in Mackenzie's Act of 1875 and that there was "a most holy horror of responsible government" in the North-West.[45] Moreover, he asserted that so long as considerable assistance from the federal government was required, "responsible government in its accepted sphere would be premature." He was supported in his stand by two of the North-West members, Macdowall and Perley. The people of Saskatchewan, Macdowall claimed, "are afraid that, with a small representation in the Council [Assembly] and with their large area, they may be taxed, and that other districts of the North-West may receive the benefit of

43*Ibid.*, p. 1476.
44*Ibid.*, p. 455.
45*Ibid.*

that taxation in a greater degree than they themselves would."[46] He hoped that in three years' time there would be sufficient development to justify a change. Perley sounded the same note: "If this Parliament will grant us a sufficient sum of money so that we shall not have to resort to direct taxation, of course we will accept responsible government. But I believe the present system, with some slight amendments, is the system that will suit the great majority of the people up there best."[47]

It will be seen that of the three main constitutional reforms sought by the North-West Council—complete representation in the legislature, an executive council, and control of the parliamentary appropriation—only the first was conceded by the North-West Territories Act of 1888. Macdonald justified his rejection of the Council's representations on the ground that they did not represent "the feelings of the people,"[48] and that it would be better to leave it to the Assembly "to suggest such amendments or improvements in the system as their experience may dictate."[49] This was simply special pleading designed to postpone the transfer of power as long as possible. It is true that there was a body of opinion in the West which assumed that a responsible executive involved an elaborate and costly administrative structure, and in Saskatchewan there was opposition to the reform on sectional grounds. But on the other hand the Council's advice had been specially solicited because of its admitted "knowledge of the wishes of the people and the requirements of the Country," and its memorial represented the views of men who had been operating the existing system and who therefore had the most accurate knowledge of the improvements which were necessary. Moreover, deference to the wishes of the Assembly was little more than a rhetorical gesture: the events of the next few years were to demonstrate that the administration was as reluctant to listen to the Assembly as it was to the Council. Above all, it was the responsibility of the government to devise a workable system however limited in its powers, and this was not provided by the section of the Act dealing with the territorial executive. ✓

The contribution of the North-West members to the Act of 1888 was not particularly impressive. They could not agree in the matter of

---

[46]*Ibid.*, p. 1478. See also petition from Prince Albert "praying that the North-West Council be continued, with enlarged powers and equitable representation; and that Responsible Government be not granted to the Territories": *Journals of the House of Commons*, 1888, p. 158. Editorials in the *Prince Albert Times* of Jan. 20, Feb. 3, and March 16, 1888 took the same line.
[47]*Commons Debates*, 1888, p. 1478.
[48]*Ibid.*, p. 1174.
[49]*Ibid.*, p. 1474.

the executive council or the ballot. Whether the compromise of a three-year term for the Assembly was suggested by them is not apparent.[50] The provision for legal experts was probably suggested by Davin, and the change in the number and distribution of the electoral districts was a victory for Macdowall. During the debate Perley made a plea for local control of the parliamentary appropriation, but this elicited no definite response from the government.[51] Davin, piqued at the rejection of his proposal for an executive council, made no comment on the bill at all during the debate, though he had no use for the proposed Advisory Council, which he regarded as "a mere toy."[52]

In regard to the general financial relationship of the Dominion to the North-West, Macdonald dismissed as premature a suggestion from the opposition that the Territories be given a per capita grant from the federal treasury similar to the provincial subsidies.[53] Another substantial increase, however, was made in the parliamentary appropriation—from $96,707.29 to $142,889.10 for 1888-9. This of course heightened the contrast between the funds at the disposal of the local legislature and those controlled by the Governor, since for the current year (1887-8) local revenues amounted to only $16,530.80.[54]

III

The people of the North-West, insofar as their attitude was reflected in the editorial columns of the Territorial papers and in the discussions during the general election, were reserving judgment of the new system until it had been observed in operation.[55] At the same time, the

[50]Macdonald argued that the three-year term was preferable because of the expected influx of population, *ibid.*, pp. 1473-4. The supporters of the four-year term felt that more frequent elections involved too much expense.

[51]*Ibid.*, p. 1478. Later Perley asked, "Will the advisory board consult with the Lieutenant-Governor as to the expenditure of money?" and Macdonald replied, "In all matters of finance" (*ibid.*, p. 1489); however, it is clear from his comments elsewhere in the debate that this did not include control of federal funds, though he appeared to approve Dewdney's practice of unofficial consultations: see *ibid.*, p. 1611.

[52]See *Commons Debates*, 1897, cols. 4116-18.

[53]The suggestion was made by Mills: *ibid.*, 1888, pp. 1174-5.

[54]*Public Accounts of the North-West Territories*, 1887-8.

[55]The campaign in most of the districts was concerned with such issues as liquor administration, previous record of the member, and rivalries between communities. The *Regina Journal* (July 5, 1888), however, expressed its gratification at the number of members who had stood for responsible government. Both the successful candidates in Edmonton, Oliver and Wilson, emphasized responsible government in their campaigns: see William S. Waddell, "The Honourable Frank Oliver," M.A. Thesis, University of Alberta, 1950, pp. 161-2. Federal political loyalties affected the result in some cases: see Dewdney to Macdonald, May 21, 1888, Macdonald Papers.

position taken by some influential journals indicated that the movement for responsible government was not to be discounted. The new Governor, the *Regina Leader* stated, "can under this bill introduce a very liberal system of government or he can fall back on the old personal government." Referring to the Advisory Council, the editorial continued: "It is perfectly clear such a Council dealing absolutely with the moneys over which they will exercise control must have the confidence of the Legislative Assembly. . . . Here we have the germ of responsible government and party organization, that is if the Governor should be in favor of ushering in responsible government."[56] Oliver of the *Edmonton Bulletin* viewed the situation in terms of the classical struggle; responsible government would be secured not as a boon conferred by the Governor, but by being grasped by a determined Assembly. The Advisory Council, he wrote, "although nominally advisory is really executive, and if it does not give responsible government in name, provides the means by which responsibility in government may be secured." The existence of the Council, he continued, "places the control of Territorial finance, which is the key to the situation, in the hands of the people's representatives, and all that remains for them is to push that control to its proper conclusion."[57] And the editor of the *Qu'Appelle Progress* wrote: "As did the old Council so must the new Legislature press upon the Dominion authorities from time to time for increased powers."[58]

Even more significant were some of the remarks of the young lawyer from Macleod, F. W. G. Haultain, who had made his mark during the last session of the Council and was elected to the Assembly by acclamation. As reported in the local press they ran as follows:

The first question that Mr. Haultain referred to was that of self-government, and he literally wiped the floor with the Ottawa authorities over their new North-West Bill. He said that we had been dealt with like a parcel of political children. For three years the old council had sent memorials to the government demanding self-government, and each time the memorial had been acknowledged in the usual way of politicians or statesmen. It was now necessary to unite, and express a strong opinion in that direction, not only through representatives, but by meetings all over the country. . . . We had asked for bread, and they had given us a stone; we had asked for a legislative assembly, and they had given us the shadow of self-government.[59]

[56]*Regina Leader*, July 3, 1888.

[57]*Edmonton Bulletin*, June 2, 1888. The *Regina Journal* took a similar stand: see editorial of June 21, 1888.

[58]*Qu'Appelle Progress*, June 21, 1888.

[59]Extract from speech reported by the *Macleod Gazette* and reprinted in the *Regina Journal*, July 5, 1888.

Obviously a new voice was being raised in the cause of responsible government—one which was destined to resound throughout the modest chamber of the territorial legislature for the next nine years, until the object so long sought was at last achieved.

Dewdney's term as Lieutenant-Governor had expired in December 1886, but the government, though unwilling on principle to grant him a second term,[60] had found it convenient to continue him in office for another year and a half. It was particularly useful to have him on hand to help the Conservative cause in the federal election of 1887,[61] and, when that was over, it was thought desirable that he should preside over the last meeting of the Council in the fall and look after the elections for the new Assembly in the following spring. His successor, Joseph Royal, did not assume office until July 4, 1888.

The selection of Royal was designed to help allay the discontent in Quebec which had been fanned to fever heat following the execution of Riel and which had resulted in severe losses for the Conservatives in the general election of 1887 and the defeat of the Quebec Conservative government later in the year.[62] Royal, a native of Quebec, had been the spokesman of the métis and French Canadians of Manitoba since 1871 when he founded the *Métis* in St. Boniface. Already well known in Montreal as a writer, publisher, and lawyer, his energy and talents soon brought him to a position of prominence in his adopted province. He became the first Speaker in the Legislative Assembly and the first Superintendent of Education. From 1872 to 1879 he held various portfolios in Manitoba cabinets as leader of the French bloc and was active in supporting the province's demand for increased financial assistance from Ottawa and for extension of the boundaries to Lake Superior and Hudson Bay. From 1879 to 1888 Royal sat in the House of Commons, and during much of this period was the most energetic of the Manitoba members. His connections were mainly with that province, but he had been a member of the first North-West Council, and during his years in Parliament interested himself in a number of issues affecting the Territories. Though adept and pertinacious in securing patronage for his French-speaking compatriots,[63] his interests were not narrowly racial.

[60]Macdonald to Dewdney, confidential, Sept. 1, 1886, Macdonald Papers.

[61]Dewdney made the arrangements for Conservative nominations under instructions from Macdonald. "We must carry the N.W.T.," the latter wrote. "Will you address yourself to this with all your astuteness": Macdonald to Dewdney, private and confidential, Oct. 19, 1886, Dewdney Papers (Trail).

[62]"Great pressure is brought to bear here for the appointment of a French successor to yourself. Girard and Royal both spoken of": Macdonald to Dewdney, private, April 5, 1887, Dewdney Papers (Trail).

[63]See his correspondence with Macdonald in the Macdonald Papers.

Rumours that Royal was being considered for the post of Lieutenant-Governor were current for some months before the appointment was announced,[64] and aroused a considerable volume of adverse
comment in the territorial press, much of it motivated by prejudice
against French Canadians.[65] Once the appointment was announced
a number of editorials appeared commenting favourably on Royal's
personal qualities, but the undercurrent of hostility was still present,
and there is no doubt that the new Governor's first approach to territorial administration was designed to overcome this handicap and
establish himself in popular esteem.

For a time it seemed as if Edgar Dewdney's connection with the
Territories would be severed with the ending of his term as Governor.
But the able and popular Minister of the Interior, Thomas White,
died suddenly in the spring of 1888, and Dewdney was selected as his
successor. The convenience of having the Territories represented in
the Senate now became apparent, for Perley was appointed to that
body and Dewdney secured his seat—Assiniboia East. In contrast to
Royal's appointment, the selection of Dewdney for this post was a
popular one. Representation in the cabinet was another territorial
aspiration of long standing, and in addition Dewdney's capacities as
an administrator were held in considerable esteem. But his attitude to
constitutional reform did not augur well for progress in this field.

[64]This rumour was circulating in Regina as early as Jan. 1886, but Royal did
not ask Macdonald for the appointment until Sept.: see Thomas White to Macdonald, private, Jan. 21, 1886, and Royal to Macdonald, private, Sept. 14, 1886,
Macdonald Papers.

[65]See also Perley's remarks, Senate Debates, 1890, p. 631. Dewdney shared the
prevailing prejudice: "I shall be very sorry to see a Frenchman here and it will
create a very bad feeling. . . . If a Frenchman is to come here the sooner a Legislative Assembly is created the better and the Indian Office should be separated
from the Lieutenant-Governor": Dewdney to Macdonald, confidential, April 11,
1887, Macdonald Papers. It was a curious argument for constitutional liberties,
but entirely typical of Dewdney's approach to the subject.

CHAPTER SEVEN

The Advisory Council and Governor Royal

1888-91

THE ACT establishing the Legislative Assembly came into force on May 22, 1888, and the elections were held in the latter part of June. On July 4 Royal took the oath of office in Regina. One of his first official acts was to appoint a commission consisting of Judge Richardson and A. E. Forget to prepare a consolidation of the ordinances (the first to be undertaken), so that the members of the Assembly would be able to know "the exact condition of the legislation of the country upon the inauguration of the new constitution."[1] On October 23 the three legal experts—Judges Richardson, Macleod, and Rouleau— were appointed, and on the thirty-first the first session of the first Legislative Assembly of the North-West Territories was opened with all due formality.

Royal's opening speech contained a reference to the constitutional situation which set the tone for the proceedings of this first session: "In the progressive evolution of our present constitution towards thoroughly representative government," he remarked, "you will find that I am in full accord with your legitimate aspirations."[2] The next day he matched his words with action by calling an informal meeting of the members to secure nominations for the Advisory Council.[3] As

[1]Royal to Macdonald, private, July 9, 1888, Macdonald Papers; see also Attorney General's files G 549 and G 915. Royal had been responsible for the consideration of the Manitoba Statutes in 1877.

[2]*Assembly Journals*, 1888, p. 9.

[3]See Royal to Macdonald, telegram, Nov. 2, 1888, and Macdonald to Royal, private, Nov. 15, 1888, Macdonald Papers. The Prime Minister was dubious about Royal's procedure, but the latter declared, "I wanted my Council to possess beyond a doubt the confidence of their colleagues. . . . Now, I am fully convinced that had I taken a different course the Board of Advisors would have been the object of all sorts and manners of attacks and adverse votes." Royal to Macdonald, private, Dec. 14, 1888, *ibid.*

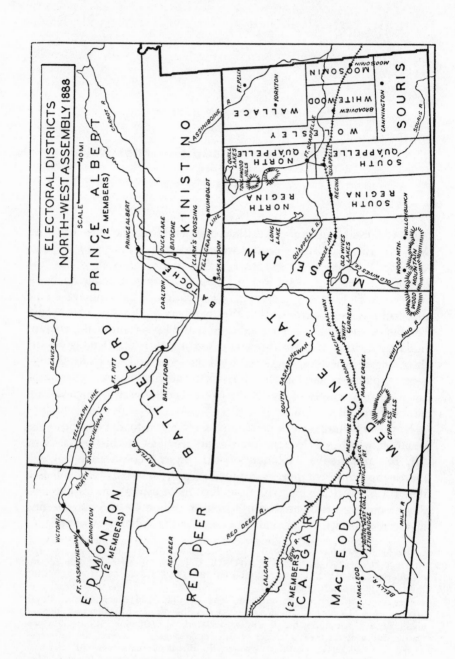

ELECTORAL DISTRICTS
NORTH-WEST ASSEMBLY 1888

SCALE ▬▬ 40 MI

PRINCE ALBERT
(2 MEMBERS)

KINISTINO

BATTLEFORD

EDMONTON
(2 MEMBERS)

RED DEER

CALGARY
(2 MEMBERS)

MACLEOD

MEDICINE HAT

MOOSE JAW

SOUTH REGINA

NORTH REGINA

SOUTH QU'APPELLE

NORTH QU'APPELLE

WOLSELEY

WALLACE

WHITEWOOD

MOOSOMIN

SOURIS

PRINCE ALBERT
DUCK LAKE
BATOCHE
CLARK'S CROSSING
HUMBOLDT
SASKATOON
CARLTON
FT. PITT
BATTLEFORD
FT. SASKATCHEWAN
VICTORIA
EDMONTON
RED DEER
CALGARY
FT. MACLEOD
LETHBRIDGE
MEDICINE HAT
MAPLE CREEK
SWIFT CURRENT
MOOSE JAW
REGINA
FT. QU'APPELLE
YORKTON
FT. PELLY
BROADVIEW
CANNINGTON
MOOSOMIN

CARROT R.
BEAVER R.
NORTH SASKATCHEWAN R.
TELEGRAPH LINE
BATTLE R.
SOUTH SASKATCHEWAN R.
RED DEER R.
BOW R.
BELLY R.
MILK R.
WHITE MUD R.
WOOD MTN.
WILLOW BUNCH
WOOD MOUNTAIN
OLD WIVES CR.
OLD WIVES LAKES
LONG LAKE
QU'APPELLE R.
ASSINIBOINE R.
QUILL LAKES
TOUCHWOOD HILLS
SOURIS R.
CYPRESS HILLS
CANADIAN PACIFIC RAILWAY
NORTH WEST COAL & NAVIGATION CO. RY.
TELEGRAPH LINE

a result of the balloting four were recommended—F. W. G. Haultain (Macleod), D. F. Jelly (North Regina), Wm. Sutherland (North Qu'Appelle), and H. Mitchell (Batoche)—and were forthwith appointed by the Governor.[4] In discussing his action with Macdonald Royal wrote,

I have learned . . . that some members came here fully decided to make an agitation in favor of thorough provincial organization. Our (4) four grit members were particularly ardent upon their cheap platform of making popularity for themselves; some of our own friends were also very much inclined that way. I thought it my duty to yourself whose liberal opinion I have learned to know and admire, as well as to the peace and contentment of the population—to anticipate such a move and to gracefully give at once and of my own free will what might have . . . appeared in time to be extracted from us.[5]

Had Royal recalled the earlier history of the federal government's relations with the Territories he would scarcely have assumed that "to give gracefully" was the Prime Minister's favourite approach to Western agitation.

If the Governor's policy was one of concession, that of the Assembly was from the very start one of vigorous assertion of constitutional rights. "It is our earnest hope and desire," ran the reply to the opening speech, "that our present powers will, before next session, be so far extended as to give us the full measure of responsible Government, which we believe the country desires. Represented as the Territories now are, fully and completely, we feel that any recommendation we may submit on the subject will be favourably entertained by the Dominion Government."[6] Obviously the members proposed to take Macdonald at his word and submit the proposals for further changes which he had promised to implement. Meanwhile, however, they had to grapple with the problem of the exercise of executive authority which had been left in such an unsatisfactory state by Parliament. The commissioners preparing the revised ordinances had already encountered the difficulty that if the Act of 1888 was followed strictly, then all executive authority other than in matters of finance would have to be vested in the Governor alone. But, as Richardson put it, "they decided that the Lieutenant-Governor must have something

---

[4]Lieutenant-Governor's Order no. 994, Nov. 2, 1888; see also *Assembly Journals*, 1888, pp. 12–13.
[5]Royal to Macdonald, private, Nov. 6, 1888, Macdonald Papers.
[6]*Assembly Journals*, 1888, p. 18.

to fall back on—somebody to advise him."[7] They therefore took a first small step in the process of conferring general administrative responsibilities on the Advisory Council: a number of duties which under the old ordinances were performed by the Lieutenant-Governor in Council were to be performed by the Lieutenant-Governor acting "with the advice and consent of the Advisory Council."[8] The Assembly accepted this solution after considerable debate on its legality and expediency.[9] It was apparent, however, that the majority were determined to invest the Advisory Council with as many of the qualities of an executive council as was possible, and, while only a modest beginning was made,[10] it left no doubt that most of the members shared the views of the North-West Council on the form which the territorial executive should take.

The circumstances connected with the preparation of the estimates and the voting of supplies revealed another aspect of Royal's policy and the Assembly's aspirations. During the period of the Council, appropriations from the general revenue fund were made by simple resolutions and no supply bills were introduced.[11] But the new law respecting revenue and expenditure envisaged appropriation by ordinance as the normal procedure, though, failing such appropriation, the Lieutenant-Governor in Council was empowered to draw on it "for any purpose of public utility in the Territories."[12] Royal paved the way for the first supply bill by his announcement in the speech from the throne that the Territorial estimates for the year 1888–9 would be prepared with the assistance of the Advisory Council. However, instead of estimates amounting to some $15,000 or $20,000 (representing the current state of the general revenue fund), those which were submitted for the approval of the Assembly totalled

[7]*Regina Leader*, Nov. 20, 1888. They limited the number of cases in which the Governor was to act with the Council to four: the bonding of civil servants and the appointment of billiard table licence issuers, members of the Board of Education, and the Queen's Printer.

[8]*Revised Ordinances*, 1888, c. 1, s. 8 (6).

[9]A few of the members favoured retaining the power of advice in the Legislative Assembly, i.e. making it to some extent an executive body. Oliver was one of the strongest supporters of the alternative course of vesting executive powers in the Council.

[10]In addition to those mentioned in footnote 7 above, the Lieutenant-Governor in Council was empowered to employ counsel to prosecute infractions of the prairie fire ordinance, to appoint (directly or by delegation) game guardians, to issue ferry licences, to appoint ferry inspectors and a registrar general and district registrars for reporting vital statistics. However, this still left numerous duties to be performed by the Governor alone, as in previous years.

[11]See for example *Council Journals*, 1886, pp. 68–9; cf. Ordinance no. 1 of 1878.

[12]*Revised Ordinances*, 1888, c. 3, s. 4.

$105,484.90.[13] The long-sought concession—control of the federal funds—had seemingly been made, as indeed was apparent from the estimated revenues which were tabled at the same time:[14]

Estimated receipts from local revenues	$ 10,750.35
Balance of the General Revenue Fund on hand Sept. 1, 1888	1,968.86
Balance of Dominion Appropriation on hand Dec. 1, 1888	92,765.69
Total	$105,484.90

The budget speech, delivered by Haultain, threw some light on this momentous development as it was interpreted by the Advisory Council:

The occasion [he is reported as saying] was one of almost historical importance, when for the first time, they had the right of controlling expenditure. When the people had the right of expenditure of money, they had free government, and, although the fact that the Assembly was at present a branch of the Interior Department and that the estimates [for the Dominion grant] were prepared and sent down to the Department by officials of the Government, rendered the position anomalous, still as far as Territorial affairs and—through the courtesy of the Lt. Governor— as far as the expenditure of the funds were concerned, they had a large measure of that responsible government for which they had agitated so long.[15]

It was clear, therefore, that the concession had been made, not by the federal government, but by Royal, and, as it proved, acting on his own initiative. As he described it to Macdonald after the close of the session,

I have had regular meetings of the Council nearly every morning from ten to twelve o'clock during the last four weeks, and it was a serious matter at first to satisfy these gentlemen that they had not an absolute control over all the expenditures of the N.W. Government wether [sic] the money come from the federal or the Territorial source. I have yielded as much as it was in my power to do, and the result I believe has been most satisfactory on the whole.[16]

Obviously in his desire to conciliate territorial opinion Royal had been out-manœuvred, for he had in fact conceded everything, yielding what he had no power to confer—control of the federal funds.

13Assembly Journals, 1888, pp. 99–100.
14Regina Leader, Dec. 11, 1888.
15Ibid. The minutes of the Advisory Council, A.S., contain no records of the discussions on the estimates.
16Royal to Macdonald, private, Dec. 14, 1888, Macdonald Papers.

Neither the minutes of the Advisory Council nor the debates in the Assembly give any information on the process by which the budget was drawn up; despite Royal's assertion a year later, it is apparent that some of the items in the departmental estimates were changed, and Haultain also declared during the debate that Parliament had approved a lump sum which they could divide as they liked.[17] Cayley of Calgary, the leading critic of the budget, pointed out the anomaly of voting funds already appropriated by Parliament on the basis of detailed estimates prepared by the Department of the Interior, while at the same time they were unable to officially advise on the preparation of these estimates for the following year (1889–90).[18] The House, however, accepted the budget as presented, and the Territories' first appropriation ordinance received the Governor's assent at the end of the session.[19]

The Assembly under the leadership of the Advisory Council had gone as far as it could in enforcing its control of local administration, but it was realized that the control was precarious unless it was formally conceded by the federal authorities. To secure this concession a number of submissions to the federal government were approved, in the hope that they would be acted upon at the next session of Parliament. After pointing out that they had been "granted control of all expenditure for the current year," they drew attention to the fact that "the North-West Territories Act does not clearly give the Assembly that control of the moneys voted by the Dominion Government for the expenses of the Government in the Territories, which, in the opinion of this Assembly, they are undoubtedly entitled to." The Parliamentary appropriation, it was asserted, "should be given in the form of a definite grant instead of a rate which lapses at the end of the fiscal year" and "should be placed at the disposal and subject to the vote of the Northwest Legislative Assembly." With respect to the local executive, they deplored the lack of a "permanent responsible body," and requested "full responsible Government."[20] The powers of the Territories should, it was asserted, be extended to include all those possessed by a province with the exception of the power to borrow money, though continued federal control of the public lands seems to have been assumed.[21] These requests were in almost the same terms

[17]*Regina Journal*, Dec. 20, 1888; see also Haultain's remarks during the session of 1890 as reported in the *Regina Leader*, Dec. 9, 1890.
[18]*Regina Journal*, Dec. 20, 1888.
[19]Ordinance no. 8 of 1888.
[20]*Assembly Journals*, 1888, pp. 105 ff.
[21]*Ibid.*, p. 111.

as those of the Council the previous year. The only dissenting voice was that of J. F. Betts, who for the next few years was to embody the opposition to responsible government in the Prince Albert district. "Let Assiniboia and Alberta have it, and let Saskatchewan go back to the old council," he declared.[22]

The Assembly also had something to say about the general financial relationship of the Territories to the federal treasury. Though Royal had permitted the Advisory Council to advise him on the preparation of the estimates for 1889–90 to be submitted to the Department of the Interior,[23] and though a larger appropriation than the previous year was requested, the Assembly was not satisfied with this formula. It was asserted that since the people of the Territories paid the same taxes and customs duties as other Canadians, and indeed contributed "a greater proportion of taxation per head," they were "entitled to receive a return on the amount paid by them into the Federal Treasury of a sum similar to that received by the various Provinces." The amount of the grant should also be determined by the high cost of administration in an area of vast distances and scattered settlements, and also by the lack of opportunity to secure revenues from the sale of public lands, timber and minerals.[24]

Before adjournment the Assembly also reiterated in a modfiied form the request of the North-West Council for power to legislate on the liquor question. Much of the time of the session had been taken up with a sharp debate on the advisability of holding a plebiscite on the issue of prohibition *versus* a licence system. The legal experts, in a written opinion, stated that the Assembly lacked the power to hold a plebiscite,[25] and a resolution was finally approved calling for a plebiscite under federal auspices, failing which the Territories should be granted "powers similar to those enjoyed by Provinces under the British North America Act in respect of the Liquor question."[26]

The events of this first session seemed to presage a prompt and easy transition to a system of responsible government. The forces of reform had been effectively organized under the leadership of the Advisory Council, with able support from Oliver and Ross among the private

[22]*Regina Journal*, Dec. 20, 1888. Clinkskill (Battleford) favoured responsible government.

[23]Minutes of the Advisory Council, pp. 6–7.

[24]*Assembly Journals*, 1888, pp. 110–11. This incorporated Haultain's budget speech suggestions for improving the financial position of the Territories.

[25]*Ibid.*, pp. 79–81. Macdonald wrote Royal, "such a thing as a Plebiscite is not known to the British Constitution, and certainly we must not set a precedent": Macdonald to Royal, private, Nov. 15, 1888, Macdonald Papers.

[26]*Assembly Journals*, 1888, p. 87.

members. They had scored notable successes in the legislation conferring powers on the Advisory Council, in the appropriation of federal monies, and in the unequivocal declarations respecting the changes to be made in the territorial constitution. The onus for furthering constitutional advance had been placed squarely on the federal government, which could no longer justify delay on the ground that the views of a completely representative body had not been available. Equally significant was the attitude of the Governor. In public utterance, in practical action, and in private communications with the federal authorities, Royal supported the movement. That his motives were partly personal and political does not lessen the merits of his policy, which was much more realistic than the obtuse and stubborn resistance to reform which characterized federal policy for the next few years.

That Royal's liberalism was genuine is revealed in his views on the nature and functions of the Advisory Council. He could have treated it as the equivalent of a committee of the Assembly (as Macdonald later recommended), to be consulted only during the session. Instead, he chose to regard it as an executive council in embryo. It was at his suggestion that a subcommittee of the Council was formed which could meet with him in Regina more or less frequently and on short notice.[27] Early in·1889 he urged that the members be paid a salary of $500, in addition to the sessional indemnity, so that he could "feel more at ease in seeking their advice and calling upon them to assist me in the administration of public affairs." The money for this purpose could be found by eliminating the legal experts, who, he wrote Macdonald, "are of no earthly use to the Assembly or to me in matters of legislation or in the discussion of bills." Such a development, he declared, "would be another step toward preparing our people to the full provincial organization and give great satisfaction."[28] That the Governor was in earnest in the matter of consulting the Advisory Council is indicated by the fact that meetings of the full Council or of subcommittees were held every month except one between the first and second sessions of the Assembly, and on a total of thirty-two days.

But if the Lieutenant-Governor was anxious to assist the constitutional evolution of the Territories, the Macdonald administration was not. No reply was made to the Assembly's representations on finance

[27]Royal to Macdonald, private, Dec. 12, 1888, Macdonald Papers.
[28]Royal to Macdonald, private, Feb. 22, 1889; see also letters of March 7 and Oct. 11, 1889, *ibid.*

and responsible government,[29] and when, during the parliamentary session of 1889, Dewdney introduced a bill (no. 136) to amend and consolidate the North-West Territories Act, the only extension of territorial autonomy was in the matter of liquor legislation which, it will be recalled, he had favoured while Governor.[30] On the other hand, centralization was to be increased by depriving the Lieutenant-Governor of the power to appoint justices of the peace and vesting it in the federal cabinet. The bill was introduced late in the session, as all amendments to the North-West Territories Act had invariably been; on this occasion the Liberal opposition became much aroused, and when Dewdney learned that he could not railroad the bill through he withdrew it, announcing that it would be reintroduced at the next session.[31]

Davin was the only North-West member who took any interest in constitutional matters during this session: he secured the tabling of the Assembly's memorials and supported the reformers' contention that the Advisory Council was not "as effective a machine of government" as an executive council would be. But he praised the "admirable manner" in which Royal had accepted the idea of making the Council "a sliding scale to responsible government."[32] Early in the session he elicited the information that the government did not intend to grant the Assembly's request for an extension of powers.[33] During the discussion of the estimates he criticized the smallness and lapsing character of the appropriation for the North-West.[34] The vote for

[29]A draft reply was drawn up by the Department of the Interior but apparently was never aproved by the cabinet. It stated that "while the existing system of government prevails in the North-West Territories it would be inexpedient to comply with the resolution of the Special Committee" and pointed out that "the grant was practically placed at the disposal of the Assembly by the Lieutenant-Governor last year." Memorandum signed by E. Dewdney, June 26, 1889, in Interior file no. 194459.

[30]Section 25 of the bill listed the powers of the Assembly—they were the same as those previously conferred on the North-West Council by federal Order in Council, except for the addition of saloon and tavern licences to the licensing powers. Section 110 gave the Assembly power to repeal the sections of the Act establishing prohibition, but this was not to be exercised before the election of a new Assembly. Section 110 also empowered the Assembly to repeal the sections of the North-West Territories Act relating to wills and the property of married women and to substitute its own legislation, and also to legislate on the powers and duties of sheriffs and clerks of court.

[31]*Commons Debates*, 1889, p. 1498.

[32]*Ibid.*, p. 355.

[33]*Ibid.*, p. 105.

[34]*Ibid.*, p. 1179.

1889–90—the first since Dewdney had assumed the Interior port-folio—was very little larger than the previous year, despite the fact that substantial increases had been the rule for a number of years; Royal's estimates, prepared with the assistance of the Advisory Coun-cil, had been pared by about $22,000.[35]

II

The unyielding attitude of the Macdonald administration towards North-West aspirations, so clearly revealed during the parliamentary session of 1889, must have caused the members of the Advisory Coun-cil to reflect seriously on their position in the interval before the As-sembly met in mid-October. During the previous session they had adopted the attitude that, as Haultain put it, "however limited their position might be, however faulty the machinery they had provided for them, they had advanced a long way towards responsible govern-ment, and instead of refusing to accept what they had because they could not get what they wanted they should make the best use of the machinery and tools they had."[36] At the time this statement was made there were high hopes that responsible government was just around the corner, but the news from Ottawa clearly indicated that the expec-tation of further constitutional change was no more substantial than a mirage on the prairie horizon. Obviously a hard and perhaps lengthy struggle was in prospect.

For the first two weeks of the session it seemed as if the *modus vivendi* of 1888 was to continue. It was only a surface calm: Haultain and his colleagues were becoming increasingly restive in the position which they occupied. Cayley had resumed his badgering of the Coun-cil on the question of Assembly control of the estimates to be sent to the Minister of the Interior.[37] Haultain gave the same reply as he had given the previous year—that these figures were of a confidential char-acter, since they were part of the federal budget, but that the Lieu-tenant-Governor had authorized him to state that he would welcome any suggestion from the Assembly on the amount to be requested. He made it plain that the Council was not prepared to stage a contest with Royal on this point, and that they regarded his attitude as a rea-sonable one.[38] On October 22 Haultain, in reply to a question on the

[35]Royal to Minister of the Interior, Nov. 28, 1888, Interior file no. 188072.
[36]*Regina Leader*, Dec. 11, 1888.
[37]*Ibid.*, Oct. 22, 1889. See also *Assembly Journals*, pp. 25–6.
[38]*Regina Leader*, Oct. 22 and Oct. 29, 1889.

position of the Advisory Council, stated that "their relations with His Honor . . . were not altered since last year" and "were pretty well understood in a general way and if any member wished for information on any particular detail he had only to ask for it."[39]

Despite these rumblings of discontent, the resignation of the Advisory Council on October 29 was a bombshell. Their letter of resignation to the Lieutenant-Governor stated that the decision had been made "reluctantly and only after serious consideration." Three reasons for the action were advanced. While there had been no "serious departures from the general principles" of the relationship of the Lieutenant-Governor to the Council, there had been, it was asserted, some departures which laid the Council open to censure "for at least grave faults of administration." Secondly they complained of the attitude of the Assembly: ". . . ever ready to criticize, and always prone to judge us by the standard of the ideal system, which they wished for, they have not given us that liberal support which in the nature of things we might reasonably have hoped for." Finally, they complained of the system itself "in which our most important powers are only granted to us in the form of concessions" rather than inherent rights. The result of their resignation, it was asserted, would "tend to bring about a more definite understanding with regard to the various powers and authorities of the Territories." Their successors, if true to the general policy outlined by the Lieutenant-Governor the previous year, would receive their "loyal and generous support."[40]

Stripped of its sophistries this statement indicated what the events of the next few weeks were to demonstrate conclusively—that Haultain and the other members of the Council wished to place themselves in a position to fight for constitutional reform unencumbered by the compromises and responsibilities which membership in the Council involved. No specific criticism was levelled against Royal: he had adhered to "the general principles" laid down the previous year; their differences with him on matters of administration were apparently not important enough to merit enumeration.[41] Altogether, Royal's

[39]*Ibid.*, Oct. 29, 1889.
[40]*Ibid.*
[41]What these "grave faults" were was not revealed until a year later during the session of 1890, when on being pressed for the reason for his resignation, Haultain undertook to list them: that a clerk who was frequently inebriated had been several times dismissed by the Advisory Council, but had been always reinstated; that the Governor had ignored the Council's advice on a printing contract; that the public accounts had not been submitted to the Council before being tabled; that a member of the Assembly had been refused payment of his expenses as an immigration agent in Eastern Canada; that a certain lawyer had been retained

interpretation of the decision was close to the truth: "I know," he wrote Macdonald, "that Mr. Haultain dreaded an hostile vote in the House, that he wanted to take the popular side in the agitation that the grit members were actively and secretly preparing, and that he had to give a pretext for his extraordinary conduct."[42]

The action of the Haultain Council in abandoning the policy of accepting the Governor's concessions and making "the best use of the machinery and tools they had," and emphasizing instead the issue of "concessions" *versus* "rights," forced Royal to re-examine his position and particularly his momentous concession of control of the federal funds. He immediately called for an opinion on this point from his legal adviser, D. L. Scott. Scott advised him that neither the Advisory Council nor the Assembly was entitled to such control. "These moneys," his opinion ran, "are not voted to the Territories, but to the Dominion Government for the expenses of the government in the Territories and by the terms of the supply bill a detailed account of the expenditures must be laid by it before the House of Commons at the next session. . . . The Lieutenant-Governor in whose hands the money has been placed is therefore the officer of and subject to the control of the Dominion Government and in the expenditure of these monies he merely acts as its agent."[43]

The soliciting of this opinion was of critical importance; up to this point there appears to have been no pressure on Royal from Ottawa to withdraw his concession, and it is reasonable to assume that he planned to continue the practice of the preceding year—the Advisory Council's letter of resignation had not indicated that any change was contemplated. Having secured this opinion, Royal felt obliged to act on it despite the storm of criticism which would inevitably ensue, and, having taken the step, he was instructed by Ottawa to stand firm in his new position. This advice, unfortunately, came in the form of a private letter from Macdonald;[44] had it been an official despatch it could have been published and thereby have saved the Governor from some of the attacks which were later made upon him. Scott's opinion, Macdonald wrote, was "sound law." The money voted by

---

as counsel against the advice of the Council; and finally, that Royal had not accepted the Council's advice in dealing with the claims of the creditors of a bankrupt bridge contractor: *Regina Leader*, Dec. 19, 1890. We do not have Royal's version of these incidents.

[42]Royal to Macdonald, private, Nov. 17, 1889, Macdonald Papers.

[43]D. L. Scott to Royal, n.d., enclosed with letter of Royal to Macdonald, private, Oct. 29, 1889, *ibid.*

[44]Macdonald to Royal, private, Nov 6, 1889, Macdonald Papers.

Parliament "must be expended under the authority of the Minister here to whose depar^t the particular vote may belong." "Now that you have made a new start," he continued, "I strongly recommend you to keep your Advisory Council within the limits of their Constitutional authority, or you will have a recurrence of the trouble you have just had experience of." The attention of the Council should be confined "to the Territorial revenues only," and it should be consulted "except in very exceptional cases" only during the sessions of the Assembly. So much for the problem of the territorial executive! In adopting this narrow view Macdonald also missed another point completely, as indicated by his statement that "in the Provinces, all such votes are expended by the Federal Gov^t without reference to or interference by the Provisional [sic] Gov^t." The two cases were wholly different; in the provinces federal funds were not spent for local purposes, while in the Territories local activities were largely financed from this source and it was only natural that the early strivings for self-government should centre about these monies. As the (Fort) Qu'Appelle Vidette put it: "It is a queer piece of business if it is necessary to appoint a council to advise the Lieut.-Governor how to spend $15,000, if he can spend the $100,000 according to the freaks of his own fancy, and the sooner it is changed the better."[45]

Royal had not yet received Macdonald's instructions when the new Council was formed, and he had continued his policy of introducing the practices of cabinet government. The leader of the new Council, Dr. R. G. Brett (the member for Red Deer) was chosen on Haultain's advice, and Brett in turn chose his colleagues, who were then approved by the Governor.[46] The other members were J. F. Betts (Prince Albert), D. F. Jelly (North Regina), and B. P. Richardson (Wolseley). They were appointed on November 5, and on the same day Brett gave a statement of policy to the Assembly. He explained that "in order that there might be no mistake, such as it was possible had existed in the past" he had asked the Governor to prepare a written statement "of the few powers the Advisory Council had under the Act." He then proceeded to read a statement, which was entered in the Journals,[47] to the effect that the Council would "exercise the functions of an Executive in matters affecting the Territorial Finances only, as well as in the discharge of the duties assigned by the Ordi-

45(Fort) Qu'Appelle Vidette, Nov. 14, 1889.
46Royal to Macdonald, private, Nov. 5, 1889, Macdonald Papers; Lieutenant-Governor's Order no. 1214, Nov. 5, 1889.
47Assembly Journals, 1889, p. 62.

nances to the Lieutenant-Governor in Council." In an obvious attempt to make the situation as palatable as possible, the statement concluded with the assurance that, in order that the views of the Assembly should have due weight in administration, the Governor would continue to consult the Council "upon all matters of the administration of public affairs" and would "comply as in the past with the recommendations of the House in a liberal and constitutional spirit." Brett then appealed for co-operation from the members even though they might be dissatisfied with the existing system. He concluded by stating that the Council would still be consulted in the preparation of the estimates to be sent to the Department of the Interior.[48]

Obviously the new Council was operating on the same basis as its predecessor had during the session of 1888—as Haultain himself admitted in commenting on Brett's statement. "Mr. Haultain," the report in the *Leader* stated, "congratulated the Advisory Council on the confidence shown in them by His Honor. The position laid down was in accordance with the Act. While trying to make the best of the present machinery he thought they should reserve the right to protest to the right quarter against the whole system."[49] When he made this statement Haultain may not have been aware of the attack on the new Council which was being prepared by the more ardent reformers in the House, and which would force him to take a stand either for or against Brett and his colleagues. For several days quiet reigned, with the Assembly devoting itself to legislative business. On November 8 the public accounts for the past fiscal year were tabled. These were in the same form as those of preceding years, being a statement of receipts and disbursements of the general revenue fund of the Territories; however, since the voting of supplies the previous year had not been accompanied by any change in the accounting system—i.e. since the federal monies had *not* been added to the general revenue fund—the accounts showed only how the revenue from local sources had been expended.[50] This was an indication of how limited the victory of the previous session had been.

On the day following the tabling of the public accounts the agitators launched their attack on the Brett Council. It took the form of a resolution in the following words: "That the position assumed by the

[48]*Regina Leader*, Nov. 12, 1889.
[49]*Ibid.*
[50]These expenditures amounted to $9,708.62 as compared with the $105,484.90 which had been voted in 1888. The *Report of the Board of Education* and the *Report on Public Works* showed how the largest part of the federal funds had been expended.

Advisory Council, as set out in the statement of their leader, when announcing the same, was asusmed contrary to the wishes of this Assembly, and the Advisory Council do not possess the confidence of this Assembly."[51] The attack was led by Clinkskill of Battleford. His speech contained little beyond the substance of the resolution: that at the previous session they had controlled the federal funds through the supply bill and that as representatives of the people they should not relinquish a right once conferred. "He would," he declared, "be acting the part of an Esau if he allowed them to hold office without remonstrance."[52] Several other members took the same line with a few additional rhetorical flourishes.

There was naturally great interest in the stand which Haultain would take. Before the want of confidence motion had been introduced, he had asked the Advisory Council whether the public accounts had been approved by them, to which Brett replied that the accounts had been presented by Message from the Governor "and spoke for themselves."[53] Haultain said nothing more until a number of speeches had been made for and against the want of confidence motion. When at last he rose in his place, it was to claim that Brett's reply to his question had forced him to support the motion—a transparent pretext, since the accounts merely reflected the system which had prevailed while he had been a member of the Council. He then shifted to the more comfortable fighting ground which had been taken by Clinkskill and the other agitators. "He did not care," he said, "whether the position of the old Council was illegal or assumption; they as representatives of the people took hold of it, and they would relinquish it very reluctantly. In his opinion they had the right to control the money granted to them from Ottawa, and they would have it if they could get it."[54]

While Haultain, Clinkskill, Ross, Cayley, Tweed, and the other agitators indulged in an orgy of indignation, the Brett Council vigorously maintained the propriety of the position which in effect Haultain had adopted the previous year. "He did not believe," Brett remarked near the end of a forceful and cogent address, "in refusing to work the system because they did not like it. It would come with just as good grace for a municipality or any district in the country to say: 'Here, we don't like this herd law or this fence law, and we are not going to carry it out, we don't want any law at all, we are going to

51*Assembly Journals*, 1889, p. 74.
52*Regina Leader*, Nov. 12, 1889.
53*Ibid*.
54*Ibid*.

kick'. That was a parallel case and that was the way the people would look at it."[55] As Betts put it, "It was a matter of regret that it should be considered that a vote of want of confidence was going to help the object so ardently desired by seven eights of the members of the Assembly."[56] Brett's supporters offered an amendment to the want of confidence motion expressing regret that it had been necessary for the Council to assume a position which was "not in the direction of responsible government,"[57] but this was voted down, and the want of confidence motion was carried by a vote of 13 to 8.

Following the vote the Brett Council resigned, at the same time expressing their belief that they had done nothing contrary to the law or the interests of the Territories. Royal refused to accept their resignation on the ground that he could not be guided by a want of confidence motion which was based, not on disagreement with any act of the Council, but on a condemnation of the Council for acceding to the requirements of the law. "Territorial matters alone," he wrote to Brett, "are intended by the statute to be placed under the control of the Assembly, and it is only in the event of you administering such affairs in opposition to the wishes of a majority of the House that your resignation, as Members of the Executive, can be entertained."[58] He emphasized his belief that the public interest would best be served by making the most of a defective constitution until improvements were introduced.

That the difference between the agitators and Brett's followers was one of tactics rather than principles was clearly revealed on November 14 when the supporters of the Council presented a motion that the Assembly ask the federal government that "full responsible government should be given to the Territories with the other powers, in addition to those already possessed by the Assembly, granted by the British North America Act to the Province[s] of Canada, with the exception of the power to raise money on the public credit."[59] Obviously the situation as it had now developed involved a contest for the political leadership of the Territories, and Brett and his followers were determined that the agitators should not monopolize the popular position of proponents of constitutional reform. But the counter attack failed: a clever parliamentary manœuvre by the "13" prevented this motion being brought to a vote, and Haultain succeeded in substituting an amendment that "the House do not consider of any further supply to

---

[55]*Ibid.*
[56]Betts made it clear that he did not favour responsible government.
[57]*Assembly Journals,* 1889, p. 74.
[58]Royal to Brett, Nov. 12, 1889, *Assembly Journals,* 1889, Appendix, p. 145.
[59]*Ibid.,* p. 93.

be granted to Her Majesty, until the supply voted last year has been properly accounted for."[60]

This historic amendment marks the inauguration of the policy of obstruction or deadlock which was henceforth to be one of the chief weapons of the agitators in their struggle for increased autonomy. Haultain's speech on this amendment was a bitter attack on the Brett Council, whom he characterized as "tottering pillars" who "should not be foisted on the House." He went on to repeat the now familiar charge that the Council should not have surrendered control over the federal appropriation. "There were certain things," he argued, "that were traditions, they might not be in black and white in the statutes, but if they were given as concessions they became vested rights."[61] Sutherland, another member of the "13," added a touch of Western humour to an otherwise acrimonious and repetitious debate. "The position of the old Council," he said, "was like a handsome new democrat in which the Council had been bowling along with a fine, spanking team. When they handed over the lines, the new Council instead of jumping into the democrat and continuing on the same course, took an old Red River cart, drawn by a shagginappy, which went crawling along with the Council lying in the bottom."[62] Brett's retort was that the previous Council had stolen the rig and had no right to be in it. The debate continued throughout the night and into the morning of November 15, when the amendment was finally passed by a vote of 12 to 7. Following this, a motion by Brett that the House go into committee of supply at its next sitting was defeated on the same division.[63] Brett and his colleagues promptly sent a letter of resignation to Royal, pointing out their failure to secure the approval of an executive act.[64] This time their resignation was accepted, though Royal took the opportunity to reiterate his view that the policy of the Council had been in conformity with the constitution.[65]

On Brett's recommendation Royal interviewed Clinkskill, Tweed,

[60]*Ibid.* The majority prevented the first amendment from being brought to a vote by securing an adjournment. Then, when the House reconvened, the Speaker ruled that a new sitting had begun. The motion to go into committee of supply was again introduced. The minority would again have moved the amendment favouring responsible government had not Haultain secured the recognition of the Speaker and moved his amendment. Parliamentary rules forbade more than one amendment to this motion: see *Regina Leader*, Nov. 19, 1889.

[61]*Ibid.*

[62]*Ibid.*

[63]*Assembly Journals*, 1889, p. 95. The majority also passed a resolution calling on the Governor to accept the resignation of the Council: *ibid.*, p. 95.

[64]*Ibid.* There is an amusing Shakespearian parody on the crisis of 1889 in *Grip* (Toronto) Dec. 14, 1889.

[65]Royal to Brett, Nov. 16, 1889, *Assembly Journals*, 1889, Appendix, pp. 147–8.

Cayley, and Neff—members of the "13"—in an effort to reconstitute the Council.[66] They refused, however, to budge from their demands for accounts covering the 1888 appropriation and full control of federal funds[67]—a position which ensured the continuance of the deadlock. The next move of the agitators was to bring the deadlock to the attention of the federal government, apparently on the theory that the desired concession could be granted by the passage of an Order in Council at Ottawa.[68] This took the form of a long resolution which the Governor was requested to telegraph to the Prime Minister and which described the recent controversies as they were viewed by the "13." "No new Advisory Council can be formed," it read, "which will have the confidence of the Assembly, until His Honor has signified his intention to accede to the just demands of the Assembly"; because of the position taken by the Governor, it concluded, "the business of the Territories is seriously impeded."[69]

The end of the session was now very near; and since it was more than likely that no reply to the telegram would be received there was a prospect of a long interval of exclusive control of the administration by the Governor; moreover, since no appropriation ordinance had been passed, there was also the prospect of the local funds being tied up for lack of a "Lieutenant-Governor in Council" to authorize their expenditure. Deadlock, in other words, was a two-edged sword which might very well strike down the "13," and they sought to avoid this result by an ingenious improvisation. Over the protests of Brett and his followers an amendment to the Interpretation Ordinance was rushed through three readings in the last two days before prorogation, which provided that the term Lieutenant-Governor in Council should no longer mean the Lieutenant-Governor acting with the Advisory Council, but instead with "two Members of the Legislative Assembly to be selected from time to time by the Assembly, and who shall hold office until their successors are appointed, and who in the first instance shall consist of the following members of the Assembly, namely:— Thomas Tweel, Esquire, Member for the Electoral District of Medicine Hat; and John Ryerson Neff, Esquire, Member for the Electoral District of Moosomin."[70] Following this the agitators met in caucus

[66]Royal to Macdonald, private, Nov. 18, 1889, Macdonald Papers.

[67]Royal to Tweed, Nov. 20, 1889: *Assembly Journals*, 1889, Appendix, pp. 148–50.

[68]See Royal to Macdonald, private, Nov. 16, 1889, Macdonald Papers.

[69]*Assembly Journals*, 1889, pp. 111–15. This motion was sponsored by Thorburn and Neff with some modifications suggested by Haultain and Cayley.

[70]Ordinance no. 24 of 1889. Brett claimed that the Assembly was placing too much power in the hands of a committee representing only one of the three districts.

and instructed Tweed and Neff to disburse the local funds in the manner suggested in the estimates tabled previously.[71] Though he naturally harboured grave doubts concerning the constitutionality of this measure Royal gave it his assent, doubtless on the theory that the federal government should assume some of the responsibility (and share some of the odium) which hitherto had fallen exclusively on him.[72]

The final action in the constitutional controversy of this session was the passage of a memorial dealing with the form of government, finance, and Dewdney's bill no. 136.[73] This memorial, which was to be sent to the Governor General in Council, to Dewdney, and to the North-West members of Parliament, referred to the resolution of the previous session in favour of responsible government and asserted:

... the experience of the past year and of the present session fully justifies the representations and the recommendation then made, but . . . although a session of the Dominion Parliament has been held since the same were made, neither by Bill No. 136, nor in any other manner, has the Government sought either to remedy the existing state of affairs or to carry into effect the recommendation above contained. . . .[74] The Assembly does not ask for the abolition of the Advisory Council, although if the number of Councillors were reduced to three, it thinks that would be sufficient, but it asks that the Advisory Council should be paid, that the Lieutenant-Governor should not be a Member of it, and that it should be definitely declared that the Dominion grant is to be expended only on a vote of the Assembly.

In regard to finance, the memorial proposed that instead of the annual vote of "an indefinite sum," a subsidy be granted similar to the provincial subsidies; the calculations on this subject resulted in a figure of $408,850 per annum for the succeeding five years.

On the subject of Dewdney's bill no. 136 the memorial contained thirteen specific recommendations. Those relating to the form of government included the following: elimination of the legal experts, lengthening the term of the Assembly to four years, giving the Governor the power of dissolution subject to the advice of responsible advisers; giving the Assembly power to deal with the franchise; transferring certain powers with respect to the administration of justice from the federal to the territorial government; eliminating the pro-

[71]Royal to Macdonald, private, Nov. 22, 1889, Macdonald Papers.

[72]See Royal to Macdonald, private, Nov. 21, 1889, ibid.: "This ordinance is not in its face ultra vires, although its application may become so. As there is a doubt I am going to assent to it. Besides it is a question of policy."

[73]Assembly Journals, 1889, pp. 125–34.

[74]Betts was the only member reported as opposed to responsible government: see debates as reported in the Regina Leader, Nov. 26, 1889.

visions regarding the use of the French language; and giving unfettered control of road allowances, trails, and non-navigable streams to the territorial government.

III

The eventful session of 1889, despite its noise, confusion and disagreements, revealed the vigour and unanimity of North-West opinion on the subject of constitutional reform. Both the "agitators" and the "moderates" were dissatisfied with the existing system. Except for a lone 'Saskatchewan representative, no one spoke against responsible government. What divided the members were differences of temperament, differences of opinion on tactics, and, to some extent at least, personal jealousies and ambitions. The agitators were men of aggressive temperament, impatient with delay and compromise, unwilling to confine their agitation to memorials. A few were Liberals who hated the Macdonald administration, and the rest, though Conservatives, were not prepared to accept dictation from Ottawa.[75] The reception which the memorial of 1888 received at Ottawa encouraged, if it did not justify, their resort to obstructionism. To some, the compromise system introduced by Royal appeared to be a liability rather than an asset in advancing the cause of greater autonomy. As Ross was reported to have said, "they were bound to leave no stone unturned to bring about a deadlock for fear that the Dominion Government might be tempted to perpetuate a system which had been working so well."[76] The motives of the moderates were equally varied: as in the other camp, there was the element of leadership ambition; there was the cautious, conservative outlook on life, the belief that the smooth functioning of the government should not be subordinated to an agitation, no matter how worthy its objectives; and for some it was an expression of loyalty to the Macdonald administration.[77]

The crisis revealed the quality of Royal's liberalism. When tested under stress it was not strong enough to compel him to correct the prejudice and ignorance of his superiors in Ottawa. From his initial error in permitting the introduction of the bill appropriating federal funds flowed a train of embarrassment and dispute which destroyed his early *rapport* with the Assembly, and blighted the reputation

[75]See G. H. V. Bulyea to Laurier, Jan. 31, 1890, Laurier Papers, P.A.C.

[76]Quoted in Royal to Macdonald, private, Nov. 17, 1889. See also editorial "North-West Government," *Regina Leader*, Nov. 1, 1889.

[77]Royal characterized Secord, Jelly, Brett and Richardson as "good sound conservatives": Royal to Macdonald, private, Nov. 16, 1889, Macdonald Papers.

which he had hoped to establish as a liberal Governor. This was brought about by an ill-advised attempt to demonstrate that no real concession of control had been involved in the budget of 1888. The inclusion of items from the parliamentary appropriation, he argued, was merely "an expression of the opinion of the Assembly respecting the apportionment of these moneys, by reason of the fact that the Assembly had not in my view any right to control their expenditure, or to alter, or divert any portion from the purposes for which they were originally voted."[78] This was certainly a different view from that expressed by Haultain during his budget speech of 1888, and the conclusion is inescapable that the Governor, instead of frankly admitting an error, was attempting to prove his infallibility and consistency by an argument which was something less than candid.[79] This involved him in a wordy and inconclusive argument with the agitators centring around his allegation that "what were merely concessions" could not be claimed as rights.[80] Floundering in his self-inflicted troubles (the federal government refused to rescue him by disallowing the appropriation ordinance of 1888), Royal became very much embittered towards the "13." Principle became obscured in his mind by dislike of the men who had manœuvred him into an embarrassing position. "I am really sorry," he wrote Macdonald, "to think that these men composed mainly of the driftwood that necessarily floats towards all new countries are doing their best to convince everybody how little they are prepared for a fuller measure of control of the public moneys."[81] Yet the critic of Royal's conduct must recognize that as a French Canadian he had few friends in the Territories, and it was natural for him to seek to retain the approval of the federal authorities.

The Governor received little support outside the Assembly: the dramatic events of the session aroused more interest in constitutional reform than had existed at any previous time, and the weight of

[78]Royal to Tweed, Nov. 20, 1889, *Assembly Journals*, 1889, Appendix, p. 149. In a letter to Macdonald he said the appropriation bill of 1888 "does not and cannot imply . . . other meaning than an expression of solemn approbation of the action of the Dominion Parliament by the North-West Legislature": Royal to Macdonald, private, Nov. 17, 1889, Macdonald Papers.

[79]Writing to Sir John Thompson from Regina on Dec. 15, 1891, Thompson Papers, P.A.C., Dewdney said: ". . . they [the members] cannot forget the mistakes he made at his first meeting, promising them all the rope he could give them and afterwards going back on his words, finding he had gone further than his powers allowed him."

[80]Royal to Tweed, Nov. 20, 1889, *Assembly Journals*, 1889, Appendix, pp. 148–50.

[81]Royal to Macdonald, private, Nov. 12, 1889, Macdonald Papers.

opinion seemed to be with the majority, "the noble thirteen." The *Saskatchewan Herald*, a steady, conservative journal, expressed the view which was widely shared by the territorial press:

Technically the Lieutenant Governor has the statutes on his side but the House contends that certain powers having been conferred on the Council they cannot be taken away at will. Whatever other results may follow, the action of the House will show the Dominion Government how firmly they are resolved that the Provincial form of government soon to be conferred upon the Territories shall embrace some provision for the management of the finances under the control of the House. Responsible government with the simplest practicable machinery is the watchword of the present House and of the country at large.[82]

Almost alone among the territorial papers, the *Regina Leader* took the part of the Governor and the moderates in the Assembly.[83] Some of the *Leader*'s contemporaries unkindly suggested that that paper saw a threat to its printing contracts if the agitators secured control of the federal funds;[84] whether this be true or not it is apparent that Davin had suddenly developed a strong dislike of Haultain and attributed his action to selfish political ambition. Reporting on the situation in a letter to Macdonald he wrote: "I asked him [Haultain] after he resigned if he were a Conservative. He replied, 'I am a mild type of Conservative.' Since that he has said he was as much Grit as Conservative and I have no doubt he means to run in the Grit interest for the Dominion at the next general election against Davis."[85] Of the majority he declared: They "have behaved with a childishness, inconsistency, want of temper, and sometimes want of decency which anger me." Part of the trouble he attributed to the machinations of the Liberals. "Some of the Conservatives," he continued, "wd. like to be able to remove the Capital; some want to be ministers; all have that vague feeling of desiring to do something—kick—bring about impossibilities—& which distinguishes the North West man."

IV

The effort of the agitators "to retain the control of the funds and the execution of the ordinances in the hands of the majority," as Frank Oliver put it,[86] was foiled by prompt action at Ottawa. Shortly

---

[82]*Saskatchewan Herald*, Nov. 27, 1889.

[83]See editorials of Oct. 29 and Nov. 1 and 26, 1889.

[84]See for example (Fort) *Qu'Appelle Vidette*, Dec. 12, 1889.

[85]Davin to Macdonald, private and confidential, Nov. 22, 1889, Macdonald Papers.

[86]*Edmonton Bulletin*, Dec. 14, 1889.

after the beginning of the new year, word was received that the ordinance creating the council of two was *ultra vires* on the ground that the creation of this council conflicted with the section of the North-West Territories Act establishing the Advisory Council.[87] Unfortunately for Royal the decision of the Minister of Justice recommending disallowance avoided the issue of control of the parliamentary appropriation; this, coupled with the fact that the appropriation ordinance of 1888 was left in operation,[88] thoroughly beclouded the situation.

Disallowance left Royal with the alternatives of reconstituting the Advisory Council (if he could secure one) not having the support of the majority, or of suspending those government services (including the expenditure of local funds) controlled by the Lieutenant-Governor in Council. He first tried to induce Tweed and Neff to accept office, but they refused in the absence of a favourable reply to the memorials of the 1889 session.[89] Tweed urged Royal to approach Brett, with the result that late in January 1890 Brett agreed to head the Council again. With the exception of Jelly, who was replaced by Secord, the other members of the former Council agreed to act again.[90]

In taking this momentous step of selecting a Council from among the members of the minority in the Assembly, Royal sacrificed principle and erred in tactics. There were two conflicting principles involved: the one, of keeping the machinery of government running smoothly; the other, of adhering to the traditions of responsible government. The Governor, though a professed liberal, abandoned the latter principle. Had it been a choice between responsible government and the complete cessation or suspension of government activities, the situation would have been different; as it was, however, only a few government activities were involved, and the inconvenience, though serious, was not overwhelming; no vital public service would have been suspended for lack of a Council. The second error was in tactics: had Royal refrained from reappointing an Advisory Council the onus for any resulting inconvenience would have been borne by the majority in the Assembly, while the Governor could have continued to occupy firm legal ground in the dispute over the control of federal

[87]Order in Council, Jan. 6, 1890, printed in *Assembly Journals*, 1890, sessional paper no. 1.

[88]*Correspondence, Reports of the Ministers of Justice, and Orders in Council Upon the Subject of Dominion and Provincial Legislation, 1867–1895* (Ottawa, 1896), p. 1251.

[89]Royal to Macdonald, private, Nov. 25, 1889 and Jan. 22, 1890, Macdonald Papers.

[90]Lieutenant-Governor's Order no. 1265, Feb. 8, 1890. The first meeting was held on Feb. 10; see Minutes of the Advisory Council.

funds. Instead, he had prepared the ground for a new dispute in which his position was much less defensible. The significance of this was not lost on the agitators: Oliver, writing in the *Edmonton Bulletin* a few days after the formation of the new Council, declared:

The recent choice of an advisory board from the minority of the house of assembly by the lieutenant-governor still further narrows down the question in dispute between himself and the majority. Instead of being a dispute regarding the unwarranted assumption by the assembly of certain powers, or regarding a demand by the assembly for the machinery of responsible government, or as to who should control funds granted by the federal parliament for Northwest government purposes, it has become simply a question of whether the majority or a minority shall rule.[91]

Royal's choice was undoubtedly based on the conviction that it was his duty to prevent any inconvenience from arising in the transaction of public business, as well as on his commendable desire to have the Council function as a quasi-cabinet. But without realizing it, he had placed Brett and his colleagues, as well as himself, in a highly invidious position.

The hostility of the federal cabinet to territorial aspirations was still firmly rooted. In a letter to Royal commenting on the formation of the new Council, Macdonald wrote:

So much difficulty has arisen from your desire to conciliate the members of your Assembly that I would strongly suggest your adhering closely to the statute. If Dr. Brett has any trouble I would advise you to appoint your own Advisory Council and if you cannot get any four gentlemen to act on the Council, it might be well for you to hint to them that the disagreeable necessity might arise of the legislature being dissolved and an appeal to the people had. It does not at all follow that you will carry out your threat, but you have it in your hands.[92]

The Prime Minister was apparently quite unaware of the fact that his Act of 1888 did not give the Governor power to dissolve the Assembly!

The supporters of territorial autonomy, however, were equally determined, and looked to the 1890 session of Parliament for legislative action which would secure their objectives. As the (Fort) *Qu'Appelle Vidette* put it: "It will be the duty of the North-west representatives at Ottawa ... to demand that the Government introduce such amendments to the Northwest Territories Act as will make the law clear and explicit ... that *all* the finances of the Territories shall be under the

[91]*Edmonton Bulletin*, Feb. 8, 1890.
[92]Macdonald to Royal, private and confidential, Feb. 1, 1890, Macdonald Papers.

control of [the] Advisory Council."[93] This hope seemed on the point of fulfilment, since the speech from the throne announced legislation to amend the North-West Territories Act. But the whole situation was changed overnight by the misguided and impetuous intervention in North-West affairs by D'Alton McCarthy, the member for the north riding of Simcoe (Ontario). McCarthy had launched a campaign against French and Catholic influence in Canadian politics the previous session in connection with the proposal to disallow the Quebec Jesuits' estates legislation. Then in July 1889 he announced his intention of proposing legislation to abolish the use of French as an official language in the Territories.[94] This change was widely favoured in the North-West,[95] but since it was a phase of McCarthy's general campaign, it aroused a formidable controversy which threatened the unity of the Conservative party, of which McCarthy was an influential and distinguished member. His bill, introduced early in the session of 1890, was prefaced by the claim "that there should be a community of language among the people of Canada,"[96] and touched off one of the most notable debates in Canadian parliamentary history, as well as taxing to the utmost Macdonald's ingenuity in maintaining unity among the divergent elements of his party. The issue was equally embarrassing to Laurier, for anything which appeared to be a concession to McCarthy's position would threaten his still tenuous hold on French-Canadian opinion, while to appear as the supporter of French-Canadian nationalism would damage his position in Ontario and other English-speaking areas. The compromise to which both party leaders finally gave their support and which carried by a three to one majority (although it did not satisfy McCarthy) provided that after the next general election in the Territories, the Assembly should possess the power to regulate the manner in which its proceedings were recorded.[97] This left intact the position of the French language in proceedings before the courts, and permitted the continuance of the practice of printing the ordinances in French. McCarthy's bill did not pass second reading, but the compromise was embodied in the amendment to the North-West Territories Act

[93] (Fort) *Qu'Appelle Vidette*, Jan. 16, 1890.
[94] See Fred Landon, "D'Alton McCarthy and the Politics of the Later 'Eighties," *Canadian Historical Association Annual Report*, 1932, p. 47. See also Sir John Willison, *Reminiscences, Political and Personal* (Toronto, 1919), pp. 174–6.
[95] See *Saskatchewan Herald*, Nov. 13, 1889, *Lethbridge News*, July 24, 1889, (Fort) *Qu'Appelle Vidette*, July 25, 1889.
[96] *Commons Debates*, 1890, col. 598.
[97] The compromise was in the form of a motion amending the motion for second reading; it was proposed by Sir John Thompson: *ibid.*, col. 1017.

which the government leader introduced in the Senate a few weeks later.

Apart from the fact that it did not consolidate the previous acts, the North-West Territories bill of 1890 resembled bill no. 136 of 1889 very closely. Though it dropped the proposal for appointing justices of the peace at Ottawa and went part way in conceding control over the liquor law, in other respects the Assembly's criticisms and recommendations were completely ignored. That the government had no intention of conceding control of federal funds is apparent from the absence of any such provision in the bill, as well as from the fact that, when the estimates for the North-West government were presented, the House was asked for the first time to vote on each item instead of on the total. Apparently, however, the two North-West Senators— Perley and Lougheed—made such vigorous representations that the government capitulated, for Senator Abbott introduced an amendment which added the following to the enumerated powers of the Assembly: "11. The expenditure of such portion of any moneys appropriated by Parliament for the Territories as the Governor in Council may instruct the Lieutenant-Governor to expend by and with the advice of the Legislative Assembly."[98] "It is proposed," Abbott stated, "to send instructions to the Lieutenant-Governor to expend a portion of the money, except what is required for routine work, such as salaries, etc., under the advice of the Legislative Assembly." He disparaged the suggestion that responsible government be introduced, claiming that there was a danger of imprudent measures being adopted in an area where the population was sparse, and where there were few newspapers and limited opportunities for holding public meetings. Having dealt with this matter to his own satisfaction, he turned with enthusiasm to his pet project of changing the name North-West Territories to "The Western Territories of Canada." The result of using the former name, Abbott explained, was that "many defects of temperature or climate, and many of the convulsions of nature which are read of constantly as applicable to the North-West Territories of the United States are attributed to our North-West Territories," and the word "North" connoted "some frigid portion of the continent north of Canada."[99]

On the second reading of the bill in the House of Commons,

[98]*Senate Debates*, 1890, p. 609.
[99]*Ibid.*, pp. 600, 605, 609. Most of the discussion of the bill in the Senate centred on the question of French language rights in the Territories and representation of the French-speaking minority in the Assembly.

Laurier, Mills, and Davin suggested that the time to inaugurate responsible government had arrived. Macdonald said that it was being withheld because territorial opinion was against "the premature introduction of the system which now prevails in the Province of Manitoba."[100] But Mills very properly pointed out that the issue was not one of granting provincial status, but of providing an efficient and stable territorial government and that the only valid distinction between territorial and provincial status lay in the powers granted to the local legislature. "But whether," Mills continued, "we give to the Territorial Legislature large power, or whether we give to it little power, whatever power is conferred upon it should be exercised, it seems to me, under the control of a responsible Administration."[101] McCarthy indicated that when the bill reached the committee stage he would renew his fight for total abolition of the use of French as an official language, and this is probably why the bill was permitted to die on the order paper. Senator Bellerose later charged that with an election pending, the Prime Minister wished to avoid any action which would jeopardize success at the polls.[102] The government's action in permitting the bill to drop prolonged and embittered the constitutional crisis, for on the one hand reform was postponed and on the other hand no open support was given to Royal in his interpretation of the existing law. The impending election was probably also responsible for the sharp reduction in the estimates submitted by Royal—from $202,423.50 to $186,910.00.[103] The largest reduction, that in the estimate for schools, forced that estimate below the amount required for grants under the terms of the School Ordinance and produced a crisis which caused much embarrassment to the Governor and had to be met by a special warrant at Ottawa the following spring.

Most territorial papers had been following the progress of the bill very closely and were greatly disappointed at the failure to pass it. "Perhaps by next year," the Saskatchewan Herald declared, "the members of the House will have learned that the Responsible Government asked for by the Assembly is not of that far-reaching kind enjoyed by the Eastern Provinces, and which they look upon as premature for the Territories."[104] As this comment indicates, and doubt-

---

[100]Commons Debates, 1890, col. 1462.
[101]Ibid., col. 4463.
[102]Senate Debates, 1891, p. 543.
[103]See Interior file no. 222961. The effect of the reduction on the school funds is discussed in Royal to Macdonald, private, Oct. 18, 1890 and Nov. 14, 1890, Macdonald Papers; see also Interior file no. 85869.
[104]Saskatchewan Herald, May 28, 1890.

less as a result of the discussions in the Assembly, there was now a much more general appreciation of the fact that responsible government did not necessarily imply provincial status or an elaborate apparatus of government. "The people of the Territories," said the (Fort) *Qu'Appelle Vidette*, "are not anxious for the appointment yet awhile, of heads of departments with their deputies, private secretaries, etc., but they would be content with things as they are if the Advisory Board could be made a responsible . . . body with executive powers."[105] Developing the same idea, Oliver wrote in the *Edmonton Bulletin*:

The matter of expense of working under this system is one for those who undertake it to consider. No doubt it can be made very expensive and very corrupt, and there is as little doubt that it can be made very cheap and very effective. The question is one of intelligence on the part of the people, to whom it gives more direct control of all matters than any other form or system. It is a matter of intellectual and moral, not of financial, qualifications.[106]

V

Since Parliament had failed to remove the source of his difficulties, Royal sought an official statement from the government which he could use at the autumn session of the Assembly. No doubt Brett favoured this too, for in an interview at Ottawa in the spring he had declared that "nothing short of getting control of the funds voted for the expense of government in the North-West Territories, together with power to elect its own executive or Advisory Council will satisfy the people of the North-West Territories."[107] Late in June, Royal wrote to the Secretary of State, asking for instructions concerning the mode of expenditure of the parliamentary appropriation "in order to settle this difference of opinion and to prevent further differences arising at the ensuing session."[108] No answer to this communication was received until the beginning of September, when a despatch from the Department of the Interior indicated that Dewdney and the Minister of Justice (Sir John Thompson) had prepared a memorandum to Council "of the effect of which you will be apprised in due time." However, the letter also conveyed the Minister's opinion that federal moneys for the payment of local officials, for schools, and for the care

---

105(Fort) *Qu'Appelle Vidette*, Nov. 7, 1889.
106*Edmonton Bulletin*, Feb. 8, 1890.
107Quoted in (Fort) *Qu'Appelle Vidette*, April 17, 1890.
108Royal to Secretary of State, June 21, 1890, Treasury Department file no. 78, A.S.

of the insane were subject to federal control, while the funds for public works "should be paid from time to time upon requisitions from His Honour and should be expended in accordance with the wishes of the Legislative Assembly so far as they are known, and on consultation with the Advisory Council according to the statute relating to the Council." "As to any other items of the appropriation made by Parliament," the letter concluded, "the Minister thinks that the mode of expenditure should be decided upon by the Lieutenant-Governor himself as he thinks to be most expedient in the public interest."[109] This did not satisfy Royal, and the expected Order in Council not having arrived, he wrote again on October 13, asking for more definite instructions before the session opened. This time, Thompson, acting for Dewdney, replied that in his opinion the federal vote "can only be disbursed upon the order of His Excellency in Council who has placed the appropriations for the current fiscal year under the control of the Department of the Interior."[110] The departmental letter of August 29, Thompson concluded, constituted all the instructions Royal required.

There was every indication that the session of 1890 would be an exciting one. Commenting on the action of Brett and his colleagues in accepting office, the Lethbridge News had written: "They are well aware that in enabling Mr. Royal to form an advisory board, they are obstructing the Assembly in their gallant fight for Territorial rights. These gentlemen have well earned for themselves the title of Jacks-in-boxes, for they are truly irrepressible. Shut them up as often as you will, on the slightest provocation, they will spring up again with a bang, to become, Jacks in office."[111] A week before the session opened, the Saskatchewan Herald predicted that "there will be some warm work before it closes." "The Advisory Board will come in for strong condemnation for the way it has overridden 'the well understood wishes of the people' in many of its doings; and some of the doings of the Lieutenant-Governor will also be made the subject of criticism."[112] A few days earlier Oliver had commented in his paper:

The special importance of the coming session lies in the fact that the dispute as to the respective powers of the legislative and executive branches of the local government which arose at last session will have to be fought out at this session, and a decision reached as to whether the Territories have representative government or not.

[109]John R. Hall to R. B. Gordon, Aug. 29, 1890, ibid.
[110]Thompson to Royal, Oct. 30, 1890, ibid.
[111]Lethbridge News, Feb. 19, 1890; see also (Fort) Qu'Appelle Vidette, April 3, 1890.
[112]Saskatchewan Herald, Oct. 22, 1890.

. . . During the past year the Lieutenant Governor has chosen to consult four certain members of the Assembly on executive matters. Either he consulted with them for the purpose of acting upon their advice or without intending to act upon it. If the former, inasmuch as the members with whom he consulted were not in accord with the Assembly his action was a deliberate insult to the majority of that body and the people whom they represent. If he consulted these members merely as a matter of form, because the statute required him to do so without intending to act on their advice, the action is an insult to the common sense of the whole country, and the members who permitted themselves to be so consulted are placed in a most unenviable light.[113]

Royal had hardly withdrawn from the chamber after delivering the speech from the throne when the battle between the moderates and the agitators broke out afresh. Brett unwisely attempted to postpone a constitutional discussion by proposing that a brief resolution thanking the Governor be drawn up and approved without debate, on the ground that the speech was not the same as one delivered in a provincial legislature—that it did not represent the policy of a government, but was the Governor's personal production "referring to the general conditions of the country, the events of the past year, etc.," and that "to discuss it was quite unnecessary."[114] In view of the fact that replies to the opening speech had been regularly prepared and discussed since 1883, it was hardly likely that this proposal would be accepted, particularly in view of the general temper of the Assembly. In rejecting Brett's proposal, Haultain took the opportunity to announce the future policy of the majority towards the Advisory Council. "On account of the unconstitutional manner in which the Advisory Council held their position," he declared, "the majority of this House did not intend to let them take any part in the business of the country, except to vote."[115] The agitators proceeded forthwith to put this policy into effect. Brett's motion to establish a special committee (representing both factions in the House) to form select standing committees for the session was defeated, and a committee was appointed composed exclusively of members of the majority. This committee presented a roster of standing committees the following day from which the members of the Advisory Council (though not their supporters) were completely excluded. Despite vigorous protests on a number of occasions during the week which followed, the members of the Council were unable to secure places on the committees.[116]

[113]*Edmonton Bulletin*, Oct. 18, 1890.
[114]*Regina Leader*, Nov. 4, 1890.
[115]*Ibid*.
[116]See reports of debates on Oct. 30, 31, Nov. 4 and Nov. 7 in the *Regina Leader*, Nov. 4 and 11, 1890, also *Assembly Journals*, 1890, pp. 28–9.

On the third day of the session, Secord, one of the members of the Council, attempted to introduce a bill. "It takes the Honourable gentleman a long time to learn things," Haultain remarked. "He ought to have understood by this time that he is simply wasting the time of the Assembly in making any motions or introducing any bills. We don't oppose his bill. It may be a very good bill, but so long as he continues to place himself at variance with the wishes of this Assembly, we do not intend to let him exercise the rights of this House."[117] The same treatment was accorded four other bills which various members of the Council attempted to introduce during the session. The arguments and protests were similar in all cases. Haultain aptly described the tactics of the majority when he declared that "they were determined if they could not as schoolmasters bring them [the Advisory Council] into a right way, they would as jailers keep them from mischief."[118]

On November 10 the address in reply to the Governor's speech was taken up, and, after a debate which lasted until 3.30 the following morning, was adopted. This remarkable document had been produced by a special committee consisting of Haultain, Tweed, Clinkskill, Cayley, and Neff, and comprised a recital of grievances and a lengthy justification of the policy of the majority.[119]

The first object of attack was the federal government. "We regret," it was stated, "Your Honor has omitted to mention the scant attention paid by the Ottawa authorities to memorials forwarded to them by the Assembly, the disallowance at Ottawa of certain Territorial Ordinances, and the unhappy differences which have existed and still exist between an overwhelming majority of the Assembly and Your Honor's Advisory Council." The treatment accorded their previous submissions to the federal government was then noticed: "The circumstances of the country and of the Assembly oblige us from year to year to make representations to the Federal Government on various matters. Our experience of the way in which these representations have been met make us little desirous of repeating them." Having disposed of the federal government, attention was next directed to the Governor and his Advisory Council. "The Assembly regrets," it was stated, "that Your Honor has not seen fit to allude to the circumstances which have led to Your Honor's selection and retention in office of an Advisory Council not in accord with, nor possessing the confidence of, the majority of this Assembly." Good government, it was asserted, re-

[117]*Regina Leader*, Nov. 4, 1890.
[118]*Ibid.*, Nov. 14, 1890.
[119]*Assembly Journals*, 1890, pp. 35–41.

quired a clear definition of the extent of the Assembly's power to control the executive, and lacking any authoritative pronouncement to the contrary, the Assembly could "do no less than assume its rights to be such as the North-West Territories Acts and constitutional usage having the force of law appear to give"—viz., "control of the executive by an Advisory Council having the confidence of the majority of the House." The reply then proceeded as follows:

The disregard for and violation of all constitutional rules, the infringement upon the rights and privileges of the House and usurpation of its prerogatives by its Members composing the Advisory Council, in our opinion, renders those Members unworthy of taking any part in the business of the Assembly.

Finally, the members of the Advisory Council were pictured as potential obstructionists:

If Your Honor's Advisers were permitted to introduce financial motions at their pleasure—while they have not the power to carry them—create debates upon them, and introduce amendments which would create further debates, a weapon of obstruction would be placed in their hands which the House has reason to believe would be used to delay the public business and without regard to the welfare of the people of these Territories.

It will be observed that, as Oliver had predicted, the agitators had seized on the selection of the Advisory Council from members of the minority as the main issue. There was no reference to the control of federal funds, except for a complaint that the management of the school funds did not conform with the provisions of the School Ordinance.[120] If control of these funds rested with the Governor and not with the Assembly, it was asserted, "it will be necessary for us to amend the present Ordinance by striking out the provisions relating to aid to Schools and thereby make known that upon Your Honour rests the responsibility of the distribution of the said fund and the support of the School system of the North-West Territories."

This sweeping denunciation and reprimand could hardly go unanswered, and Royal proceeded to prepare a reply. "I have endeavoured," he wrote to Macdonald, "to place the whole situation in its true light so as to clear it from all side issues and sophistry with which Mr. Haultain and his friends are for their own ends trying to confuse it."[121] He was badly handicapped in preparing his answer,

[120]This arose from the reduction in the parliamentary appropriation for 1890–1; see above p. 187, also Royal's reply, *Assembly Journals*, pp. 50–1.
[121]Royal to Macdonald, private, Nov. 14, 1890, Macdonald Papers.

both by his action in reconstituting the Council and by the lack of an authoritative official statement from Ottawa on the financial situation. He was still awaiting the promised Order in Council,[122] and meanwhile he apparently felt that he could not make public the correspondence which he had received from Hall and Thompson. The best he could do was to refer to the Order in Council disallowing the ordinance creating the council of two, which, while it might be interpreted as supporting his contention, was so ambiguous that the agitators were able to ignore it. He then proceeded to argue that the refusal of Tweed and Neff to accept office following the previous session had forced him "to select a Council from amongst those willing to comply with the law, irrespective of the fact whether they possessed the confidence of the House or not."[123] This situation was not of his choosing, he argued, but was due to the unyielding attitude of the majority on the control of the federal funds. Altogether it was not a very effective reply, and, instead of silencing the agitators, it produced a rebuttal which occupies over ten pages of the journals of the House.[124]

This time the whole field of the controversy was covered—the question of control of the federal funds, as well as the propriety of appointing a Council from among the minority. With regard to the former, it was asserted that no authoritative statement from the federal government had been laid before them proving unequivocally that they did not have the right to control the federal funds. Until such a statement was forthcoming, the reply ran, "we are compelled to interpret the law, both statutory and constitutional, for ourselves and to assert by every legitimate means our right to that measure of control of the public funds of these Territories which was exercised by us at the first session of this Assembly, and of which we are now deprived by the action of Your Honour in ignoring the majority of this House, without, so far as we are yet aware, any change in the law on the subject having been made." The reply claimed this right on four grounds. First, the funds were "in general terms appropriated for the purposes of the local Government" and the North-West Territories Act required this government to be carried on by and with the advice and consent of the Assembly. Secondly, there was an intimate connection between legislative power and financial control, the federal funds being apportioned to purposes such as education and public printing

[122]See telegram, Royal to Macdonald, Nov. 26, 1890, *ibid.*
[123]*Assembly Journals*, 1890, p. 50.
[124]*Ibid.*, pp. 111–22.

which were controlled by, or dependent upon, ordinances of the Assembly. "We must," the reply ran, "be made aware from year to year of the amount of funds which can be depended upon to give effect to that legislation, and we can only properly become aware by the exercise of concurrent, if not absolute control." In the third place, the federal appropriation should, it was contended, "be considered as of the same nature as the subsidies received from the Federal Treasury by the several Provinces." Finally, it was pointed out that the Assembly already possessed the power of appropriating certain revenues (from liquor licences and permits) derived from federal legislation and which were therefore, strictly speaking, federal funds.[125]

This reply was the most elaborate justification of the policy of the majority which was produced during the constitutional controversies of these years. It sought at one and the same time to demolish the Governor's arguments, to interpret existing law, and to rationalize the claims of the majority. It was composed by the same committee which had prepared the first reply and indicates that there was no lack of dialectical skill and inventiveness of argument in the Assembly, even though the weight of legality (with respect to the financial dispute) lay with the Governor.

The discussion of the two addresses in reply to the Governor, though lengthy, contained little that had not already been said during the preceding session. Both Brett and Richardson expressed willingness to resign their positions as members of the Council if the majority would accept the Governor's view on the financial question.[126] Both of them expressed the hope that at its next session Parliament would confer control of the federal funds; meanwhile, they had accepted office in order to permit the expenditure of local funds and thus satisfy the people. Among the agitators "majority rule" was the most popular fighting slogan, since responsible government still seemed for some to have overtones of an expensive administrative structure.[127] Haultain, however, declared that they were fighting for it "within the various limits of our constitution." "Ever since the year 1886," he stated, "the North-West Council and the North-West Assembly have moved

---

[125]In 1886 the North-West Council asked that fines under the liquor law be paid into the territorial rather than the federal treasury on the ground that "more general interest would be taken in exposing and prosecuting infractions of the law": *Council Journals*, 1886, p. 37. This request was granted by Order in Council of Oct. 5, 1887; see Interior file no. 132024 and Attorney General's file no. G 772, A.S.

[126]*Regina Leader*, Nov. 14, 1890.

[127]See speeches of Turriff, Davidson, and Cayley, *ibid.*, Nov. 14, Dec. 9, 1890.

in favour of responsible government. This was argued against responsible government that we have not 'trained men', but in English speaking countries men are always ready to assume the duties of responsible government."[128] For the first time there was sharp criticism of Royal—during the previous session the Advisory Council had borne the brunt of the agitators' anger. "The Assembly," Tweed cried, "had a right to know by what authority His Honour took away the control of those funds. It was never the intention of the Dominion Government to withhold this control and to bring twenty-two members to Regina to legislate on nothing but bulls and fences."[129]

The debates on the addresses constituted the two main battles of the session of 1890. There were other sharp skirmishes, but they did not produce prolonged debate. When Brett attempted to have the House resolve itself into a committee of supply to consider the estimates, the result was a foregone conclusion. The motion was defeated and for the second successive session no appropriation ordinance was passed.[130]

Despite the doubts which had been expressed concerning the efficacy of representations to the federal government, another memorial was approved near the end of the session. After pointing out the government's neglect of the constitutional proposals of 1889, the memorial declared that the Assembly was reiterating its previous views on the subject.[131]

VI

In considering the results of this extraordinary session, it is clear that the majority had failed either to budge the federal government or to create a deadlock by dislodging the Advisory Council. Brett and his colleagues clung to their position tenaciously, and seemed confident of continued success. Under these circumstances, the agitators could only hope that public opinion would support them and induce the government to proceed with some legislative remedy at the next session of Parliament. Despite Brett's claim that there had been a re-

128Ibid., Nov. 14, 1890.
129Ibid., Dec. 9, 1890. Macdonald's remark about financial control during the debate of 1888 (see above p. 157, footnote 51) was frequently cited as proof that Royal was responsible for the policy of withholding control of the federal funds.
130See Assembly Journals, 1890, pp. 78, 130. For the estimates see ibid., sessional paper no. 13.
131Ibid., pp. 129–30.

vulsion of feeling in favour of the Advisory Council, in so far as the press was concerned the majority had seemingly held their own. The *Saskatchewan Herald* declared, "The session will mark an important era in the history of the Territories, and show a degree of unanimity among both press and people not often met with."[132] None of the papers which had supported the agitators in 1889 modified their stand in 1890. Of the fifteen papers published in the Territories at this time, only the four rabidly Conservative organs took the side of Royal and the minority—the *Regina Leader*, the *Calgary Herald*, the *Prince Albert Times*, and the *Moosomin Courier*.[133] The *Calgary Herald* indulged in a veritable orgy of indignation at "the factious and revolutionary spirit exhibited by the Haultain Ring at Regina." "The people," it declared, "respect men who show fair play—men who respect themselves—men who act decently in all things. But with the immoral principles propounded by Haultain and Company in the name of the Ring, with the ridiculous airs and assumptions which these men are wearing for a brief hour, with their attempt to play the petty tyrant at the expense of the good name of the Legislature, they can have no sympathy."[134] The critics of the minority could also be harsh. *The Saskatchewan*, published in Prince Albert, declared: "Had it not been for the unpatriotic action of these five councillors in accepting a position which should have been spurned with contempt the Territories Act would have been amended at the last session of the Dominion House and the disgraceful farce now going on at Regina would not be taking place."[135]

The Macdonald administration received highly critical versions of the tactics of the majority from Royal and Davin. "These thirteen with Haultain at the head," Royal wrote Macdonald, "are obstinate and will not concede an inch, the more so now that they are so egregiously blundering together. . . . How Mr. Haultain and his friends are thus showing their understanding of the *role* of responsible institutions is not for me to say."[136] Writing to Thompson, Davin announced in characteristically grandiloquent fashion: "The history of the world does not afford such another exhibition of childishness, perversity, and want of everything like moral elevation. If any more

[132]*Saskatchewan Herald*, Nov. 19, 1890.

[133]The papers supporting the majority in the Assembly were the *Calgary Tribune, Edmonton Bulletin, Lethbridge News, Medicine Hat Times, Macleod Gazette, Moose Jaw Times, Regina Journal, Qu'Appelle Progress,* (Fort) *Qu'Appelle Vidette, Saskatchewan Herald,* and *The Saskatchewan* (Prince Albert).

[134]*Calgary Weekly Herald*, Nov. 12, 1890, "That Circus at Regina."

[135]*The Saskatchewan*, Nov. 20, 1890.

[136]Royal to Macdonald, private, Nov. 6, 1890, Macdonald Papers.

powers are given it would be better to give full responsible government. Responsibility would steady a little, and perhaps some better men would come forward—tho' I don't know where they are."[137] But the thunder in Regina seems to have produced few echoes in Ottawa and certainly no disposition to regard the situation as a grave one. "Right will prevail," Macdonald assured Brett, ". . . Meanwhile all that the Advisory Board has got to do is to be quiet and firm."[138] "I fancy," he wrote Davin, "that when the tyrant majority go to their several homes they will find that they have not strengthened themselves by their extraordinary course."[139]

Whether the Prime Minister was right or not, constitutional questions did not play a large part in the federal election campaign of 1891. The movement for provincehood for Alberta, launched by the *Calgary Herald* in the fall of 1890,[140] was reflected in the campaign in that district: Davis favoured the move as soon as adequate funds were in sight to prevent a recourse to direct taxation, while his opponent plumped for immediate provincehood with adequate subsidies.[141] In Assiniboia East, Turiff raised the issue of control of the federal funds in his campaign against Dewdney, while in Assiniboia West, Tweed, one of the most active members of the "13," ran as an independent Conservative against Davin. Since all the sitting members were returned, there was little hope of any new point of view being brought to bear on the constitutional position of the Territories by North-West representatives in the Commons.

For two years in succession the government had introduced a bill to amend the North-West Territories Act, and with the approach of the 1891 session there was a prospect that some legislation would finally be passed. Up to this point the Brett Council had concerned itself with administrative activities, in fulfilment of its contention that the public interest demanded that the Governor should not be deprived of advisers. Now, however, it went a step further, and constituted itself the official spokesman for the North-West on constitutional changes.[142] The assumption of authority in relation to such a vital matter was, under the circumstances, highly improper, particularly since the two "delegates" who were sent to Ottawa advocated changes

[137]Davin to Thompson, private and confidential, Nov. 10, 1890, Thompson Papers.
[138]Macdonald to Brett, Dec. 2, 1890, Macdonald Papers.
[139]Macdonald to Davin, Dec. 6, 1890, *ibid.*
[140]See *Calgary Weekly Herald*, Sept. 24, Oct. 1, and Oct. 22, 1890.
[141]*Ibid.*, Feb. 18, 1891.
[142]Minutes of the Advisory Council, March 26, 1891. The expenses of the "delegates" were to be paid out of territorial funds.

not contained in the Assembly's 1889 memorial on constitutional reform, and some which had not even been discussed in the Assembly. It was, said the *Saskatchewan Herald*, a "One Horse Delegation"— its members (Brett and Betts) "represent only themselves."[143]

The two "delegates" later reported to the Governor on the negotiations which took place.[144] At a meeting at which Dewdney and the other North-West members of Parliament and senators were present, the two delegates recommended that "the greater portion of the amount voted annually by Parliament for expenses of Government in the North-West Territories should be given in the form of a grant to the Legislative Assembly of the North-West Territories and would not lapse at the termination of the fiscal year for which it is voted." This grant, they proposed, should include amounts for schools, roads and bridges, printing and advertising, salaries of territorial government employees, care of the insane, legal expenses, the government library, well boring, stationery, immigration promotion, and aid to hospitals. As for the executive, it was proposed "that a committee of the Assembly should exist as a responsible body to the Assembly whose business it would be to prepare legislation for the consideration of the Assembly and act as an executive in matters of finance and in carrying out the provisions of the Ordinances, and provision be made for the payment of such services." The Governor should be empowered to dissolve the Assembly, and the North-West Territories Act should not restrict the powers of the Assembly with respect to liquor control, use of the French language, and the school system. It was also proposed that the legal experts be dispensed with and three new electoral districts created.

However improper it may have been for the Brett Council to submit these proposals, there is no doubt that the main principles were favoured by all members of the Assembly. Nevertheless, it seems that the North-West senators and members were not prepared to endorse them fully.[145] Under these circumstances Betts saw an opportunity to advance a proposal which would realize Prince Albert's dream of emancipation from a government located in Assiniboia.[146] His plan called for the abandonment of a common administration for the North-West except for the office of Governor; the three provisional

---

[143]*Saskatchewan Herald*, April 24, 1891. See also further editorial on July 3, 1891 and editorials in *Calgary Herald*, May 13, 1891, and *Edmonton Bulletin*, July 18, 1891.

[144]Report dated July 5, 1891, sessional paper no. 11, 1891–2, Legislative Assembly records.

[145]*Regina Leader*, May 26, 1891.

[146]See report "North-West Matters," *ibid.*, June 2, 1891.

districts were each to have an elected council possessing executive and legislative powers, including all those proposed under the former scheme, and parliamentary grants for the expenses of government;[147] as soon as any district attained a population of 50,000 it should, upon application, "be received into Confederation as a Province and become possessed of all the rights and privileges of other Provinces." Sir John A. Macdonald's death on June 6 delayed the negotiations, but before the two "delegates" left Ottawa near the end of the month they had received assurances from Prime Minister Abbott that legislation based on one or other of the two schemes would be submitted to Parliament. Since Betts's proposal would undoubtedly have involved a larger financial outlay by Ottawa and would have imposed an impossible burden on the Governor, it is not surprising that it did not form the basis of the bill which was introduced by Dewdney early in July.[148]

In its main principles the North-West Territories Amendment Act of 1891 resembled the bills of 1889 and 1890. The Assembly was empowered to legislate on certain aspects of property law hitherto governed by provisions in the old Act, and on the use of the French language in its proceedings.[149] In future it could regulate the use of intoxicants in that portion of the Territories included in the provisional districts. It was permitted to alter the boundaries of the electoral districts, although the power to increase their number was withheld.[150] The legal experts were dispensed with. Since some changes in constituency boundaries were being made and since Parliament still retained control over the number of electoral districts, Davis and Macdowall seized the opportunity to introduce amendments increas-

[147]Assiniboia was to have a council of 12, Alberta, 9, and Saskatchewan, 8.

[148]54-55 Vict., c. 22. Much of the debate on this bill centred on the question of separate schools, although no change in the existing law on this subject had been proposed. Earlier in the session McCarthy had introduced a bill, which did not go beyond first reading, giving the Assembly unrestricted control over the use of the French language and the school system: *Commons Debates,* 1891, col. 174.

[149]54-55 Vict., c. 22, s. 18. The power of the Assembly in this matter was not to be exercised until after the forthcoming territorial general election. The Assembly, however, could not touch the use of the French language in court proceedings.

[150]*Ibid.,* s. 2. In order to remove doubts, the powers of the Assembly to establish election regulations were set forth (sections 5 and 6). At Mills's suggestion the issuance of writs of election and the appointment of returning officers were placed within the control of the Assembly, as well as the power to incorporate tramway and telephone companies; he also argued for a change in the nomenclature of the legislation passed by the Assembly, claiming that since it was a representative body, the word "act" should be substituted for "ordinance." See *Commons Debates,* 1891, cols. 3930-1, 3935.

ing the number of seats for Alberta and Saskatchewan, so that, when the bill finally emerged from the committee, the membership had been increased from 22 to 26 members: Assiniboia and Saskatchewan were each given one additional member, and Alberta was given two, to bring the totals to 12, 6, and 8 respectively.[151]

The Act only partially embodied the constitutional principles advocated by the Brett Council. Included in the bill was the Abbott amendment of the previous year respecting the financial powers of the Assembly, and it was indicated that these powers could be exercised through a committee of the House. This concession was contained in the following item in the enumerated powers of the Assembly:

(12) The expenditure of territorial funds and such portion of any moneys appropriated by Parliament for the Territories, as the Lieutenant-Governor is authorized to expend by and with the advice of the Legislative Assembly or of any committee thereof.

While this provision opened the way for territorial control of the Parliamentary appropriation, and thus is a major landmark in the autonomy movement, the Act was provokingly indefinite in regard to the status of the committee which might be set up to exercise these financial powers. Apparently the committee, whenever it was established, would replace the Advisory Council,[152] but no direction was given regarding its numbers, name, or method of appointment. Moreover, the Minister of Justice, Sir John Thompson, who had charge of the bill, rejected the idea that the committee would be a responsible executive. "While the powers of the North-West Territories and the functions of their Government are limited," he declared, "this Government is the executive for the North-West Territories. . . . We do

---

[151]The boundaries of two districts, St. Albert (Alberta) and Batoche (Saskatchewan) were drawn so that French-speaking electors would form a majority: see *Senate Debates*, 1891, pp. 556–7. The question of electoral district boundaries aroused considerable discussion and exhibited the usual conflict between the provisional districts on the number to be given to each; there was a belated attempt by the government to eliminate one Saskatchewan seat, but this was not carried out before the end of the session. See *Commons Debates*, 1891, cols. 3912, 3921–2, 4298, 6307–8, 6325–7; also *Senate Debates*, 1891, pp. 563, 581, 657–9.

[152]*Commons Debates*, 1891, col. 1760. The section of the Act of 1888 establishing the Advisory Council was not repealed at this time on the ground that it would "have led to confusion, in view of the Ordinances imposing certain duties on the Lieutenant-Governor acting by the advice of the Advisory Council, and in view of the fact that some time must elapse before the election of the new Assembly and the enactment by it of Ordinances by which a new method of managing the finances of the Territories would be established": memorandum of the Deputy Minister of Justice, Dec. 7, 1891, *Assembly Journals*, 1891–2, sessional paper no. 4. He held that the power to constitute a committee to deal with finance implied that the Assembly could in effect repeal the section relating to the Advisory Council.

not propose that there shall be an executive in the North-West Territories itself. . . ."[153] Mills was unable to convince the Minister with his now familiar argument that the powers which had been conferred on the legislature, even though limited, "ought to be exercised in connection with a responsible executive." Thompson was most positive in his rejoinder that the system was and must continue to be one of crown colony rule until provincial status was granted. He implied that there was no halfway house between subordination to Ottawa and provincial status. Any attempt to confer executive powers would create "divided executive responsibility" and resulting dissatisfaction and agitation.[154]

This summary dismissal of the need for permanent advisers for the Governor was motivated by a determination to strike at the agitators in the Assembly by denying the Territories an executive body which could be made responsible to the legislature. With the same object in view the ministry induced Parliament to place the weapon of dissolution in the hands of the Governor. "Anyone," declared Thompson, "who has listened to or has read the debates which have occurred in reference to North-West matters during the last year or two can realize that an occasion might arise when the dissolution of the Assembly would be very convenient in the interests of the administration of the affairs of the Territories."[155]

The debates on this bill proved beyond doubt that little reliance could be placed in the private members from the North-West as supporters of responsible government. Though all Conservatives, they never achieved that harmony and mutual trust which would have permitted them to influence federal policy. As in 1888 they accepted the government measure without demur, and busied themselves chiefly with drawing the boundaries of the electoral divisions to give as many members as possible to their respective districts. In this matter they did not reflect the weight of informed opinion in the North-West. The Act of 1891, like all its predecessors, was a tardy and inadequate response to the constitutional requirements of the Territories. Like the Acts of 1875 and 1888, it had a liberal feature—the promise of local control of the federal appropriation; but this was offset by the inevitable defect—in this case, inadequate provision for local executive authority. That this was not an imaginary need was to be demonstrated by the promptness with which the Assembly took up this problem at its next session.

153*Commons Debates*, 1891, col. 3926.
154*Ibid.*, cols. 3927, 3929.
155*Ibid.*, col. 3926.

CHAPTER EIGHT

The Executive Committee and Governor Royal

1891-93

CONSTITUTIONAL REFORM did not figure prominently in the territorial general election of October 31, 1891. The prospective grant of control over federal funds eliminated this as an issue, while the grant of power to legislate on the liquor question provided material for much of the discussion during the campaign. In some constituencies, proposed changes in the law relating to the use of the French language, separate schools, and the election procedure (the introduction of the ballot) received attention; in others, interest was focused on the amount of public works expenditures which certain areas had or had not received. The question of the form of the territorial executive was not an issue, apparently because it was assumed that the Assembly would be able to establish some workable and generally acceptable system.[1] Royal encouraged this view when, in an interview with the *Regina Leader* in July, he stated that it would be "for the House to say by what means the funds will be spent, whether by a finance committee, an Advisory Board or a small Ministry." "Either of these," he stated, "the Assembly will have power to appoint and to pay."[2]

There was evidence during the campaign, however, that the struggles in the Assembly had not been forgotten. Members of the majority in the old House campaigned boldly on their record as proponents of popular rights. Clinkskill, referring to the powers sought by the first Assembly, declared in his election address: "I am prepared to advocate . . . the extension of these powers, so that the North-West Terri-

---

[1]At J. R. Neff's nomination meeting in Moosomin, one speaker claimed that the Assembly was trying "to foist full responsible government with the expensive accompaniment of a ministry upon an unwilling people"; Neff repudiated this charge. See *Moosomin Courier*, Nov. 5, 1891. He was elected by acclamation.

[2]*Regina Leader*, July 21, 1891.

tories may be granted complete autonomy in all its affairs so far as the constitution of the Dominion will allow."[3] At the same time, the campaign evoked no criticism of the record of the agitators in the Assembly, and the results seemed to indicate that the electors approved their course of action: of the eleven members of the majority who stood for re-election, seven were returned by acclamation while the other four won their contests; of the seven members of the minority group who ran, only one (Brett) was returned by acclamation, and three were defeated including two members of the Advisory Council, Richardson and Secord.[4] While the stand of these various members on constitutional issues was not the only determining factor in these contests, the result as a whole was impressive, and justified the jubilance of those papers which had been supporting the agitators. "The composition of the Legislative Assembly," wrote the editor of the *Saskatchewan Herald*, "is a grand endorsement of the policy of the majority of the last one."[5]

Royal's speech at the opening of the first session of the second Assembly on December 10 referred to the amendment of the North-West Territories Act and promised his cordial and ready co-operation in the establishment of any committee which was deemed necessary for the control of territorial revenues and the portion of the parliamentary appropriation to be transferred to the control of the Assembly. The Brett Council had been allowed to pass quietly from the scene. In the opinion of the Department of Justice it continued to exist until a new executive was established by the Assembly,[6] but it had not been reconvened after its meeting on May 7.[7] When the Assembly met, Haultain and his associates assumed the leadership of the House from the opening day, naming one of their number, J. H. Ross, as Speaker. There was no further need, however, for them to resort to the tactics which had been adopted during the previous year, and Brett and Betts were not excluded from the privileges of the House.

The first task which faced the Assembly was the creation of the "committee" which was suggested by the Act of 1891, and Haultain was deputed to prepare the necessary legislation. The feeling of the House on this matter was revealed in its reply to the Governor's open-

[3]*Saskatchewan Herald*, Oct. 23, 1891.   [4]There were seven new members.
[5]*Saskatchewan Herald*, Nov. 20, 1891.
[6]See Deputy Minister of Justice to Deputy Minister of the Interior, Dec. 7, 1891 in *Assembly Journals*, 1891–2, sessional paper no. 4.
[7]This is the last meeting recorded in the Minutes. Dr. Brett was of the opinion that the Advisory Council ceased to exist on June 30, when the Assembly was dissolved: *Regina Leader*, Oct. 15, 1891.

ing speech. "The models furnished in the Constitutions of the various provinces," it declared, would be followed "as far as possible," with slight deviations "on account of the differences which still exist in the measure of responsible government possessed by them and by ourselves."[8] The bill presented by Haultain provided for the establishment of a body to be known as The Executive Committee of the Territories, "to aid and advise in the Government of the Territories, so far as the same is vested in the Lieutenant-Governor and the Legislative Assembly of the Territories by any Act of Parliament, or Order-in-Council, of Canada."[9] This Committee was to consist of not less than four members of the Assembly "chosen and summoned by the Lieutenant-Governor," who might receive salaries without being disqualified from sitting and voting in the Assembly.

The significance of this measure was that it went beyond the establishment of a simple committee on finance chosen by the Assembly, and beyond the Tweed-Neff "council of two" of 1889. It created a body which was a close approximation to an executive council operating according to the principles of responsible government. The members were to be named by the Governor, and, unlike the members of the old Advisory Council, were required to take an oath of office; moreover the Governor was excluded from membership, and the practice was subsequently adopted of designating one of the members as chairman. Haultain even proposed that the members should follow the contemporary practice of cabinet government by seeking re-election upon being appointed to the Committee, but he was persuaded that this refinement was unsuited to the existing stage of constitutional development.[10]

During the discussion of this measure Dr. Brett expressed some doubt that the terms of the Act of 1891 gave them the power to vest the appointment of the Executive Committee in the Governor, and he proposed that it should be chosen by the House.[11] His amendment was not accepted, although his opinion proved to be the correct one, and his proposed method of choosing the Committee had to be adopted the following year. Except for Brett's comments, the bill aroused very little discussion in the Assembly, and was passed without a dissenting vote.[12] Royal assented to it early in the session in order to permit the speedy appointment of the Committee.

[8]*Assembly Journals*, 1891–2, p. 46.   [9]Ordinance no. 1 of 1891–2, s. 1.
[10]See the *Regina Leader*, Dec. 21, 1891.
[11]*The Standard* (Regina), Dec. 25, 1891.
[12]Oliver and Brett favoured a Committee of three members; *Regina Leader*, Dec. 29, 1891.

In considering whether he should assent to this bill, Royal had been placed once again between two fires—Ottawa's antagonism to autonomy aspirations, and general approval of the measure in the Territories. He had consulted the Prime Minister,[13] who took the view that the measure was probably *ultra vires* because the Assembly did not have power "to establish what would practically be an executive Council whose functions would extend to all matters of Government." He had been given much the same opinion by his local legal adviser, D. L. Scott. On the other hand, he had a keen enough sense of administrative necessities to recognize the need for a body "to form with the Lieutenant-Governor the Executive Branch for the carrying out of the Ordinances of the Assembly; and second, to have charge of the expenditure of the Territorial moneys and to be responsible at all times for every one of its acts in connection with such expenditure to the Assembly." He admitted that such a body would doubtless "unceasingly try and increase its importance, magnify its own *status* and grasp for more power," but this tendency, he assured Abbott, would be restrained by his own vigilance and by the opposition of all the members of the Assembly to an expensive executive apparatus. His assent to the bill, he explained to the Prime Minister, was based on the following considerations:

1st. Because of the unanimity with which the Assembly have passed it after full and long discussion by the Members both in conference (caucus) and in the House;
2nd. Because of the universal approval which the Press of all shades of opinion has given it;
3rd. Because the objections found against the organization contemplated by the Bill, raised only a doubt as to the extent of the powers assumed and conferred;
4th. Because I believe that sound policy made it most desirable that I should not appear to oppose the action of the Legislature unless such action be clearly against the Law.

Thus Royal refused to become involved in a further quarrel with the Assembly merely to satisfy petty legal objections. In giving his assent to the ordinance he placed the onus for disturbing the new structure on the Abbott administration.

Royal followed the traditions of cabinet government in selecting the first Executive Committee. The day after assenting to the bill he invited Haultain to form a Committee, and on December 31, 1891,

13The consultations on this bill are set forth in a letter from Royal to Abbott, Jan. 7, 1892, Abbott Papers, P.A.C.

the latter announced that Clinkskill, Tweed, and Neff had agreed to serve with him.[14] By an amendment to the Interpretation Ordinance the Committee assumed the authority previously exercised by the Advisory Council wherever action by the Lieutenant-Governor in Council was required by territorial legislation.[15] And before the session ended some significant additions were made by the Liquor License Ordinance and the School Ordinance to the powers exercised by the Lieutenant-Governor in Council. But no attempt was made to strip the Governor of all his administrative powers, as this would have required a careful review of all existing legislation. Haultain and his colleagues preferred to make progress slowly, and wisely refrained from assuming additional duties until they had some experience with the new organization.

During the course of the session Haultain outlined his conception of the nature of the Executive Committee and the proper relationship between it and the Assembly.[16] The powers of the Committee, he contended, were confined to matters of finance and to administrative work devolving on the Lieutenant-Governor in Council under the ordinances. "They were not posing as a government," he declared, "and did not intend to pose as a government in matters of legislation generally affecting the country." In the introduction of all legislation not involving finance, every member of the Assembly was on an equal footing. Moreover, members of the Committee could vote as they chose on such legislation: except for bills involving the expenditure of money, there would be no "government measures" which they would be bound to support. He declared that the Committee did not object to opposition if conducted fairly, but that "it was not their intention to be put up as a target for any member to fire at whenever he felt so inclined." This statement meant that the rather haphazard system of introducing legislation would continue, and Cayley and Brett argued that the Committee should begin to assume responsibility in this regard.[17]

The way in which the Committee was to be organized for the performance of its functions was described by Haultain in the course of

[14]See Lieutenant-Governor's Order no. 1578, Dec. 31, 1891; see also Royal to Abbott, Dec. 29, 1891, Abbott Papers.

[15]Ordinance no. 3 of 1891–2.

[16]See his remarks as reported in the *Regina Leader*, Jan. 5 and Jan. 12, 1892. Royal reported them to Abbott as further justification for assenting to the ordinance establishing the Executive Committee: Royal to Abbott, Jan. 9, 1892, Abbott Papers.

[17]*Standard*, Feb. 5, 1892.

his budget speech. "We considered," he stated, "that one member of the Executive Committee should give up practically the whole of his time to the duties of the Committee; the other members going home during recess but being subject to recall if occasion should demand it."[18] They were to be paid at the rate of eight dollars per day plus travelling expenses. Haultain became the first "resident member" of the Committee.

The portion of the federal funds to be controlled by the Assembly had been made known a few days after the opening of the session, when a federal Order in Council was tabled which transferred control of the unexpended balances for 1891–2 for schools, roads and bridges, well boring, printing and advertising, elections, travelling expenses of officials, and a few smaller expenditures.[19] In total these items represented about 73 per cent of the sum voted by Parliament. This left the funds for the payment of the territorial civil service, the care of the insane, the administration of justice, "contingencies," and a few other items, to be handled by the Governor and the Department. Royal had recommended that the items to be transferred to the control of the Assembly should be such as "would only require the occasional presence at Regina of the Members of the Assembly chosen as a Committee thereof,"[20] but the order seems to have been prepared at Ottawa without much reference to his suggestions, although the largest items were the same in both cases. The budget which Haultain presented towards the latter part of January proposed a total expenditure for the half year ending June 30 of $87,110.46. "On this occasion," he told the members, "I can . . . without any doubt whatever congratulate the House on having obtained a large measure of responsible government." The result of the struggles since 1888, he stated, "has been the legislation of the last session of the Dominion [Parliament] and the Order in Council which received so much applause when laid before this House in the early part of the session."[21]

After the sharp controversies of 1889 and 1890, the session of 1891–2 must have seemed relatively uneventful to those who had been members of the former House. The longest debates, and the greatest number of divisions, were concerned with the change in the liquor law, which was the subject of one of the most important

---

[18]*Ibid.*

[19]Order in Council, Dec. 8, 1891, *Assembly Journals*, 1891–2, sessional paper no. 3. The amount transferred was $157,660.58 as compared with a total appropriation by Parliament of $219,790.58.

[20]Royal to Abbott, Nov. 10, 1891, Interior file no. 276358.

[21]*Standard*, Feb. 5, 1892.

bills of the session. Betts, in order to place on record the views of the late Advisory Council in favour of responsible government, secured the tabling of papers connected with the delegation to Ottawa, but this move roused only faint echoes of the heated exchanges of the previous session.[22]·The address in reply to the speech from the throne was adopted after the briefest of debates. The voting of supplies, preceded by an excellent budget speech by Haultain, produced considerable discussion but no controversy. A resolution favouring the introduction of the ballot received unanimous assent, although legislation on the subject was left till the succeeding session. As had been expected, the use of French in recording and publishing the proceedings of the Assembly was abolished by a resolution introduced by Haultain and Tweed, although an attempt was made by the members from Prince Albert, St. Albert, Batoche, and Mitchell to retain the existing system.

A comprehensive review of the financial position of the territorial government and a plea for a fixed subsidy was contained in a resolution addressed to the Prime Minister and the Ministers of Finance and the Interior. The Assembly had every reason to be concerned about this matter since for three successive years the parliamentary appropriation had been reduced below the amount requested by Royal. For the fiscal year 1891–2 he had submitted estimates to Dewdney totalling $253,467.50, but these had been reduced to $219,790.58.[23] The largest reduction was in the amount for schools, since Dewdney wished to force down the comparatively high salary scale enjoyed by teachers in the North-West, and hoped to induce the school districts to bear a larger share of educational costs.[24] The financial proposals approved by the Assembly at this time[25] were based on the same principles which had been adopted in presenting the case in 1889:

1. A subsidy of 80 cents per head (as allowed the provinces) on an estimated population of 125,000.[26]

[22]*Regina Leader*, Jan. 5, 1892.

[23]See Interior file no. 247952. The discussion of the North-West estimates during the parliamentary session of 1891 was much more thorough than in previous years, with the opposition referring to the public accounts and criticizing Royal for his expenditures for "frills" in connection with Government House: *Commons Debates*, 1891, cols. 5067–71.

[24]See Order in Council, June 22, 1891, also Burgess to Dewdney, Nov. 18, 1890, Interior file no. 85869. It was claimed in the Order in Council that the average salary in the Territories was $620 per annum, whereas in Ontario it was $469 and in Quebec (outside Montreal) $282.

[25]*Assembly Journals*, 1891–2, pp. 126–31.

[26]In 1889 the estimate had been 150,000.

2. Interest on a debt allowance of $27.77 per capita for an actual population of 67,500.

3. A grant for government of $50,000 (the same as Manitoba's).

4. A grant of $125,000 because of the lack of revenue from public lands, grass, timber and minerals, which revenue accrued to the federal government and was enhanced by local enterprises undertaken by the territorial government; the high cost of administration in a vast area of scattered settlements was adduced as another reason for this grant.

The total annual grant if made up on this basis would be $368,723.75, as compared with the $232,410 which it was calculated the federal government was currently spending in the Territories on activities which elsewhere in Canada fell within provincial jurisdiction. It was proposed that the grant should be paid at this rate for four years, and that a census of the Territories should be taken in 1896 to permit a readjustment in the subsidy. A strong protest was entered against the reduction of the moneys for school purposes.

The absolute necessity of adequate provision for the education of the children resident in the Territories [it was stated] rests mainly on two grounds:
1. That such provision is a powerful immigration attraction to intelligent and educated people, who are the most desirable settlers, and
2. That it is the most powerful agency in bringing the whole future population of the Territories up to a high standard of intelligence, and therefore of ability to make the most of their surroundings.[27]

The argument concluded with a description of the special problems and needs involved in the organization of a system of public education in the North-West.

Since the financial position of the territorial government was to become the dominant element in later federal-territorial relations, the submissions by the Assembly in 1889 and 1892 are of particular significance as the initial presentations of the case for more generous treatment; there was the matter of efficiency as well, for it was very properly pointed out that the existing system of lapsing grants was not conducive to "economical expenditure," since it prevented the savings of one year from being carried forward to the next. The amount of the proposed grant was not unreasonable if compared with the settlement which was made with British Columbia when it entered Confederation in 1871. At that time it was agreed that the province should be paid $214,000 annually, though its population num-

27*Assembly Journals*, 1891-2, p. 129.

bered less than 35,000, of whom about 25,000 were Indians; moreover the bulk of its public lands remained under provincial control.[28]

II

The Executive Committee held its first meeting on January 4, 1892, while the Assembly was still in session. It did not formally elect a chairman, although undoubtedly Haultain acted in this capacity. No distinction was drawn between members of the Committee: Haultain refused to assume the title of "Premier" and like the other members signed his correspondence as "member of the Executive Committee."[29] Before the session ended the Committee appointed Haultain as "a sub-committee for the transaction of all business,"[30] thus fulfilling the announced intention of having one member give constant supervision to the work. In the interval before the next meeting of the Assembly, Neff and Cayley (who became a member of the Committee following Clinkskill's resignation) alternated with Haultain in this capacity. To provide administrative assistance, two members of the territorial public service, R. B. Gordon (Clerk of the Assembly) and Victor Dodd were designated as Clerk and Assistant Clerk respectively of the Executive Committee. Like the Advisory Council, the Committee kept minutes, but in addition a new series of executive documents appeared—the Committee's recommendations to the Lieutenant-Governor, which, upon his approval, became orders in council.[31]

Though the purpose of the Act of 1891 was to give the Assembly a free hand with respect to the transferred funds, Ottawa did not relinquish the controls imposed by the federal Audit Act and the Auditor General's regulations.[32] One of the first moves of the new territorial executive was to press for release from these restrictions. Haultain and his colleagues contended that the increased financial autonomy given

[28]*Report of the Royal Commission on Dominion-Provincial Relations* (Ottawa, 1937), Book II, pp. 234–5.

[29]See the *Regina Leader*, Jan. 5, 1892, "The New Executive," also Haultain's correspondence in the Attorney General's G series files, A.S. Even at this early date, however, the title "premier" was given to him by the press: *Regina Leader*, April 11, 1892; *Standard*, Jan. 1, 1892.

[30]Minutes of the Executive Committee, Feb. 22 and March 17, 1892, A.S.

[31]The earliest of these recommendations appear in a volume in the custody of the Clerk of the Executive Council of the Province of Saskatchewan. The first is dated January 26, 1892. The first recommendation in this volume bearing the Lieutenant-Governor's signature is dated Sept. 16, 1892.

[32]A. M. Burgess to R. B. Gordon, telegram, Jan. 7, 1892, Interior file no. 276358.

by the Act of 1891 involved the right to control the method of expenditure and the audit of accounts, that the old system of monthly statements and requests for funds should be abandoned, and that the whole sum should be paid over at once. The Governor, they pointed out, could still see that the money was spent for the purposes specified in the parliamentary appropriation.[33] This proposal, however, was rejected by the federal authorities on the ground that no such exception could be made to the principle of control through the Auditor General of the sums voted by Parliament. The Executive Committee was not willing to accept this decision as final, and countered with a formal memorial to the cabinet requesting a new system whereby Parliament would vote the appropriation for the expenses of government in the Territories in the form of a lump sum, non-lapsing grant.[34] A detailed vote by Parliament, it was argued, did not permit sufficient flexibility and could not reflect an accurate knowledge of local requirements. The "enormous distances and difficulty of communication" prevented the expenditure of money before the vote lapsed on September 30. The existing system of accounting, they pointed out, involved an unnecessary duplication of records and clerical assistance. Full control by the Executive Committee would be just as efficient as the old system and more satisfactory to the people of the Territories. They also presented an analysis of the estimates for the current year and argued that a greater proportion of the items should have been transferred to the control of the Assembly.

The government responded to this pressure by inviting Haultain to visit Ottawa during the spring session of Parliament for a full discussion of the questions at issue.[35] A subcommittee of the cabinet, consisting of Dewdney and the Minister of Finance, examined the situation with Haultain, and reported in favour of a grant or subsidy of $250,000, which would be at the disposal of the Assembly.[36] This recommendation, however, was not accepted by the government on the ground that "it was not desirable to give the Territories a Provincial status by granting a subsidy."[37] Defeated on this issue, Haultain

[33]See Interior file no. 276358. Cheques were to be signed by the Governor and countersigned by a member of the Executive Committee: Haultain to Dewdney, Feb. 22, 1892, Interior file no. 286540.
[34]Memorial of Feb. 29, 1892, Interior file no. 376358; also printed in *Assembly Journals*, 1892 (2nd session), pp. 56–62.
[35]See Interior file no. 293112.
[36]See draft recommendation to the Governor General in Council, by the Ministers of Finance and the Interior, April 23, 1892, Interior file no. 284083.
[37]Haultain's statement in the Assembly, Aug. 23, 1892, as reported in the *Standard*, Aug. 26, 1892.

pressed for a lump sum vote instead of an itemized vote,[38] and this change was made, perhaps because Dewdney's deputy, A. M. Burgess, view it with favour.[39]

The estimates for the North-West voted at this session consisted of only seven items; one of these (called "schools, clerical assistance, printing, etc.") consisted of all of the items which had been transferred to the control of the Assembly by the Order in Council of 1891 plus most of those whose transfer was proposed in the Committee's memorial, including the salaries of the employees in the North-West government offices in Regina.[40] In addition to increasing the number of expenditures under Assembly control, this change enabled the Assembly to subdivide it freely, being no longer bound by a detailed parliamentary appropriation.[41] It also had the effect of reducing the amount of discussion of the estimates in Parliament, most of whose members lacked the knowledge if not the inclination to discuss local problems in the Territories.

During the first half of 1892, while Haultain was pressing the case for fiscal autonomy with the federal government, Royal attempted to apply at least a partial brake to the movement. The estimates for the year 1892–3 which he had submitted in February[42] had apparently not been drawn up in consultation with the Executive Committee.[43] He also seems to have been unaware of the nature of Haultain's consultations in Ottawa and of the significance of the lump sum vote approved by Parliament, for on July 11 he wrote to the Minister of the Interior requesting that a number of items in the estimates be not transferred to the control of the Assembly, but be continued under his personal supervision. These included the funds for the government library and for the salaries of the employees in the North-West government offices in Regina. The reason for retaining control of the latter item, he argued, was that while the staff (hitherto appointed by the

38Ibid.

39Burgess to Dewdney, April 18, 1891, Interior file no. 91587.

4055–56 Vict., c. 2. A parallel change took place in the reporting of expenditures in the Dominion public accounts. Beginning with the fiscal year 1892–3, the *Auditor General's Report* segregated expenditure under the following heads: "Expenditure by Department of Interior," "Expenditure by the Lieutenant Governor," and "Expenditure by the Legislative Assembly."

41See Dewdney's remarks in *Commons Debates*, 1892, col. 999; and Haultain's remarks as reported in the *Standard*, Aug. 26, 1892, and in *Assembly Journals*, 1892 (1st session), pp. 53–6.

42Interior file no. 281513.

43See Haultain to Dewdney, July 18, 1892, Interior file no. 242756, in which he requests a copy of the estimates submitted by Royal; also John R. Hall to Haultain, Aug. 4, 1892, in Interior file no. 284083.

Governor) had recently been confirmed in their positions by a federal Order in Council, they nevertheless might suffer by "that tendency of all newly created bodies . . . to look round for opportunities of effecting radical changes and often, in the hope of obtaining credit for economy, to sacrifice efficiency for the sake of cutting down expenses."[44] In total, the money which he wished to control amounted to $34,700 as compared with the $6,000 appropriated as "expenditure connected with the Lieutenant-Governor's office."[45] His representations, compared with those advanced by the Committee in its February memorial, indicate that a marked divergence of views existed.

There was no possibility of the Committee accepting Royal's views on this matter, for as Haultain pointed out to Dewdney, "the work that most of the clerks do is incidental to the expenditure of money controlled by us or to the carrying out of our ordinances."[46] In this instance the government accepted the views of the Executive Committee, and the Order in Council passed on July 25, 1892, transferred to the control of the Assembly the whole of the lump sum vote, except $5,000 to be expended by the Governor on schools outside the provisional districts.[47] At the same time Dewdney wrote to Haultain that they expected the Executive Committee would "deal justly, and even generously with the employees whom they find in office" and who had been appointed under the old order of things.[48]

III

During the first half of 1892 several changes took place in the composition of the Executive Committee which presented the issue of responsible government in a different form than it had hitherto assumed. Two weeks after the prorogation of the Assembly, James

[44]Royal to Dewdney, July 11, 1892, *ibid.*

[45]The sums which Royal wished to spend were as follows: library, $1,000; clerical assistance, $11,800; travelling expenses of Lieutenant-Governor and Secretary, $2,000; stationery, telegrams, postage, telephones, and newspapers, $1,500; messengers and caretakers, $3,900; light and fuel, $3,900; contingencies, $4,000; legal adviser, $1,200; addition to salary of Clerk of the Legislative Assembly, $400; schools in unorganized districts, $5,000; total, $34,700.

[46]Haultain to Dewdney, July 12, 1892 (Interior file no. 242756) and July 26, 1892 (Interior file no. 284083).

[47]Order in Council, July 25, 1892, *Assembly Journals*, 1892 (1st session), sessional paper no. 4. See also A. M. Burgess to R. B. Gordon, July 18, 1892, Interior file no. 284083. The schools outside the provisional districts are listed in an enclosure with R. B. Gordon to Secretary, Department of the Interior, Nov. 9, 1891, Interior file no. 85869.

[48]Dewdney to Haultain, July 22, 1892, Interior file no. 242756.

Clinkskill resigned on the ground that he could not agree with Haultain's education policy, which had taken the form of an amendment to the School Ordinance modifying the system of inspection to achieve a greater uniformity in educational standards irrespective of the religion of the pupils.[49] Clinkskill later claimed that he had not been consulted before the introduction of the legislation by Haultain. Haultain invited Thomas McKay of Prince Albert to join the Committee, but McKay declined. At this time Haultain knew of no other member from the district of Saskatchewan who favoured this education policy, and some were unacceptable on other grounds: Betts was rejected because of his record as a member of the Advisory Council, and Meyers because of his lack of political experience.[50] By early March it became essential to secure a new member because of Haultain's projected visit to Ottawa, and the inability of either Neff or Tweed to reside in Regina during his absence. Haultain then turned to Cayley of Calgary, who agreed to act during his absence. On Haultain's return he resigned.[51] A little over a month later and just before the Assembly met he was succeeded by Hillyard Mitchell, representing the constituency of Mitchell in Saskatchewan, who Haultain discovered was not opposed to the education policy.[52]

The problem of securing a Committee which was united on certain basic policies and also representative of the three provisional districts was really the issue of responsible government in another guise: whether the principle of "cabinet solidarity" (one of the essential features of responsible government) should be sacrificed to extraneous considerations, in this case district representation. Haultain's policy was to secure district representation provided it did not conflict with the principle of having a Committee whose members were personally competent and united on certain important issues. The *Lethbridge News* felt that he had yielded too much in this respect, and argued that the Committee should be composed of the ablest men in the Assembly irrespective of what district they came from.[53] The *Prince*

[49]Clinkskill's resignation was accepted by an order of the Lieutenant-Governor (no. 1580½) on February 6, 1892. The reasons for the resignation were discussed during the first session of the Assembly in 1892: see the *Standard*, Sept. 2, 1892. See also the *Saskatchewan Herald*, Feb. 5, 1892.

[50]See Haultain's statement in the Assembly as reported in the *Standard*, Sept. 2, 1892.

[51]Cayley was appointed on March 17, 1892, and resigned on June 18, 1892: see Lieutenant-Governor's Orders nos. 1596½ and 1626.

[52]Mitchell was appointed on July 29, 1892: see Lieutenant-Governor's Orders no. 1654.

[53]*Lethbridge News*, April 6, 1892. Its choice for the Committee was Haultain, Cayley, Oliver, and McKay.

Albert Times, on the other hand, asserted that district representation should be the overriding consideration in forming the Committee, and complained vociferously that Saskatchewan's interests had been sacrificed.[54] But the *Edmonton Bulletin* and the *Saskatchewan Herald* took the position that the principle of collective responsibility was more important than district representation.[55] However, this issue as it was aired in the press during the spring of 1892 appeared to have been settled by the selection of Mitchell as a member of the Committee.

The session of the Assembly which opened on August 2, 1892, had been convened as soon as possible after the prorogation of Parliament in order to facilitate the appropriation of the federal grant.[56] Royal's speech contained no references to constitutional matters and the House proceeded directly to the consideration of legislative measures.

TABLE D

I. INTRODUCTION OF BILLS: SESSIONS OF 1888 TO 1890

Session	By Advisory Council	By legal experts	By private members	By committee	Total
1888	2	1	5		8
1889	6		31	2	39
1890	1	3	25		29
Total	9	4	61	2	76

II. INTRODUCTION OF BILLS: SESSIONS OF 1891–92 TO 1896

Session	By Executive Committee	By private members	Total
1891–92	4	39	43
1892	7	21	28
1892 (2nd)	6	37	43
1893	17	28	45
1894	15	32	47
1895	16	22	38
1896	19	19	38
Total	84	198	282

[54]*Prince Albert Times*, March 30, 1892.

[55]*Edmonton Bulletin*, April 16, 1892; *Saskatchewan Herald*, April 22, 1892. Cf. editorial in latter paper Nov. 30, 1894.

[56]Royal to Dewdney, July 11, 1892, Interior file no. 284083. Haultain later claimed that he had advised the Governor to call the Assembly: see remarks at the nomination meeting at Yorkton as reported in the *Standard*, Nov. 18, 1892.

The most important of these from the constitutional point of view was a bill introduced by Haultain to provide that a considerable number of executive functions hitherto performed by the Governor under territorial legislation should in future be performed by the Lieutenant-Governor in Council, i.e. by the Executive Committee.[57] Members of the Committee introduced only seven bills during the session, and when criticized for this, Haultain stated that, as he had pointed out during the previous session, he did not regard the Committee as a government, and consequently they "would not assume responsibility for the general legislation of the House, nor indeed for any legislation which did not directly deal with our finances."[58]

This statement, however, must have left the members somewhat confused, since it was apparent that Haultain was giving a wide meaning to "legislation dealing with finance," i.e. a money bill. He had made conformity to a particular education policy (the change was not primarily a question of finance) a measure of eligibility for membership in the Executive Committee.[59] At the same time one of the most important bills of the current session was a school bill which proposed to abolish the Board of Education and place control of education in the hands of the Executive Committee, and this was introduced by a private member, Daniel Mowat of South Regina.[60]

The proceedings of the first three weeks seemed to indicate that this session would be similar to the one held six months earlier. Certainly nothing occurred which indicated that a political crisis was pending. There had been no significant criticisms of Haultain and his colleagues on the Committee. Consequently the want of confidence motion which was introduced following Haultain's budget speech was a bombshell. It was moved by Betts of Cumberland and seconded by Mowat of South Regina. The result was equally unexpected. "After a fierce debate of more than seven hours," the *Regina Leader* reported, "in a House crowded with spectators, the Assembly divided and the result was the defeat of the Haultain administration by the small

[57]"The result of this [bill]," said Haultain, "will be to give the Executive Committee control over a large number of matters that hitherto have been in the hands of the Lieutenant-Governor. It is another step in the direction of full responsible government." *Regina Leader*, Aug. 11, 1892.

[58]The *Standard*, Sept. 2, 1892.

[59]The *Saskatchewan Herald* on March 25, 1892 commented: "Looking at the position of parties in the Assembly, where the vote is about four to one in favour of a national system of education, we had hoped that this would have been taken as a question on which freedom of opinion might have been permitted."

[60]There is some evidence that Haultain had a hand in framing Mowat's bill: see Oliver's remarks as reported in the *Standard*, Sept. 2, 1892.

majority of one" (thirteen to twelve).[61] The motion declared that the House could not approve "the conduct of the Executive Committee towards the District of Saskatchewan, and in other respects."[62] Saskatchewan, it was alleged, had not been treated fairly because no member from that district had been on the Committee in the period between Clinkskill's resignation and Mitchell's appointment. That all districts should be represented on the Committee, it was contended, was the "tacit understanding" at the time the first incumbents were chosen.[63] Haultain's opponents, however, could produce no evidence that Saskatchewan had suffered during the five and a half months when it had had no Committee member, nor were they able to produce any substantial criticisms of the Committee's conduct "in other respects."

The real source of the opposition to Haultain is not to be found in the reported statement of grievances, nor indeed can it be traced to any one influence. That the remnants of the Brett "party" voted against Haultain is understandable,[64] for their memories of conflicts during the first legislature were still vivid. To these four can be added five members who had opposed Haultain's school legislation of the previous session.[65] Two others, Cayley and Meyers, had indicated that they were opposed to further changes in the education system.[66] The motives of the remaining two members, Mowat and Lineham, are not evident, particularly those of Mowat who had introduced the controversial school legislation and who now was associating himself with its chief opponents. There is no doubt that the personal rivalry between Cayley and Haultain was a contributing factor.[67] Cayley had been the leading critic of the first Advisory Council and had only been prevented from assuming the leadership of the agitators by Haultain's timely resignation in 1889. Altogether it appears that the downfall of the first Haultain Committee was due to a combination of sectional jealousies, clashing political ambitions, personal dislikes, and

[61]*Regina Leader*, Aug. 25, 1892.
[62]*Assembly Journals*, 1892 (1st session), p. 70.
[63]See debates as reported in the *Standard*, Sept. 2, 1892.
[64]This group consisted of Brett, Betts, Reaman, and Jelly.
[65]These were McKay, Prince, Boucher, Davidson, and Clinkskill. Boucher, the member for Batoche, had not been a member the previous session, but his predecessor Nolin had been of this group and on such an issue their views would probably coincide.
[66]Cayley and Meyers were among those voting against the abolition of the Board of Education: see *Assembly Journals*, 1892 (1st session), p. 30.
[67]"Cayley and Haultain are the two ambitious ones," Dewdney wrote to Thompson during a visit to Regina in 1891: Dewdney to Thompson, Dec. 15, 1891, Thompson Papers.

disagreement on educational policy, with no one cause predominant.[68] That Saskatchewan's temporary exclusion from representation in the Committee was not a serious complaint is evidenced by the fact that no hint of dissatisfaction on this score was expressed during the first three weeks of the session. There is little evidence available on the organization of the opposition. Its leading members were Betts, Brett, Clinkskill, and Cayley; that these four at least were acting in concert is fairly certain, but there is no evidence of the existence of a caucus at this time, nor do we know whether the leaders had exact foreknowledge of the strength of their group.

Royal immediately called on Betts to form a Committee, but after some consideration the latter withdrew in favour of Cayley.[69] Three days later the membership of the new Committee was announced: Cayley, McKay, Mowat, and Reaman, with Cayley as the leading or "resident member."[70] Meanwhile, however, Haultain and his associates had not been inactive, and on the day after Cayley announced the formation of the new Committee they struck back in dramatic fashion. When the House convened on August 30, Mr. Speaker Ross stepped down from the chair and called on Mr. Deputy Speaker Sutherland to take his place. He then announced that he was resign-

[68]Royal gave his version of the dispute in a letter to Thompson, Sept. 1, 1892 (Thompson Papers):

"Of course, several elements are mentioned as having combined to bring about the present crisis; foremost, is stated a pedantic manner on the part of Mr. Haultain in dealing with the Members, an offensive tone in debate and a strong tendency to perform by himself alone the various functions pertaining to the Executive Committee.

"On the other hand, Mr. Haultain has created a very considerable distrust in the minds of the Conservative Members of the Assembly by his intimate relations with the Grits, who are one and all his most faithful followers and ardent admirers. His party is no doubt composed of a majority of Conservative Members, but it is claimed that Messrs. Oliver and Ross are his confidents [sic] and well known lieutenants.

"The School question, in my opinion, enters into this combination of causes as an infinitesimal element, supporters of non-denominational Schools being found in both camps. Besides, the School Bill before the house had emurged [sic] from the Committee of the Whole in a shape, which rendered it unobjectionable to every one."

Cayley later claimed that he had been approached during the first session with the proposal that he lead an opposition group, but that he had refused: see remarks made at the nominating meeting at Yorkton as reported in the *Standard*, Nov. 18, 1892.

[69]See Royal to Thompson, Sept. 1, 1892, Thompson Papers; also Betts's remarks in the Assembly as reported in the *Standard*, Sept. 2, 1892, and *Regina Leader*, Aug. 29, 1892. Haultain gave no advice on the choice of his successor: see his remarks during the nomination meeting at Yorkton as reported in the *Standard*, Nov. 18, 1892.

[70]Lieutenant-Governor's Order no. 1676, Aug. 27, 1892.

ing his position because he regarded the Haultain Committee as the recognized spokesmen for the principles of responsible government, and that he wished to place himself "in such a position as to be able by voice and vote to advocate those principles" and to protect the interests of his constituents.[71] As soon as Ross had completed his statement Mr. Deputy Speaker Sutherland, also a Haultain supporter, announced his resignation, with the result that the House was faced with the necessity of choosing a new Speaker from a membership which was evenly divided between the supporters of Cayley and Haultain. When the members assembled on the following day, Cayley nominated Sutherland for Speaker despite that gentleman's protests[72] but the result was a tied vote, 13 to 13. Cayley thereupon announced that the day's business was over and the members dispersed without any formal motion of adjournment.[73] The following morning Haultain, Tweed, and Magrath called on the Lieutenant-Governor to inform him that they were willing to have one of their group, Magrath, elected Speaker. In proposing this course (which involved a reversal in tactics) they claimed to be activated by the desire to secure the passage of the legislation then before the House, but this may not have been the sole or even the chief motive, for they were preparing to charge Mowat with attempting to bribe Sutherland to support the Cayley Committee. They probably anticipated that this charge would sap Cayley's strength in the Assembly and result in a return to office for Haultain and his colleagues. But their plans, whatever they may have been, were blocked by the Governor, who informed them that he had already prorogued the House by proclamation.[74]

Though Royal's tactics during the first Assembly had left an undercurrent of distrust in the minds of many members of the new House, there had been no open conflict during the past year.[75] This action in so precipitately proroguing the Assembly, without even calling the members together to hear the reading of the proclamation, produced the bitterest of all the attacks which were made upon him during his governorship. The Haultain group immediately issued "an address

[71]*Assembly Journals*, 1892 (1st session), p. 80.
[72]*Regina Leader*, Sept. 1, 1892.
[73]*Assembly Journals*, 1892 (1st session), p. 81.
[74]Lieutenant-Governor's Order no. 1677: proclamation of Sept. 1, 1892; also printed in *Assembly Journals*, 1892 (1st session), pp. 83–4.
[75]Writing from Regina late in 1891 Dewdney reported: ". . . what they [the members] fear is that any committee they appoint will have no power to curb the Lieutenant-Governor during the recess and no matter what they do during the session when their backs are turned His Honour will do just as he pleases": Dewdney to Thompson, Dec. 15, 1891, Thompson Papers.

to the People of the North-West" which was published in the territorial press.[76] It described their proposal to end the deadlock over the choice of a Speaker and went on to charge that prorogation had been carried out on the advice of an executive which had been unable to transact the business of the House, that prorogation had placed the administration until the next session in the hands of an executive which did not possess the confidence of the Assembly, had killed much important legislation, and had prevented the airing of the bribery charges. The address then concluded with the following broadside:

Because of the action taken by His Honour the Lieutenant-Governor as above recited, we, the undersigned members of the North-West Assembly specifically charge the Honourable Joseph Royal, Lieutenant-Governor of the North-West Territories with having taken the position of a political partizan by his action in thus unnecessarily and unjustifiably proroguing the House to the injury of the public business and in defiance of constitutional law and usage.

The situation which confronted Royal after the failure of the Assembly to elect a Speaker was one of those occasions when the Sovereign or his representative can properly give advice to political leaders. Royal's duty under the circumstances was to encourage the completion of the business of the session and to secure a group of advisers having the confidence of the majority of the House. There was therefore no excuse for his precipitancy. Before resorting to prorogation he should have exhausted all the possibilities of ending the deadlock. It was his duty to accept just such an offer as the Haultain party had prepared, irrespective of its political results.

Royal made no public defence of his action, but in a despatch to Sir John Thompson on September 1, he gave his version of the crisis.[77] It appears that he had acted on his own initiative and not on Cayley's advice. He claimed that during the previous evening (a few hours after the sitting where the tie vote had occurred) and after "diligent and impartial inquiry," he had concluded "that time alone would afford means for altering the condition of the two parties and put an

[76]See the *Standard*, Sept. 9, 1892. C. A. Magrath, reminiscing about this episode at a later date, wrote: "The committee [preparing the protest] were in an adjoining room for half an hour and occasionally Frank Oliver's language almost shattered the intervening wall through which it penetrated to us; if anything he could be original": C. A. Magrath, *The Galts, Father and Son . . . and How Alberta Grew Up: Brief Outline of Development in the Lethbridge District* (Lethbridge, n.d.), p. 48.

[77]Royal to Thompson, Sept. 1, 1892, Thompson Papers; see also his telegram to Thompson of Sept. 2, 1892, *ibid*.

end to the deadlock created by Speaker Ross' resignation." He had become convinced, so he stated, that the situation "threatened to last indefinitely" and quoted conversations with Haultain and Cayley in support of this contention. He then entered a very grave charge against the integrity of Haultain, Tweed, and Magrath, by asserting, "I have no doubt that these gentlemen were perfectly aware of what had been done [the prorogation] when they sought this interview." Since by his own admission only an hour had elapsed between the issuance of the proclamation and the interview, it is possible that the members were quite unaware of what had happened. In any event Royal stands condemned for precipitate and injudicious action, probably inspired by personal dislike of the Haultain group.[78] His contention that the situation was "monstrous" and required "to be treated without a moment's hesitation," was absurd. "The interests of the public and the good government of the Territories," which he claimed he had protected, would have been better served by withholding his ·power of prorogation pending further negotiations. Instead of placing the responsibility for the deadlock on the members of the Assembly, he played into the hands of his critics; as in 1890, he created an issue in which he occupied the weaker ground.

Of the three parties involved in this situation the Haultain group occupied the strongest position. Ross's action in resigning was criticized as expressing a spirit of partizanship which contradicted the traditions of the office of Speaker,[79] and there was certainly no very substantial basis for his charge that the Cayley group was opposed to the principles of responsible government. But Canadian political tradition had not isolated the Speaker from politics to the extent which prevailed in Great Britain, and consequently there was no reason why Ross should not have resigned in order to give his support to the group with which he had been associated as a private member.

Cayley justified his retention of office on the ground that it was not the duty of the Executive Committee to elect a Speaker.[80] The tied vote on his motion to elect Sutherland did not, he held, constitute a vote of want of confidence in the Committee. He was confident, at

[78]See Haultain to Dewdney, Sept. 3, 1892, Dewdney Papers (Trail).
[79]See the editorial, "The Political Situation," in *Regina Leader*, Sept. 1, 1892.
[80]Cayley's justification of his position regarding the speakership is contained in a long letter published in the *Regina Leader*, Sept. 26, 1892, in reply to a letter by Senator Perley published in the *Standard* on Sept. 23, 1892. He argued that the choice of a Speaker in the Canadian House of Commons was not an act for which the government assumed responsibility, and also cited British practice in this matter.

least in his public utterances, that the deadlock would not exist at the following session. They would stand or fall on their efforts to improve the administration. "If," he declared, "we can show that in every respect there has been a distinct advance, we are convinced from the class of men who are in the Assembly that no old quarrels nor personal differences will prevent their giving us just the support we deserve."[81] Cayley's defence was weak because his position was weak; his elevation to office was not a result of any revulsion of public opinion against the Haultain Committee. His supporters were a heterogeneous group of individuals whose ambitions or grievances, rather than common beliefs, had led them to coalesce.

The people of the Territories, in so far as their opinions were voiced by the press, were not nearly so evenly divided as the members of the Assembly, and were by no means prepared to reject Haultain's leadership. The attack on Royal contained in the manifesto of the Haultain group was repeated in less restrained language in the editorial columns of a number of territorial papers. The *Moose Jaw Times* used such terms as "the man who now disgraces the Lieutenant-Governor's seat" and "unscrupulous partizan."[82] The *Lethbridge News* discussed the question of "whether Mr. Royal is a fool or a knave."[83] Other papers were less vituperative but the majority either criticized Royal or condemned the Cayley Committee for retaining office.

It does not appear that the Abbott administration took much interest in this political crisis, despite Nicholas Flood Davin's private report that sinister Grit designs inspired the Haultain group.[84] The temperamental Irishman's version of the situation was quite different from that given to the government by Senator Perley. "Royal made a great mistake in that act," he wrote to Thompson regarding the prorogation. The deadlock, he asserted, "would have cured itself in a day or so had he not prorogued. . . . Royal is very unpopular."[85] Thompson, who was shortly to succeed Abbott as Prime Minister,[86] was, characteristically, more concerned with the legality of the ordinance creating the Executive Committee than with political and administrative realities of territorial affairs.[87] Nor was Dewdney much concerned, since

---

[81]Statement given in an interview with the *Regina Leader*, Sept. 8, 1892.
[82]Quoted in the *Standard*, Oct. 14, 1892.
[83]Quoted in the *Standard*, Sept. 23, 1892.
[84]Davin to Thompson, private and confidential, Sept. 19, 1892, Thompson Papers.
[85]Perley to Thompson, Nov. 26, 1892, *ibid*.
[86]He became Prime Minister on Nov. 25, 1892.
[87]See Thompson to Royal, private, Sept. 12 and 20, 1892, *ibid*.

he was preparing to relinquish the Interior portfolio in favour of the lieutenant-governorship of British Columbia.[88]

IV

The sudden prorogation of the Assembly left the Cayley Committee in control of the treasury and with full power to make appropriations by Order in Council.[89] Following their appointment they had prepared a set of estimates for submission to the Assembly, but were not in a position to table them before prorogation.[90] Despite Cayley's claims for the superiority of these estimates, they were substantially the same as those submitted by Haultain. The chief innovation was the introduction of an item "special public works, not specified," which was designed as the first step in the introduction of centralized management of public works expenditures; the sum allotted to the members for expenditure in their districts was reduced by this amount ($10,000). Cayley's critics refused to regard this as an honest reform and characterized it as a means of providing the Committee with funds to be expended in districts represented by its supporters or in districts whose members might be weaned away from the Haultain group.[91]

The precise nature of the Cayley Committee's relations with the Governor is not apparent, but it is obvious that they did not press for further administrative autonomy.[92] This, coupled with the position which they occupied as beneficiaries of Royal's ill-advised action in proroguing the Assembly, sealed Cayley's fate and foreshadowed his disappearance from the field of territorial politics. The first, and what proved to be a decisive test of his position, came sooner than either he or anyone else anticipated. On October 3 Joel Reaman, who had been made a "resident member" in addition to Cayley, died of typhoid fever which was raging at that time in the unsanitary territorial capital. This necessitated a by-election in Wallace, which was called for November 12. The supporters of the Haultain group in the constituency nominated F. R. Insinger, while the Cayley nominee was Thomas McNutt. Both the rival leaders engaged actively in the campaign,

[88]Dewdney resigned as Minister of the Interior on Oct. 16, 1892, and assumed the lieutenant-governorship on Nov. 2, 1892.
[89]Under the terms of Ordinance no. 2 of 1891–2.
[90]They were published in the *Regina Leader*, Sept. 12, 1892.
[91]See *Moose Jaw Times*, Sept. 7, 1892, and *Edmonton Bulletin*, Sept. 15, 1892.
[92]See below, p. 229.

addressing joint meetings all over the constituency.[93] At a meeting in Yorkton, Haultain was reported as attacking the record of the Committee, while Cayley concentrated his appeal on a programme of administrative reforms. Haultain made much of the alleged opposition of the Committee to the principle of national schools. "Cayley," he claimed, "was unable to introduce salutary school legislation because he was tied hand and foot by the clerical party upon whom he depended for his support and political existence."[94] Cayley denied this charge, and his candidate McNutt declared that he was a supporter of national schools,[95] but it is probable that the charge stuck since Haultain's supporters could point to the voting record of the Cayley group on the school legislation.[96] Though Cayley denied having had anything to do with Royal's decision to prorogue the House, his denial was less effective than his opponents' claim to be the defenders of the principle of responsible government.[97] Apparently the voters were not greatly impressed with Cayley's move to introduce centralized supervision of public works projects and his pledge that the Committee would assume a more active role in preparing legislation than its predecessor had done.

The result of the voting was a substantial majority for Insinger, the Haultain candidate. It was a verdict which Cayley could not ignore. "I will advise His Honor," he declared in a press statement, "to call the House together as soon as possible, and I will resign on the day the House meets."[98] Both Royal and Cayley were now in a very embarrassing position; however, they were able to take cover under a decision of the federal government on the constitutionality of the ordinance creating the Executive Committee.[99]

As we have already seen, Royal had received an unofficial opinion

[93]See Cayley's remarks reported in *Regina Leader*, Nov. 17, 1892. Frank Oliver defined the issues of this election as (1) the personal qualities of Haultain and Cayley, (2) the issue of district representation on the executive, (3) the school question, and (4) the question of the privileges of the Assembly and the prerogative of the Governor: *Edmonton Bulletin*, Nov. 24, 1892. See also "Political Reminiscences of Dr. T. A. Patrick, Yorkton," microfilm copy, A.S.

[94]Report of a meeting at Yorkton on Oct. 14 in the *Standard*, Oct. 28, 1892. See also Haultain's remarks at the nomination meeting in Yorkton, *ibid.*, Nov. 18, 1892.

[95]See report of the same meeting in *Regina Leader*, Oct. 24, 1892.

[96]See letter to the editor by T. A. Patrick, Oct. 31, 1892, in the *Standard*, Nov. 4, 1892, and report of nomination day speeches, *ibid.*, Nov. 18, 1892. See also Cayley's remarks as reported in *Regina Leader*, Nov. 17, 1892.

[97]*Ibid.*   [98]*Ibid.*

[99]Order in Council, Oct. 1, 1892, *Assembly Journals*, 1892 (2nd session), sessional paper no. 1.

from Abbott that the Assembly did not have power to create an executive with power to advise the Governor generally on the administration of territorial affairs. He had, nevertheless, given assent to the ordinance, and the Executive Committee had been functioning effectively for nine months when Sir John Thompson, the Minister of Justice, reviewed the legislation. Thompson's decision was that the ordinance was *ultra vires* in so far as it implied that the Lieutenant-Governor was to administer the government on the advice of the Committee; only on the expenditure of territorial funds and the portion of the parliamentary appropriation at the disposal of the Assembly could the Committee properly tender advice. He did not recommend disallowance, but suggested that the ordinance should be amended "in order that confusion and misinterpretation be avoided." Immediate action was not required, but Royal seized on this part of the opinion as an excuse for summoning the Assembly to meet on December 7.[100]

V

As soon as the House met, J. H. Ross was nominated for the speakership by the Haultain group, and was elected unanimously. Later in the same day Cayley announced that the Executive Committee had resigned, not because of the defeat of his candidate in Wallace, but because of the opinion of the Minister of Justice that the ordinance establishing the Committee was *ultra vires*.[101] The Minister's opinion did not go this far, but Cayley was seeking an excuse for the executive to retire more gracefully than would otherwise have been possible.

The Assembly was now faced with the problem of reconstituting an executive and defining its duties. In this connection the opinion of the Minister of Justice was of little help: he had said nothing about the method of selecting a Committee. Haultain and his associates apparently decided that it would be best to abandon the method of appointment by the Lieutenant-Governor, with its suggestion of cabinet status, in favour of a Committee appointed by the House—a system which

[100]Royal had gone to Ottawa shortly after the close of the previous session. What advice he received from the ministry is not apparent, although Thompson wrote to Senator Perley, "We have had interviews with Mr. Royal and I have no doubt that he will call the Legislature together and get rid of the difficulty which has made deadlock there": Thompson to Perley, private, Oct. 14, 1892, Thompson Papers.
[101]*Assembly Journals*, 1892 (2nd session), p. 13. An order of the Lieutenant-Governor (no. 1730, Dec. 7, 1892) cancelled their appointments.

they had adopted during the crisis of 1889. They were determined, however, to give this new Committee the same measure of executive authority which they had sought for its predecessor under the ordinance of 1891–2.

On December 12, Haultain secured the passage of a resolution proposing the appointment of four members to advise the Lieutenant-Governor "in relation to the expenditure of Territorial funds and such portion of any moneys appropriated by the Parliament of Canada for the Territories as the Lieutenant-Governor is authorized to expend by and with the advice of the Legislative Assembly or of any Committee thereof."[102] On the following day two members of the Haultain group, Campbell (Whitewood) and Insinger (Wallace) moved that the Committee be composed of Haultain, Neff, Tweed, and Mitchell (i.e. the same members who had been ousted from office in August). Clinkskill and Betts thereupon moved an amendment to the effect "that the Committee should be so composed that representation shall be given to both parties which have recently existed in this Assembly," but this was defeated by a vote of 14 to 12.[103] The Cayley group suffered one defection from its ranks, Lineham of Calgary, otherwise the membership was divided in the same way as the preceding session.

Haultain and his associates now turned to the second problem, that of defining the powers of the new committee. The debate had indicated that there were some who felt that it was similar to a standing committee of the House, and the *Regina Leader* advanced the view that it would cease to exist as soon as the Assembly prorogued.[104] Yet territorial legislation since 1878 had specified that certain executive acts should be performed on the advice of a Council having a continuing existence, and the majority of the members were determined to maintain this principle and extend it to cover still more of these acts.[105] About a week after the appointment of the Committee, Haultain sought to clarify the position by introducing a resolution in the following terms: "That this House claims the right of the House, through its Committee, to advise the Lieutenant-Governor in relation to all Executive Acts and Appointments made necessary by Territorial Ordinances."[106] Royal was requested to telegraph the Assembly's views on this point to the Prime Minister and the Minister of the

102*Assembly Journals*, 1892 (2nd session), p. 23.
103*Ibid.*, p. 26, and *Regina Leader*, Dec. 22, 1892.
104See editorials of Dec. 22, 1892, and Jan. 5, 1893.
105See Ordinance no. 35 of 1892.
106*Assembly Journals*, 1892 (2nd session), p. 44.

Interior.[107] "It was never the intention of the Assembly," Haultain declared in referring to the opinion of the Minister of Justice, "to interfere with the prerogatives and duties of the Lieutenant-Governor as defined by the Federal enactments. But the right here referred to was one which the Assembly had exercised unquestioned during the past four years, and as doubt had been cast upon that right it was well that the Assembly should assert it, for the guidance of its Committee in case any difficulty arose."[108] In a letter to Royal, Haultain stated the problem even more precisely:

The Assembly [for the past four years] has delegated the power of making appointments and doing various things under the ordinances and I submit that they possess the right either of making these appointments and doing these acts directly by ordinance or of indicating how and by whom they shall be made and done.[109]

He therefore proposed that a bill be passed making the Committee a permanent body ("the members thereof shall severally hold office until their successors are appointed"), fixing its size at four persons, giving it a name ("The Executive Committee of the Territories"), and permitting it to make a quorum of one or more of its members (to strengthen the position of the resident member at the capital).[110]

Royal referred this proposal to Ottawa,[111] but the government was evidently not prepared to become involved in a further dispute at this stage. "Our time to act," T. M. Daly, the new Minister of the Interior, told Thompson, "is when these ordinances come down to you in due course."[112] Thompson was perhaps not uninfluenced by the state of opinion in the Territories as represented to him by W. W. Macdonald, the new Conservative member who had been elected in Assiniboia East following Dewdney's resignation. Referring to rumours which had been current before the Assembly met, Macdonald wrote:

I may say there is a very strong feeling in favor of the system begun last January—the Governor inviting a member to choose his colleagues and

107Ibid., pp. 44–5.
108Debates as reported in the Standard, Dec. 23, 1892.
109[Haultain] to Royal, Dec. 20, 1892, Attorney General's file no. G 848, A.S.
110Ordinance no. 1 of 1892, "An ordinance respecting Expenditure." Ordinance no. 23 of 1892 repealed the ordinance respecting the former Executive Committee. By a resolution of Dec. 31, the Committee chosen on Dec. 13 was designated as the Executive Committee referred to in Ordinance no. 1: Assembly Journals, 1892 (2nd session), pp. 101–2.
111Royal to Thompson, telegrams, Dec. 21 and Dec. 26, 1892; see also Royal to Thompson, private, Jan. 5, 1893, Thompson Papers.
112Daly to Thompson, Dec. 22, 1892, ibid.

for an Executive Committee who shall act as the Governor's advisers so long as they retain the confidence of a majority of the Assembly. This system satisfied the Assembly, and gave general satisfaction in the country. It is inexpensive and a continuance of it will keep of [sic] agitation for provincial Government.

. . . I feel very strong on this question knowing so well the feelings of the Electors on the subject. . . .

. . . I sincerely trust you will see your way clear not to make any change until every chance is given to see how the Assembly works out the constitutional system.[113]

Haultain's bill did not produce any sharp controversy, though Betts opposed the principle of a quorum of one, and Clinkskill questioned the right of the Committee to act when the Assembly was not in session. One member observed that since a vacancy by death could not be filled without the consent of the House, "prayers should be offered up daily in their behalf."[114] The new Committee was indeed an extraordinary body, for an executive chosen by members of the legislature is foreign to British constitutional practice. Yet this was the only procedure open to the Assembly in view of the uncompromising and uncomprehending attitude of the federal government to the problem of the executive branch of the territorial government. Despite the incongruity, the Committee thus constituted continued to exist until cabinet government was established in 1897.

The session of 1892 as a whole was a quiet one. The Cayley group had tested its strength on the amendment to the motion appointing the new Committee and also on the appointment of a deputy Speaker and was defeated on both occasions.[115] There were complaints of discrimination against the minority in the formation of the standing committees, but no extended controversy developed. Although the estimates for 1892–3 had, under Cayley's régime, been adopted by order of the Lieutenant-Governor in Council, the new Haultain Committee was determined that the House should have an opportunity to vote them for the remaining seven months of the fiscal year. Although many of the items were merely unexpended balances of votes in the Cayley Committee's estimates, there were a number of changes, the most important being the elimination of the item "special public works" except for those already authorized by Cayley.[116]

113W. W. Macdonald to Thompson, Nov. 26, 1892, *ibid.*
114The *Standard*, Dec. 30, 1892.
115See *Assembly Journals*, 1892 (2nd session), p. 27, and report of debates in *Calgary Weekly Herald*, Dec. 21, 1892. The vote on the deputy-speakership was 13 to 10.
116Ordinance no. 38 of 1892 (Supply Ordinance).

VI

The first Haultain Committee, starting from the basis of the North-West Territories Act of 1891, had attempted to extend territorial autonomy to the whole system of financial administration. While the Cayley Committee held office, however, this movement had suffered a set-back: the theory of federal responsibility for the proper expenditure of the funds transferred to the control of the Assembly had been successfully asserted by the Auditor General of Canada;[117] and the preparation of the estimates for the Department of the Interior for 1893-4 (on which the parliamentary appropriation was based) had been undertaken by Royal without consulting the Committee. Moreover, in his speech proroguing the Assembly he made it plain that he regarded himself as personally responsible for the proper expenditure of the moneys voted in the supply bill.[118]

Haultain refused to submit meekly to these arrangements, which involved a serious limitation of the power and importance of the Executive Committee. The Committee's first move was a recommendation to Royal that "the advice of the Committee for any expenditure proposed to be made will be conveyed to His Honor by the recommendation of a Member of the Committee on each voucher."[119] To this proposal, by which the Governor would be called on to ratify expenditures already incurred, Royal objected. Instead, he insisted "that before any liability is incurred . . . the particulars of the proposed expenditure shall be submitted for His Honor's approval in the form of a Report from the Committee."[120] Royal also insisted on receiving a report before cheques were issued. At the same time he expressed doubt regarding the possibility of the Committee having a quorum of one member, which was the system whereby Haultain was

---

[117]Haultain had inaugurated a system whereby cheques issued against federal funds were signed by the Governor and countersigned by a member of the Executive Committee. Due apparently to pressure by the Auditor General, the federal funds were, in October 1892, placed at the disposal of the Governor and R. B. Gordon, Secretary to the Governor and Clerk of the Assembly, although with the proviso that expenditures should be approved by the representative of the Executive Committee. Cayley does not seem to have objected to this change. See Interior files nos. 284083 and 286540.

[118]*Assembly Journals*, 1892 (2nd session), p. 106.

[119]Victor Dodd, Secretary to the Executive Committee, to R. B. Gordon, Secretary to the Lieutenant-Governor, Dec. 17, 1892, Interior file no. 284083. See also Royal to Bowell, Acting Prime Minister, April 26, 1893, *ibid.*, and Attorney General's file no. G 848, A.S.

[120]R. B. Gordon to Executive Committee, Dec. 19, 1892, in Royal to Bowell, April 22, 1893, Interior file no. 284083.

enabled to perform certain routine duties for the Committee without having to bring the other members to Regina.[121]

The next move in this contest was made by the Committee early in the new year, when a lengthy resolution was submitted to the Prime Minister and the Ministers of Finance and the Interior.[122] It reiterated the plea contained in the Assembly's memorial of January 1892 for "a fixed amount in the nature of a subsidy." It cited the difficulties encountered during the fiscal year 1891–2 because of the lapsing character of the grant. Finally, it complained that the estimates for 1893–4 which were then before Parliament had been prepared by the Governor without any advice from the Assembly or its Committee and were "altogether inadequate for the needs of the Territories."[123]

Shortly after these representations were made, Haultain undertook a mission to Ottawa to press the views of the Committee through personal interviews.[124] Although he did not succeed in obtaining any increase in the parliamentary appropriation or the establishment of a subsidy, he did secure two concessions. The first took the form of a special section in the supply Act which provided that "the amounts granted . . . for the government of the North-West Territories shall not be deemed to have lapsed if not expended within the year for which they are granted."[125] The second concession related to the method of payment and expenditure of the parliamentary appropriation. During the period of the first Haultain Committee this had been paid by letters of credit issued to Haultain and Royal jointly, and during the period of the Cayley Committee, at the insistence of the Auditor General, it had been paid to Royal and Gordon, Secretary

[121]Royal to Haultain, Dec. 22, 1892, Attorney General's file no. G 848, A.S.
[122]Resolution of Executive Committee, Feb. 4, 1893, signed by Haultain, in Interior file no. 276358.
[123]*Ibid.* The estimates for 1893–4 were sent to Ottawa on Dec. 6, 1892 (see Interior file no. 312513). Royal patterned these on the Cayley Committee's budget for 1892–3, adopting the same figures in most instances, but he changed certain items. These estimates Haultain later characterized as "deliberately and maliciously unfair and insufficient": Haultain to Daly, Aug. 5, 1894, sessional paper no. 1, 1894 session, in records of the Legislative Assembly. One of the features of these estimates was the Governor's attempt to retain control over the government library on the ground that he was "necessarily more familiar with the contents and wants of the Library than anyone else can be." His effort was unsuccessful, since the Assembly adopted a recommendation that the library be placed under the direction of the Executive Committee: *Assembly Journals,* 1892 (2nd session), p. 91; *ibid.,* 1893, pp. 85–7.
[124]See report "Going to Ottawa" in *Regina Leader,* Feb. 16, 1893.
[125]56 Vict., c. 1, s. 3. Due to Haultain's representations, the period for closing accounts for the year 1892–3 was extended to September 30, three months beyond the end of the fiscal year for which the funds were voted by Parliament: see Interior file no. 91587.

to the Lieutenant-Governor and Clerk of the Assembly, who was also a federal appointee. Though Cayley advised on the expenditure, the change in procedure was retrogressive in so far as fiscal autonomy was concerned. This was an arrangement which Haultain would naturally oppose, and a federal Order in Council of March 22 met his views by specifying that in future the credits were to be made in favour of the Clerk of the Legislative Assembly and "the chief member of the executive committee."[126]

Royal's reaction to this move, which eliminated him from an active role in financial administration, is a further evidence of the more conservative attitude to territorial autonomy which he was adopting during the latter part of his term. On April 26, 1893, he sent a dispatch to Mackenzie Bowell, the Acting Premier, protesting that the Order in Council deprived him of "the necessary control which the Lieutenant-Governor is expected and instructed to exercise over the expenditure of the federal monies placed at the disposal of the Assembly."[127] His protest, however, was unavailing. The attitude of the government was embodied in a memorandum of the Minister of the Interior which stated that the purpose of the order was "to relieve the Lieutenant-Governor of the labour and trouble attending the signing of cheques, and to avoid delays which might be caused by his absence"; further that the signature of all cheques by Gordon, a federal officer, "was a sufficient safeguard"; and finally "that the desire of the government is to lean towards giving the Committee of the North-West Assembly as full control as possible of the money voted to them, and every facility to deal with the same."[128]

The Thompson administration may well have been prompted to adopt this more liberal approach because of the sharp criticism voiced by members of the opposition during the session of that year. In discussing the supplementary estimates for the expenses of the Lieutenant-Governor's office, a number of Liberal members expressed surprise that his position had not been equated with that of the Governor of a province. Control over local affairs, including the expenditure of the sums voted by Parliament, they urged, should be granted at once. "The system," one member argued, "should be one thing or the other.

---

[126]Order in Council, March 22, 1893, in Interior file no. 284083. Haultain's letter to Royal of April 6, 1893, Attorney General's file no. G 848, is also indicative of the importance he attached to the question of fiscal autonomy.

[127]Royal to Bowell, April 26, 1893, in Interior file no. 284083. He claimed that the regulations which he had imposed the previous December for the expenditure of the federal funds had "been found both simple and effective."

[128]John R. Hall, Acting Deputy Minister of the Interior to Mackenzie Bowell, May 17, 1893, Interior file no. 284083.

It is a hermaphrodite institution as it is now."[129] The government spokesmen, Daly and Thompson, were on the defensive throughout the discussion.

The last session of the Assembly during Royal's term opened on August 17, 1893. He had solicited the views of the Committee on the most appropriate date, and Haultain conveyed them informally, since he believed that it was "not within the province of the Committee to advise" on this matter.[130] The choice of a date was still restricted by the fact that the sum at the disposal of the Assembly was not transferred until after the beginning of the fiscal year of the federal government (July 1), and its amount depended upon the terms of the federal Order in Council.[131] The session of 1893 exhibited almost no partizan conflict and no challenge to Haultain's leadership.[132] There were only five recorded divisions and in none of these was there any evidence of party lines; in every one of the votes members of the Executive Committee were to be found on opposite sides. As in previous years the private members played a large part in the introduction of legislation: of the forty-five bills, less than half (17) were introduced by members of the Committee.

The session produced little in the way of constitutional change. The only legislation bearing on the subject was an ordinance introduced by Haultain which greatly circumscribed the power of the Lieutenant-Governor in Council to appropriate funds; the action of the Cayley Committee in this respect could not be repeated—no general appropriation could in future be made by Order in Council.[133] The other development reflected the increase in government business and the effect of the transfer of administrative responsibilities from the Governor to the Committee: Haultain's budget provided for the salary of a second resident member.[134]

In his parting message to the Assembly, Royal made a brave effort to recapture the reputation for liberalism which at the start of his

[129]*Commons Debates*, 1893, col. 1739.

[130]Haultain to Royal, June 15, 1893, Attorney General's file no. G 848. Cayley had taken the same stand on the Governor's exercise of this prerogative of the Crown: see letter to the editor of the *Regina Leader*, Sept. 23, 1892, in issue of Sept. 26, 1892, also his remarks on the result of the Wallace by-election, *ibid.*, Nov. 17, 1892.

[131]At this session the end of the territorial fiscal year was changed from June 30 to Aug. 31 (Ordinance no. 2 of 1893, s. 2) with the result that the moneys which were appropriated included portions of the federal grants for two successive years.

[132]Cf. Royal to Thompson, Sept. 16, 1893, Thompson Papers.

[133]Ordinance no. 2 of 1893, s. 1.

[134]See report of debates in *Regina Leader*, Sept. 7, 1893.

term he had hoped to establish, but which his own errors in judgment and the policy of his superiors at Ottawa had denied him. "The Law," he asserted, had placed him "in a somewhat invidious position of appearing to oppose the popular interests." He then continued:

When on the 4th July, 1888, I was sworn in as Lieutenant-Governor of the North-West Territories, the functions of that Office were as totally different from those of the Lieutenant-Governors of the Provinces, as they will be from those to be performed by my successor. I was responsible to the Privy Council of Canada alone for all executive acts done in the Territories. The Assembly had hardly a voice in the Government of the Country and the Lieutenant-Governor was practically a Political Commissioner under whose direct supervision and authority the affairs of the Territories were conducted and administered.

Now all this has been materially changed and hence my satisfaction.[135]

The "material change," however, had not been achieved without a struggle, and there were objectives in the battle for territorial self-government which had yet to be won.

[135]*Assembly Journals*, 1893, pp. 108–9.

CHAPTER NINE

The Achievement of Responsible Government

1894-97

DOWN TO 1893 the men who had held the office of Lieutenant-Governor of the North-West Territories had all possessed some particular quality of character or background which justified their appointment. It was perhaps an indication of the decrease in the administrative responsibilities of the office that Royal's successor, Charles Herbert Mackintosh, was chosen primarily because of faithful service to the Conservative party, for he had had no previous connection with Western Canada, and possessed no abilities which specially marked him out for the position. The territorial press generally had favoured the selection of a local man, and after the appointment was announced the *Regina Leader* wryly remarked: "It seems a kind of tradition as a new country is opened up to give as much as may safely be given to eastern aspirants."[1]

Mackintosh, an Ottawa journalist, was a former mayor of that city and at the time of his appointment was representing it in the House of Commons.[2] As a member of Parliament he attained some prominence as a controversialist, but displayed scant interest in the practical aspects of legislation and administration. Endowed with a more than ordinary sense of self-importance, he was firmly convinced that his appointment was a boon to the uncouth society and politics of the

[1]*Regina Leader*, Sept. 28, 1893. See also *Saskatchewan Herald*, Jan. 20, 1893, and Daly to Thompson, Aug. 21, 1893 (Thompson Papers) reporting on the views of the Prince Albert Liberal-Conservative Association. N. F. Davin applied for the post (see Davin to Thompson, private and confidential, May 25, 1893, *ibid.*) and he was very much opposed to the choice of Mackintosh: see his private letters to Thompson May 19, 20, and July 1, 1893, *ibid.*

[2]Mackintosh had been editor of the *Ottawa Citizen* since 1874, and had edited *Canadian Parliamentary Companion* from 1877 to 1882. He was the author of a number of pamphlets on political subjects.

North-West. "I find it rather lonesome here," he wrote Thompson three months after his appointment, "but am working hard, too hard, I fear. I know almost everyone in the Territories, either meeting them personally or writing to them—and my feet are pretty solidly set."[3] Obviously a person of Mackintosh's pretensions would not be satisfied with the quiet role of constitutional Governor, and he was soon busy improving the tone of North-West politics. One of his first concerns was the agitation of the small but aggressive Patrons of Industry movement. "I am glad to say," he reported to Thompson, "that the settlers here are tractable and reasonable, and that the newspapers are prepared to do what is fair. It is important that I see them all and arrange for the publication of such editorials as promise to bring the hot-heads back to their senses."[4] At the same time he was lecturing the population on the constitutional situation: responsible government, he told a Moosomin audience early in 1894, they now possessed "in a large measure," but further advances should be made with caution as it was "possible to have responsible government at too great a cost."[5] At first he was sure that the pioneers wanted nothing but to "get rich upon the smallest amount of either mental or physical effort," but after a few weeks further reflection he concluded that "really they are a fine all around lot—and I want to be proud of them."[6]

In view of all this it was fortunate for the peaceable conduct of local administration that the executive responsibilities of the Lieutenant-Governor had been trimmed down during Royal's régime. On the other hand, the Governor still occupied an influential position in the field of federal-territorial relations, and his views on territorial politics were bound to influence the ministry at Ottawa to some extent. "I find the Executive Committee very reasonable," he reported to Thompson, "save and except our young friend Haultain, the Chairman, who is rather inclined to pigheadedness. I fear power was yielded and privileges granted before the proper time."[7] The result, he claimed, was a tendency to be defiant—" 'The Dominion Government

[3]Mackintosh to Thompson, private, Feb. 7, 1894, Thompson Papers.
[4]Ibid.
[5]Reported in *Regina Leader*, Feb. 8, 1894.
[6]Mackintosh to Thompson, private and confidential, Jan. 4 and Feb. 7, 1894, Thompson Papers.
[7]Mackintosh to Thompson, private and confidential, Jan. 4, 1894, ibid. In view of the Governor's own conceit his judgment of Haultain may be taken with some reservation: "an honest fellow, very vain and extremely crochety [sic], and self confident" (ibid.); similarly his characterization of the North-West legislators: "I find that many of the representatives devote much time to reading the British North America Act, and discuss intra vires and ultra vires with an air as profound as one of my Lords of the Privy Council . . ." (ibid.).

236
236

put us here, they have accepted the responsibility of controlling this
North-West—now let them find the funds *we* consider necessary for
the management of affairs.' " He then added: ". . . the sooner both
the Committee and Assembly are given to understand that a halt
must be called and stock-taking be demanded, the sooner will the
machinery run smooth and effectually."[8]

Mackintosh's reports doubtless affected the stand of the Thompson
administration in the dispute with the Haultain Committee over territorial finances and responsible government which developed during
the first half of the year 1894. This notable controversy was conducted
by correspondence and in conference, with the result that it did not
receive much publicity. In its financial aspect it concerned the amount
and nature of the parliamentary appropriation for 1894–5. It will
be recalled that the estimates for the previous year had been prepared
by Royal without consulting the Executive Committee. This action
had been criticized by the Committee in its resolution of February 4,
1893, and it was to be expected that it would challenge any attempt
to repeat this proceeding. The arrival of a new Governor provided
an opportunity to change the procedure: the estimates for the expenses
of the Governor's office were prepared by him, while those under Assembly control were prepared by the Executive Committee and submitted to Mackintosh for transmittal to Ottawa.[9] Haultain grasped
this opportunity to present the case for increased financial assistance.
He pointed out the Committee's resolution of the previous February
requesting a subsidy instead of an annual vote still embodied the basic
claims of the territorial government.[10] He then proceeded to urge
several important financial and administrative changes which in his
opinion were made necessary by the "large measure of self-government" already granted. The most important of these was a substantial
increase in federal aid, if not in the form of a subsidy then by an
enlargement of the annual grant. Haultain appended detailed, annotated estimates of the requirements for the coming year, totalling
$403,640, or about twice the amount currently received. The largest
portion of the proposed increase was made up of a 26 per cent increase
in the item for public works and a 30 per cent increase in the item for
schools. He also urged the elimination of the double audit at Regina

[8]*Ibid.*

[9]The Governor's estimates were transmitted in a despatch to the Minister of
the Interior on Dec. 28, 1893, Interior file no. 343549. The Executive Committee's
estimates were submitted to Mackintosh by Haultain on Jan. 25, 1894, and forwarded to Ottawa on Jan. 31: see Treasury Department file no. 80, A.S.

[10]*Ibid.*

and Ottawa of the vote placed at the disposal of the Assembly, which, he asserted, "necessitates a large amount of extra labour in our Offices, with no apparent corresponding advantage." A single local audit was the proper system for a vote which was in the form of a lump sum and which did not lapse at the end of the fiscal year.

Following the opening of Parliament in March 1894, Haultain made another pilgrimage to Ottawa to make direct personal representations to the ministry. There were a number of meetings with Thompson and Daly, at some of which Mackintosh and the North-West senators and members were present.[11] Haultain appears to have gained the impression that the government was prepared to meet the territorial requests, but when the estimates were submitted to Parliament there was a mere $1,300 increase in the sum controlled by the Assembly, although an additional $25,000 was subsequently voted, chiefly to defray the cost of the forthcoming general election.[12] The subsidy proposal was rejected. These estimates, Daly informed Haultain, "will be supplemented in the Supplementaries for 1894–95 to meet some of the pressing necessities to which you referred when you were in Ottawa—otherwise they will be in exactly the same position as they were last year."[13] This was a keen disappointment to Haultain, and he protested vigorously that he had been depending "upon a specific agreement, made by yourself and Sir John Thompson that our Vote would be in the form of a subsidy this year."[14] In a later letter he characterized the supplementary vote of $25,000 as "a satire on both the generosity of the Government and the development of the Territories."[15] Daly, however, denied that any specific agreement or promise had been made, though he admitted that he and Thompson "may have expressed ourselves as being favourable to that idea."[16] He did not explain why, under these circumstances, the concession was withheld.

[11]*Regina Leader*, Aug. 5 and 19, 1894.

[12]See Interior file no. 363132. The main appropriation was $199,200 for 1893–4 and $200,534 for 1894–5: 56 Vict., c. 1, and 57–58 Vict., c. 1. The main discussion of the estimates for 1894–5 in the committee of supply centred around the item for the Governor's office, with the Liberals urging a reduction and criticizing Mackintosh's "political" speeches: *Commons Debates*, 1894, cols. 4921–7.

[13]Daly to Haultain, June 29, 1894, sessional paper no. 1, 1894, records of the Legislative Assembly.

[14]Haultain to Daly, July 18, 1894, *ibid.*

[15]Haultain to Daly, Aug. 5, 1894, *ibid.* Apparently Haultain and Neff were not in agreement on the financial position. Mackintosh reported that Neff believed the only increase required was for election expenses: see Mackintosh to Thompson, private and confidential, April 14, 1894, Thompson Papers.

[16]Daly to Haultain, July 26, 1894, sessional paper no. 1, 1894.

Information received from Mackintosh had doubtless played a part in this decision. He was alarmed by the increase in the number of schools, which he claimed was a consequence of the large grants and the small share of the cost borne by taxation:

While this goes on, schools will continue to increase and demands upon the Dominion Exchequer follow. Meanwhile, funds for really practically developing the Territories are being swallowed by this lusty young giant— Education, with all his attendant fads and freaks. . . . If there is any method by which the Dominion vote could be safe-guarded, it would be proper to do so, for you have no guarantee that other services will not be sacrificed to the constant demand for new schools, heavily subsidized. The money of the Dominion is a trust fund, and given to develop the Territories. If the Executive goes on spending every dollar for education . . . a violent agitation will follow for further sums from Parliament.[17]

During the discussion of the estimates by the cabinet, Daly had argued for a $50,000 increase ("It is too near the election to contract"), but he too was disturbed by the high cost of education and referred to the need "for the North-West Territories to give a helping hand to themselves" in the matter of local public works by increasing the number of statute labour districts.[18]

II

When he made his financial proposals Haultain had also urged the replacement of the Executive Committee by an Executive Council operating on the principles of responsible government.[19] The Committee, he contended, had been created by the Assembly "to meet the actual necessities" and "although appointed directly by the Legislature, fulfills many of the functions, and has most of the responsibilities of a Provincial Executive Council." He and Neff (the second "resident member") devoted their whole time to government business. He also proposed that the Assembly be empowered to fix the size of its membership and the indemnity of the members. These matters were also discussed during the Ottawa meetings, and before he left for Regina Daly asked him to draft an amendment to the North-West Territories Act which would remove existing anomalies. "Your experience and familiarity with the Act and the working of the same," Daly wrote, "gives you a peculiar knowledge of the subject, and I should like to take advantage of your presence in Ottawa by getting

[17]Mackintosh to Thompson, private and confidential, April 14, 1894, Thompson Papers. See also Mills's remarks in *Commons Debates*, 1894, col. 5170.
[18]Daly to Thompson, confidential, April 11, 1894, Thompson Papers.
[19]Treasury Department file no. 80, A.S.

an expression of your views in writing."[20] Haultain accordingly prepared a memorandum proposing the creation of an Executive Council to be chosen by the Lieutenant-Governor.[21] Other recommendations included lengthening of the term of the Assembly from three to four years and granting the Assembly the power to fix the number of its members. "The creation of an Executive Council," Haultain stated, "does not involve provincial powers or a provincial establishment. It simply creates territorial autonomy within the well defined limits imposed by the several federal Acts respecting the North-West Territories."[22] Haultain later claimed that both Thompson and Daly had agreed to his suggestions;[23] in any event he appears to have been satisfied with the draft bill which was sent to him by the Deputy Minister of the Interior.[24] However, by the time it was introduced by Daly it had become a typical North-West Territories bill, with one clause establishing an Executive Council[25] and another establishing an Executive Committee.[26]

Haultain did not see this bill until over three weeks after its introduction, whereupon he wired to Daly, Thompson, and Davin pointing out the inconsistency of the measure and urging that his draft be adhered to.[27] In reply to this Daly telegraphed: "Clause twelve relating to the Executive Council will not form part of bill got there without my knowing. Fourteen relating to the Executive Committee will stand as it is and this is the most you can expect."[28] Haultain followed up his telegram with a letter voicing a vigorous but dignified protest. He began by pointing out that the re-enactment of the ordinance regarding the Executive Committee, which provided that its members should remain in office until their successors were appointed, did not meet the situation which would shortly arise with the dissolution of the Assembly.[29] "Except by a straining of every known Parliamentary rule," he wrote, "the Executive Committee cannot exist when the Assembly of which it is a Committee has come to an end." "Why,

---

[20]Daly to Haultain, April 9, 1894, sessional paper no. 1, 1894.

[21]Haultain did not keep a copy of this memorandum, which is undated, but a copy was sent to him by A. M. Burgess on June 29, 1894, ibid.

[22]Haultain to Burgess, May 14, 1894; Haultain to Daly, Aug. 5, 1894, ibid.

[23]Haultain to Daly, June 23, 1894; Haultain to Davin, June 25, 1894, ibid.

[24]Burgess to Haultain, April 19, 1894, ibid.

[25]Bill no. 133, s. 12.

[26]Ibid., s. 14. This section reproduced the provisions of the territorial ordinance establishing the Executive Committee: Ordinance no. 1, of 1892.

[27]Telegrams dated June 22, 1894: copies in sessional paper no. 1, 1894.

[28]Daly to Haultain, telegram, June 22, 1894, ibid.

[29]Mackintosh had emphasized the same point in a letter to the Prime Minister: Mackintosh to Thompson, private and confidential, April 14, 1894, Thompson Papers.

I would ask," he added, "in dealing with North-West matters should you continually resort to heroic and unprecedented remedies when you have such familiar examples to follow as the English, Federal, and Provincial Constitutions." He continued:

The Clauses which I drafted and which I might remind you were approved by both Sir John Thompson and yourself, are a simple and practical solution of all of our difficulty. They provide us with machinery suitable to our circumstances, analogous to that in use in the Dominion and in the Provinces, which can be worked along well known and generally recognized lines. I went over this ground so often with both Sir John Thompson and yourself that I feel it unnecessary to discuss it at length again, and I can only express my surprise and disappointment at the reluctance displayed by the Government in meeting our wishes in a matter which concerns us very closely and practically, especially when the granting of what we ask cannot possibly embarrass or compromise the Government in any way. . . .

You must pardon my insistence with regard to the Executive Council Clauses, but this is a matter which involves the actual working of our institutions, the importance of which can not be fully realized by anyone who is not familiar with our everyday work.[30]

Commenting on this bill in a letter to Davin, Haultain gave way to his feelings of annoyance and frustration. The provision regarding the Executive Committee, he wrote, "is a tardy and useless recognition of machinery actually now in use":

Why can't the Government put an end to this constitution mongering? Is there any practical difference between an Executive Council chosen by the Lieutenant-Governor and an Executive Committee created by the House which does not count in favor of the former? . . .

In their apparent dread that with the assumption of a portion at least of the toga virilis we should become too independent, the Government keep forcing upon us a fantastic constitutional costume, which is good for neither use nor ornament.[31]

Haultain's protests might have had some effect had they been supported by the North-West members and senators, but this support was withheld. The retention of the Executive Committee, Davin told him, "seems to us Perley and myself satisfactory."[32] Davin's enthusiasm for responsible government had long since evaporated over the fire of his hostility to Haultain.[33]

[30]Haultain to Daly, June 23, 1894, sessional paper no. 1, 1894.
[31]Haultain to Davin, June 25, 1894, *ibid*. Neff forwarded Haultain's criticisms to W. W. Macdonald, M.P., commenting, "we are in the best position to know what is required": letter of June 26, 1894 in Thompson Papers.
[32]Davin to Haultain, telegram, June 25, 1894, sessional paper no. 1, 1894.
[33]See for example Davin to Thompson, strictly private, Sept. 15, 1894, Thompson Papers.

Meanwhile the government had withdrawn the original bill and introduced another which incorporated the terms of the ordinance relating to the Executive Committee.[34] The only result of Haultain's criticisms was an amendment in committee which empowered the Assembly to provide a method for the filling of vacancies whether "occasioned by death, resignation, or otherwise," provided that the appointment of the new members should be approved by the Assembly at its next session.[35] This, Daly stated in a letter to Haultain, would eliminate the necessity of calling the Assembly immediately upon a vacancy arising or following a general election.

While the Prime Minister remained adamant in his opposition to the creation of an Executive Council,[36] he was prepared to make some concessions in respect to the powers of the Assembly. Control over the number of seats, the size of a quorum, and (by implication) over the salary of the Speaker and the sessional indemnity, was conferred.[37] The term was extended to four years, and the power to incorporate tramway and street railway companies was granted. These liberal features only heightened the incongruity of the government's position on the question of the executive, and Mills was able to repeat the criticism which he had made on similar occasions in the past. "The honorable gentleman," he remarked, "is still deferring the day when responsible government will be introduced into the Territories. When you confer upon them the power of electing a Legislature, I do not see why the principle of responsible government, to the extent of their authority, however little that may be, should not be introduced."[38] Thompson retorted that the existing system was working satisfactorily, while Daly asserted that "the feeling on the part of the present Council, as well as the Legislature is that . . . they do not want responsible government,"[39] a statement which revealed his con-

---

[34] 57–58 Vict., c. 17, s. 17.

[35] Ibid., s. 17, ss. 3. See also Daly to Haultain, July 26, 1894, sessional paper no. 1, 1894.

[36] See Daly to Haultain, June 29, 1894, ibid.

[37] See Commons Debates, 1894, col. 5168. There were also a few clauses repealing sections of the Act of 1888 which had become inoperative, including the section relating to the Advisory Council. Mackintosh's contribution was the provision establishing property qualifications for justices of the peace; he opposed the extension of the term of the Assembly and the grant of power to increase the membership: see Mackintosh to Daly, April 21, 1894, and to Thompson, April 28, 1894, Interior file no. 235355. On the third reading of the bill McCarthy proposed the removal of the provision in the North-West Territories Act guaranteeing separate schools; after a lengthy discussion this was defeated by a vote of 114 to 21; of the three North-West members who voted, Davin supported the amendment on the principle that the Assembly should not be restricted in its power to deal with education. See Commons Debates, 1894, col. 6089 ff.

[38] Ibid., col. 5168.   [39] Ibid., col. 5170.

fusion over the difference between responsible government and provincial status.

The Minister of the Interior, though a Queen's Counsel, seems to have been unable to appreciate this simple distinction which was so well understood in the little territorial capital on the bare plains of the North-West. "In one voice you people shout for provincial autonomy," Daly wrote Haultain about this time, "in another you say you don't want it. You have got the nearest approach to it that can be given without your having the full authority that is vested in the Legislative Assemblies of the different Provinces."[40] To this Haultain replied:

We have never shouted for provincial autonomy, but have consistently said that we did not want it. Allow me to suggest that "provincial autonomy" is not the only sort of autonomy suitable to these Territories. We want the autonomy of any self-governing organization, be it School district, Municipal Council or Territory.[41]

Daly's reply to this reveals the depths of his confusion:

You cannot have complete autonomy without responsible Government. You say you do not want responsible Government. . . .There is no analogy whatever between the present constitutional condition of the Territories and that of any Province in the Dominion and there cannot be until such time as you are given full autonomy.[42]

Again Haultain, though he had almost lost patience by this time, tried to teach the minister a few elementary constitutional axioms:

I did not say that we do not want responsible Government. We *do* want responsible Government, not provincial institutions.

What we want is management of our own affairs, be they large or small. That management can best be had by means of a responsible body chosen in the same way as responsible advisers are chosen, either in the Dominion or the Provinces.

Our Executive machinery, within well defined limits, can be exactly the same as that of a Province, can be conducted by analogy and worked according to precedent, without any other approach to provincial institutions or the elaborate establishment and extensive jurisdiction of a Province.[43]

III

Since the three-year term of the Assembly had almost expired, the session of August and September 1894 was to a considerable extent

[40]Daly to Haultain, June 29, 1894, sessional paper no. 1, 1894.
[41]Haultain to Daly, July 18, 1894, *ibid.*
[42]Daly to Haultain, July 26, 1894, *ibid.*
[43]Haultain to Daly, Aug. 5, 1894, *ibid.*

concerned with measures relating to the forthcoming general election. Two of the ordinances were based on the increased powers conferred by the Act of 1894: the first provided that vacancies occurring in the membership of the Executive Committee when the House was recessed or between sessions should be filled by the Governor on the advice of the remaining member or members, subject to subsequent confirmation by the Assembly;[44] the second increased the membership of the Assembly from twenty-six to twenty-nine, giving one more to Assiniboia and two to Alberta.[45] Neither of these measures aroused any controversy. The election ordinance was also consolidated:[46] the first election law, sponsored by Frank Oliver, had been passed in 1892 and amended the following year, but, except for the Whitewood by-election of February 1894, it had not yet been tested in operation. Its most significant feature was the use of the so-called "Oliver ballot," involving the use of a blank ballot paper and coloured pencils—a colour being assigned to each candidate. It was claimed that the virtue of this novel system was that it enabled illiterate persons to vote and reduced the number of spoiled ballots,[47] although economy may also have been a factor since the expense of printed ballots was avoided.[48]

An echo of the recent contest with the federal government was

[44]Ordinance no. 25 of 1894, "An Ordinance respecting the Executive Committee of the Territories."

[45]Ordinance no. 4 of 1894. An unusual feature of this redistribution was that district boundaries were not completely respected: three constituencies in Assiniboia and Alberta included small adjoining parts of Saskatchewan. This drew an anguished protest from the Saskatchewan Times (Prince Albert): see issue of Nov. 27, 1894.

[46]Ordinance no. 2 of 1894. It consolidated Ordinances no. 21 of 1892 and no. 4 of 1893.

[47]See editorial in the Edmonton Bulletin, Oct. 25, 1894. Oliver wrote: "The idea is to get over the difficulty that exists in the case of an ordinary ballot with people who cannot read. In the Territories there is a large foreign population many of whom cannot read, and therefore cannot vote intelligently." Actually the number of naturalized foreign-born who would be voting at this time would not be large (see Table A, p. 105); possibly the métis were being considered in this connection.

[48]Mackintosh ridiculed the ballot law in letters to Ottawa ("the most peuerile [sic] production," "this extravagance," etc.), and claimed that a general election would cost at least $30,000 instead of $10,500 without the ballot (the 1888 election cost between $9,000 and $10,000): Mackintosh to Thompson, private and confidential, Jan. 4 and Feb. 7, 1894, Thompson Papers. He was quite wrong in his prediction—the election cost only $14,367.68 (see Public Accounts of the North-West Territories, 1894–5, pp. 42–3) and the system on the whole gave general satisfaction, being used in two succeeding territorial general elections and in the first provincial elections in Alberta and Saskatchewan in 1905. For comments on the ballot, see editorials in Edmonton Bulletin, Nov. 8, 1894, Moose Jaw Times, Nov. 23, 1894, and Regina Leader, July 16, 1896, and Dec. 16, 1905.

heard during the budget debate. Mackintosh, in a style reminiscent of Dewdney, had attempted in his speech from the throne to palliate the government's failure to increase the grant, but Haultain in presenting the estimates stated flatly that despite the representations of the Committee the required increase had been refused. Moreover, he pointed to the insecurity involved in annual grants. "Parliament," he said, "is given to its moods and it might happen that parliament, or a section of parliament, might assume an attitude which would affect our vote."[49] Haultain doubtless had in mind the opposition by the Roman Catholic bishops to the School Ordinance of 1892 and certain school regulations, which had reduced the amount of sectarian control of education. These changes, though overwhelmingly favoured in the Territories, had caused considerable agitation in other parts of Canada, and the Thompson administration had been asked to disallow the legislation. One of Mackintosh's first tasks had been to act as a mediator between the federal and territorial authorities to secure some compromise in this matter.[50]

Since Haultain's recent passage at arms with Daly, relations had been further strained by a crisis arising from a crop failure in Assiniboia which brought the farming population in the Moose Jaw, North and South Regina, and North and South Qu'Appelle districts to the verge of destitution. The federal government volunteered no assistance, and Haultain very properly contended that territorial resources were inadequate even for ordinary expenditures, though he promised that, failing federal action, the Committee would use what funds it could.[51] Finally, a delegation from the Assembly obtained a qualified promise of assistance from Daly, on the understanding that the initiative in launching public works relief projects would be taken by the territorial executive.[52]

---

[49]See *Regina Leader*, Sept. 6, 1894.

[50]See his correspondence with Thompson in the Thompson Papers. The Roman Catholic complaints were supported by three members of the Assembly: *Assembly Journals*, 1894, pp. 126–30.

[51]See report of public meeting in Regina, *Regina Leader*, Aug. 23, 1894, and report of debates in *Moose Jaw Times*, Sept. 7, 1894.

[52]*Assembly Journals*, 1894, pp. 91–2. Daly, writing to Haultain on Aug. 27, stated: ". . . you may rest assured that if in dealing with any unusual conditions . . . you find your resources inadequate to meet the demands made upon your local exchequer, that you will find me ready to meet the necessities of the occasion, and the Government at Ottawa will, I am sure, act upon my recommendation in the premises": copy in Daly to Thompson, confidential, Aug. 28, 1894, Thompson Papers. It appears that the policy of the administration was to refuse to admit the principle involved in earmarking federal funds for relief purposes (see Thompson to Davin, Sept. 8, 1894, *ibid.*); hence the insistence that the matter was a territorial responsibility and the qualified promise of federal aid.

During the budget debate Haultain announced his intention to press for a basic administrative reform following the general election—the abandonment of the practice of spending equal sums in each electoral division for public works under the direction of the local member. This system he had disliked from the start,[53] and he described it as inequitable, liable to abuse, and greatly disliked by the federal authorities.[54] As an evidence of future intentions a small sum was included in the estimates for public works projects undertaken by statute labour districts and municipalities. This would introduce the principle of central control, and at the same time encourage the formation of statute labour districts, which the Minister of the Interior was very anxious to promote.[55]

Had there been any considerable dissatisfaction with the Haultain Committee, it would have manifested itself during the course of this session as well as during the Whitewood by-election of the previous February.[56] But while Brett, Betts, and Clinkskill advanced a few criticisms during the budget debate, their rather vague allegation that the Committee had been inefficient attracted little attention, and they made no attempt to organize an opposition.[57] The same situation prevailed during the October general election. There were fewer acclama-

[53]See Haultain's 1888 budget speech, *Regina Leader*, Dec. 11, 1888. Haultain also admitted at this time that "a large amount of the revenue was expended on work which would properly come within the duties of municipalities."

[54]*Regina Leader*, Sept. 6, 1894. Not all of the members shared Haultain's dislike of the existing system. Frank Oliver in his election address of 1894 claimed that equal division of the funds "gave every member a direct interest in keeping down other expenditures with a view of increasing the amount available for public works in his district; and also a system which left every member free to vote for every measure that came up on its merits without the possibility of pressure being brought to bear upon him by the offer of money for expenditure in his constituency." The system, he claimed, resulted in a larger proportion of public funds being returned direct to the people in aid to schools and public works than in any of the provinces: *Edmonton Bulletin*, Oct. 8, 1894. See also *Saskatchewan Times*, Aug. 20, 1895.

[55]See Daly to Thompson, confidential, April 11, 1894, Thompson Papers. Haultain stated that there were 36 statute labour districts at this time. There were only four rural municipalities in the Territories in 1894. See A. N. Reid, "Local Government in the North-West Territories," *Saskatchewan History*, vol. II, no. 1, pp. 1–13; no. 3, pp. 1–14.

[56]The by-election was made necessary by the expulsion of the member, Daniel Campbell, who had been accused of forgery and embezzlement and had fled the country: see *Assembly Journals*, 1893, p. 71, 90, and sessional paper no. 7, 1893, *ibid.* The Whitewood campaign revolved around sectional interests within the constituency and the policies of the Executive Committee were not mentioned in any of the reported speeches. For a report on the first use of the ballot in this election see *Regina Leader*, Feb. 22 and March 15, 1894.

[57]Supporters of Haultain (including members of the Executive Committee) were to be found on opposite sides in almost every recorded division.

tions than in 1891,[58] but unlike 1891 there were no issues which were discussed generally throughout the country. The Patrons of Industry, then strong in Assiniboia, avoided official participation except in Moose Jaw constituency. Except in South Regina, where Haultain supported Mowat's opponent, the candidates conducted their campaigns without intervention or assistance from outside their districts. The *Saskatchewan Herald* commented on the difficulties of the candidates in finding a policy:

Irrigation, freight rates, immigration and a few other topics have been put up in some districts as planks likely to bridge the way to power. The candidates for re-election generally point to what they have done and promise to follow up the course best calculated to ensure prosperity to the country; new candidates, not having a record to refer to mostly content themselves with timorously pleading, "Send Me!"[59]

Haultain and Mitchell were elected by acclamation, and Neff had a substantial majority in Moosomin. Tweed was defeated, but not, it appears, upon his record as a supporter of the Haultain group. Cayley had left the Territories, but the other leading critics of the Haultain Committee—Brett, Betts, Mowat, and Clinkskill—were returned. Of the twenty-nine members of the new Assembly, eighteen were members of the old; of these, eleven had supported Haultain in the contest of 1892. Altogether, Oliver's post-election pronouncement was a fair commentary on the result: "The issues involved in the elections," he wrote, "seem to have been personal and local rather than general and therefore they cannot be claimed as a great victory, moral or otherwise, for any one except the members elected; unless indeed the fact that the present method of carrying on the government of the Territories was never brought in question may be taken as evidence of the general satisfaction with that method of government."[60]

To fill the vacancy caused by Tweed's defeat the other committeemen recommended J. H. Ross, who was appointed on April 8, 1895.[61] Ross subsequently resigned the speakership and was confirmed in his new position by the Assembly at the following session. Ross's appointment had several advantages from Haultain's point of view: he had been a vigorous advocate of autonomy; he was a prominent member of the increasingly potent territorial Liberal organization; and, representing a constituency in Assiniboia, he did not disturb the existing

[58]Six in 1894 as compared with eleven in 1891.
[59]*Saskatchewan Herald*, Oct. 26, 1894.
[60]*Edmonton Bulletin*, Nov. 5, 1894.
[61]Order in Council (N.W.T.), April 8, 1895.

balance in the Committee. To succeed Ross as Speaker, Haultain proposed his old opponent Betts. Their previous disagreements, he declared, were "occasions of the past, and he trusted it was not the intention of the Assembly to keep alive the troubles and dissentions of the past."[62] The "Premier" was never more adroit than in this shuffle by which he gained a powerful ally and silenced one of his sharpest critics.

Meanwhile, during the fall of 1894, the Executive Committee had proceeded with its first venture in relief administration. Relying largely on the usual methods of public works expenditure, special relief projects were launched in the five electoral districts affected by the drought. These projects were mostly well managed, despite the temptation to corrupt practice presented by the election contests which were being waged at the same time.[63] Nearly $45,000 was expended, involving payments to some 1,650 persons.[64] This extraordinary expenditure, succeeded in the early part of 1895 by demands for seed grain advances, threatened to dislocate the territorial budget, and gave Haultain a new argument to add to those previously presented in his annual submissions on financial requirements.[65]

The estimates for 1895–6, which were transmitted to Ottawa, came to about the same amount (less election expenditure) as those submitted the previous year. The Committee's resolution of 1892 was again advanced as the charter of territorial claims, but the current crisis arising from relief expenditure underlined the old argument for an increase in the federal grant. "The annual amount hitherto voted," Haultain wrote, "has been barely sufficient to provide for the ordinary expenditure of the Territories and has left no margin available for meeting any unforeseen and extraordinary needs which arise from time to time."[66] At the same time he found no fault with the principle of administering relief under territorial auspices, stating that it was the most economical and convenient system, besides having the advantage

[62]Report of debate in Assembly in the *Saskatchewan Times*, Sept. 10, 1895.

[63]See budget debate as reported in *Regina Leader*, Sept. 26, 1895.

[64]See *Public Accounts of the North-West Territories*, 1894–5, pp. 207 ff. Haultain in his statement to the Assembly on relief in 1895 reported the same sum, but gave the number assisted as 1,800, *Regina Leader*, Sept. 26, 1895.

[65]In the end, seed grain relief was administered by the federal authorities: see Interior file no. 371987. For political reasons Davin was very anxious that it not be placed in the hands of the territorial government: see Davin to Thompson, private and confidential, Jan. 29, 1894, and Thompson's reply, Feb. 2, 1894, Thompson Papers.

[66]Haultain to Lieutenant-Governor of the North-West Territories, Jan. 25, 1895, Treasury Department file no. 81, A.S. The amount requested by Haultain was $375,640.

of educating the people "to look to the Assembly, and to the Assembly vote, for a solution of purely local questions, and not to Parliament for special votes from year to year." Haultain also referred to his proposed programme of placing public works administration more directly under the Committee, thus "ensuring a more proper system of expenditure." The submission concluded with a renewed plea for the abolition of the double audit.

This year Haultain spent over two months at Ottawa,[67] but to singularly little purpose. No supplementary vote was provided to recoup the territorial treasury for relief expenditure, and the net increase in the grant was only about $27,000.[68] Daly justified the government's refusal to make any substantial increase by "the depressed condition of the revenues of the country, which have rendered necessary a substantial reduction in the cost of all the services of the Government."[69] The only results which he could show for his visit, apart from the small increase in the grant, were a few minor changes in the North-West Territories Act enabling the Assembly to incorporate cooperative associations for irrigation projects and local omnibus and baggage transfer companies.[70] The prevailing outlook in the capital was well expressed by the Minister of the Interior when he declared: ". . . the North-West Territories Government is still in leading strings."[71]

IV

During its 1895 session the Assembly devoted much of its time to various aspects of the financial relations of the Territories and the Dominion. The Committee's main concern at this time was to improve certain phases of local administration which, apart from their inherent merits, would strengthen the territorial case in future negotiations with Ottawa.[72] The system of treasury administration and audit, hitherto

[67]See sessional paper no. 16, 1897, records of the Legislative Assembly.

[68]The appropriation for 1894–5 was $200,534 plus $20,000 for the election; the appropriation for 1895–6 was $242,879, but this included $15,500 previously paid under statute for sessional indemnities, Speaker's salary, and travelling expenses. The net increase was therefore approximately $27,000.

[69]Daly to Mackintosh, May 1, 1895, Treasury Department file no. 81.

[70]58–59 Vict., c. 31, ss. 1 and 2. The irrigation districts were defined as "associations of the land owners, and persons interested in the lands" as distinguished from irrigation companies. The federal Companies Act and the North-West Irrigation Act did not permit the organization of mutual organizations: see Daly to Bowell, June 5, 1895, Bowell Papers, P.A.C.

[71]*Commons Debates*, 1895, col. 3721.

[72]The only request directed to the federal government during this session pertaining to the territorial constitution was for power to incorporate hail insurance

governed largely by executive regulation, was brought under a comprehensive audit ordinance.[73] This legislation created the office of Territorial Auditor and provided that this official could only be dismissed on an address of the Assembly. Also with a view to the stricter management of public funds, Haultain secured the assent of the Assembly to a more complete control by the Executive Committee over public works projects recommended by the members.[74] At the same time he did not find it possible to go any farther than he had the preceding year in abandoning the system of equal expenditures in all districts, "in the absence," so he claimed, "of specific information members had been requested to supply." "He hoped," he continued, "that next year the House would not only be disposed to accept but would insist on a policy of voting the money specifically by the House."[75] A school grants policy was also recommended, designed to reduce the proportion of school costs paid from the territorial treasury.[76] Neff sponsored an amendment to the Statute Labor Ordinance, and urged the members "to impress upon their various districts the importance of these organizations." "The necessity for local organization," he argued, "was very great. . . . Hitherto a large amount of money had been spent for minor works," which should be saved "by the people taking upon themselves the doing of the work."[77]

While admitting the necessity of putting their own house in order, Haultain still contended that the Territories "were practically ground down to an amount that was not sufficient for bare necessities."[78] In "the general cutting down" of expenses at Ottawa, he said, "the Government had not used that discretion which they had a right to expect." "Unfortunately," he added, "they had no representative of the Territories in the House of Commons who would enter his protest against the extremely inadequate amount which was being voted to the Territories, either in this or any other year."[79] This criticism of the

companies, hail losses being a matter of serious concern at this time: *Assembly Journals*, 1895, p. 47–8.

73Ordinance no. 13 of 1895.

74See *Regina Leader*, Sept. 26, 1895, p. 6.   75*Ibid.*, p. 1.

76Haultain reported that the grant per pupil was $3.94 in Manitoba and $12.77 in the Territories, and stated that there would be no great hardship if the grants were gradually reduced: *ibid.*

77*Ibid.*, Sept. 12, 1895.   78*Ibid.*, Sept. 26, 1895, p. 1.

79*Ibid.*, p. 4. As a result of this remark Haultain became involved in a sharp controversy with Davin in which the latter charged him with ignoring the North-West senators and members during his recent visit to Ottawa: see *Regina Leader*, Oct. 10, 17, and 24, 1895. Senator Perley also criticized Haultain's failure to consult with them: *Senate Debates*, 1896 (1st session), pp. 97–8.

federal members was prompted in part by the fact that Haultain and the Committee were under fire from Frank Oliver for proceeding with relief expenditures without having secured a firmer guarantee from Ottawa, and for having failed to press strongly enough for a complete reimbursement during the current year. With a view to capitalizing on the discontent over this issue, Brett and Clinkskill introduced what amounted to a want of confidence motion,[80] but withdrew it when it became apparent that the majority (including Oliver) did not wish to defeat the Committee. But one of the Committee's supporters, Magrath, issued what appears to have been a timely warning to Haultain against wasting time in Ottawa. "If his appointments with the Ministers there could not be arranged for early and kept, Mr. Haultain should come home. He would lose no support in the House by maintaining the dignity of the House."[81] The debate on the relief issue, the liveliest since the session of 1892, indicated that it would not be long before the Assembly would renew its request for a larger grant from the federal treasury.

The Executive Committee, viewing the turbulent state of federal politics at this time, no doubt deemed it inadvisable to invite the Assembly to present any comprehensive proposals to the government on the constitutional and financial position of the Territories. In the spring of 1895 the Manitoba school controversy had come to a head, and Senator Sir Mackenzie Bowell, who had succeeded to the prime ministership following Thompson's death in 1894, was faced with the prospect of a formidable split within his party. At the same time the Liberals were becoming increasingly aggressive, confident that the accumulated discontents and major and minor scandals of eighteen years of Conservative rule would sweep them into office in the election which had to be held in 1896. Shortly after Parliament met in January of that year the Prime Minister was faced with a revolt in his cabinet, and was forced to agree to retire in favour of Sir Charles Tupper at the close of the session. This dramatic development, coupled with the Liberal filibuster of the government's Manitoba school measure (The "Remedial Bill") made the session one of the most turbulent and least productive in Canadian parliamentary history. Only a small part of the estimates were passed, and these did not include the North-

[80]*Regina Leader*, Sept. 26, p. 1.

[81]Mowat had accused Haultain of "having a picnic at Ottawa" and the latter had asserted that "a greater part of the time he had nothing to do there but enjoy himself, as he was kept waiting to finish business on which he was sent." *Ibid.*, p. 6.

West grant, although $25,000 was voted in fulfilment of Daly's prom-
ise to make an adjustment in connection with the relief expenditures
of 1894.[82] Among the numerous government measures which died on
the order paper was a bill increasing territorial representation in the
House of Commons by giving a second member to Alberta, as well as
a bill which would permit Saskatchewan to be represented in the
Senate.[83]

Had Parliament approved the budget, there would have been no
improvement in the financial position of the North-West government
apart from the aforementioned $25,000. Though Haultain had sub-
mitted estimates totalling $378,760,[84] the figure which the cabinet
adopted was the same as the previous year—$242,879,[85] and since
the Laurier administration made practically no change in the estimates submitted to the special session called after the 1896 election to
vote supply,[86] this was all that the Territories received for the year.
While the Conservatives were still in power Haultain betook himself
to Ottawa, but apart from the $25,000 he accomplished nothing.
During the special session J. H. Ross made the pilgrimage, doubtless
despatched by the Committee with the hope that Laurier and his
Minister of Finance would not refuse a fellow Liberal, but he returned
empty-handed.[87]

The Manitoba separate school controversy, which played such a

---

[82]See *Commons Debates*, 1896 (1st session), col. 7129 ff. The failure to vote
supplies was a great hardship since the expenses of the last two months of the
territorial fiscal year were met by a portion of the appropriation voted by Parliament in the spring of each year; this year however the appropriation did not
become available until after the end of the territorial fiscal year: see Haultain's
budget speech, *Regina Leader*, Oct. 22, 1896, and editorial comment, *ibid.*, Aug.
20, 1896.

[83]Under the Liberal administration territorial representation in the House of
Commons was not increased until 1903 (effective 1904) and no additional senators were appointed until 1904.

[84]Treasury Department file no. 82, A.S.

[85]Senator Perley criticized the estimates as inadequate, and also told the government that they should consult Haultain rather than Mackintosh on the financial
needs of the North-West: *Senate Debates*, 1896 (1st session), pp. 176–8. In the
Commons, Davin, with an eye to the election campaign, introduced a vaguely
worded resolution proposing that the Territories "be treated on a different footing
from that heretofore" and "not be treated on a plane of inferiority" which, he
explained, meant (among other things) provincial status. He was opposed to more
than one province, and stated that the agitation for separate provinces originated
with "people who have moneyed interests in certain towns," viz., Calgary,
Regina, and Prince Albert. *Commons Debates*, 1896 (1st session), cols. 1871–88.

[86]*Commons Debates*, 1896 (2nd session), cols. 316–17.

[87]See *Regina Leader*, Aug. 20 and Sept. 17, 1896. See also Ross to Sifton, private, Oct. 14, 1896, Sifton Papers, P.A.C.

large part in the federal election campaign in other parts of Canada, was not the dominant issue in the Territories. Matters much more closely related to the everyday life of the pioneers, the tariff on agricultural implements, land policy, freight rates, and developmental projects by the federal government, attracted the most attention, and the strongest stirrings of agrarian unrest yet felt in the North-West were an important factor in the result. The Conservative candidates were everywhere on the defensive: Davin, the government standard bearer in Western Assiniboia, frankly admitted the shortcomings of recent federal policy, referring in his official address to "the utter want of originality of mind that has characterized the management of the Department of the Interior in the past."[88] Both he and his opponent, who was backed by the Patron organization, referred to the inadequacy of the funds available for the North-West government.

Haultain, who had been a candidate for the Conservative nomination in Alberta, participated in the campaign. Speaking at a mass meeting in Calgary he pictured the Conservative party as the one more likely to be sympathetic to the pressing financial needs of the North-West. "The Conservatives," he declared, "have been trying to help the West, but the Liberals have done nothing, they have simply been hopeless, faithless and unbelieving."[89] J. H. Ross assisted the Liberal effort, arguing that the opposition would do more for the Assembly than had the government.[90]

The outcome of the election, in the Territories at least, was as much a protest vote as an endorsation of the Liberal party. Davin was the only Conservative who retained his seat—by a majority of one; Oliver won in Alberta on an independent platform with Liberal support; in Eastern Assiniboia another independent accepted by both Patrons and Liberals secured the seat. In Saskatchewan, Laurier was elected by a narrow majority, but later relinquished this seat for one in Quebec, and was succeeded by a local Liberal.

V

The 1896 general election marked the beginning of a new era in Canadian politics, and provided a natural opportunity for the North-West Assembly to restate its constitutional aspirations and bring its

[88]*Regina Leader*, June 18, 1896. Davin had relinquished his interest in the *Leader* in 1895 but for the period of the election campaign it was under his control; thereafter it became a Liberal journal.

[89]*Calgary Herald*, June 11, 1896.

[90]Ross to Sifton, private. Oct. 14, 1896, Sifton Papers.

views on federal-territorial relations to the attention of the new government. The performance of this task was the most important feature of the 1896 session. At the same time there was a further development of the policies which the Committee had espoused the previous year: the old system of equal division of public works moneys was finally abandoned, and the foundations of a system of centralized public works administration were laid.[91] Coupled with this was a measure which permitted compulsory organization of statute labour districts.[92] By these two reforms the Assembly placed itself in a strong position to argue for better financial terms in its negotiations with Ottawa.

The memorial on constitutional and financial matters which was prepared for submission to the Laurier administration gave rise to the most notable debate in the parliamentary history of the North-West up to that time. The chief participants—Ross, Haultain, Brett, Insinger, Magrath, Fearon, and Clinkskill—dealt with the subject in such a comprehensive and thoughtful fashion that all the issues were soon clearly defined. The debate was indeed the ripe fruit of a decade of agitation and discussion, which, it was apparent, had produced a wealth of political leadership.

The subject was introduced by J. H. Ross, the senior member of the legislature and propónent of North-West rights in the Council and Assembly since 1883. Since his retirement from the speakership he had again become a powerful figure in the deliberations of the Assembly, and had given Haultain very effective support during the previous session. With his party in power at Ottawa, he had become the most influential politician in Assiniboia.[93] In moving the resolution for a committee to prepare a memorial, he reviewed the struggles and achievements of the past decade, and then proceeded to outline the needs of the present: an executive council, the power to appoint the magistrates and coroners, freedom to deal with real property law, and a federal grant suited to "their needs at the present time and the services which would accrue from year to year."

And every member of the House, [he asserted] no matter what his opinions may have been in regard to those who from time to time may have held the reins of government at Ottawa, had on every occasion striven

91See Haultain's budget speech, *Regina Leader*, Oct. 22, 1896, and the appropriation ordinance (no. 1 of 1896). The need for a change was underlined by certain irregularities which had occurred in the Battleford and North Qu'Appelle districts: see *Assembly Journals*, 1896, p. 64–5, 89; Attorney General's file no. G 552, and *Regina Leader*, Oct. 22, 1896.

92Ordinance no. 26 of 1896.

93See his correspondence with Clifford Sifton in the Sifton Papers.

in the interests of that House, and he hoped that would continue. What was a difficult solution for them in 1891 was far more difficult in 1896–7; what was a grievance in 1891 was a grievance of greater extent in 1896–7. The time had come when the Dominion Parliament must deal with the Territories in a more liberal spirit; the time had come when they must get out of leading strings; the time had come when they must assert themselves; and the time had come when the Dominion Parliament, . . . if proper representations were made to it,—if that Parliament knew its duty and would see its way, would give the Territories the reasonable and just demands they claim.[94]

The memorial of 1896 followed very closely the lines of Ross's argument.[95] Referring to the petitions and memorials of the past, it admitted that Parliament had been "willing partly to accede from time to time to some of their just requests"; but, it was claimed, they were "not in a position to use the limited powers they do possess to the best advantage, and . . . their legislation on subjects coming strictly within the duties of a Territorial Assembly has not the necessary quality of security or completeness. . . . While they do not ask for some rights inherent to provinces, notably the rights to raise money on the public credit, the chartering of railways, and the administration of justice with relation to criminal matters, they can see no good reason why other privileges of a territorial or provincial nature should be withheld from their administration." To achieve these objectives it was suggested that the powers conferred on the Assembly should be *exclusive* powers,[96] and that they should be further extended to include complete control over real property, the power to incorporate insurance companies, and the power to establish, maintain, and manage "hospitals, asylums, charities and eleemosynary institutions." Also requested was the power to control the appointment and qualifications of justices of the peace, and the appointment, duties, and salary of the clerk of the Assembly; the Lieutenant-Governor in Council moreover should be empowered to appoint sheriffs and clerks of court and their deputies. To remove existing "uncertainties and difficulties" connected with road management (arising from federal control of the public lands) the same arrangement as had been made with Manitoba should be adopted.[97]

[94]*Regina Leader*, Oct. 15, 1896.

[95]*Assembly Journals*, 1896, p. 67–76.

[96]The use of the term "exclusive" was not meant to be quite the same as in section 92 of the British North America Act, for it was admitted that the supremacy of Parliament in the Territories could not be challenged.

[97]Dissatisfaction with territorial powers over roads and trails was a grievance of long standing, having first been expressed in the North-West Council's memo-

The anomalous character of the Executive Committee ("a creation without precedent to guide it" and without "the well defined constitutional status which political development during a long course of time in Great Britain and her colonies has given to Executive Councils") made it desirable, it was contended, to have an executive of the latter type. Their action in making the best of the situation by con-

TABLE E

POPULATION OF THE PROVISIONAL DISTRICTS, 1895
(exclusive of Indians)

District	White	Half-breed	Total
Assiniboia	33,925	867	34,792
Alberta	26,185	2,598	28,783
Saskatchewan	5,763	4,168	9,931
Total	65,873	7,633	73,506

SOURCE: *Report of the Commissioner of the North-West Mounted Police*, 1895 (Ottawa, 1896), p. 2. A census taken by the police.

ferring executive powers on a committee of the House was, it was stated, of dubious legality—"Besides, the present machinery does not admit of development, as for instance in the direction of division into departments with responsible heads," and the Committee had no power to control the exercise of the Governor's prerogative powers and those conferred by federal legislation.

The financial proposals in this memorial were based on the same principles which had been adopted in the memorials of 1889 and 1892—a four-year subsidy made up of a per capita grant, a per capita debt allowance, a grant in aid of government, and a grant in lieu of lands. For this last, however, they were not prepared to set a figure "until such time as they enter confederation," although it was argued that since a larger proportion of public lands in the Territories than in Manitoba was reserved for national purposes, the Territories were entitled to a comparatively larger amount than was allowed to Manitoba ($100,000). But without any grant in lieu of lands the other three items amounted to $346,038, as compared with the

---

rial of 1883; minor changes were made in the law—54–55 Vict., c. 22 (1891), 55–56 Vict., c. 15 (1892), and 57–58 Vict., c. 17 (1894), but even after all these the Territories still lacked the advantages which Manitoba possessed under the act 39 Vict., c. 20 (1876).

$309,359 voted for 1896–7, of which $242,879 only was at the disposal of the Assembly.

There was no difference of opinion in the Assembly on the desirability of these various proposals, and the members devoted their attention to the broader issue of provincial *versus* territorial status. The memorial made only a passing reference to this matter when it stated that existing constitutional difficulties did not require "the granting of a full provincial status" and that "till the time arrives, which may be at a not distant day when the Territories should be taken into Confederation (as one or more provinces)" a few amendments to the North-West Territories Act would meet the needs. Dr. Brett opened up this phase of the question by proposing that "they should tell the Dominion Government in unmistakable terms that at the expiration of this Assembly,—two years hence,—they would expect full provincial powers would be given to the Territories, either as a whole or divided."[98] He admitted that public opinion was opposed to immediate provincehood on the ground that it would bring direct taxation either on a provincial basis or through the spread of municipal organization, but neither of these developments, he contended, were inevitable accompaniments of provincehood. The further objection that they were not strong enough to make a proper financial bargain with the federal authorities was also, he believed, invalid. Much of the "bargain" was fixed by the terms of the British North America Act, and the grant in lieu of public lands could be a temporary arrangement without prejudicing a final settlement at a later date.

After developing these arguments at some length, Brett proceeded to advance a case for provincehood for Alberta, including Athabasca. Since early in 1895 the *Calgary Herald* had renewed its efforts to mobilize public opinion on this subject, and had achieved some success. A provincial autonomy committee had been formed, public meetings had been held at various points to discuss the matter, and a number of influential Alberta citizens had rallied to the cause.[99] In supporting this, Brett argued that a difference in the economy of the eastern and western portions of the Territories had developed. The full utilization of Alberta's rich resources, he claimed, could only be achieved by the exercise of provincial powers. The "secession" of Alberta would not, he admitted, be popular elsewhere—Alberta was

[98]*Regina Leader*, Nov. 12, 1896. Subsequent quotations, unless otherwise noted, are from this issue.

[99]The committee issued a pamphlet *Provincial Government for Alberta, Its Meaning and Necessity* (Calgary, 1895).

contributing too much to local revenues—but the necessity of province-hood for Alberta and other parts of the Territories would soon be universally admitted. Brett was ably supported by Magrath of Lethbridge, who argued that they should begin to educate the people on the subject of the future form of government even though there was no immediate prospect of securing provincehood.

The position taken by Brett and Magrath received qualified support from Fearon of Medicine Hat. He disliked the present "indefinite" state of affairs and denied that the borrowing of money was "so much of a bugbear as it was popularly supposed to be." Like a farmer with a large undeveloped property who refused to use credit, they were "allowing their natural resources to remain dormant." However he rejected the proposal to establish Alberta as a province—"There was," he declared, "no argument advanced why Alberta should be separated from the Territories and formed into a province that could not be advanced in favor of any other part of the Territories." "In fact it was disintegration, a principle opposed to the spirit of the age." United, "they certainly would be of more importance than they would be divided."

The defence of the "gradualist" approach represented by the memorial was opened by Insinger of Yorkton. He ridiculed Brett's claim that they could make an "open end" contract with the federal government on the natural resources issue. And, he asserted, they were not sufficiently strong, with only four members of Parliament, to make a full contract—"to fight all the other parts of Canada, because fight they must." "Would the Parliament at Ottawa give them full consideration for the large amount of public lands which had been taken from them for the general benefit of Canada? The Parliament at Ottawa would simply give what they thought proper, and not what the Territories wanted." If they made the contract now "they would get left." They should not ask, he contended, for more than they really wanted—this would prejudice their whole case. It was a positive advantage that the requests contained in the memorial were not a contract, "but only an arrangement that would hold good for a few years, or until such time as they might want something else." "Their principle," he declared, "should be to go and ask for those things in detail;—show why they wanted these things, and prove that they really wanted them. If they showed that they understood what they wanted, and that they knew how to handle it, they stood a very good chance of getting it. He did not believe in asking for a whole lot of things in the chance of getting a little."

Haultain's defence of the memorial was largely taken up with a criticism of Brett's proposal that the Alberta partner should withdraw from the firm.[100] He did not know, he said, "what the honorable member meant when he spoke of a partnership existing between what was one single united country, and he believed would remain so." Instead of provinces based on distinct economies, they should have "a good strong province" with a diversity of resources. There was no greater conflict of interest between sections of the Territories than there was between sections of the older provinces. The policy south of the border of having small compact states was not one which should have great weight with them. "So far as they knew anything about American institutions, he (Mr. Haultain) thought that was not exactly the part of the world to which they were going to look for precedents." There were no obstacles to intercommunication between the districts, and the sectional argument was capable of indefinite extension—they could "cut the whole country into small plots so that every man might be a province unto himself with three acres and a cow."

He believed [he said] they should have one province, but that they need not have it yet. He believed they should go on, as they had been going on, with gradual development of their present institutions, here and there gaining a little more power, here and there extending their jurisdiction, here and there getting a little more money. These were the practical questions for consideration. . . .

If they must dream, he concluded, let them dream of "one large province with all its varied resources." "A dream of one large province holding its own in confederation, the most powerful province in confederation, would be a much more desirable thing to think about, and to speculate about, than a number of small areas confined in their powers and in their influence." Haultain's peroration practically concluded the debate. Magrath and Brett withdrew their amendment[101] and the memorial passed unanimously.

VI

The attitude of the new Minister of the Interior, Clifford Sifton, seemed to augur a favourite response in Ottawa to the Assembly's proposals. In an address at Moosomin early in December he declared that

[100]*Regina Leader*, Nov. 19, 1896.

[101]The amendment proposed the insertion of the following clause, "The Assembly is of the opinion that until the Territories are admitted into Confederation as two or more provinces which they consider is necessary at an early date for the compact government on local lines of such a vast country, that the passage of a few amendments . . ." etc.: *Regina Leader*, Nov. 12, 1896.

"the swaddling clothes plan of treating the North-West had come to an end." "He was satisfied," he continued, "there would be no longer any attempt made to prevent the people of the North-West from doing business which can be done better by themselves than by people at Ottawa."[102] This declaration was encouraging, and, armed with the memorial, Haultain went east in the early part of 1897. He soon discovered, however, that the Laurier administration was no more willing than its predecessors to meet the territorial requests in full, and J. H. Ross was hurriedly summoned to assist in "educating" the ministers and the members regarding the needs of the North-West.[103] The amendment to the North-West Territories Act which issued from these negotiations[104] bore the impress of a more liberal attitude than had prevailed in Ottawa for some years; at least the old suspicion of a responsible executive had disappeared with the overthrow of the Conservative régime. The measure was introduced by Sifton, and provided for the establishment on October 1, 1897, of "the Executive Council of the Territories," whose members were to be chosen by the Lieutenant-Governor—it being understood that their status and tenure of office would conform to the well-understood principles of responsible government.[105] The Executive Committee, Sifton said, was a body "without precedents in our constitutional system." "The bill," he said, "will give the people of the Territories a government which shall not have the full powers of a provincial government, but in so far as they have power to deal with subjects, they shall do it in the same way as the other provinces. They will have Ministers who are responsible to the legislature, and the rules and precedents that apply to the provincial governments will apply to the government of the Territories."[106]

In the years since 1892 the North-West Assembly had clothed the Executive Committee with so many of the vestments of a responsible executive that the establishment of the Executive Council seemed to many to be but a change of name—a formal recognition by Parliament of a system which had béen developed by the North-West itself. As the

---

102*Ibid.*, Dec. 10, 1896.
103*Ibid.*, April 8, 1897. See also Ross's remarks during the budget debate, *ibid.*, Dec. 9, 1897.
10460-61 Vict., c. 28. Assented to June 29, 1897.
105Section 9 introduced the contemporary practice of having members resign their seats and seek re-election upon being appointed to the cabinet.
106*Commons Debates*, 1897, cols. 2797, 4115. Mackintosh invited Haultain to form the first Executive Council and on October 7, 1897, the following were appointed: F. W. G. Haultain (Macleod), J. H. Ross (Moose Jaw), Hillyard Mitchell (Mitchell), C. A. Magrath (Lethbridge), G. H. V. Bulyea (South Qu'Appelle). Only Haultain and Ross held portfolios at the start.

Regina Leader described it in its review of the constitutional history of the Territories:

The real machinery of government for daily control, and providing for the active intervention of men responsible to the Assembly in all matters of administration and expenditure coming within the jurisdiction of the Assembly, has had to be conceived, made and carried out by the House itself. The North-West administration has been confronted with primary, primitive conditions. They have had precedents to follow in a way, but no specific Parliamentary authority to guide them. They may fairly claim no small credit for originating and independently making a constitution under most adverse circumstances.[107]

The other provisions of the Act of 1897 and the financial arrangements of that year fell short of what the Assembly had requested. The proposed extensions of legislative authority were all refused except in regard to the qualifications of justices of the peace; there was some further extension of control over road allowances and trails. The power to appoint sheriffs was refused, but the positions of clerks of court and clerk of the Assembly were placed under local control. The financial proposals were rejected. "They were met," Haultain later reported, "with the statement that the Dominion was paying for many services in the Territories which were paid for in the provinces by the provinces." The government's attitude, he said, was that if they were given a subsidy they should "undertake all the services which the provinces carry on."[108] The subsidy proposal was therefore dropped, and the two territorial representatives fell back on a statement of their actual requirements, which came to about the same amount. Their arguments produced an increase of $40,000, but this was far short of the amount which was deemed necessary.[109] "Constitutionally," Haultain commented later, "we have approached close to provincial basis, but financially we are a long distance from that basis. . . . If the arbitrary amounts voted by Parliament are to be based not upon present requirements but upon the worn out estimates of earlier requirements, then [we] . . . will go in for full provincial establishment in order to

[107]*Regina Leader*, Oct. 14, 1897.

[108]Remarks during the 1897 budget debate: *Regina Leader*, Dec. 9, 1897.

[109]During the second session of 1896 Oliver had made a vigorous plea for an increased grant to the Territories: *Commons Debates*, 1896 (2nd session), cols. 412–18, 2394–6. In the 1897 session Davin outlined the terms of the Assembly's memorial and supported them with the qualification that there should be a federally appointed auditor in Regina: *Commons Debates*, 1897, cols. 1030–41. As spokesmen for North-West "rights," Davin and Oliver were bitter rivals, see *ibid.*, cols. 1041–3.

get financial recognition."[110] In this declaration the Premier defined the issue which dominated the next period in the political development of the Territories.[111]

VII

The evolution of self-government in the Canadian North-West Territories during the twenty-seven years following the union of 1870 displays many features which might be compared and contrasted with American and British territorial or colonial administration. The similarity between the cautious approach to colonial self-government displayed by the British authorities before 1846 and the territorial policy of the Conservative administration at Ottawa is perhaps the most striking feature of the situation. The mantle of "imperial" pretensions was donned with alacrity in Ottawa, and only put off with reluctance. There were influences which contributed to this apart from the mere existence of dependent territory and the prestige of the British colonial system, notably the distinctive features of Canadian federalism and Macdonald Conservatism. The financial assistance given to the provinces by the federal government, the federal power of disallowance of provincial legislation, the position of the Lieutenant-Governors and the judiciary as federal appointees, were among the more tangible evidences of the relatively high degree of centralization which prevailed in the Canadian federation. And it was Macdonald's policy to emphasize the pre-eminence of federal authority whenever constitutional issues arose, so that his territorial policy may be regarded as an extension of his philosophy of federal-provincial relations. Then too, his administrative policies involved a large measure of government intervention in support of the national economy, one phase of which was western development, so that the pervasive character of federal administration in Western Canadian economic life also helped to cultivate an autocratic approach to territorial administration. Moreover, the exigencies of party politics made Ottawa reluctant to relinquish command over means of patronage which properly belonged to the territorial government.

The spokesmen for North-West rights, while not unmindful of earlier struggles for responsible government, were more concerned with practical issues than with historic parallels; in general they

[110]Remarks during the 1897 budget debate: *Regina Leader*, Dec. 9, 1897.
[111]See C. C. Lingard, *Territorial Government in Canada: The Autonomy Question in the Old North-West Territories* (Toronto, 1946).

adopted a practical rather than a doctrinaire approach in their contests with the federal government. In promoting their ideas they had to contend with sectional jealousies within the Territories, national party loyalties, personal political ambitions, and an indifference to local politics begotten by the dominant role of the federal government in the more important concerns of pioneer life. A further handicap was the widespread confusion over the implications and interrelationship of responsible government, provincehood, direct taxation, and municipal organization. Nevertheless the autonomy movement did have a wide measure of popular support: speaking of the situation in the 1880's on one occasion Senator Perley remarked, "I admit that the people were, perhaps, rather impatient to have self-government while the population was so sparse, but still that was the opinion all over that country that we should have self-government."[112]

The example of the United States was far less important in the field of territorial policy than in other aspects of western administration. Adherence to British constitutional forms was the very essence of Canadian political life, with the result that there was little interest in or knowledge of the American system, either in Ottawa or the North-West. One consequence of this was the prevailing misconception that the American system involved the same degree of territorial subordination as that which prevailed in Canada, and that it was, if anything, less liberal. In reality, Canada had adopted a system which resembled the primitive one which had long since been discarded by the United States; after 1827 the terms of the Ordinance of 1787 had been abandoned to the extent that no territory had been established without an elective legislature. "The newer form," one American scholar writes, "was less a unit of control than a framework for self-government."[113] Moreover, in the United States there was less detailed supervision by the federal government: "control was ineffective rather than either tyrannical or generously moderate"[114]—a statement which could hardly be applied to the Canadian system. Nevertheless the closer control by Ottawa was not without its advantages in the earlier years, and as time went on the Canadian territory, like the American, "tended increasingly to be a frontier unit in that it was dominated and molded by the frontier and by frontiersmen."[115]

The demand for provincial status voiced by Louis Riel in 1870 and

[112]*Senate Debates*, 1896 (1st session), p. 97.
[113]Earl S. Pomeroy, *The Territories and the United States, 1861–1890, Studies in Colonial Administration* (Philadelphia and London, 1947), p. 97.
[114]*Ibid.*, p. 106.   [115]*Ibid.*, p. 94.

1885 did not represent the main stream of the autonomy movement in the Canadian North-West. Similarly, the agitation in the early 1890's for the establishment of provinces represented the appetite of rival towns for self-aggrandizement rather than the viewpoint of the settlers as a whole. The more characteristic expression of western aspirations was the sober, steady movement whose object was to keep constitutional progress in step with social and economic development. This movement achieved a notable success in 1897, and from this went on to its natural culmination in the formation of the provinces of Saskatchewan and Alberta in 1905.

CHAPTER TEN

Reflections on Territorial Government

1897-1970

POLITICAL INSTITUTIONS are shaped by social forces—by the traditions, psychology, and vital interests of the people composing a community. Moreover, prevailing geographic and economic conditions also have a profound effect on politics and constitutional arrangements. All this is vividly illustrated in the history of the old North-West Territories from 1870 to 1897 and in the Canadian North in subsequent years. Where a concentrated population existed with its own social system and traditions of government and strong sense of community, as was the case in the Red River Settlement, it was not possible for the federal authorities to force it into a constitutional structure which was repugnant to the majority. Hence, under Louis Riel's leadership, the province of Manitoba was created out of a part of the North-West Territories. But for the remainder of the area—a vast, empty land with a scattered white population—it was not inappropriate that a primitive form of colonial government should be established, with Ottawa assuming the role of London as the seat of imperial authority. But once this imperial-colonial relationship was established, the easiest course in later years and in other parts of the Northwest was to regard it as the norm. Ottawa settled into a comfortable lethargy in its dealings with the Territories.[1]

As soon as Manitoba was largely settled and the C.P.R. was constructed between Winnipeg and Vancouver, settlement flowed west into

[1]The political rights of the original people of the Northwest, the Indians, were non-existent under the terms of the Indian Act despite the fact that they composed the majority of the population until probably 1890. Thereafter they became a cultural minority, isolated on reserves set aside for them under the terms of the numbered treaties negotiated in the 1870's, in order to permit the Canadian frontiersman to occupy the soil.

the available land in the provisional districts of Assiniboia, Saskatchewan, and Alberta. "Improved communications, and the presence of an intelligent and articulate leadership ... created a steadily growing sense of community in problems, interests, and possibilities," a later commissioner of the present-day Northwest Territories has noted.[2] It was in this context that the struggle for responsible government took place. The territorial community, comprising the settled areas of the three provisional districts, was united on this objective, and the imperial authority was forced to make this constitutional change in 1897, after the Liberal victory of 1896.

But this unanimity of political objective was lacking in 1905. A sufficiently strong "district consciousness" of sense of community had developed in Alberta that any attempt to create one large province between Manitoba and the Rockies was foredoomed to failure. The Regina bureaucracy, headed by Premier Haultain, was unresponsive to the metropolitan ambitions of Calgary and Edmonton. This played into the hands of the federal government, which had no wish to create another large, strong province which might well challenge its policies. Hence two provinces were created—Alberta and Saskatchewan—neither of which, like Manitoba, was given control of its natural resources. This latter provision was a serious departure from the principles of federalism as then understood. The federal union created in 1867 was founded on the principle of two co-ordinate levels of sovereignty, but the restrictions placed on the three prairie provinces were a departure from this principle.[3] The new provincial governments in Alberta and Saskatchewan did not contest this violation, but in later years it created great acrimony, as it had in Manitoba beginning in the 1880's.[4] The imperial mentality triumphed over principle.

In eastern British North America the confederation movement had an economic dimension which was decisive—the ambition of the economic group dominant in the Province of Canada to dominate also the Maritime region and more importantly the unexploited Northwest. This was the reason for federal control of the natural resources of the three prairie provinces. But both before and after 1905 a clear pattern emerges of a federal authority which responded to the constitutional require-

[2]R. G. Robertson "The Evolution of Territorial Government in Canada" in J. H. Aitchison, ed., *The Political Process in Canada* (Toronto, 1963), 139–40.

[3]It should be noted that the constitutions of Alberta and Saskatchewan also restricted the power of the province in education, the provision for separate schools being made mandatory.

[4]The control of natural resources was transferred to the provinces in 1930. See Chester Martin, *"Dominion Lands" Policy*, The Carleton Library no. 69, edited by Lewis H. Thomas (Toronto, 1973), pp. 204–26.

ments of the Territories and its people only when the exploitation of a newly discovered natural resource aroused central Canadian cupidity.

The first constitutional change after 1897 was the creation of Yukon Territory. Widespread placer gold mining activity in the Yukon district began in the 1880's along the Yukon River. Access to the area was chiefly from ports in the Alaska panhandle, and the issue of collecting customs on goods imported from these ports arose, as well as the enforcement of federal mining regulations. There was also the problem of maintaining law and order in an area where a large alien population had assembled along the river close to the American boundary. The American miners, who formed a majority of the population, were disposed to regard the country as American territory, particularly since the 141st meridian (the western boundary of the North-West Territories) had never been surveyed. The situation posed the threat of American annexation. In 1894 a detachment of North-West Mounted Police was sent to investigate the need for law enforcement and for the extension of federal services and regulations. They found that the miners had, through the device of "the miners' meeting," assumed the powers of local government and particularly the enforcement of rough justice. The following year the police succeeded in abolishing this institution and substituting their own police and judicial powers. But as late as 1896 the inspector in charge of the Yukon detachment was insisting that civil courts "should be established with the least possible delay" and that a gold commissioner and registrar were "urgently needed." "The want of them," the inspector continued, "creates a distrust in the administration of government and there is an idea spreading that the country is occupied by the government solely for the purpose of revenue."[5] Wm. Ogilvie, the Canadian government surveyor sent to the Yukon in 1895, in a report to the government echoed these sentiments. A police post was built very close to the Alaska–Yukon boundary in 1895. The boundary was surveyed in the vicinity of the diggings by Ogilvie. During 1895–6 he also surveyed the land along the river and its tributary creeks where the miners had staked out claims, and he inevitably became involved in surveying the claims and settling disputes as best he could. Ogilvie urged that a more elaborate and permanent arrangement be made for further surveys and the registration of claims, with the result that in 1897 a gold commissioner-surveyor-land agent was appointed, along with a staff of surveyors. The following year was one of intensive movement and activity by the gold seekers, culminating in August with the famous discoveries on Bonanza Creek, near the confluence of Bonanza Creek and the Klondike and Yukon rivers.

[5]North-West Mounted Police Annual Report, 1896, *C.S.P.* 1897, no. 15, p. 235.

The response of the federal government activity was painfully slow and hesitant, particularly during the last years of the Conservative régime. But even the new Liberal Minister of the Interior, Clifford Sifton, thought Ogilvie's reports too optimistic.[6] The Yukon had been created a provisional district of the North-West Territories in 1895, but this involved no semi-autonomous territorial government. In theory it was still subject to the government at Regina. It was not until the late summer of 1897 that a federal officer who was to co-ordinate and supervise all federal government employees was appointed, with the title of Commissioner of the Yukon. By now large sums of revenue were being paid to the federal treasury in the form of fees, gold royalties, and customs duties. That fall Sifton and a large party travelled to the Yukon, but the Minister confined himself to the southern part of the district and did not visit the mining camps.

Since the centre of population and mining activity was so far removed from the territorial authorities in Regina it was deemed appropriate to convert the provisional district into the Yukon Territory, and the centre of political authority shifted to Ottawa. By this time the centre of mining activity had moved upstream from the vicinity of the American boundary and was centred at Dawson City near Bonanza Creek. The Mounted Police barracks, the gold commissioner's quarters, the post office, and residence quarters for government officials were the first buildings to be constructed beside the miners' shacks and tents. Dawson City became the capital of Yukon Territory.

The act of 1898[7] created a territorial government similar in some aspects to that which prevailed in Battleford from 1876 to 1882, except that the head of the administration was designated as commissioner rather than lieutenant-governor, thus robbing him of the powers and prestige of being the local representative of the Crown. Although the commissioner of the provisional district had recommended the creation of a council of three appointed and three elected members, the federal government rejected the elective principle. The Yukon Act provided for the appointment of a council of up to six members with executive and legislative powers. This was a reversion to the pre-1875 territorial constitution—the most primitive form which had ever existed in the Northwest. Irrespective of which party was in power in Ottawa there was a rooted aversion to popular democracy in the territories excused in this case by the presence of so many aliens in the population.

The legislative powers of the commissioner and council were to be the same as those possessed by the lieutenant-governor and Legislative

[6]D. R. Morrison, *The Politics of the Yukon Territory, 1898–1909* (Toronto, 1968), p. 15.
[7]61 Vict., c. 6.

Assembly of the North-West Territories, except those withheld by the federal authority. The powers of the commissioner were unprecedented—in addition to heading the local administration he was given authority over all officers of the federal government in the territory, because of the obstacles to communication with Ottawa. He was also given the traditional power to reserve approval of any ordnance and send it to Ottawa for decision by the federal cabinet.

The Canadian Parliament had shown no interest in the gold rush before 1898. This probably is to be explained by the distance of the area from Ottawa, the inefficient mail service, and the indifference of Canadian businessmen until late in 1897. There was no Canadian newspaper representative in the territory in 1898, whereas there were nearly two hundred from American, British, French, and German newspapers.[8] The Yukon District commissioner had noted caustically that "While the American papers have heaped on us a great deal of abuse, our thanks are certainly due to them for advertising our country, as without the assistance of their press and population, comparatively little would be yet known of the British Yukon." The combined effect of remoteness of the country from central Canada and the characteristic lack of bold initiative of the Canadian businessman probably explain this anomalous situation.

To keep the polygot but largely American population under Canadian control finally became a high priority for Sifton and his colleagues. Conditions in the Yukon were chaotic, verging on anarchy by 1898. That year saw a flurry of federal government activity. First was the passage of the Yukon Act followed by the appointment of the first commissioner (William Ogilvie) and four councillors, all of them employees of the government in Dawson City. Secondly there was the dispatch of 200 militiamen—the Yukon Field Force—to back up the activities of the North-West Mounted Police. In the same year also the Public Works department decided to construct a telegraph line linking Dawson with the American port of Skagway, Alaska. The link was completed in the autumn of 1899, and using the fast steamer service permitted the officials to communicate with Ottawa in four days. An all-Canadian line through northern British Columbia was constructed in 1901, cutting the time lapse in half. A plan to encourage the construction of a rail link with British Columbia had to be abandoned, much to Sifton's disgust, by unilateral American action on the boundary issue in the panhandle.[9]

[8]*C.S.P.* 1899, no. 13, p. 331 (Report of Commissioner J. M. Walsh, 1898).

[9]For a discussion of Sifton's strongly nationalist position on this railway issue see D. J. Hall, "The Political Career of Clifford Sifton 1896–1905" (unpublished Ph.D. thesis, University of Toronto, 1973), pp. 239–63, particularly 258–63. Dr. Hall is currently engaged in preparing a complete biography of Sifton.

The impetus to federal action was provided by the emergence of a self-conscious community which possessed many of the characteristics of a turbulent American-style frontier. Dawson City itself when Ogilvie arrived numbered 17,000, and the total Yukon population was 40,000. Despite its name, neither Dawson City nor any other settlement along the river had the benefit of municipal organization. Just as was the case in the North-West Territories from 1870 to 1883, municipal functions had to be assumed by the commissioner and council. The situation in the Yukon settlements was particularly acute. Squalid housing, disease, the threat of fire, and prostitution were rampant. The federal government was more concerned with collecting revenue, and Sifton was restricted by the necessity of limiting federal expenditures in his department. In short, the situation in the Yukon from 1896 to 1900 was chaotic.

Political activity began in 1897 with numerous mass meetings which protested federal mining regulations and the partisan activities of some federal government officials. In 1898 these miners' association meetings began an agitation for two elected members in the territorial council and representation in Parliament, and a petition was forwarded to the federal government. The pre-1897 style of constitutional agitation in the North-West Territories reappeared.

The press, which was a potent poiltical force in territorial affairs in the south, also emerged in 1898—three American-owned newspapers and one Canadian. Two were anti-Ottawa in their editorial policy. Uninhibited vituperation was characteristic of the Yukon press, and its chief targets were the Minister of the Interior, Commissioner Ogilvie, and the majority of the council. In addition there was plenty of good copy in reporting on the feuds among the councillors and among the resident federal officers. The strong sense of regional self-consciousness which all these events produced is well expressed in the following perceptive editorial in the *Klondike Miner* early in 1899:

A great deal has been said and written about the apparent lack of wisdom shown in the governing of this territory and in the laws and regulations under which we operate. After all is said and done does not the greater part of the trouble arise from the government of Canada attempting to keep this distant country directly under its own eye and control through local officers who of very necessity, do not feel their responsibility to the people of the locality as they do to their own immediate superiors, the Dominion officials—the source of their authority here. It is not the first time in the history of the world when an ignominious failure has followed the attempt to pass laws for the government of a country at an enormous distance from the place of execution, and it reflects no particular discredit by reason of its failure. ... The two principles that are being violated in the government of this country ... [are] that of the necessity ... to have the opportunities to easily present grievances for speedy redress ... and [that] the citizens ... if they are to continue to be taxed ... shall be permitted to have a voice in the spending of their money and that it shall be used for their good and for the development of this land and not to make good ... deficits in the general running expenses of the Dominion.[10]

To counter this sort of criticism, and that voiced by the miners' association, Sifton secured an order in council in 1899 forbidding any person on the federal payroll from holding land or acquiring mining claims in the Territory. Later in the year he sponsored an amendment to the Yukon Act which elaborated the court system and made the Supreme Court of British Columbia the court of appeal, a system which had prevailed in the North-West Territories when the Manitoba court had performed the same role. Under Senate pressure, provision was made for the election of two councillors when the federal cabinet saw fit to implement the arrangement. The powers of the council were augmented to permit the imposition of taxes on shops and taverns and the performance of municipal functions and to levy charges to meet their costs. The council could also empower any municipality to levy taxes for the performance of similar functions.

The federal government delayed action on implementing the elective principle, causing hostility to Ottawa to reach fever pitch. A citizens committee emerged from mass meetings of the miners to act as a lobby or pressure group for the Yukon in its relations with the federal government. The committee was bitterly critical of the commissioner and the majority of the council for refusing to endorse its requests and for holding their sessions in secret. Fuel was added to the fire when the crown prosecutor, who was the first registrar of lands and a political friend of Sifton, charged that the committee was an instrument of the Conservative party. Liberal ministers and their appointees in the public service were suspicious of all local critics of federal policies. The Conservative opposition, despite their own party's indifference before 1896 to conditions in the Yukon, launched a major campaign in the Commons in 1899 and the succeeding year, condemning the government for gross inefficiency and dishonesty in handling Yukon affairs.

The government, in an effort to counter the impact of the opposition's criticism of Yukon administration, announced in July, 1900, that an election would be held for two members of the council as provided in the previous year's amendment of the Yukon Act. Four candidates

[10]*Klondike Miner*, Feb. 3, 1899, printed in D. R. Morrison, *The Politics of the Yukon Territory 1898–1909* (Toronto 1968), p. 27.

were nominated for the October election—two of them by the citizens committee which created the "Citizens Yukon Party." Its candidates won by a substantial majority. The success of the party prompted the Liberals in the Yukon to found a Liberal party, whose leaders were chiefly federal officials.

The council of the Yukon Territory after the addition of the elected members became an active legislative body. Moreover, as in the North-West Territories, memorials were sent to Ottawa requesting federal action on matters of concern to the population, particularly mining regulations. In 1901 the Yukon Party members sent a minority petition calling for parliamentary representation and a wholly elected council.

Commissioner Ogilvie was dismissed on Sifton's initiative after a little more than two years in office because of his limitations as an administrator and failure to defend Liberal policies vigorously. His successor, James H. Ross, appointed early in 1901, had been a member of Haultain's cabinet and was noted for administrative capacity and Liberal party leadership in the Territories.

Ross took the initiative in promoting legislation for the adoption of municipal institutions in Dawson and other centres, and at long last Dawson City was given a mayor and council. Thus after four years the Yukon council was relieved of the difficult and time-consuming activities which more properly belonged to municipal governments. In addition to sponsoring this reform locally, Ross was able to convince the federal government in 1902 to enact a further amendment to the Yukon Act increasing the elected membership to five, and to provide one member in the House of Commons. Ross, who had been forced to resign as commissioner because of ill health in July, 1902, was elected as the first member of Parliament for the Yukon that same year, in a campaign which was notorious for irregularities and corrupt practices. The election for five members of the territorial council was held in January, 1903 largely on non-partisan lines. It was in this year that the elected members of the council first advocated responsible government.

F.T. Congdon, the third commissioner, had first come to the Yukon as legal adviser to the territorial government in 1901. He was a Liberal machine politician, much more so than Ross. He became embroiled in a quarrel with the residents and the council of Dawson City which ended in the revoking of the city charter and direct rule from the commissioner's office. By flagrant patronage he built a personal following, and in 1904 resigned to contest the federal election. He was defeated by a Conservative, largely because of his maladministration of Yukon affairs and feuds with other Liberals, and corrupt election practices. In the summer of 1905 Frank Oliver, Sifton's successor as Minister of the

Interior (1905–11), visited Dawson City and met many citizens, and announced a number of reforms in mining regulations to satisfy complaints. The next commissioner was a British Columbia politician and reformer, who initiated many administrative improvements, but resigned after a year and a half to re-enter provincial politics.

In the 1905 session the Conservative member for the Yukon argued vigorously for a ten-member elected territorial council and responsible government. He was opposed to provincial status at this juncture. Laurier responded as follows:

... Is the government, or is parliament at all derelict in its duty in regard to that matter? It is only eight years since the Yukon was discovered and brought into civilization. Up to that time it was an unknown country. All of a sudden, in 1897, there was a rush of population from all over the world, ... [It] would have been extremely unwise to have given at once an elective council to the new community.[11]

Agitation for representative institutions and responsible government continued, and in 1908 the Yukon Act was amended[12] to provide a constitution closer to the provincial model. Frank Oliver in sponsoring the amendment said:

There is naturally a desire on the part of every community in this country to have the fullest possible measure of self-government. In the organization of new territories it has not always been thought desirable, nor has it always been possible, to give entirely elective legislatures. When the Northwest Territories were first organized it was necessary to have a legislature partly elective and partly appointed, and when the Yukon government was organized that system was followed. ... [We] have hopes of the future development of the country; ... The proposition before the House is to give the territory today an entirely elective Council and a form of government generally that will be in accord with the general principle that pervades our constitution namely, that the people shall govern in certain well-defined affairs and within well-defined limitations. ...

Laurier in 1905 and Frank Oliver three years later turned a blind eye to the need in the Yukon to control the carrying out of the legislation which the council was empowered to enact. Their talk about self-government was the sort of pious platitude so beloved of politicians in power. In 1888 Laurier had criticized the bill establishing an Assembly for the Territories on the ground that "a local Legislature, which has not at the same time the power of controlling the Executive, cannot and

11*Commons Debates*, 1905, cols. 7078–9.
127–8 Edward VII, c. 76.

did not ever work satisfactorily."[13] Oliver, the radical territorial councillor and assemblyman before 1897, had been in the forefront of the struggle for responsible government. But after the Liberals came to power, the ambitions of the Yukon councillors were firmly resisted.

The Yukon Act amendment of 1908 is a curious departure from the course of constitutional evolution which prevailed in earlier years in the Yukon and in the old North-West Territories, in that it strongly resembled a provincial constitution. The commissioner occupied the same position as a lieutenant-governor, but was not responsible to the elected legislature. A ten-man elected council was provided, to hold office for a three-year term, unless dissolved by the commissioner. The council was to be presided over by a speaker, rather than by the commissioner. Money bills were initiated by the commissioner. There was no executive council,[14] but the same arrangement as that of the 1891 amendment to the North-West Territories Act was made – viz. that the expenditures of funds should be made by the commissioner and council "or any committee thereof." In the North-West Territories Haultain and his associates had used the committee to advance the cause of responsible government, but no such leadership emerged in the Yukon, in part, probably, because of the drastic decline of the population to less than nine thousand in 1911.

In reflecting on the constitutional history of the Yukon to this point, several influences can be detected. First, it is obvious that the Laurier ministry drew on earlier, more primitive forms of territorial government adopted by the Conservative régime. Implicit in these earlier forms was the principle of an imperial-colonial relationship and government by remote control. Second, there was the reluctance to establish semiautonomous democratic forms of government, until popular pressure reached crisis proportions. Moreover, the desire to secure partisan political advantage was even stronger than before 1896, with the result that territorial politics was not conducted on a non-partisan basis. Finally, it appears that the threat of American expansionism was a more potent influence on federal policy than the needs of a self-conscious community within the region.

The settlement of the Yukon took place without a treaty with the Indians, and the federal government did not initiate negotiations. But the gold rush was directly responsible for Treaty No. 8, negotiated in 1899 and 1900. Many gold seekers converged on Edmonton in 1898, determined to reach the gold fields by starting by either the Athabasca or the Peace rivers. Some of the hundreds taking the former route were

[13]*Commons Debates*, 1888, col. 1475.
[14]*Commons Debates*, 1907–8, col. 10529.

diverted to Great Slave Lake by rumours of finds there. The gold seekers and trappers included many lawless men, and the Indians and the half-breeds were their victims. Unrest steadily increased as the Indian saw his hunting grounds invaded by this horde.

The first response of the federal government was the same as that in the Yukon. A N.W.M.P. patrol was sent to the region, and their reports, supplemented by representations from Roman Catholic and Anglican missionaries, prompted the government to decide on treaty negotiations. As was the case in the earlier numbered treaties, the document with which the commissioners were supplied was drawn up in Ottawa by bureaucrats who knew nothing of the country or the way of life of the original people. Contributing to the decision to take early action was the fear that if minerals were discovered, the demands for compensation for the surrender of land ownership would escalate.[15]

The commissioners were given only limited authority to negotiate (it was hardly a treaty in the strict sense). And the terms resembled those applied to the plains tribes—a very different group of Indians. The area involved was immense, comprising all the land drained by the Athabasca and Peace rivers and their tributaries along with a portion of north-eastern British Columbia, the Slave River, and the south shore of Great Slave Lake. The Indians were widely scattered throughout the region as family groups with no permanent residence. Their chief concerns were hunting rights (which had not been included in the draft treaty), food supplies in years of famine, and freedom of movement instead of confinement on reserves. The commissioners, with their growing knowledge of the situation, accepted the Indians' demands, though they had no authority to write them into the treaty. The surrender of title to the land was not explained, and the Indians saw the treaty as a friendship pact which would guarantee peaceful settlement.

From what one can observe in the history of the two regions so far considered it is apparent that the central government has had great difficulty in responding quickly, effectively, and with well-defined principles to situations far removed physically from the national capital. It could almost be characterized as "out of sight, out of mind." Only where a local situation had reached crisis proportions in a community, or where Americans threatened to intervene, had a response been forthcoming.

The next region which illustrates this fact was the Canadian Arctic. The area, including the Arctic Islands, was transferred to Canada by

[15]See R. Fumoleau, *As Long As This Land Shall Last: A History of Treaty Eight and Treaty 11, 1870–1939* (Toronto, 1975), pp. 56–7.

Britain in 1880.[16] The federal government did nothing to assert Canada's sovereignty. "There was ... an atmosphere of complacency, or lack of interest regarding these remote regions, and effective control was slow to be exerted."[17] The American presence in this region took the form of whaling expeditions which since the 1860's had ranged far and wide in the eastern Arctic—a no-man's-land where the whalers were a law unto themselves, reaping a rich harvest. They established year-round stations and employed Eskimos as hunters, labourers, and guides. They not only killed hundreds of whales but also traded with the Eskimos for seal skins, musk-ox hides, whale bone, and the ivory of the walrus and narwhal. The profits of the New England ship owners were fantastic, based on the exploitation of the ships' crews and on the small value of the goods traded with the Eskimos. Eskimo women were employed as seamstresses on the ships and for sexual relationships. Compared with the whalers, the numerous northern explorers – Canadian, American, and Norwegian – had no social impact during the latter quarter of the nineteenth century. The Canadian attitude changed after 1900 as fear developed that the activity of the whalers posed a threat to Canadian sovereignty.

Meanwhile, in the western Arctic from Herschel Island eastward American whalers carried on similar activities. In 1903 Ottawa finally responded by sending the police to Herschel Island. This resulted in the establishment of police posts on the island and at Fort Macpherson on the lower Mackenzie River. In the same year the steamer *Neptune* was sent to the eastern Arctic. The expedition was commanded by a distinguished geologist, A. P. Low, and a six-man detachment of the N.W.M.P. with extensive administrative powers. During 1903 and 1904 most American whaling stations on the northwestern shore of Hudson Bay were visited. Regulations regarding Canadian criminal law, customs entries, and immigration were publicized and enforced; a ban on the export of musk-ox hides (an animal threatened with extinction) was promulgated. Several proclamations of Canadian sovereignty were recorded in the upper Hudson Bay-Southampton Island region, and the officer commanding the N.W.M.P. detachment recommended the establishment of five posts in the region, serviced by a specially constructed steamer. The high Arctic did not figure in the activities of the *Neptune* expedition. While this region was explored in succeeding

[16]Imperial Order in Council, July 31, 1880, in *Statutes of Canada*, 1880–1, pp. ix–x.
[17]W. G. Ross, "Canadian Sovereignty in the Arctic: The Neptune Expedition of 1903–04," *Arctic*, June, 1976, p. 88.

years, Canadian sovereignty continued to be challenged in the absence of visible occupancy.

The creation of the provinces of Alberta and Saskatchewan left the remainder of the Northwest Territories east of the Yukon to the boundary of Labrador under direct federal control. For the government of this vast, sparsely settled region bounded on the south by Manitoba, Ontario, and Quebec, an amendment to The Northwest Territories Act was passed in 1905.[18] It provided for the appointment of a commissioner as the chief executive officer and an appointed council of not more than four members to aid the commissioner in executive and legislative matters. The powers of the commissioner in council were the same as those possessed by the Legislative Assembly of the Territories prior to 1905. The court system, however, reverted to that provided by the Act of 1875 – stipendiary magistrates appointed in Ottawa with appeals to be heard by a judge in one of the provinces. Seven years later the boundaries of the Northwest Territories were drastically altered by adding to Manitoba the area south of the 60th parallel to the west shore of Hudson Bay, and by giving Ontario and Quebec northern boundaries on Hudson and James Bays. The inducement for this generosity, at territorial expense, was provided by businessmen in the three provinces, particularly by entrepreneurs interested in the forest and mining resources. Unilateral exercise of the power to alter territorial boundaries had existed since 1871 when an amendment to the British North America Act had conferred it on Ottawa.[19] After the legislation of 1912 the boundaries of the Territories were the 60th parallel on the south, the Arctic Islands on the north, Hudson Bay on the east, and the Rockies on the west.

In view of the fact that the only official Canadian presence in the Northwest Territories after 1905 was provided by the Mounted Police and its patrols, it is not surprising that the comptroller of the force was appointed commissioner of the Territories in 1905, with headquarters in Ottawa. He continued to serve in this capacity until his death in 1918. During that period no council was appointed and hence no legislation was passed. As commissioner of the police he directed the detachments at eight posts in the North. It must be noted that in addition to their law enforcement function, the police performed executive and regulatory functions for various departments of the federal government.

In 1920 the Deputy Minister of the Interior was appointed commissioner, a practice which continued for the next forty-three years. In 1921 an amendment to the Northwest Territories Act was passed increasing

18 4–5 Edward VII, c. 27.
19 The British North American Act, 1871, 34–35 Victoria, c. 28.

the council from four to six.[20] The first appointees, in addition to the commissioner of the R.C.M.P., were all senior civil servants, who acted more as an interdepartmental committee than as a legislative body. This sudden reorganization of the almost moribund territorial government was a consequence of the oil discovery at Norman Wells on the Mackenzie in 1920. The discovery also resulted in the negotiation of Treaty No. 11 in 1921, the last in the series of Indian treaties which it had taken half a century to negotiate.

During the preceding fifteen years the commissioner of the Northwest Territories ignored the periodically destitute tribes of this area, who lacked any of the services which Indians covered by treaty enjoyed. But at the end of World War I prospectors began to invade the Mackenzie and the north shore of Great Slave Lake in search of precious metals. They were followed by itinerant traders and trappers. All these white men were invading a region which the Indians regarded as their own. The oil discoveries at Norman Wells drew national attention to the region and caused great excitement among prospectors and speculators.[21] Now at long last the requests of Indian spokesmen, their friend Bishop Breynat of the Diocese of Mackenzie, and even a senior official of the Indian Affairs department were heeded in Ottawa.[22]

In many of its essential features the negotiation of Treaty No. 11 resembled that of No. 8. When the commissioners visited the eight trading posts (a few having police detachments), along the Mackenzie they encountered a mixed reaction among the Indians. Many spoke no English, and in the absence of an interpreter scarcely understood the terms of a treaty drafted in Ottawa. Whether the Indians fully understood the meaning of surrender of title is extremely problematical. And no treaty has ever been made with the Indians and Eskimos living east of the Coppermine River.

The 1920's and 1930's were not a particularly happy period in the Yukon and the Northwest Territories. Local government had been almost completely liquidated in the Yukon by Arthur Meighen, then Minister of the Interior, in 1918. An amendment to the Yukon Act[23] that year empowered the government to abolish the elected council and replace it with a two-member appointed council. Any territorial government office could be abolished by federal order in council. The result was the elimination of all officials with the exception of the commissioner and the gold commissioner. Second thoughts the following year per-

[20]11–12 George V, c. 40.
[21]Fumoleau, *op. cit.*, pp. 135 ff.
[22]Report of the Superintendent-General of Indian Affairs, 1921, *C.S.P.* 1922, no. 27, pp. 35, 152–5.
[23]8–9 George V, c. 50.

mitted the creation of a three-member elected council,[24] with the commissioner remaining the chief executor for both territorial and federal legislation. Silver was discovered at Mayo, and the council in 1923 petitioned for the addition of a fourth member, but this was refused. In these same two decades the Yukon was subject to almost complete control by the paternalistic federal bureaucracy in Ottawa and by officials of seven or more departments in the territory.

Meanwhile in the Northwest Territories the council met infrequently. It was chiefly concerned with services for a new element of the population—white immigrants from the south, mostly trappers and traders who joined the handful of police, missionaries, nuns, and Hudson's Bay Company employees. The trappers moved steadily down the Mackenzie River as far north as Arctic Red River, denuding the area of furs. "The Indians had no protection against the competition of the white trappers,"[25] and the Indian Agent at Fort Simpson reported in 1926 that many fur-bearing animals were practically extinct. But the territorial council did nothing to protect the interests of the Indians. The period was also marked by spectacular material changes. The discovery of rich deposits of uranium ore at Great Bear Lake and gold at Yellowknife brought hundreds of prospectors into the Territories and the establishment of successful mining operations. Steamboats began to ply the Mackenzie, followed by air travel (the twenties and thirties were the heyday of the bush pilots). Gasoline boats and radio communication also appeared.

From the 1930's on the agitation for constitutional reform was taken up by the white immigrants who complained about taxation without representation in Parliament and the territorial council. This entrepreneurial pressure was resisted in Ottawa by a well-founded suspicion that an autonomous territorial government would be a white man's government and the interests of the majority of the population, the indigenous people, would be ignored. However, from the 1940's on the federal authorities slowly and hesitantly capitulated to local pressure. The last five Ottawa-based commissioners, beginning with Charles Camsell who had been born in the Northwest Territories, were well-educated, sophisticated members of the bureaucratic élite, more aware than any of their predecessors of the aspirations and complexities of the situation in the North and the socio-economic position of the Indians and Eskimos. This viewpoint was generally shared by their ministers, particularly Jean Lesage, Alvin Hamilton in John Diefenbaker's ministry, with its "northern vision," Arthur Laing, and Jean Chrétien of

[24]9–10 George V, c. 9.
[25]Fumoleau, *op. cit.*, p. 247.

the Trudeau ministry—undoubtedly the most active minister in charge of territorial affairs since Confederation. The progress towards limited autonomy was slow but steady, except for fully responsible government.

In the 1930's more frequent and productive sessions of the council were held. Changes in constitutional law followed increases in the white population and economic productivity. The first resident member was appointed in 1946. In 1951 the council was increased to eight members; and for the first time there were elected members—three for a three-year term.[26] The territorial government established three constituencies, all in the Mackenzie valley, where the articulate and discontented white immigrants were largely located. Three whites were elected, although Indians and Eskimos were entitled to vote under the franchise ordinance passed by the territorial council.[27] This amendment also required that one of the sessions each year should be held in the Territories. Members of the opposition in the House of Commons criticized the bill because it was such a small step towards representative government. Later in the same year at Yellowknife, the first of a number of sessions was held outside Ottawa. In 1952 the Northwest Territories Act was consolidated[28] (proclaimed in 1953) with an updated enumeration of the legislative powers of the council, which by now were much the same as those possessed by a province under the B.N.A. Act, with the important exception of ownership and control of natural resources, local works and undertakings, the incorporation of companies, amendment of the constitution, and the administration of justice, all of which remained under federal control. In 1954 Parliament granted an increase in the council to nine members, four of them elected.[29]

Meanwhile the Department of Resources and Development was finding that its authority in the North was being complicated by the service activities of over a score of other departments, with a staff of many hundreds of permanent and seasonal workers.[30] This was in marked contrast to the pre-1905 North-West Territories, and before the era of the welfare state. The need for co-ordination was obvious, and in 1948 the Advisory Committee on Northern Development was

26 15 George VI (1951), c. 21.

27 *Ordinances of the Northwest Territories*, 1951, c. 18.

28 1 Elizabeth II (1952), c. 46.

29 2–3 Elizabeth II (1954), c. 8. This act was sponsored by Jean Lesage, who in 1953 became the first minister of the new Department of Northern Affairs and National Development and who held office until 1957, when the Liberal government was defeated by the Progressive Conservatives.

30 By 1965 the numbers were approximately 2500 full-time and 2200 seasonal workers: see *Report of the Advisory Commission on the Development of Government in the Northwest Territories* (Ottawa, 1966), pp. 27–46. Hereinafter cited as Carrothers.

established, consisting of deputy ministers of the departments involved, to co-ordinate federal activities and provide advice to the cabinet.[31]

During the Lesage régime, supreme courts were established in the Yukon and the Northwest Territories with headquarters at Whitehorse and Yellowknife.[32] Of the two, the latter was the more onerous, for Judge Sissons was determined to go on circuit throughout his vast district comprising one third of Canada.[33] During his eleven years of devoted service in the North, he adapted Canadian law to Eskimo customs and values—one of the great sagas of Canadian history. The Progressive Conservative Minister Alvin Hamilton introduced an amendment in 1959[34] which enabled the territorial council to designate the place in the Territories where one of the annual sessions would be held, as well as empowering the federal cabinet to dissolve the council "to bring the principles relating to dissolution in the territories to accord with the principles followed in the provinces and in this house." "We are moving," he continued, "step by step toward assuring that the administrative and judicial aspects of these expanding territories will grow as the economics of these territories change."[35]

In the Yukon the membership in the council was increased from three to five in 1951.[36] In 1958 the territory was granted the power to borrow, subject to approval by the federal government.[37] The council was increased from five to seven in 1960.[38] The amendment also provided that the council should recommend for appointment by the commissioner three councillors to be "an Advisory Committee on Finance" who should be consulted by the commissioner in preparing the budget for the territory.[39] But as in previous years, the commissioner was to act on his own on other areas of administration, and was responsible only to Ottawa. The council was certainly not satisfied, and in succeeding years resorted to obstructionist tactics, much to the consternation of the commissioner.

In 1947 a part of the Northwest Territories was granted representation in Parliament by extending the Yukon constituency eastward to include most of the district of Mackenzie.[40] Five years later the electoral district of Mackenzie was created as a separate constituency,[41] having an estimated population of 16,000, a majority of them Indian and Eskimo. It should be noted that these acts benefited only the white

---

[31]Carrothers, p. 46. For a critique of the record of the Committee see *ibid.*, 183.

[32]3–4 Elizabeth II (1955), c. 48, s. 18. Assented to on July 11, 1955.

[33]See Jack Sissons, *Judge of the Far North* (Toronto, 1968).

[34]7–8 Elizabeth II, c. 7.   [35]*Commons Debates*, 1959, col. 1355.

[36]15 George VI (1951), c. 23.   [37]7 Elizabeth II (1958), c. 9.

[38]8–9 Elizabeth II (1960), c. 24.   [39]*Ibid.*, s. 3, ss. (1) and (3).

[40]11 George VI (1947), c. 71.   [41]1 Elizabeth II (1952), c. 48.

population, since it was not until 1960 that Canadian Indians were enfranchised.[42] The members elected for the Mackenzie constituency have all been effective advocates of constitutional reforms and the improvement in the socio-economic condition of the Indian and Eskimo people.

During the Conservative régime the Northwest council (whose appointed members were in a majority) called for the division of the Territories into two separate political units. The pressure for this action came from the white population in the Mackenzie district which expected that the western territory (to be named Mackenzie) would make a rapid advance to responsible government.[43] Commissioner Robertson and other Ottawa officials on the council spent considerable time in 1959 and succeeding years in promoting the project. In 1962 the council passed a resolution which finalized their deliberations on the boundaries and form of government. The latter proposed that for both the western and eastern territories there be a commissioner and council with the same powers as those in the existing Northwest Territories. For the new Mackenzie Territory the commissioner should reside at a territorial capital, and the council should consist of nine members, five elected and four non-resident appointees "to provide experience and knowledge of administration, business and other affairs that may not be readily available in the Territory."[44] The other new territory should bear an Eskimo name, and its commissioner should live in Ottawa, assisted by an appointed council of seven, three of them residents of the territory, at least one of them an Eskimo. This commissioner was to co-ordinate territorial government policies with the policies and responsibilities of all federal departments. It was the quintessence of benevolent imperial control.

Following the defeat of the Progressive Conservatives in 1966, the new Minister of the Interior, Arthur Lang, sponsored two bills which embodied his predecessor's plans for the North and the proposals of the bureaucrat-dominated Northwest council.[45] But there was vigorous criticism of the bills by some of the elected councillors, by representatives of a number of settlements, some in the eastern Arctic, by the territorial members of Parliament, and by the outspoken judge of the Supreme Court, Jack Sissons. The controversy raged for months, and the bills never passed beyond first reading.

The government's retreat was short lived, however, for there was so

42 8–9 Elizabeth II (1960), c. 7 and 8. See also *Commons Debates* 1960, p. 1912.
43 Northwest Territories, *Votes and Proceedings*, 17th Session (July, 1959), p. 2.
44 *Ibid.*, 22nd Session (Jan., 1962), p. 112.
45 *Commons Debates*, 1965, pp. 114–45.

much southern Canadian interest in the search for oil and metals that any neglect of constitutional problems was likely to have serious political repercussions. In the Territories political consciousness was increasing, particularly among the white population, but also among the Indians and Eskimos. In 1964 there was a bitter and heated conflict at the June session of the council between the assistant commissioner and the other appointed members (with the exception of Dr. Frank Vallée, professor of Anthropology at Carleton University) and two of the elected members – those from the lower Mackenzie valley. The latter criticized the over-centralization of Indian administration in Ottawa and opposed the proposed division of the Territories[46] "which is not known or understood by a great number of the people."[47] It was significant that the other two elected members, who represented predominantly white constituencies, voted with the appointed members. When Dr. Vallée moved for a reorganization of the territorial government along democratic lines, the assistant commissioner blocked approval by demanding postponement.[48] The only victory for the elected members was approval of a motion by Vallée at the November session requesting that all residents of the Territories be enfranchised by the enlargement of the number of elected councillors.[49]

The controversies which arose from the projected legislation for dividing the Territories, and a growing appreciation of the complexities of providing government services to the widely scattered Métis, Indians, and Eskimos whose familiarity with existing and alternative forms of government varied widely, induced the government in 1965 to appoint an Advisory Commission on the Development of Government in the Northwest Territories, headed by A. W. R. Carrothers, Dean of Law at the University of Western Ontario.[50]

The year 1966 was the most momentous in the history of the Northwest Territories since 1905. The first development was the amendment of the Northwest Territories Act[51] increasing the number of elected members to seven, giving them a majority in the council, and permitting the creation of two constituencies in the region situated east of Mackenzie and including the high Arctic. Another legislative move was the act creating the Department of Indian Affairs and Northern Development,

[46]Northwest Territories, *Votes and Proceedings*, 27th Session (June, 1964), pp. 141, 161–2.

[47]*Ibid.*, p. 161.

[48]*Ibid.*, pp. 163–4.

[49]Northwest Territories, *Votes and Proceedings*, 28th Session (Nov., 1964), pp. 83, 84. Parliament added two elected members to the council in 1966: 14–15 Elizabeth II, c. 22.

[50]*Commons Debates*, 1965, p. 1144.

[51]See above, fn. 49.

thus transferring the management of Indian affairs from the Department of Citizenship and Immigration.[52] The logic of this move was compelling, since the two territorial governments counted so many native citizens in their population. In the same year the new Liberal administration departed from tradition in the appointment of a new commissioner to succeed Robertson, B. G. Sievertz who was not a deputy minister, but the director of the northern administration branch of the department. This was a small step in the direction of territorial autonomy.

The Carrothers commission travelled widely throughout the Territories collecting opinions. It also held hearings in Ottawa and solicited the views of southerners who had an interest in the North. It commissioned studies by experts on the North in the fields of economic forecasting, physical geography, sociology, and anthropology. The commissioners also examined commissioned investigations of socio-political structures of indigenous peoples in Greenland, Alaska, the Soviet Union, Australia, and New Zealand. It was undoubtedly the most thorough investigation of its type which had ever been undertaken in Canada.

There had been occasional suggestion during the previous thirty years, emanating from all four western provinces, that their northern boundaries be extended to the Arctic Ocean. The Ontario–Quebec boundary extensions of 1912 were invoked as a rationale for these proposals. In 1937 the British Columbia premier advocated the annexation of the Yukon, and two years later the Alberta legislature urged the northern extension of its boundary to include the Mackenzie valley to the Arctic. In 1966 the latter province seized the opportunity provided by the deliberations of the commission to present an elaborate brief calling for this enlargement in the areas of the four western provinces.[53] Although the case was for the alleged benefits which would be enjoyed by territorial citizens, the peculiar socio-economic problems of the native people were ignored. The chief point of the brief was the benefits which the business community in the south would enjoy. This brought a prompt response from the Yukon member of Parliament who declared: "We in the Yukon, and I know the feeling is the same in the Northwest Territories, do not wish to become any province's back-yard."[54] This view was echoed by the member for the Northwest Territories who called Alberta's proposal "somewhat rude and intolerable" and "nefarious." He continued: We find it somewhat strange and disconcerting that

52 14–15 Elizabeth II, c. 25, s. 40–1. See also remarks of R. J. Orange, *Commons Debates*, 1966, pp. 336–9.
53 Government of Alberta, *Submission to the Advisory Commission on the Development of Government in the Northwest Territories* (Edmonton, 1965).
54 Eric Nielson (P.C.) *Commons Debates*, 1966, p. 3162.

this interest has been generated only after the oil and mineral potential of the Yukon, Mackenzie and Arctic have become a reality."[55]

The Carrothers report stressed that forms of government should be functional, and are designed "to bring about, through a political process, the solving of social and economic problems and the pursuit of values of a more general nature."[56] Thus, while not ignoring the political aspirations of the white community in the North, the report placed great stress on the life style of the indigenous people—the Indians and Eskimos who constituted 60 per cent of the territorial population— and their existing and anticipated political reactions. Over 20 pages of the 214-page report dealt with this subject. Unlike the approach of many southern politicians and bureaucrats, the commissioners were the first to see the situation of the North in human terms. The Indian and Eskimo were in a process of transition, some retaining the old life style, others combining the old with the life style of the whites. There was a visible generation gap. There was a further complication in that some Indians lived under Treaties 8 and 11 and others (as well as the Eskimos) had never signed a treaty. Some of the former claimed that the treaties had not been fulfilled. This, among many others, is a major cause of hostility of the Indians to the whites.

Other causes appear to be lack of economic opportunity, social rejection and physical isolation in communal enclaves where the Indian lives on the fringe of white dominated communities. . . . He lives near subsistence, in a poor white sub-culture and in an irreversible state of dependence on the white man's way of earning a living, unwilling ward of the state and victim of custodial care.[57]

The Eskimos occupied a similar position, having recently gone through a period of rapid change from nomadism to settlement near trading posts, missions, schools, and places where there were opportunities to earn wages. Nevertheless it would take time "to induce a race who for thousands of years lived by the seasons to live by the clock."[58] The Eskimo and Indian population comprised three-fifths of the potential labour force but only one-sixth of the employed. While many of the older native people had no education, the youth were being educated, but were unemployed, and discontent was rising. "The passive role of the Indians throughout the north is disappearing, as it has disappeared in other nations throughout the world. ... The condition of the native people is improving. But the gap between the economic condition of the

[55]R. J. Orange, *ibid.*, p. 337.   [56]Carrothers, p. 96.
[57]*Ibid.*, pp. 64–5.   [58]*Ibid.*, p. 68.

native and that of the white man may well be widening."[59] In human terms, the commissioners concluded, "The North is Canada's neglected backyard."[60]

The report continued with an examination of the geographic characteristics of the Territories, with its areas of boreal forest, tundra, and perpetually frozen lands in the high Arctic and adjacent islands, their geological features, mineral resources, their waterways, and the climatic restraints. The huge area and low population density were all relevant to the problems of the form of government.

The Carrothers commission's recommendations were not formulated as immutable final answers, and it was urged that, in view of the rapidity of socio-economic change in the Territories as described above, the situation be reassessed in 1976. This may explain why the recommendations were neither conservative nor radical but a judicious blend of the two philosophies.

The commission noted that the paramountcy of the federal power in Yukon and the Territories meant that it was not bound to provide a local constitution in any way similar to that of a province. This was best illustrated in the executive branch of the territorial government, which in no way resembled that prevailing in a province. On the other hand the territorial government had been given powers not possessed by a province—to levy taxes on furs to be sold in the south and to govern Indian and Eskimo hunting of game.

The commissioners noted also that it was legally possible to create a system of territorial government having all the legislative powers then enjoyed plus most federal powers—a unitary form of government subject to federal control. Of the various forms of territorial government that might be chosen, the commission favoured one "that is more likely to mature" into provincial status.

The commission flatly rejected the proposal that provincial boundaries be extended to absorb the territories.[61] It rejected the proposal to divide the Territories and create two territorial governments,[62] although not ruling out the possibility at some later date. Division, it was pointed out, would have the accidental effect of isolating the Eskimos from gaining experience and sophistication in public affairs, and would have a similar effect in Mackenzie, where a white-dominated government would emerge. Moreover, it had found that only a minority favoured division. Some of the majority, including the councillors, had abandoned

59*Ibid.*, pp. 175–6.
60*Ibid.*, p. 78.
61*Ibid.*, p. 152.
62For all its recommendations, the report elaborated on the reasons for its choice; their omission from this chapter is in the interest of conciseness and brevity.

their former opinion. Provincial status for the Mackenzie district was also ruled out on financial grounds. The understandable desire for greater self-government, the commissioners concluded, "can be satisfied almost as fully at the present time without division as with it."[63] And "two attenuated governments are less likely to attain their claims against the central government [in Ottawa] than is one consolidated government."[64]

The last fifty pages of the report consist of specific recommendations, each accompanied by a supporting rationale. The capital and the residence of the commissioner should be moved from Ottawa to Yellowknife. On the structure of government, it was recommended that the office of commissioner be continued and that he be chairman of a legislative assembly and of an executive council, and exercise increased powers subject to ministerial control at Ottawa. He was empowered to appoint a deputy commissioner with the consent of the minister. Responsible government was to be postponed for the present, but "at an appropriate time" the commissioner would withdraw from the assembly, and become, with Ottawa's consent, a lieutenant-governor. The deputy commissioner would be an elected member of the assembly and gain from the commissioner the power possessed by the premier of a province. The executive council was to be chosen by the commissioner from either elected or appointed members of the assembly. Each councillor would head one or more of seven proposed departments. The legislative assembly was to number eighteen, four appointed by the commissioner. Electors were to be all citizens of nineteen years of age (reduced from the existing age of twenty-one). The appointed members would provide valuable knowledge and expertise in the proposed restructuring of the government, but their existence should be reconsidered by the minister at a later date. The legislative powers of the council should be the same as those of a province with the exception of the amendment of the constitution, the restrictions then existing on the powers of the territorial government and confinement of control of public lands to surface rights only, and certain restrictions on the administration of justice. Since the economy development of the territories was so basic to the future evolution of its government, the commission recommended that its administration should include a department of economic development, that there also be a Northwest Territories development board composed of territorial and federal officials, including members of the Economic Council of Canada, and a Northwest Territories develop-

[63]*Ibid.*, p. 146.
[64]*Ibid.*, p. 149.

ment corporation with an initial capital of $10 million, to assist businesses in the private sector of the economy.

In summary, the commission concluded that the form of government should remain flexible and capable of modification. "We conclude," the commissioners said, "that what is required now is not provincehood, but the means of growth to provincehood."[65]

Although there was some criticism of its conservatism, the Carrothers commission's report was favourably received by the press, members of parliament, and the majority of the Northwest council. The council had submitted a brief to the commission calling for the removal of the capital to the territories and the early establishment of responsible government culminating in provincial status in ten year's time. Parliament's enlargement of the council that year[66] resulted in the election of three members for the area east of Mackenzie, including an Eskimo. Legislative activity was extensive and important in the two sessions of that year.

Meanwhile in the Yukon the council continued its turbulent demand for increased autonomy, coupled with criticism of federal policies. The Minister responded by sponsoring legislation increasing the financial powers of the council[67] and appointing the first resident of the territory to be commissioner of the Yukon. But he would not meet the council's demand for an increase of membership to fifteen and agreement for provincial status in fifteen years. As in the Territories, these constitutional proposals were accompanied by much constructive legislation.[68]

Canada's centennial year was one of notable mineral production in the two territories but of much political controversy in Yukon. Both the territorial and federal administrations were harshly criticized, and the council refused to approve the budget. Political controversy was less evident in the Territories. Two recommendations of the Carrothers commission were implemented when Yellowknife was designated as the territorial capital and Stuart Hodgson was named on March 2 as the first resident commissioner.[69] He and a group of former federal officials and their families arrived in the capital in September. Meanwhile the territorial elections had returned seven elected members, four in constituencies in the Mackenzie valley and three in various areas in the Arctic. The first session with Hodgson in the chair was a lively one, with the council calling for full implementation of the Carrothers report

[65]*Ibid.*, p. 151.
[66]See p. 00
[67]14–15 Elizabeth II, c. 28.
[68]Ordinances of the Yukon Territory passed in the year 1966.
[69]Hodgson had been deputy commissioner in Ottawa, 1965–7.

—a view which had been vigorously expressed earlier in the year by former Commissioner Sievertz. Another motion called for a strict accounting of revenues from the natural resources when provincial status was achieved.

The last two years of the sixties revealed the persistence of the problems which had begun to emerge in the Yukon and the Territories after the end of the Second World War: the tensions created by the newly arrived white southerners; high crime rates among the native people; miniscule employment opportunities for native people in government service and in the mining and gas and oil drilling activities of gigantic American oil consortiums; the question whether the native people would share the profits from the exploitation of the natural resources. There was a vast Canadian and international press attention to resource development in the North, and numerous conferences in the south, which included pronouncements by Prime Minister Trudeau and Jean Chrétien. But there was also the expression of the old resentment at the colonial position of the north *vis-à-vis* Canada and at the layers of federal bureaucracy, with its constantly changing personnel and overlapping activities.

Concern for the native peoples and their future, their employment, protection of the environment, and land claims appeared more frequently in the speeches and policies adopted by the Minister of Indian Affairs and Northern Development. This did not mean, however, that Chrétien endorsed all the reforms in the territorial constitution proposed by the Carrothers commission. In November, 1969, the Progressive Conservatives sponsored a resolution harshly condemning the Trudeau government for not ending "the colonial form of government which exists in the Territories."[70] Although the motion was defeated, it produced a high level of debate, since the rival party spokesmen shared a similar philosophy of the significance of northern development which was well expressed by the Liberal member for Mackenzie:

... much must be done. We have started to recognize what the north means to us as Canadians. I suggest that if anything will make us different from our neighbours to the south, if anything will give us a distinctive Canadian character, it is the fact that we are a northern nation, a people who inhabit the northern half of North America. That is something that can be the mainstay of our personality for years to come.[71]

The year 1970 was the centennial of the Northwest Territories and the Yukon—the anniversary of the acquisition by Canada of the vast

[70]*Commons Debates*, 1969, p. 1093.
[71]*Ibid.*, p. 1108 (R. Orange).

area between Ontario and British Columbia. Attrition had reduced the area of the Northwest Territories, but it was still over a million square miles, over twice the area of Quebec, and the Yukon was approximately the same size as Manitoba.

It was a notable year in terms of territorial constitutional evolution, even if it fell short of what many citizens of the North desired. Chrétien introduced legislation early in the year[72] creating an executive committee in the Yukon which would include two of the elected members. Subsequently the council gave portfolios to them, one an education "ministry" and the other for health and welfare. In the Territories the elected membership was increased from seven to ten, and the appointed reduced from five to four. "This supports," Chrétien said, "the principle that eventually the appointed members should be replaced entirely by elected residents of the territory ... I hope that increasing the number of elected representation will lead to greater involvement of Indian and Eskimo people in territorial affairs for the Territorial Government is theirs too."[73] The term of the two councils was extended from three to four years, the period during which legislation might be disallowed by the federal government was reduced to one year (as was the case with provincial legislation) and they were given the power, hitherto exercised by Parliament, to legislate on the qualifications of candidates and electors, and the administration of justice. Chrétien stressed the great imbalance in the budgets of the two territories between expenditures and local revenues, which was underwritten by the federal government.

The amendment of the Territorial Lands Act was designed particularly to guard against the danger of pollution by industrial activity. "We are determined," Chrétien declared, "that the north shall not fall victim to the evils of uncontrolled exploitation. We are currently meeting representatives of the oil industry, the mining industry and the forestry interests because they are the people who know what they want to do. We are also meeting with conservationists and the territorial government because they are the ones who know what they do not want to see happen. Hopefully, the regulations will be acceptable to all these widely diverse interests. If they are not, the government must and will accept its responsibilities."[74]

The first gas discovery was made in 1970 on an island in the high Arctic, and talk of pipelines to serve southern Canada and the United States, which had begun the previous year, was intensified. This

[72]18–19 Elizabeth II, c. 69, An Act to amend the Yukon Act, the Northwest Territories Act, and the Territorial Lands Act.
[73]*Commons Debates*, 1970, p. 6924.
[74]*Ibid.*, p. 6925.

prompted the organization of a militant organization among the territorial Indian and Eskimo population COPE (Committee for Original Peoples Entitlement) who stressed their claim to a country which they had controlled for countless thousands of years. The Indians of the northernmost of the Yukon joined the agitation, demanding "guarantees that oil exploration would not disturb their hunting, fishing and trapping grounds."[75] In general "there was rising militancy among the Eskimos, Indians, and Métis in the north that led them to challenge the federal government, at conferences, and through the press, over matters of aboriginal rights and land claims."[76] Jim Lotz, the distinguished authority on the north, describes the situation in the following terms:

Ever since the new thrust towards northern development began in 1954 with the creation of the Department of Northern Affairs and National Resources, a ding-dong battle has been fought in Canada over the "right" way to develop the North. For a long time, it seemed, development was just a matter of mines and roads, of building schools and educating the native peoples. But over the past few years the process of northern development has become highly politicized. The North has become the ground upon which a number of national conflicts are being fought out: conservationists against developers, modernists against traditionalists, humanists against technocrats, evolutionaries against revolutionaries. From being a remote and romantic land, Canada's North has suddenly become a mirror to the nation. ...[77]

This review of the complex constitutional developments in the Yukon and the Northwest Territories from 1897 to 1970 has touched on the highlights, and is by no means a complete narrative of all the accompanying events and the part which individuals played in the story. Considering the period as a whole one is struck by the continuity of the imperial-colonial relationship, by the resort to formulas of the 1870–97 years, and the continuity of political dissent which was so notable in the old North-West from 1885 to 1905. This dissent belongs in the same category as the classical constitutional struggles which began in the provinces of the old British Empire. "Were not its failings," writes Professor Zaslow, "the failings of Canada as a whole—the pragmatic approach heedless of intellectual consistency, the confusion about ends and means, the concern for practical results of a most material sort?"[78]

The situation of Canada's dependencies in the twentieth century was

[75]*Canadian Annual Review*, 1970, p. 306.
[76]*Ibid.*, p. 307.
[77]Jim Lotz, "Northern Alternatives," *North*, vol. XXVIII, no. 1 (1975), p. 3. See also his *Northern Realities* (Chicago, 1971).
[78]In F. H. Underhill, ed., *The Canadian Northwest: Its Potentialities* (Toronto, 1959), p. 104.

much more complex than that of the old North-West Territories because the sense of community identity was absent, except in a few urban communities. The white man's world co-existed with the native peoples' life style and value system. The latter, who were almost as numerous as the whites, strenuously resisted assimilation and the acceptance of southern Canadian values, and occasionally resorted to confrontation tactics. Only with mutual tolerance, forbearance, and respect would a united northern community emerge, and in turn produce autonomous political units within the Canadian federation. It is essential that not only the federal government but southern Canadians generally should understand these northern realities.

Note on Sources

The chief sources used in the preparation of this study are the records of the federal and territorial governments (both printed and manuscript), collections of personal papers, and contemporary newspapers. Numerous secondary sources have been consulted and have yielded some useful details; where specific information has been obtained from them, acknowledgement is made in the footnotes. Research in the field of post-Confederation politics is still handicapped by the scarcity of critical studies of federal policy, and the quality and quantity of biographical works and the literature of recollection and reminiscence, both national and local, is such that comparatively little background information could be secured relating to the events narrated.

I. Federal Government Records

Extensive use has been made of the official publications of the federal government—statutes, journals, official debates of the House of Commons and Senate, sessional papers, departmental reports, and census reports. Of the unpublished government records the most important were the files of the Department of the Interior, now in the custody of the Department of Resources and Development, and in process of transfer to the Public Archives of Canada. Transcripts or microfilm copies of most of these files relating to the territorial government are in the Archives of Saskatchewan. The records of the Secretary of State for the Provinces in the custody of the Secretary of State for Canada have also been consulted for the period prior to the organization of the Department of the Interior. Federal Orders in Council pertaining to all matters under the supervision of the Department of the Interior are available in a series of printed volumes, and a microfilm copy in the Archives of Saskatchewan has been used in this study.

II. Territorial Government Records

The publications of the territorial government are not extensive. Those which were of most use were the Council and Assembly journals, the ordinances, and the public accounts. A complete listing of territorial government publications may be found in C. MacDonald, comp., *Publications of the Governments of the North-West Territories 1876–1905 and of the Province of Saskatchewan 1905–52* (Regina, 1953). Of the unpublished material, the official correspondence of the Lieutenant-Governor of Manitoba in the Public Archives of Manitoba has been most useful for the period when the government was located in Winnipeg. Much of the correspondence originating in the Governor's office in Battleford and Regina has not survived, and it is particularly fortunate that some of it can be reconstructed from the Department of the Interior files. Fortunately too, some of it is to be found in the files transferred to the departments of the Attorney General and the Territorial Treasurer when these were organized in 1897. These files (now in the Archives of Saskatchewan) also contain material pertaining to the activities of the Executive Committee. Of the territorial government records which have survived the following were the most useful:

Minutes of the North-West Council, 1873–5. P.A.M.

Lieutenant-Governor's Papers, 1870–6. P.A.M.

Oaths Book, North-West Territories, 1873–6. P.A.M.

North Western Territory, Register of Commissions. P.A.M.

Account Book for the North-West Territories, 1873–5. P.A.M.

Proclamations and Orders of the Lieutenant-Governor of the North-West Territories, 1876–97. A.S.

Orders in Council, 1892–7 (microfilm copy). A.S.

Minutes of the Advisory Council in Matters of Finance, 1888–91. A.S.

Minutes of the Executive Committee of the North-West Territories, 1892–4; 1895–8. A.S.

Oaths Book, 1877–97. A.S.

Unpublished sessional papers of the Council of the North-West Territories and the Legislative Assembly of the North-West Territories (microfilm copy). A.S.

Attorney General's files, G series, 1876–1905. A.S.

Treasury Department files, 1877–1905. A.S.

III. PRIVATE PAPERS

For this study the most important collections of private papers were the Sir John A. Macdonald Papers, the Sir J. J. C. Abbott Papers, and the Sir John Thompson Papers in the Public Archives of Canada, and the Alexander Morris Papers in the Public Archives of Manitoba. The following collections provided occasional items of value: the Alexander Mackenzie Papers, the Sir Mackenzie Bowell Papers, the Edgar Dewdney Papers, the Sir Clifford Sifton Papers, the Sir Wilfrid Laurier Papers, and the Louis Riel Papers, all in the Public Archives of Canada; the David Mills Papers in the Library of the University of Western Ontario, the Edward Blake Papers in the Library of the University of Toronto, the Sir Richard Cartwright Papers, and the Alexander Morris Papers in the Archives of Ontario, and the David Laird items in the Archives Division, Legislative Library of Saskatchewan. Of considerable value as a supplement to the Macdonald Papers were the Edgar Dewdney Papers in the possession of Mr. F. H. B. Dewdney of Trail, B.C.

IV. NEWSPAPERS

Contemporary newspapers were of great value with respect to matters of fact and opinion. The following were consulted on specific points: *Globe* (Toronto), *Mail* (Toronto), *Gazette* (Montreal), *Ottawa Times, Nor'Wester* (Fort Garry), *New Nation* (Fort Garry), and *Manitoban* (Winnipeg). The following territorial papers were used for the periods noted: *Calgary Tribune*, 1885-95; *Calgary Weekly Herald*, 1884-97; *Edmonton Bulletin*, 1880-97; (Fort) *Qu'Appelle Vidette*, 1884-97; *Grenfell Sun*, 1894-7; *Lethbridge News*, 1889-92; *Macleod Gazette*, 1887-92; *Medicine Hat Times*, 1887-92; *Moose Jaw Times*, 1889-97; *Moosomin Courier*, 1884-92; *Moosomin Spectator*, 1892-7; *Prince Albert Times*, 1882-92; *Qu'Appelle Progress*, 1885-97; *Regina Journal*, 1886-90; *Regina Leader*, 1883-97; *Saskatchewan* (Prince Albert), 1889-92; *Saskatchewan Herald* (Battleford), 1878-97; *Saskatchewan Times* (Prince Albert), 1892-7; *Standard* (Regina), 1891-7. The Regina papers and the *Calgary Weekly Herald* provide the fullest reports of the debates in the Council and Assembly. The Provincial Library of Manitoba possesses the most complete files of Manitoba and North-West Territories newspapers; microfilm copies of many of these are in the Archives of Saskatchewan.

Index

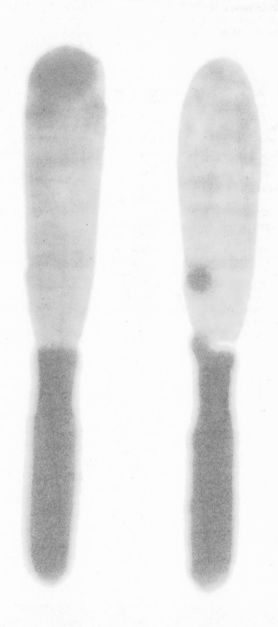